ON THE FORM OF
THE AMERICAN MIND

PROJECTED VOLUMES IN THE SERIES

1. *On the Form of the American Mind*
2. *Race and State*
3. *The History of the Race Idea*
4. *The Authoritarian State*
5. *Political Religions; The New Science of Politics; and Science, Politics, and Gnosticism*
6. *Anamnesis*
7. *Published Essays, 1922–*
8. *Published Essays*
9. *Published Essays*
10. *Published Essays*
11. *Published Essays*
12. *Published Essays, 1966–1985*
13. *Selected Book Reviews*
14. *Order and History,* Volume I, *Israel and Revelation*
15. *Order and History,* Volume II, *The World of the Polis*
16. *Order and History,* Volume III, *Plato and Aristotle*
17. *Order and History,* Volume IV, *The Ecumenic Age*
18. *Order and History,* Volume V, *In Search of Order*
19. *Studies in the History of Political Ideas,* Volume I
20. *Studies in the History of Political Ideas,* Volume II
21. *Studies in the History of Political Ideas,* Volume III
22. *Studies in the History of Political Ideas,* Volume IV
23. *Studies in the History of Political Ideas,* Volume V
24. *Studies in the History of Political Ideas,* Volume VI
25. *Studies in the History of Political Ideas,* Volume VII
26. *Studies in the History of Political Ideas,* Volume VIII
27. *The Nature of the Law, and Related Legal Writings*
28. *What Is History? And Other Late Unpublished Writings*
29. *Selected Correspondence*
30. *Selected Correspondence*
31. *Miscellaneous Papers*
32. *Miscellaneous Papers*
33. *Autobiographical Reflections*
34. *Index*

THE COLLECTED WORKS OF

ERIC VOEGELIN

VOLUME 1

——— ❧ ———

ON THE FORM OF
THE AMERICAN MIND

TRANSLATED FROM THE GERMAN BY

RUTH HEIN

EDITED WITH AN INTRODUCTION BY

JÜRGEN GEBHARDT

AND

BARRY COOPER

LOUISIANA STATE UNIVERSITY PRESS

BATON ROUGE AND LONDON

Designer: Albert Crochet

Typeface: Trump Mediaeval

Typesetter: Impressions, a Division of Edwards Brothers

Printer and binder: Thomson-Shore, Inc.

Library of Congress Cataloging-in-Publication Data

Voegelin, Eric, 1901–
    [Über die Form des amerikanischen Geistes.   English]
    On the form of the American mind / translated from the German by
Ruth Hein ; edited with an introduction by Jürgen Gebhardt and Barry
Cooper.
        p.   cm. — (The Collected works of Eric Voegelin ; v. 1)
    Includes index.
    ISBN 0-8071-1826-5 (alk. paper)
    1. Philosophy—United States.   2. United States—Intellectual
life.   I. Title.   II. Series: Voegelin, Eric, 1901–   Works.   1989 ; v.
1.
B3354.V8813 1989 B3354. V883U 1995
191—dc20   95-34016
                                                              CIP

Jürgen Gebhardt and Barry Cooper would like to thank the Earhart Foundation,
and Barry Cooper also thanks the Social Science and Humanities Research
Council of Canada and the Alexander von Humboldt-Stiftung, for financial
support for research on the political philosophy of Eric Voegelin. John von
Heyking provided able research assistance in identifying many of Voegelin's
English-language resources.

Contents

Editors' Introduction   ix

Editors' Note   xliii

Preface   1

Introduction   2

1. Time and Existence   23

2. On George Santayana   64

3. A Formal Relationship with Puritan Mysticism   126

4. Anglo-American Analytic Jurisprudence   144

5. On John R. Commons   205

Index   283

Eric Voegelin in the early 1930s
Courtesy of Lissy Voegelin

Editors' Introduction

On the Form of the American Mind was published by J. C. B. Mohr of Tübingen in 1928. This first book from Voegelin's hand has remained virtually unknown to the American public; its reception in German academic life was neither cordial nor based on a deep understanding of Voegelin's interpretative strategy. As readers familiar with Voegelin's later work will discover soon enough, his language exhibits little of the limpidity and power of his mature prose. In 1928 Voegelin was but six years beyond the completion of his Ph.D. and still a prisoner of German sociological and academic political usage. Notwithstanding a certain opacity of style and, at first blush, eccentricity of content, *On the Form of the American Mind* can still be read with profit by those in search of an understanding of the spiritual life of the United States.

To assist contemporary readers in gaining access to this work, the editors have divided the introduction and their labors. In the first section the text is situated in the context of methodological debates current at the time of writing; in the second, the context of Voegelin's experience in America is indicated and some comparisons drawn with similar studies from the post–World War I era.

The German Context

"The intellectual history of the first half of the twentieth century is extremely complex because it is the history of a slow recovery (with many trials that have ended in impasses) from the thorough destruction of intellectual culture in the late nineteenth century." In his retrospective remarks to the concise programmatic lectures published as *The New Science of Politics*, Voegelin states that this process of recovery had "reached the point where one can say that at least the foundations for a new science of order have been laid."[1] Voegelin considered a well-developed philosophical anthropology and a theory of the spirit the most important ingredients of a rejuvenated science of politics which is truly concerned about the human predicament. From his scholarly beginnings in the 1920s Voegelin had been engaged in a grand and multifaceted intellectual discourse arising from the attempts of the German-speaking academic world focusing on the problem of a science of sociohistorical reality.

This book is a part of that tradition. The publication in 1928 fell into the last phase of a spirited debate that was ended abruptly by the destruction of free academic discourse after Hitler's rise to power. The particular German quest for a scientific foundation for humanistic scholarship, and especially for a scientific foundation for historical and social disciplines, was carried on by the university-centered social and cultural elites—the "German mandarins," as Fritz Ringer called them. Ringer points out that "the German *Wissenschaft* is not the equivalent of the English *science*," because "the latter implies the use of methods analogous to those of the natural sciences," whereas in German usage, "any organized body of information is referred to as *eine Wissenschaft*, with the indefinite article." And Ringer continues: "At the same time, all formal knowledge, and the collective activity of scholars in obtaining, interpreting, and ordering it, may be rendered *Wissenschaft* or, more commonly, *die Wissenschaft*, with the definite article. Hence, *die Wissenschaft* must be translated as 'scholarship' or 'learning,' rarely as 'science,' and *eine Wissenschaft* simply means 'discipline.' "[2] So Wilhelm Windelband, a leading neo-Kantian, insisted in his lecture "Was ist Philosophie?" (1892) that "the German word *Wissenschaft* . . . fortunately includes much more than the English or French *science*." Referring to the Hellenic notion of episteme he defined scientific thinking (*wissenschaftliches Denken*) as rational cognition directed at any object whatsoever solely for the sake of knowledge itself.[3] Ringer, commenting critically on Windelband's

1. Eric Voegelin, *The New Science of Politics* (Chicago, 1952), 26.
2. Fritz Ringer, *The Decline of the German Mandarins: The German Academic Community, 1890–1933* (Cambridge, Mass., 1969), 102–103.
3. Wilhelm Windelband, *Präludien* (2 vols.; Tübingen, 1919), I, 13, 20–23.

idea of *Wissenschaft*, states questioningly: "Why fortunately? Evidently because the German academics preferred to find in learning itself a dimension of philosophical contemplation and wisdom."[4] Indeed, they did. Learning in terms of searching for truth involved the strictly personal element of self-cultivation, as the German *Bildung* may be rendered. This general idea of *Wissenschaft* originated with German idealism and neohumanism. It became the organizing principle of the reformed university system that Wilhelm von Humboldt inaugurated in Prussia in 1810 and that was imitated by the other German states in due course.

This state-sponsored university system integrated the mathematical-physical sciences and the humanistic disciplines (including theology) under the direction of philosophy into the "scientific" system of institutionalized free research and instruction.[5] Guided by the concept of self-cultivation, these institutions of higher learning aimed at the scholarly education of a cultural elite. A *Professor* was to be the scholar par excellence, and his educational product was the unique social figure of the *Bildungsbürger*.[6] This revolutionary concept of unified research and instruction brought forth novel organizational forms of scholarship, which resulted in a differentiation and professionalization of the whole range of scientific disciplines, the natural sciences as well as the historical and social sciences.

The overall success of the German university system established the high international reputation of German scholarship and made German universities models that were studied and imitated all over the world. But the natural sciences and the applied sciences, as impressive as were their results and notwithstanding their influence upon the formidable economic progress of Germany during this period, did not significantly influence the cultural composition of late-nineteenth-century Germany. The development of systematic history-based humanistic disciplines increasingly played a leading role in the self-interpretation of the society after the decline of the idealist philosophies. These empirically oriented interpre-

4. Ringer, *Decline of the German Mandarins*, 103.
5. Franz Schnabel, *Deutsche Geschichte des 19. Jahrhunderts* (4 vols.; Freiberg, 1948), I, 445–57.
6. Werner Conzel and Jürgen Kocka, eds., *Bildungsbürgertum im 19. Jahrhunderts* (2 vols.; Stuttgart, 1985, 1990); Ulrich Engelhard, *Bildungsbürgertum* (Stuttgart, 1986).

tative sciences of man in society and history postulated "that they—and not a philosophical system—ascertained and revealed the truth about the world, indeed the truth of the world."[7] After German unification in 1871 the universities were the unquestioned social and intellectual centers of the cultural life of the nation, and the professoriate functioned as the guardians of the national culture. Therefore the claim of the humanistic disciplines to reveal scientifically the meaning of the sociohistorical reality entailed more than a matter of academic dispute—it aimed at the formation of the social and cultural identity of the nation in a time of crisis.

This idea of the intellectual leadership of the interpretative sciences of man forced upon them an intensive search for their theoretical and methodological foundations. In the late nineteeenth century two alternative conceptions, neo-Kantian *Kulturwissenschaft* and Dilthey's *Geisteswissenschaft*, emerged from the discourse engendered by this search. Those two approaches evolved from a set of experiences, motivations, sentiments, attitudes, and ideas that were common to the German mandarins and formed their self-understanding in thought and action. First of all, both approaches elaborated epistemological and methodological foundations of the historical and philosophical disciplines in order to safeguard their theoretical status as *Wissenschaften* in terms of their claim to truth and at the same time to distinguish them from the natural sciences. This quest for a common frame of reference for the rapidly developing empirically oriented special disciplines involved a renunciation of the grand designs of idealistic philosophy as well as a refusal of all "positivistic" attempts at transforming the humanities into "hard sciences" analogous to the natural sciences.[8] A second important motive that transcended the scope of a discourse concerned with purely epistemological questions bore a relation to the social function that the professoriate expected the humanities to fulfill in the German society—namely, to be instrumental in the creation of a national cultural community. Being by and large culturally liberal Protestants (with a certain dislike for Socialists, Jews, and Catholics, and with a strong attachment to the

7. Thomas Nipperday, *Deutsche Geschichte, 1835–1866* (Munich, 1983), 532.
8. Wilhelm Windelband, "Geschichte und Naturwissenschaft" [1894], in Windelband, *Präludien*, II, 136–60; Wilhelm Dilthey, *Einleitung in die Geisteswissenschaften* (2d ed.; Berlin, 1923), 3–86.

Bismarckian state), the German mandarins were beset by anxieties over a cultural crisis brought about by the emerging forces of social change in Germany. If this crisis could successfully be met, it would revitalize the great traditions of the eighteenth-century German classics to which all humanistic scholarship was committed and provide a sound moral and spiritual basis to the new nation-state. The mission of *Kultur-* and *Geisteswissenschaft* made sense because it was based on the shared assumption that the concept of *Wissenschaft* and the ancillary concept of *Bildung* embodied the historically most progressive unfolding of humanity, which had been manifest in the German philosophy and literature of the 1800s. Consequently the new sciences of the sociohistorical world seemed most suitable to accommodate this tradition in a rational way with the conditions of a rapidly modernizing society and to supply the badly needed cultural and social cohesion in terms of the specific *German* ideal of order: the cultural and legal state.

Upon closer inspection, however, the questionable character of both concepts becomes obvious. They reflected a precarious tension between the cosmopolitan spirit and the national spirit that marked the intellectual movement of the 1800s, which in turn reflected the absence of a common national experience of politics. The sciences of the sociohistorical world, therefore, took as their points of reference either *culture,* understood as the embodiment of a cultured humankind, or the *objective spirit,* understood as objectification of the historical life of the human world. Culture was to be the subject matter of *Kulturwissenschaft* and the intellectual world that of *Geisteswissenschaft.* There was room neither for the specific political quality of human existence in community, nor for the idea of political man within the natural-law tradition, nor for the paradigm of the political nation in the Western sense.[9] The notion of politics conceived in terms of the *state* involved, first, a "meta-political apperception" of the political realm, as Ernst Vollrath noted, and the realities of political life were permanently measured critically against the image of a morally autonomous community.[10] Hence, "the emphasis was always upon the ultimate

9. Heinrich Rickert, *Kulturwissenschaft und Naturwissenschaft* (Tübingen, 1899), 51–52, 62–68; Wilhelm Dilthey, *Der Aufbau der geschichtlichen Welt in den Geisteswissenschaften* (Göttingen, 1968), 146–56.

10. Ernest Vollrath, "Die Kultur des Politischen: Konzepte politischer Wahrnehmung in Deutschland," in *Der Begriff des Politik,* ed. Volker Gerhardt (Stuttgart, 1989), 268–90.

purposes of government [*i.e.*, of the state]. In the tradition of the legal and cultural state, these theoretical objectives were generally stated in moral and spiritual terms. The analysis of political realities was neglected, and relatively little attention was paid to the questions of political techniques. . . . Indeed the suggestion was that the details of everyday politics were ethically as well as intellectually beneath the notice of the cultivated man."[11] But this exalted paradigm of an "idealistic" politics was modified by "real political apperception" of the *state*, which, in the jurisprudential *Staatswissenschaften*, considered the state as the subject of domination exclusively in terms of the personification of power and rulership. Since, however, cosmopolitan universalism and formal universalism combined in the scientific quest for truth and reinforced each other, the "metapolitical apperception" generally prevailed.

The crucial difference between the neo-Kantians and Dilthey and his students arose from their respective epistemologies and methodologies. In the present context we can provide only a summary outline of essential features of this complex subject. The starting point of the neo-Kantians lay in the expansion of Kant's epistemology from the realm of nature to the realm of culture, first of all by eliminating the thing-in-itself from consideration. This eventually led to the conclusion that generally valid knowledge of any domain of reality is constituted by a priori categories or logical forms inherent in pure thought and detached from the reality under investigation. The validity and objectivity of cognition is guaranteed solely by the functions of thought (*Denkfunktionen*) and grounded in a nonexistent pure subject, or transcendental ego—a status never fully attained by empirical man.

Thus the objects of cognition are intellectually generated. Concepts provide the selective principle "with which reality is investigated . . . [A]ll disciplines of knowledge must be more or less tightly organized around selective principles or goals which they set for themselves and not by the content-area they investigate." Only by means of transcendent a priori categories can reality, which is in itself chaotic and formless, be ordered to yield knowledge.[12] Hence, the principal distinction between the natural sci-

11. Ringer, *Decline of the German Mandarins*, 121.
12. Jeffrey T. Bergner, *The Origin of Formalism in Social Science* (Chicago, 1981),

ences and the humanistic disciplines for the neo-Kantians is founded upon the methodological difference of the modality of cognition (*Erkenntnisweise*). The Southwest German originators of *Kulturwissenschaft*, Windelband and Rickert (and following them, Max Weber) interpreted the logical prius as a theoretical value. This meant that *Kulturwissenschaft* amounted to the embodiment of truth both as an account of knowledge of culture and as an object of culture insofar as culture is defined in terms of the entirety of all culturally valued objects. This a priori valuation of culture as absolute and universally valid (*unbedingt allgemeingültiger Wert der Kultur*) provides the principles for conceptualization and selection in any rational study of the cultural life of historical humankind because it incorporates the historical universality that is embodied in the individual and in particular cultural phenomena. By relating specific phenomena to the leading cultural values, their cultural relevance surfaces and the formless chaos of reality is transformed into ordered knowledge. "The unity and objectivity of *Kulturwissenschaften* depends on the unity and objectivity of our understanding of culture and this in turn is conditioned by the unity and objectivity of our values."[13] By means of this value-relating activity, the scholar approximates the function of the transindividual evaluating subject (the transcendental ego) of cognition, if and insofar as he himself incorporates the cultural value of being a cultivated person (*Kulturmensch*).[14] For this reason Max Weber concludes: "A transcendential prerequisite for all *Kulturwissenschaften* is . . . that we are cultural persons with the ability and the will consciously to take an attitude towards the world and to give it meaning."[15] The other major concept emerging from the rich and manifold field of German scholarly self-reflection, Dilthey's *Geisteswissenschaft*, insisted, contrary to neo-Kantianism, on a content-based difference between the natural sciences and the sciences of the sociohistorical world and likewise on a difference

88; Werner Flach and Helmut Holzney, eds., *Erkenntnistheorie und Logik im Neukantianismus* (Hildesheim, 1980), 9–14; Klaus Christian Köhnke, *Entstehung und Aufsteig des Neukantianismus* (Frankfurt, 1986).

13. Rickert, *Kulturwissenschaft und Naturwissenschaft*, 63.

14. Jürgen Gebhardt, "Die Werte," in *Anodos: Festschrift für Helmut Kuhn*, ed. R. Hoffmann *et al.* (Weinheim, 1989), 35–54.

15. Max Weber, *Gesammelte Aufsätze zur Wissenschaftslehre* (Tübingen, 1968), 180.

in their respective methods.[16] Dilthey's multilayered and in some respects contradictory project aimed at transforming the moral and political sciences into a modern empirical science of the intellectual world. The project was carried out under the auspices of the German philosophical tradition and the historicism of the great German historiographers, and was intended to reconcile the postulate of objective knowledge with the historical notion of relativity. It would do so by means of an epistemological synthesis of philosophical self-reflection (*Selbstbesinnung*) and historical understanding (*Verstehen*) that would result in a unified hermeneutical logic of empirical research. The a priori of any cognition is the coherence of human life (*Lebenszusammenhang*) as presented in the whole range of human experience. The fundamental experience of a common intellectual world of mutual understanding evolves from the specific human awareness of reality. Dilthey designated this sphere of community as the realm of the objective spirit (*Geist*) comprising all manifestations of life in the mode of objectifications of the spirit. This world of the spirit is an interrelation of effects (*Wirkungszusammenhang*) permanently generating values, realizing goals, and producing goods by the interaction of individuals, communities, and cultural systems. The intellectual world constitutes the sociohistorical world in terms of these structural units in time and space.

By turning toward the sociohistorical world, the reflecting human mind moves in a common intellectual world, thereby enabling man to understand and decipher the historical sediments of the spirit as documented in the testimonies of the past. "The context of the intellectual world becomes apparent in connection with the subject, and it is the movement of the spirit up to determining the contexts of meaning of this world, which connects individual logical processes with one another. Thus, on the one hand, this intellectual world is created by the conceived subject and, on the other hand, the movement of the spirit is directed towards attaining objective knowledge in it."[17] In philosophical self-reflection the sociohistorical world, expressing the world of the spirit, attains an objective knowledge of itself, enlightening itself on itself. Thus the virtually formless chaos of reality reveals an underlying structur-

16. Dilthey, *Aufbau der geschichtlichen Welt*, 244–58.
17. *Ibid.*, 191.

ally ordered meaningful whole by means of the hermeneutical logic of empirical research. "History is the most powerful tool for giving speech to one's own inner self and to make it speak and explain. Whatever man finds in himself, he can at first see reflected by history, because it reveals everything that is inside of man and lets him become aware of it. Self-reflection is the foundation for knowledge about the deepest points and positions of the *status humanitatis* and how they influence man's view of himself and of knowledge. The *humanities* [*Geisteswissenschaften*] in turn are the deepest point of the essence of inner experiences and of man."[18] In the course of the ongoing process of empirical research, the *Geisteswissenschaften*, as interpretative sciences of man, bring forth ever-expanding knowledge of the sociohistorical reality along with a growing understanding about man's position in the whole of reality. The *Geisteswissenschaften* disclose to modern man under the open horizon of history the common ground of all human life.[19] The *Geisteswissenschaften* accomplish the purpose of philosophy in the present time: "Man's self-reflection, society's reflection about itself—these should help develop the strength and direction of actively intervening thought and action."[20] In a sense Dilthey's *Geisteswissenschaft* is a substitute for a defunct practical philosophy, but one regrettably devoid of any concept of the political. As Ringer pointed out, this methodological debate of the 1880s and 1890s "cut across disciplinary lines, influencing every field of knowledge outside the natural sciences. It affected the very language of scholarly discourse in the social studies and humanities."[21] The theoretical positions involved, and in particular neo-Kantianism, evoked criticism of the varied intellectual movements that were engaged in recasting the central philosophical problems and solutions that had been previously formulated in this debate. Before World War I, and especially after the defeat of 1918, German intellectual life was again marked by a widespread feeling of profound cultural and sociopolitical crisis. The sense of crisis reani-

18. Wilhelm Dilthey, *Grundlegung der Wissenschaften vom Menschen, der Gesellschaft und der Geschichte* (Göttingen, 1982), 276.
19. See Manfred Riedel, "Hermeneutik und Erkenntniskritik," in Riedel, *Verstehen und Erklären* (Stuttgart, 1978), 64–112; Hans Georg Gadamer, *Wahrheit und Methode* (Tübingen, 1875), 205–28.
20. Dilthey, *Grundlegung der Wissenschaften*, 304.
21. Ringer, *Decline of the German Mandarins*, 316.

mated the quest for grounding the spiritual life in reality in order to reach a synthesis of learning with the realities of human existence in the midst of a deeply troubled Weimar Republic. In this complex intellectual and political situation, the borderline between philosophical reflection and the *Weltanschauung* of a politically alienated conservative intelligentsia often became blurred. But such outstanding intellectual figures of this movement of intellectual renewal as Edmund Husserl, Max Scheler, and Karl Jaspers were committed to a critical revision of the antecedent paradigms and focused on the central question of the cognitive and rational explication of the human world.

A whole generation of young scholars during the early 1920s was under the spell of this thriving intellectual culture that absorbed Nietzschean radicalism, French vitalism, scientific positivism, traditional historicism, phenomenology, critical realism, the revived classical idealism, Freudianism, and even the new theories of physics. This situation involved new challenges to any conceptualization of a science of man in society and history, and new responses were required.

When Eric Voegelin entered the scientific community he was confronted with a strange mixture of new trends and traditional conventions in scholarship. His dissertation "Wechselwirkung und Gezweiung" (1922)[22] discusses and compares two theoretical concepts, the one developed by Georg Simmel, who along with Max Weber was a founding father of German sociology, and the other by Othmar Spann, the Viennese representative of an organicist social science rooted in German romanticism. Although Voegelin originally was a student of Spann, very soon he began to work with the famous law professor Hans Kelsen, the foremost exponent of the jurisprudential discipline dealing with law and government that the Germans call *Staatslehre*. In Kelsen's work the traditional *Staatswissenschaft* had been reshaped into a "pure theory of law" (*Reine Rechtslehre*), purged of all sociological and speculative elements by means of neo-Kantian logic. Without denying the scientific accomplishments of Kelsen, Voegelin became increasingly critical of the implications of this approach for empirical research because, in his eyes, generating the object of inquiry by logical a

22. Eric Voegelin, "Wechselwirkung und Gezweiung," in Voegelin Papers, Box 51, Folder 5, Hoover Institution Archives, Hoover Institution, Stanford, California.

xviii

priori eliminated the empirical formative elements of the state as a "historical meaningful unit" (*historische Sinneinheit*).[23] While still interpreting the humanities in terms of the neo-Kantian concept of the "sciences of cultural objectifications of the spirit" (*Kulturobjektivationen des Geistes*), Voegelin distanced himself from the specific epistemology of Kelsen's *Staatslehre*. It should, however, be noted that only many years later did Voegelin identify the positivistic metaphysics in Kelsen's thought.[24] Very much under the impact of Max Weber's fundamental search for the meaning of any historical science,[25] Voegelin went his own independent way and directed his academic work toward "a reconstruction of the complete science of the state," which would include the "cognition of the essential core of state formation" (*Wesenskern der Staatsbildung*).[26]

This reconstruction begins with a history of the dogmatics of German historical and juridical *Staatslehre*, told backward (*Dogmengeschichte nach rückwärts*) in order to explain how the developmental history of the *Staatslehre* implied a "destruction of the problem complex" to be found in the highlights of the political philosophy of Plato and Aristotle in antiquity, of the scholastics, of the Enlightenment, and of German idealism. Voegelin transformed the historian's unsystematic quest for the essential elements of state formation by means of Weber's concepts of "social relationship and meaningful oriented action" into a critical analysis of community formation. The "idea of community," signifying the fact of political cohesion, is to be denoted by the term "meaningful unit" (*Sinneinheit*): "the variety of actions is combined into a unified entity of meaning in the 'community.' "[27] Community is not to be put in psychological terms since it is not present in the consciousness of every single individual all the time but unfolds in the entirety of individual actions. Individual actions coalesce into

23. Eric Voegelin, "Zur Lehre von der Staatsform," *Zeitschrift für öffentliches Recht*, LXIV (July, 1927), 572-608; see also Eric Voegelin, "Kelsen's Pure Theory of Law," *Political Science Quarterly*, XLII (1927), 268–76.

24. An extensive discussion of Kelsen is in Eric Voegelin, *Der autoritäre Staat* (Vienna, 1936), 102–17.

25. See Eric Voegelin, "Über Max Weber," *Deutsche Vierteljahresschrift für Literaturwissenschaft und Geistesgeschichte*, III (1925), 177–93.

26. Eric Voegelin, "Reine Rechtslehre und Staatslehre," *Zeitschrift für öffentliches Recht*, IV (1924), 124, 131.

27. *Ibid.*, 120.

the unity of a community by means of such symbols as monarchy or democracy. Those symbols are not part of the individual's consciousness but constitute a reality of their own, which is sociopolitical reality. The unity of political action achieved by symbols is determined by the idea of the meaningful unit in the sense of Kant's regulative idea. The meaningful unit, Voegelin said, unfolds at (am) the historical substratum and thus comes to constitute the state capable of general political action (gesamthandlung Staat).[28] This reconstruction of the science of the state (Wissenschaft vom Staat) was to culminate in the tenet of the "idea of the state" (Lehre von der Idee des Staates), which is the supreme conditioning form of the state (höchste bedingende Form des Staates). The presupposition of the ideas links up the theories of the different cultural objectifications (relating to the state, religion, art, economics) in a system of social philosophy.[29]

These early studies reflected the "crisis of the Staatslehre"[30] that was triggered by the unsettling experiences of the revolutionary change of regime in Germany after the end of World War I. The ruling theoretical and methodological paradigm was challenged by the rival approaches of sociology and Geisteswissenschaft. Voegelin's search for a theoretical grounding for Staatslehre was at first very much informed by interpretative sociology. Voegelin focused, however, on the signification of symbols and ideas in forming the meaningful intellectual composition of the reality of the state as a political unit. The inquiry into those meaningfully structured social units grounded in typical forms of the mind conflicted with neo-Kantian a priorism since the meaning that constituted the object of the inquiry, namely the state, evolved from the sociohistorical reality itself. Voegelin, therefore, broke away from the neo-Kantian underpinnings of interpretative sociology and—in the course of his extensive and elaborate exposition of the manifold currents of contemporary and traditional thought—undergirded it by means of a revised epistemology of Geisteswissenschaft. The published, and in particular the unpublished, writings of Voegelin in the late 1920s and the early 1930s testify to his continuing at-

28. Ibid., 126–27.
29. Ibid., 131.
30. Hermann Heller, "Die Krisis der Staatslehre," Archiv für Sozialwissenschaft und Sozialpolitik, LV (1926), 289–316.

tempt to work out a *"geisteswissenschaftliche Staatslehre."*[31] Reviewing Carl Schmitt's *Verfassungslehre* in 1931, Voegelin explicitly stated his epistemological concern: "In my opinion, the principle of purity of methods cannot be applied to a field of the *Geisteswissenschaften* such as *Staatslehre*, because the subject that is to be the object of scientific research has its own fundamental characteristics irrespective of the epistemological context of the science, and scientific objectification cannot be carried out independently according to its own principle, but needs to be an imitation of the model in the subject."[32]

The decisive step of this reorientation, which gave Voegelin's concept of *Geisteswissenschaft* its highly original and distinctive mark, occurred as a result of his American experiences. This book considers these experiences in terms of an interpretative understanding of the American mind. In the Introduction, Voegelin wrote that his book was intended not as "an inspired riddle-solving synthesis of the American mind" but as "a first attempt at extracting the instruments of interpretation as well as the meaning from the material itself."[33] Presenting unknown material and interpreting it at the same time considerably impedes the understanding of the intimate correspondence of the different sections of the book. Indeed, some of the German reviewers shared this impression and they made it a main point of their critiques.[34] Voegelin, however, meant his extensive Introduction to be a commentary that was to summarize the substantial and methodical patterns of meaning that result from working on the material and that are to be found fragmented in the text.[35]

The dense and complicated Introduction was intended to explicate Voegelin's hermeneutical approach to the analysis of national mental types and shed light on a crucial phase in his intellectual life. In particular the assimilation of the American experience into the theoretical and methodological framework of the revised *Geis-*

31. Eric Voegelin, *Staatslehre als Geisteswissenschaft*, in Voegelin Papers, Box 53, Folder 8.
32. Eric Voegelin, "Die Verfassungslehre von Carl Schmitt: Versuch einer Konstruktiven Analyse ihrer staatstheoretischen Prinziplien," *Zeitschrift für öffentliches Recht*, XI (1931), 89–109; quoted from p. 90.
33. Eric Voeglin, *On the Form of the American Mind*, herein, 3.
34. See the review of M. Palyi, in *Archiv für Rechtsphilosophie*, XXII (July, 1929), 645–47.
35. Voegelin, *Form of the American Mind*, herein, 3.

teswissenschaft provided a firm epistemological basis for a hermeneutical science of the sociocultural world distinct from all that
concerned neo-Kantian transcendentalism.

The theoretical intention, as indicated by the Introduction, is
integrated directly with the key sections of the interpretative presentation of the material. The Introduction is not, however, a
model of clarity. Accordingly, in order to clarify the conceptual
apparatus, we will draw on some unpublished lectures, written in
English, that discuss "the problem of national types of mind." What
occasioned this text was a series of lectures on international relations given in Geneva in December, 1930.[36] The language is matter-
of-fact. The argumentation avoids philosophical problems *sensu
stricto*. But in some important points Voegelin's objective comes
more clearly into focus, if this material is used with some care as
a supplement to the Introduction. Nevertheless, for the reader to
see how they were adapted to his special investigative purposes,
Voegelin's principles and categories have to be placed in the context
of the intellectual discourse from which he had taken them. This
context is not spelled out in the book, and often it is difficult to
discover it in the midst of Voegelin's vast and varied reading. It
may be specified as follows.

The subject matter of Voegelin's scientific inquiry—namely, the
form or, broadly speaking, the type of the American mind—does
not constitute an a priori determined (neo-Kantian) transcendent
object of a specific scientific discipline. Rather, the subject matter
emerges from an analysis of what Voegelin termed *geistige Gestal-
tungen*. In the text we have translated this technical term as "intellectual formation," which is even less self-explanatory in English than was Voegelin's German. Nevertheless, the meaning he
intended can be made tolerably clear. Examples of an intellectual
formation include such things as philosophy, law, and economic
theory. These are understood to be expressions of a common form
and style, which in turn bind together disparate intellectual formations into a meaningful whole, a "mental network" that can be

36. Eric Voegelin, "National Types of Mind and the Limits to Interstate Relations," in Voegelin Papers, Box 51. This text is unidentified in the Voegelin Archive.
It is referred to, however, in a list of publications appended to a letter from Voegelin
to the Paris Office of the Rockefeller Foundation: Voegelin to J. Van Sickle, June 19,
1931, in RF 705/5/46, Rockefeller Archive Center, North Tarrytown, New York.
The occasion for the Geneva lectures is not mentioned.

interpretatively apperceived and described. This analysis dissolves disciplinary borders and orders the material according to its immanent meaning. In other words, meaningful interrelationships among intellectual formations are clarified in light of the common mental form, so that a wide range of intellectual, cultural, and social phenomena fall into a comprehensive pattern.

Voegelin's concept of mental forms owes much to Ernst Cassirer's modification of the neo-Kantian approach to the *Geisteswissenschaften*. Cassirer aimed at providing "an adequate methodological basis for the cultural sciences," that is, the *Geisteswissenschaften*. Proceeding from the neo-Kantian investigation of the conditions of the scientific cognition of the world, he sought to describe the various fundamental ways of "understanding" the world in order to grasp their specific direction and their characteristic mental forms. "Only when such a 'morphology' of the human spirit was established, at least in general outline, could we hope to arrive at a clearer and more reliable methodological approach to the individual cultural sciences."[37] Cassirer "sees . . . the unifying element in the unity of the mind as the unity of its forming and of the rules inherent in its objectification and 'directions.' "[38] Being products or self-revelations of the spirit (*Geist*), the mental forms materialize by way of the symbolizing capacity of consciousness. The Kantian distinction between the "intelligible" and the "sensual," between "idea" and "appearance," dissolves. We are caught in a world of images (*Bildwelt*). "Through it alone do we see that which we call 'reality.' "[39] Culture conditions the creation of particular worlds of images, particular symbolic forms. The intent of philosophy is to understand those images and forms in their formative fundamental principle.[40] Voegelin too insists that all "reality" is mediated by the symbolic. The existence of symbols as signs (*symbolisches Sein*) and the existence of the things that the symbols refer to (*existentiales Sein*) cannot be divided neatly into separate realms that exist per se. The morphological analysis draws close to existential being,

37. Ernst Cassirer, *Philosophy of Symbolic Forms*, trans. Ralph Manheim (3 vols.; New Haven, 1953), I, 69.
38. Massimo Ferrari, "Das Problem der Geisteswissenschaften in den Schriften Cassirers für die Bibliothek Warburg (1921–1923)," in *Über Cassirers Philosophie der symboliscen Formen*, ed. Hans Jörg Braun *et al.* (Frankfurt, 1988), 114–33, quoted from p. 122.
39. Cassirer, *Philosophy of Symbolic Forms*, I, 111.
40. *Ibid.*, 202.

which, however, retreats. What remains are again only symbols. Existential being and symbolic being penetrate each other, so that all being is always symbolic. The duality of symbol and existence represents in its tensional relationship the unity of being. There is "no actual intrinsic reality over which a structure of nonreality rises" by means of symbolization. The inspection of the realm of mental forms discloses only symbolic being, the inner composition of which alone is to be experienced and interpreted.[41] Voegelin detached Cassirer's conceptualization from its systematic classification of symbolic forms (myth, religion, science, ethics, art, etc.) and connected the notion of the universal objectifying function of language to his own concept of the mental morphology of sociocultural units; he did so on the assumption that they are determined by an underlying formative principle of the mind. This sociological specification of Cassirer's tenet of culture followed from Voegelin's prior designation of the state as a meaningful unit: "every intellectual formation that arises in a social body reveals traces of its origin in its form. . . . But such a social body is itself merely the embodiment of intellectual formations held together by traits peculiar to the form."[42]

Now, the aforementioned lecture on "national types" stated that the aim was to outline a "science of types of mind" that "acknowledges the substantial homogeneity of all cultural units to be investigated, as well of the fundamental differences between them according to the principle of mind that is embodied in everyone, and gives them their *morphé*, their unique style from the innermost and essential phenomenon to the last and almost negligible detail."[43] The "morphological postulate" implies that the whole apparatus of everyday life, the organization of the state as well as the works of science and of art, reveal the properties of the style and mental form (*Formeigentülichkeiten*). But these materials do not lend themselves easily to an analysis of the form itself, since they are peripheral to the morphological center from which the categories, structure, and motives of all intellectual figurations emerge. "The central sphere of material is therefore the realm where the mind expresses itself in speculations on the meaning of life, the

41. Voegelin, *Form of the American Mind*, herein, 23–24.
42. *Ibid.*, 5–6.
43. Voegelin, "National Types of Mind," 17.

place of man in society and the universe, etc."[44] These materials are more suitable for morphological analysis because they entail exclusively "entities of linguistic expression of a theoretical nature." Accordingly, Voegelin said, theory is supposed to mean "an attempt claiming to order a field of problems rationally,"[45] which is a Weberian formulation.

The selection of this kind of textual material for interpretative analysis of mental forms is justified insofar as the language of a theoretical text comes closest to the conceptual language of the analysis proper. Since language is the medium of both the object of inquiry and the inquiry itself, linguistic expressions of a theoretical nature best reveal the formal specifics of intellectual figurations. This holds true in particular for those linguistic-theoretical phenomena (sprachlich-theoretische Erscheinungen) that are preeminently "self-expressive" because unlike the natural sciences, whose objects transcend the medium of expression, they are philosophical by nature—that is, they inherently involve self-reflection (Selbstbesinnung) about their subject matter and about themselves.

The "subject matter is essentially immanent, and its medium—the epistemological process in its multifarious forms—is also the medium in which it is studied."[46] Voegelin fuses Cassirer's "morphology of the mind" with the Diltheyan hermeneutical science that is defined as "the art of understanding written manifestations of life."[47] Dilthey's hermeneutical method relies on the self-expressive character of the objects to be interpretatively understood. In 1924 Georg Misch, Dilthey's student, son-in-law, and editor, clarified the underlying theoretical assumptions as follows:

> The logical characteristic of the Geisteswissenschaften is based . . .
> on the expressive nature of its objects; on the assumption that these
> mental objects . . . can speak to us of their own volition, that they do
> not merely bear meaning in formative being and express it. . . . And
> we can understand the language of these objects, which all have their
> own self, because the spiritual life that is expressed objectively in this
> work of real proceeding history is basically one with the formative
> powers in the soul of the cognitive person who, despite his individu-

44. Ibid., 204.
45. Voegelin, Form of the American Mind, herein, 4.
46. Ibid., 7.
47. Wilhelm Dilthey, Die geistige Welt (Göttingen, 1957), 333.

ality, is in real contact with the whole of humankind precisely because his own life is of historical nature.[48]

The epistemological key to a hermeneutical understanding of the sociohistorical reality is the self-reflective act, *Selbstbesinnung*. Helmuth Plessner, who explicitly rooted *Geisteswissenschaft* in a philosophical anthropology, defined "philosophical hermeneutics as the systematic response to the question regarding the possibility of achieving self-understanding of life through the medium of experiences gained through history."[49] Constituting the hermeneutics as philosophical anthropology meant a specification of *Selbstbesinnung* that owed much to Husserl's phenomenology. Husserl always viewed *Selbstbesinnung* as going beyond its particular function in the phenomenological enterprise as an element in man's meditative quest for the essence of his personality and the meaning of his existence.[50] This anthropological aspect of *Selbstbesinnung* was very important for Voegelin because it was instrumental in his philosophical analysis of mental forms. *Selbstbesinnung* reaches into the self-conscious center of the human personality, thus gaining access to the centers of meaning of any web of symbolic forms. When it is applied to the mental forms of a sociocultural unit, this procedure identifies the morphological center of a national type of mind.

From the hermeneutical point of view, *Selbstbesinnung* works on the historical material in order to get it to speak on its own terms. The categories of the analysis are therefore, as Voegelin states, "purely empirical" and not formulated a priori. Under the anthropological aspect, *Selbstbesinnung* pinpoints the organizing principles underlying the categorical expressions of mental forms. For this central sphere of meaning Voegelin uses the categorical concept of the *personal*. Personal meanings relate to the central attitudes of life and denote the dialectics of self-consciousness.[51] Other spheres of life that are peripheral to the personal crystallize

48. Georg Misch, "Die Idee der Lebensphilosophie in der Theorie der Geisteswissenschaften" [1924], in *Materialien zur Philosophie Wilhelm Diltheys*, ed. Frithjof Rodi and Hans Ulrich Lessing (Frankfurt, 1984), 132–46; quoted from p. 141.
49. Helmut Plessner, *Die Stufen des Organischen und der Mensch* (1928; rpr. Berlin, 1975), 23.
50. See Gerhard Pfafferoth, "Die Bedeutung des Begriffs Selbstbesinnung bei Dilthey und Husserl," in *Dilthey und die Philosophie der Gegenwart*, ed. Ernst Wolfgang Orth (Freiburg, 1985), 351–80.
51. Voegelin, *Form of the American Mind*, herein, 9–11.

around this center of meaning. This categorical distinction between the *personal* and the *peripheral* permits morphological analysis to trace the formulation of the mental form into all social ramifications.

The structural shape of the modes of self-consciousness in its relation to social or economic structures (property, economic and administrative institutions, social mores) comes to light and can be presented in terms of a morphological uniformity of style of the personal as well as of the peripheral structures in society. This fundamental categorical frame describes morphologically determined patterns of meaning to be found in such different areas of inquiry as the intellectual biography of a philosopher (George Santayana), the life and work of a political figure (John R. Commons), and the development of concepts (the concept of time).

This hermeneutical approach to the mental forms oscillates between the study of "personal and anonymous processes" (*persönliche und anonyme Abläufe*), the personal one being more important. "Because even if the thought of an impersonal movement of the mind can be grasped, its life is nevertheless empirically bound to that of man, which expresses itself and moves in a mental form. The form is not an inflexible boundary for a subject, causing its edges to be clearly delineated against the background; . . . Rather, all form is dissolved in the movement of the mind itself, and consequently the shadow can be caught for a moment only in the medium of history, which follows the movement."[52] This theoretical explication of the fundamental principle of morphological analysis indicates again that Voegelin works with the fundamental premise of the hermeneutical *Geisteswissenschaft:* All manifestations of human life are objectifications of the spirit that materialize in the historical and social world. The "context of activity of the spiritual world" grounded in the movements of the objective spirit is disclosed by the logic of hermeneutical research insofar as the human mind discovers its own in the historical creations of the intellectual world. The historical forms of the mind express the historical movement of the spirit, Voegelin insists, and the selection of the historical objects to be investigated is made by history itself. "Any cross section of life contains an infinite variety of possible contin-

52. *Ibid.,* 17.

uations to the next point on the historical continuum. Of these only one is chosen—not by the historian, but by life itself. The historical line of meaning runs like a rope across the abyss into which everything that cannot stay on the rope plunges. Lines of meaning can be of varying length and varying universality. . . . But the one attribute they all have in common is that each subsequent moment is a continuation of the preceding moment and is meaningfully connected with it."[53] Consequently the historical movement of the spirit articulates itself in the intellectual formations in terms of lines of meaning that are made visible by means of the categorical framework.

But the categories never exhaust the richness of the realm of mental forms. They only bring out more clearly the interplay of structural variations and the typical motives from which the intellectual formations arise. Those motives, however, that occasion all intellectual formations spring up from the primary problems of life: "sorrows of loneliness, yearning for the company of others, for intimacy and love, the emotional adventures of youth, the disillusionment of old age, the expectation of death."[54]

The projected hermeneutical inquiry into the form of the American mind starts out with an elaborate and demanding discussion of the concepts of time and existence in European and American philosophy in order to lay bare the structure of American self-consciousness and the implied notion of the human person. The comparative approach is methodologically necessary, Voegelin argued in his lecture on the problem of national mental types, in order "to separate the fundamental structure common to all units from the morphological element and by this separation single out the national features."[55] Taking his point of departure from David Hume's philosophy, Voegelin juxtaposes the modes of thought and motivating experiences operative in European (S. H. Hodgson, Franz Brentano, Husserl) and American (William James, Charles S. Peirce) philosophizing on time and existence. The extended interpretation of Santayana that follows demonstrates the peculiar American-European synthesis of the two morphological worlds in the intellectual biography of an outstanding philosophical thinker.

53. *Ibid.*, 18.
54. *Ibid.*, 22.
55. Voegelin, "National Types of Mind," 206.

Even if the problems and the materials that the philosophers worked on are identical, Voegelin concludes, their respective philosophical accounts present different worlds, as is revealed in their participation in the typical world of ideas of a specific large social body.[56] In order to indicate structural differences between the constitutive concepts of personality, Voegelin distinguishes between the "open self" and the "closed self," terminology adapted from Henri Bergson's *personne ouverte.* "If we conceive the European tradition, with its mania for conceptualizing the mystery of the person rationally, as a doctrine of a *closed* self, the philosophy of the type of Peirce's and James's can be called the doctrine of the *open* self."[57] The form of the open self adopted by the American dialectics of self-consciousness is the meaningful center from which all other forms radiate into society, namely: the fundamental principles of democratic community formation and economic life; the religious notions of God; the emphasis on the practical purposes of all scientific work; and, as a result of a certain disparagement of theory, an empty intellectualism.[58]

The historical depth of the form of the open self is examined in Voegelin's study of the Puritan mystic Jonathan Edwards. This chapter brings into focus the Christian roots of the American ideas of the person and the community. In terms of morphological analysis, the form of the American mind centering around the open self can be traced back to the beginnings of the formation of American identity in colonial times.

The formative impact of the personal structure on the legal culture is indicated in the chapter on Anglo-American jurisprudence. The Americanization of English jurisprudence, Voegelin argues, led to the natural-law tradition of American constitutionalism. It remodeled English legal culture on the image of a free and democratic individual whose needs are supposed to be served by a pragmatically and empirically conceived law and who, defined by his rights, becomes the organizing center of community life.

The final chapter, on John R. Commons, expands the presentation of the life and work of this representative of political and economic reform into a multifaceted analysis of the idea of a demo-

56. Voegelin, *Form of the American Mind,* herein, 72.
57. *Ibid.,* 63.
58. *Ibid.,* 11–14.

cratic community. Here Voegelin considers the mental, political, social, and economic aspects of democracy in the context of modern urban and industrial America. Voegelin's exposition of the subject was colored by his close personal relationship with Commons. Indeed, his work with Commons in Wisconsin left an indelible mark on Voegelin's understanding of America: Commons and the "Wisconsin Idea" of the Progressive movement shaped his view of American democratic politics for all his life.[59]

Commons' biography, his social ideas, and his political practice concentrate in microcosm the events and forces of the great social and political transformation in the 1890s, which were a great watershed of American history. As a consequence of the end of the frontier and the beginning of industrialization, the life of the pioneer and settler was on the wane. The growth of the industrial system of production and of the working class, of trusts and of political machines, required a reconstruction of the democratic citizen community that would include the whole nation. "In his pragmatism, his opportunitism, his talent for compromise and for common sense, his shrewdness and curiosity, his humor and simplicity, his suspicion of theory and of theorists, his versatility and industry, and his idealism," said the American intellectual historian, Henry Steele Commager, "Commons was one of the representative men of his generation."[60] Voegelin does not exaggerate when he claims that the life of Commons became "the collector and the expression of the history of a nation and of its meaning."[61] In Commons' "philosophy of the concrete life" that emerges from the depth of American society, Voegelin sees the ongoing efficacy of the open self in all areas of American life. The whole range of cultural and social phenomena, from John Dewey's philosophy and Giddings' sociological thought to the basic conceptions of politics as well as to economic and legal institutions, trade unionism and industrial relations, is conditioned by the interrelationship of personal and peripheral structures. And again, Voegelin describes the structural difference in the whole complex of social life that separates the American mental form from the European.

59. See Eric Voegelin, "La Follette und die Wisconsin-Idee," *Zeitschrift für Politik*, XVII (1927), 309–21.
60. Henry Steele Commager, *The American Mind* (New Haven, 1963), 246.
61. Voegelin, *Form of the American Mind*, herein, 15.

John R. Commons *ca.* 1920
Courtesy of Lissy Voegelin

In his concluding remarks Voegelin discusses the structural difference between social types of mind in a very instructive way, returning to the fundamental epistemological problem of the hermeneutical *Geisteswissenschaft* that prided itself on its empirical "philosophy of life" (*Lebensphilosophie*). Commons' "philosophy of life" differs from

> all European attempts, especially those of Bergson and Simmel, primarily by one trait that on first glance looks like dilettantism. The thoughts are developed without any significant prior philosophical education. The technique of treating the concepts is highly inadequate, and the intention of putting down in writing a philosophical system is missing completely. It almost looks as though this theory of law and economics had accidentally grown into a major philosophy. But it is precisely the apparent dilettantism and the inadvertent element in forming the system that have their origins in the typically American approach to the problems; that is, they originate not in the structure of the system, as is true in the writings of Bergson and Simmel, but in its tangibly experienced everyday events.[62]

62. *Ibid.*, 280–81.

By means of investigating the history of the American worker, as well as his present condition, or by analyzing the decisions of the Supreme Court, the American confronts his problem of life; where the analysis is most penetrating, it brings to light the metaphysical content of the problem in a splendid way.

> The same philosophy of life that presents itself in Europe as the final product of individual philosophical culture, seen by selected people and aimed at an intellectual elite, is discovered in America by an exceedingly modest and amiable man who, coming from a farmers' and workers' environment, spent decades working through his historical and political experiences. His perspective was so astute that, almost without being aware of what he was doing, he needed only to say what he saw in order to give the highest philosophical expression to the significance of the society in which and for which he lived.[63]

Beyond Voegelin's obvious admiration for Commons, this statement clearly proved to be seminal for Voegelin's projected *hermeneutics* of the sociohistorical world. The claim of *Geisteswissenschaft* to be an empirical philosophy (*Erfahrungsphilosophie*) of reality and of life grounded in the universal and "unmutilated" experience (Dilthey) can only be justified if in fact the analysis of intellectual formations is firmly placed in the context of political life. Moreover, the objectifications of the mind are not manifestations of life per se, but are bound up intrinsically with collective and transpersonal modes of human socialization.

The realm of the spirit takes shape historically in the political forms of human existence, which includes a wide range of cultural and social ramifications. The human experience of life revolves around the modes of the sociopolitical embodiment of mental forms, and as was indicated, its morphological center of meaning was denoted by the category of the *personal.* The personal indicates the area where the realm of the objective spirit intersects with the minds of individuals, thus constituting a transpersonal unity of meaning that is understood as the mental form of the political community. In a sense Voegelin recast *Geisteswissenschaft* in political terms that smoothed the way for his own *geisteswissenschaftliche Staatslehre,* which in turn anticipated the philosophy of politics of his later years.

Analysis of *On the Form of the American Mind* indicates that

63. *Ibid.,* 281.

Voegelin integrated the approaches of *Lebensphilosophie* into what Georg Misch called the "philosophical combination of anthropology and history" that was characteristic of the new trends in the discourse of the *Geisteswissenschaften* and that finally resulted in a theoretical paradigm of philosophical anthropology. Under the impact of the experience of western European and American intellectual and social worlds, Voegelin had become aware that his project of a *geisteswissenschaftliche Staatslehre* was bound up with the "particular movement of the German mind." In a speech on Max Weber (1930) he spelled out this specific historical condition of a German scientist. "The national communities of the West, France, England, and those taking shape in America, live in the tradition of the idea that has been forming their political societies and people since the seventeenth century." Because the social sciences are connected to political ideas, no self-reflection (*Selbstbesinnung*) about their ethical and metaphysical preconditions will take place. But Germany is different: "The nation lacked political unity, and, therefore, it never created an image of the political life of the citizens, of the public relations of the Germans to one another and to the leaders of their state, which would have been embossed in the existence of each individual in such a way that it would have seemed natural and beyond all doubt as was the case in the West. . . . Whereas each of us bears the responsibility for the maxims of our individual actions within the community, Western man can move freely in the forms of his tradition."[64] The German scientific and social culture is chiefly molded by the modern "separation of cognition and belief" that necessitates self-reflection on the ethical and metaphysical conditions of responsible public and communitarian action and makes it the central motive of scientific activity. Science is, therefore, says Voegelin, quoting Weber, "reasonableness for self-reflection and the knowledge of actual conditions."[65] There Voegelin is in agreement with Dilthey's original motive for founding the *Geisteswissenschaft:* "Man's self-reflection, society's reflection about itself."[66] But contrary to Dilthey's unreflected universalism, Voegelin had become aware of the specific German relationship of politics to philosophy, and he made it the

64. Voegelin, "Über Max Weber," 14.
65. *Ibid.,* 15.
66. Dilthey, *Grundlegung der Wissenschaften,* 304.

leitmotiv of his philosophizing. Self-reflection, in Voegelin's view, opens the empirical horizons of human existence and its orders. In order to accomplish this task, Voegelin meant to break away from the speculative world of the closed self and to establish a model of self-reflection on the experience of the open self.

This is the quintessence of the German-American synthesis in his intellectual biography. An anthropologically grounded concept of "openness" become the centerpiece of his hermeneutical project. The spirit "is open to the world not only by reaching out and acting but also open as the place for the eruption of the spiritual reality that lies beyond the person. It has insights and inspirations. It is immediately bound up with the world ground, and it is embedded in the spiritual communities at all levels: humanity, the nation down to the family circle, and close bonds of friendship."[67] These formulations encapsule Voegelin's philosophical anthropology of the open self. The meeting point where the personal mind encounters the realm of the transpersonal spirit is meditatively opened up in a "boundary experience" (*Grenzerfahrung*). This experience is constitutive for human existence insofar as it illuminates the cognitive and existential center of the human personality. An unpublished text of Voegelin's written in 1931 offers the following explanation: "A person is the experience at the boundary at which a finite of this world is contrasted against an infinite of the other world."[68] This experience has persons attain the certainty of their own essence, their personal core (*Personskern*). The empirical determination of the essential core of the person is realized in the course of philosophical self-reflection. Thus, contours of a philosophical anthropology based on a theory of the spirit emerge in Voegelin's conceptualization of a science of national types of mind. It is closely connected to the broad intellectual movement in Germany that converges on the fundamental quest of philosophical anthropology that motivated such different thinkers as Edmund Husserl, Ernst Cassirer, Georg Misch, Helmuth Plessner, Karl Jaspers, Max Scheler, and Martin Heidegger in the 1920s. It is the quest for an interpretative self-assertion in the light of empirical knowledge about ourselves. The concept of philosophical anthropology

67. Eric Voegelin, *Rasse und Staat* (Tübingen, 1933), 68–69.
68. Eric Voegelin, "Herrschaftslehre," in Voegelin Papers, Box 53, Folder 5, p. 17.

welded anew the philosophical to the empirical.[69] But Voegelin aimed not at freewheeling speculations about man as such but at a heuristic means for the investigation of the multifaceted historical concretions of the spirit in the social world. The scholar, he notes in the text quoted above, cannot grasp the spirit in its timeless *an sich* but only "by dealing with his historic reality scientifically."[70]

Only a few of the German reviewers came to terms with the theoretical intentions of the author[71] or realized at least the innovative potential of the study.[72] Other reviewers did not understand the guiding principles and methodological implications of Voegelin's morphological approach from the outset. They therefore criticized mainly the selection of material and the formal structure of its organization. Nearly all reviewers noted the very demanding and occasionally opaque literary style of Voegelin's language. In general this book by an aspiring young scholar gained only cursory attention by the scholarly public, as was customary in German academic life. However, one enthusiastic American reviewer concluded: "As a whole, the inquisitive and sympathetic enquiry outweighs carloads of other foreign interpretations of America."[73]

The American Context

The Laura Spelman Rockefeller Memorial provided a short-lived opportunity for outstanding young European scholars to undertake postdoctoral work in the United States. The memorial was established in October, 1918, for general philanthropic purposes. In 1922 its mandate was changed to focus on specific social problems— welfare, child study, interracial relations, and so on—but also to support social science research. By 1929, however, the memorial was reconsolidated with the Rockefeller Foundation. Eric Voegelin

69. See Herbert Schnädelbach, *Philosophie in Deutschland, 1831–1933* (Frankfurt, 1983), 268–69; Wolfgang Lepenies, "Wandel der Disziplinkonstellationen in den Wissenschaften vom Menschen," in *Der Mensch und die Wissenschaften vom Menschen* (Innsbruck, 1983), 67–82; Karl Siegbert Rehberg, "Philosophische Anthropologie und die 'Soziologisierung' des Wissens vom Menschen," in *Soziologie in Deutschland und Österreich*, ed. Rainer M. Lepsius (Opladen, 1981), 160–98.

70. Voegelin, "Herrschaftslehre," 20. See also Jürgen Gebhardt, "Erich Voegelin und die neuere Entwicklung der Geisteswissenschaften," *Zeitschrift für Politik*, XXXVI (1989), 251–63.

71. Günter Sauermann, in *Nationalwirtschaft*, V (1929), 666–67.

72. Carl Brinkmann, in *Historische Zeitschrift*, CXL (1929), 109–11.

73. G. Müller, in *University of Oklahoma Books Abroad*, July, 1933.

received his doctorate from the University of Vienna in December, 1922; he spent the first part of 1923 studying German constitutional law at Berlin and Heidelberg and took up a post in October, 1923, in Vienna, as assistant to Hans Kelsen. Later that year he was proposed by Dr. Pribam of the University of Vienna as a suitable recipient for the prize, and on October 4, 1924, Voegelin arrived in the United States with a stipend of $1,800 a year and a travel allowance—by the standards of the day, an ample source of support.[74] Voegelin was, then, one of the earliest recipients of this important award.

It is clear that he had developed a well-thought-out program. He began work at Columbia University in the fall of 1924, studying sociology with Giddings, educational theory with Dewey, and public administration with J. H. Macmahon, all of whom were leaders in their respective disciplines. Voegelin moved to Madison for the 1925 summer session at the University of Wisconsin, where he first met Commons and Selig Perlman, who introduced him to American labor history, American populism, and American political history and institutions. Following an extensive tour of the United States, Voegelin was appointed a research fellow in economics for the fall term at Harvard, where he began a concentrated study of American jurisprudence with Roscoe Pound and attended Alfred North Whitehead's lectures in philosophy. He returned to Wisconsin after Christmas and spent the summer session of 1926 at Yale Law School. In short, for a period of twenty-four months Voegelin was able to work with some of the most creative scholars in America and at several of its great universities.

In retrospect, Voegelin wrote, "these two years in America brought the great break in my intellectual development."[75] In fact, his later account occasionally distorts the original specifics of his intellectual posture at that time, and the details of his studies as reported to the Rockefeller Foundation are not in exact agreement with his recollection. Nevertheless, these years undoubtedly had a lasting influence on his scholarly and personal outlooks. "There was," he said, "a world in which this other world in which I had

74. When Voegelin returned to Vienna in December, 1927, he received $30 a month as Kelsen's assistant and supported himself chiefly by journalism and tutoring.
75. Eric Voegelin, *Autobiographical Reflections* (Baton Rouge, 1989), 28.

grown up was intellectually, morally, and spiritually irrelevant."
In the encounter with American social, political, and academic life,
Voegelin "gained an understanding . . . of the plurality of human
possibilities realized in various civilizations, as an immediate experience."[76] Two aspects of that experience may be singled out for
brief elaboration: his encounters with Commons and with the philosophy of George Santayana.

Consider, first, Santayana. In his Introduction to the present volume Voegelin indicates that, for him, Santayana summarized the
English skeptical tradition just as Commons completed the development of the transformation of America from a pioneer and agricultural society into an urban and industrial one. The *Autobiographical Reflections* contains the following observation:

> This account of my American experience would be incomplete with-
> out mentioning the strong influence of George Santayana. I never met
> him, but I got acquainted with his work in New York, partly through
> the suggestion of Irwin Edman. I studied his work with care and still
> have in my library the books that I bought that year in New York. To
> me, Santayana was a revelation concerning philosophy, comparable
> to the revelation I received at the same time through common sense
> philosophy. Here was a man with a vast background of philosophical
> knowledge, sensitive to the problems of the spirit without accepting
> a dogma, and not interested at all in neo-Kantian methodology. Grad-
> ually I found out about Lucretian materialism as a motivating expe-
> rience in his thought, and this was of considerable importance for my
> understanding later, in Paris, the French poet Paul Valéry and his Lu-
> cretian motivation. Santayana and Valéry have remained for me the
> two great representatives of an almost mystical skepticism that in fact
> is not materialism at all. The emotional impact of this discovery was
> so strong and lasting that in the 1960s, when I had an opportunity to
> travel in southern France, I went to see the Cimetière Marin in Cette
> where Valéry is buried overlooking the Mediterranean.[77]

Santayana's influence, then, was indirect and mediated by his
works. As Voegelin later became, Santayana was a European
thinker of the first rank who also became American; both men
were, so to speak, professionally skeptical of doctrines and dogmas
and ever searching for the experiences that lay behind the formulations. For Santayana this impulse was expressed as much in his
poetry as in his philosophical prose. Voegelin, too, had a poet's sen-

76. *Ibid.*, 32–33.
77. *Ibid.*, 31.

sitivity to the power of language. Indeed, Voegelin even tried his hand at translating several of Santayana's sonnets that he discusses in chapter 2.[78] These brief hints regarding the influence of Santayana's "almost mystical skepticism" will have to suffice for the present.

Regarding John R. Commons we have available more direct information. From this book and from the *Autobiographical Reflections* it is clear that Voegelin had great respect for Commons.[79] Even so, we remain in the dark as to the detailed reasons for Voegelin's affection and admiration for the man. Commons' own autobiography and a somewhat sparse archival record indicate he was a man of great intellectual integrity and virtue.[80] He was in several respects the embodiment of what Voegelin typified in this book as the open self. One may see this not only in the evidence Voegelin adduced in the chapter herein devoted to Commons, but more immediately in the reception Commons accorded visiting European scholars whose training, if not their disposition, was more likely to exemplify what Voegelin called the closed self. Let us consider some additional evidence.

It was mentioned above that during the late summer and early fall of 1925, Voegelin undertook an extensive tour of the United States. He did so in the company of Heinrich Pollak, a Czech Rockefeller Fellow.[81] Both Voegelin and Pollak became regular members of the "Friday-Nighters," a group of students and faculty who would gather at the Commons home for serious and occasionally less than serious discussion.

There exists, for example, a delightful report on a mock litigation

78. These texts are interleaved with Voegelin's copy of Santayana's *Poems* (New York, 1923) and are stored in the Voegelin Library at the University of Erlangen.
79. In addition, Voegelin translated two of Commons' articles: "Farm Prices and the Value of Gold," *North American Review*, CCXXV (January–February, 1928), 27–41, 196–211, appeared as "Landwirtschaftliche Preise und Goldwert," *Nationalwirtschaft* 2:1 (1928). "Anglo-American Law and Economics" was translated as "Das Anglo-Amerikanische Recht und die Wirtschaftstheorie"; it was written especially for a festschrift to honor Friedrich von Wiesen, *Die Wirtschaftstheorie der Gegenwart*. See Commons, *The Economics of Collective Action* (New York, 1950), 399–400, and Commons to Edward W. Morehouse, April 14, 1926, in USS Mss 21A/3, Commons Papers, Wisconsin Historical Society.
80. See John R. Commons, *Myself: The Autobiography of John R. Commons* (Madison, Wisc., 1963).
81. LSRM/S.III-6/52/548, in Rockefeller Archive Center. Pollak subsequently published *Die Gewerkschaftsbewegung in der Vereinigten Staaten* (Jena, 1927) on the basis of his American experience.

between Dr. Heinrich Pollak of the German University of Prague and "the so-called Henry who was born in this country." Dr. Pollak had, it seems, wasted his time in Madison by having been replaced by plain Henry Pollak, and he wished to sue his replacement personality for damages because he was about to return to Europe, where Henry would be quite out of place. Henry excused the eclipse of the severe Heinrich by the fact that Henry had fallen in love—with America, but also with a young American woman. One of the judges at this tribunal was Voegelin, whose contribution was to expound at length on "formal logic." Much learned nonsense led to the esteemed Dr. Pollak's being sentenced to return to Europe:

> Suddenly a lady who watched the proceedings from the beginning until this sad end rises before the court and addresses it. Her name may be Mrs. Commons; let it live with future generations: "Henry, never mind, Henry. You are a fine fellow. We like you always, cheer up and don't appeal to the supreme court."
> Henry smiles, thanks the chief justice for the decision. Everybody seems to be satisfied. Dr. Heinrich Pollak disappeared. We hope to hear from him when back to Europe.[82]

Pollak's good humor appeared in a report he sent to the Friday-Nighters regarding the trip he took with Voegelin: "Then I travelled ten thousand miles through thirty-five states quarreling with Erich Voegelin, sight-seeing, and studying the profitable nature of the American Plan of hotel management and industrial relations. Let me say in passing that I prefer the former to the latter."[83] An earlier and more extensive report outlined their itinerary over the six-week period. According to Pollak they had three aims: to visit several universities, to see the natural beauty of America, and to gather information on labor conditions—the "American Plan" referred to in his earlier letter. They traveled west from Minneapolis to Denver. As Pollack wrote to Commons, "Erich took several snapshots from the train and I assure you that they look all alike: a sad plain without any vegetation or cultivation." In Denver they met officials and workers of the Colorado Fuel and Iron Company, and Voegelin read up on American trade unionism, which was one of Pollak's areas of specialization.

82. USS Mss 21A/15, Commons Papers, Wisconsin Historical Society.
83. Dorothy Whipple, Heinrich Pollak, and Ewan Clague to J. R. Commons, November 9, 1926, in USS Mss 21A/3, Commons Papers, Wisconsin Historical Society.

As a practical consequence of our railway-extension-division course in labor problems, Voegelin insisted on seeing all the unions we could possibly locate and listened very attentively to their officials, but whenever we visited a company or employers' association, he expressed very advanced opinions, though he is certainly not a radical. Sometimes I wished he would have been silent and not explaining "that in Europe it is much better, because the workmen are all organised" (he may be right), but the following incident was highly amusing to me: we were at the famous Industrial Association of San Francisco and the manager of these union-fighting promoters of the American Plan spoke about the manifestations of public opinion, apparently represented by the Board of Directors of the association. Erich remarked on this and when our dear Industrial Relations Manager tried to prove that public opinion in matters of industry were truly represented by the manufacturers and bankers . . . Voegelin got really excited and said that this was nonsense and he would rather accept the building trades' council of San Francisco as arbiter![84]

They visited Salt Lake City, the Pacific Northwest, and Stanford before pushing on to Los Angeles:

This name has something mysterious for many Europeans, but in reality it is nothing more than the city of the super-boosters. We could not find there anything of interest, thus we proceeded to Hollywood, where we obtained access to the wonders of filmdom, namely Universal City. A German manager took us around and found great pleasure in introducing us to many feminine stars. I shall never forget how Erich was engaged, during lunch, in conversation with one Laura la Plante and declared afterwards that she is really pretty, "aber so dumm, so dumm."[85]

From Hollywood the two turned back east via the Grand Canyon, the Southwest, and Texas to Baton Rouge and New Orleans. Voegelin then proceeded to Berea (a liberal-arts college in Kentucky) and New York, Pollak to Chicago and Detroit to inspect the famous slaughterhouses and stockyards and Henry Ford's automobile plants.

The otherwise trivial details of an obviously pleasant trip are relevant to more philosophical considerations for two reasons. First, because the itinerary corresponds to a common pattern of German visitors: *quer durch*, straight across. On the surface, then,

84. Heinrich Pollak to John R. Commons, October 12, 1925, in USS Mss 21A/3, Commons Papers, Wisconsin Historical Society.
85. *Ibid.*

they were simply a pair of young foreigners on tour. Second, how-ever, the attitude of Voegelin and Pollak was not that typical of German travelers. This is indicated indirectly by the good humor expressed in Pollak's letters, but also in the interest they showed in obtaining firsthand, genuinely empirical evidence, upon which experience their later scientific work drew.

Earl Beck has made an extensive survey of accounts by German travelers of the United States during the 1920s.[86] His description of much of this literature provides a striking contrast to *On the Form of the American Mind*, which Voegelin says in his Preface is "an expression of sympathy and respect for the life of a nation." In con-trast, most German visitors were decidedly unsympathetic. A com-mon theme was that America had no culture. "Few observers," Beck remarked, "found it necessary to define the term or set forth their frame of reference. Culture—Germany had it; America did not!" This common judgment of America by German visitors was tempered by two considerations: first, they knew very little of American cultural achievements—in art and literature, for exam-ple; second, they kept mainly to the large cities, and even to the German immigrant communities within them. "What irritates is, of course, the exaggeration and the superficiality, the willingness to generalize from surface manifestations. And then there is also the unspoken frame of reference, the so much prized German Kul-tur. The conception that a differently formed civilization and cul-ture must be judged by more universal standards, that one nation appraising the accomplishments of another must be prepared at the same time to submit its own to careful scrutiny, found little re-flection in the myriad German writings on America."[87]

Likewise, American philosophy was unfavorably compared with German philosophy, American high schools with the German *Gymnasium*, Beethoven and Bach with jazz! Since American reli-gious sentiments remained untouched by the higher criticism, they appeared to German eyes as naïve and childish. A predominant theme was that Americans were purely materialist in their aims in life, that they were "big children" without spirituality. During Pro-

86. Earl R. Beck, *Germany Rediscovers America* (Tallahassee, 1968). Beck sum-marizes Pollak's book but says nothing of Voegelin's. It was, however, listed in Beck's bibliography.
87. *Ibid.*, 153, 189.

xli

hibition they were without spirits as well, which many visitors took as evidence of the narrowness of American puritanism.[88] Activists without a thought in the world, their highest emotional achievement was sentimentality without depth: in a word, they were *Spiessbürger*—self-satisfied, mindless consumers. This extensive array of negatively critical books, Beck concluded, was "one clear sign of the decline of German scholarship." His reason was equally clear: "Few German scholars really looked beneath the surface of things in America; few sought empathy with Americans. Confronted with that which was different, they drew back within themselves in shocked dismay and voiced horror, not understanding."[89] In this respect, as in many others, *On the Form of the American Mind* is clearly exceptional.

In this first major work Voegelin combined his astute powers of observation and analysis with a conceptual vocabulary that was struggling to find its own coherence and form. Viewed from the perspective of his mature political philosophy, terms such as *open self* appear less than adequate to the reality they describe. Voegelin himself pointed out to his publisher's son in 1953 that the book was of a "decidedly fragmentary and occasional character."[90] Even so, *On the Form of the American Mind* was a major achievement for a scholar in his mid-twenties. Using categories such as "open self," Voegelin was able to show the significance and interrelationship of such disparate phenomena as undergraduate "petting parties," the mysticism of Jonathan Edwards, and the actions of the Federal Reserve Board. If Voegelin's conceptual terminology is open to criticism today, the reasons for arguing against it can be found in large measure in Voegelin's later work. Even in 1928, it would seem, Voegelin was in the van of political science.

JÜRGEN GEBHARDT
BARRY COOPER

88. See, however, Eric Voegelin, "Die Verfassungsmässigkeit des 18. Amendments zur United States Constitution," *Zeitschrift für öffentliches Recht*, V (1926), 445–64.
90. Voegelin to Hans G. Siebeck, September 18, 1953, in Voegelin Papers, Box 36, Folder 13.
89. Beck, *Germany Rediscovers America*, 256–57.

Editors' Note

Discursive material in Eric Voegelin's notes is given in full as translated; documentation or commentary by the editors is set off in brackets. This approach reflects the editors' desire to preserve Voegelin's notes in their original form insofar as possible. The author's purely documentary notes, however, required different treatment if they were to be most useful to the reader. In *On the Form of the American Mind* Voegelin was quite casual in citing sources, often giving only a fragmentary reference. The editors and translator have endeavored in all such cases to provide full standard information in conventional footnotes. In doing so, we have dispensed with brackets, judging that they would clutter the page to no very useful purpose.

ON THE FORM OF
THE AMERICAN MIND

Preface

The materials for this book were collected during a two-year stay in the United States as a Laura Spelman Rockefeller Memorial Fellow. It gives me great pleasure to express my gratitude for the fellowship, with special thanks to those members of the fellowship committee whose advice in scholarly matters and assistance in all technical questions contributed so crucially to the completion of my research.

My work was made infinitely easier by the kindness extended to me by Harvard University and the University of Wisconsin. Both enabled me to make full use of their facilities, one by appointing me a Research Fellow in Economics, the other by conferring on me the title of Honorary Fellow.

My greatest debt of gratitude, however, goes to Professor John R. Commons. During the few months I was fortunate enough to spend with him, his inexhaustible fund of knowledge and his experience of a lifetime spent participating in the development of American democracy provided a context for my scattered bits of knowledge and gave them a coherence that can never be attained from studying the literature alone.

Even more meaningful than his scholarly help was the example of Commons himself. The stranger to any culture always faces the difficulty of making his way from the periphery, where isolated details perplex him, to the center where they can be understood. And only rarely is he lucky enough to find this deepest meaning embodied in a living person, so that almost effortlessly he obtains direct access to the center of a culture. That my work is more than a collection of disparate facts and has instead become an expression of sympathy and respect for the life of a nation—this I owe entirely to Commons, whose stature is such that one has to love it in order to be defended against its superiority.

Eric Voegelin
Vienna, January 29, 1928

Introduction

The traits peculiar to American economic and political institutions and to intellectual life in the United States have in the last 150 years given rise to more interpretations of America than of any other nation. These studies have intensely scrutinized virtually all the available materials and have created a general picture from these resources. There is little need to make corrections in the broad outlines of the resulting works.

Outstanding among the early views is Goethe's twelve-line poem, "Amerika, du hast es besser . . . " [America, you are better off . . .]. Its attitude seems recently to have become the slogan of the country that never experienced the Middle Ages. By introducing the concept of *Raumvolk* [spatial people] into political geography, Friederich Ratzel provided another approach to extrapolating individual intellectual traits from the American scene. Ever since the extent of American economic power became obvious, numerous studies have attempted to pinpoint the essence of "Americanism" in mass production, and Henry Ford's assembly line became the symbol of a new world—a symbol that is admired even as it seems somewhat uncanny.

It is reasonable that such fundamental concepts as time, space, and mass production were chosen as springboards for interpretation; if now the descriptive powers of these concepts seem exhausted, it is not because they are inadequate but merely because they have fulfilled their purpose and have steered interpretations of the American mind to a point that calls for new methods if the task is to be mastered.

New methods are needed—but they have not yet been found. Nor is it easy to find them, because what distinguishes them from the old methods of a priori categories and generalized slogans is their intimate connection to the materials, which only exhaustive familiarity with the materials can ensure. The reader should therefore not look to this book to provide an inspired riddle-solving synthesis of the American mind. My detailed analyses are intended as a first attempt at extracting the instruments of interpretation as well as the meaning from the material itself. Since the book is dedicated to a twofold task—to cite materials that must be assumed to be unfamiliar to the [German] reader and to elaborate them through interpretation—it may be difficult to follow the context and connection of the various sections. These introductory remarks are therefore intended as a commentary on the essential factual and methodological development that resulted from examining material that may appear in the text as disjointed segments.

❧

On the surface the book is divided topically into two parts. The discussions of time and existence, of George Santayana, and of Puritan mysticism are all concerned with what is commonly called philosophy or metaphysics. Because the presentation of analytical jurisprudence is necessary to an understanding of several sections in the study of John R. Commons, the last two chapters are likewise connected.

Beyond this external division into chapters, when we approach the actual contents, we find not sharper definition but greater confusion. When judged from the traditional perspectives of political science and philosophy, a diversity of themes seems only loosely connected. A brief history of the concepts of time and existence as treated in British and American philosophy is followed by a detailed study of the concepts of perception articulated by S. H. Hodgson, William James, Charles S. Peirce, Edmund Husserl, Franz Brentano, and Santayana. Next comes an almost self-contained section dealing with Santayana's poetry. Additional chapters offer an examination of the growth of Puritan mysticism from Calvinist dogmatics, a detailed depiction of problems in legal theory, remarks on the development of American political doctrine, economic theory, the stabilization of the dollar and the policies of the Federal Reserve Board, the problem of social classes in the United States, the history and philosophy of the labor movement, administrative authorities, and an examination of philosophy of history.

3

We must step back from this apparent chaos to note that these diverse subjects all belong to a single class; though the category is large, there is overall unity: all the topics deal with language. In my study of the form of the American mind, I have left aside all formations that employ any means of expression other than language—music and the plastic arts, agriculture and horticulture, the mass arrangements of commercial production. I have narrowed the field even further by the elimination of artistic formations, except for the few pages devoted to Santayana's poetry. Otherwise the text contains no discussion of the novel, drama, film. I also leave aside consideration of language as a means of mass education as used in schools, radio, and newspapers. I deal only with entities of linguistic expression of a theoretical nature—*theory* being defined as an attempt claiming to order a field of problems rationally and thus to render it comprehensible. From this broad group I eliminated all attempts that are commonly considered part of the natural sciences. What remained was further stripped of works of history and philology. Thus a small number of theoretical works in philosophy, law, politics, economics, political science, and sociology were available for my investigation. From these I chose a smaller group that furnished examples which seemed particularly suitable to this first attempt at a study of form.

It is important to stress that the materials studied are offered as examples. In selecting them I applied specific criteria and did not attempt to exhaust all sources. Nowhere do I present the materials simply as information. The sections that follow the development of an idea over a period of time should not mistakenly be seen as a history of dogmatics. A reader may complain that the analysis of American metaphysics concentrates on the works of Peirce, James, and Santayana, never mentioning Royce and Dewey; or that Jonathan Edwards and Peirce are separated by a period of time that was not without its own significance. But such criticism does not address the objective of my work. It does not aim at presenting academic intellectual history and, if only for technical reasons, cannot, given the mass of material, mention every phenomenon for no better reason than that it exists.

The principle by which I selected materials—in short, the method used to study the form of the American mind—cannot be developed on the basis of a priori principles. Neither the book itself nor this Introduction is intended to engage in arguments concerning methodology, and I will neither accept nor refute theories about the purity of methods, the correlation of method and object, and a ban on methodological syncretism. Of necessity something will have to be said concerning the method employed here, but I do not intend to produce the impression that my thesis expresses scientific a priori principles; its sole purpose is to explain why particular rules spontaneously grew out of the material studied. It is almost too much to say that rules were followed; they were not followed so much as found. And the fact that they proved useful in this instance is no guarantee that they could successfully be employed on other occasions. Listing them is an empirical summary, not the development of an a priori system.

The statement that may be taken to be the guiding principle of this study—that every intellectual formation that arises in a social body reveals traces of its origin in its form—illustrates my method. Such an assertion cannot be made a priori, no matter how probable it seems. And the attempt to apply it arbitrarily to one or another formation, relying on its absolute validity, would run into a number of problems. By the term *intellectual formation* we refer not only to the larger, obvious phenomena, such as political institutions, art works, factories, railroads, psychological therapies, and the like. The study must also take into account all aspects of everyday life, no matter how trivial: for example, the ships on the Hudson River tend to be painted a smudged red color, rather like a bloodsausage, while boats on the Seine seem to prefer a more gentle tint; one must also consider the smooth oils used to paint houses in Zurich and Basel, the elegance of the gray-black bricks found in some quarters of London, the reddish-brown twice-baked bricks in the United States, and the long windows and balconies that characterize the urban landscape in Paris; the type of suits, selling for $22.50, made of a fabric never used in Germany for men's wear; the imperturbable calm with which the Parisian theater ticket sellers detach the revenue stamp from the sheet, lick it conscientiously, paste it on the ticket made of shoddy paper, and finally cancel it with the stroke of a pencil, while in New York the cardboard tickets are clean and thick and smooth, with the excise tax printed and included in the price. As a rule, all these phenomena will probably exhibit traces of their origin, and perhaps in fact they do; but we cannot say so with certainty. And if we should attempt to analyze forms by using only these materials, we may perhaps manage to produce a charming essay; but it is unlikely that we would achieve significant and rational results.

According to this rule, intellectual formations should show traces of their origin in a particular social body. But such a social body is itself merely the embodiment of intellectual formations held together by traits peculiar to the form. Thus, what the rule states is that when an intellectual formation belongs to an embodiment with particular formal features, it also displays these same formal features. But the argument seems circular. Only *seems*, however; in practice the argument results in a very clear rule—which states that the interpretation of various phenomena must not be undertaken according to a preconceived scheme but must follow from the material itself, finding in the material its inherent meaning and the method best suited to clarifying it. In every instance, therefore, interpretation must proceed immanently and may never be subject to a transcendental value system.

A few empirical reference points may be useful here. Evidence has shown, for example, the probability that related forms are found in intellectual formations belonging to the same language; but this is by no means a certainty, as shown by British and American differences in English usage. Relations of forms, furthermore, are probable among formations in adjacent areas of time and space. But even this principle of contiguity is very flexible; because we find connections based on past experience among phenomena separated by centuries, it seems permissible to call the space of a century a neighborhood in time. Nor is there any a priori assurance that the works of a thinker who lives abroad will exhibit the intellectual forms of his homeland. Homeland or birthplace may often serve as a good point of reference; but particularly in the very significant case of Santayana, who was Spanish by birth, this rule turns out to be invalid.

It is not possible, therefore, to articulate any general principles; at best we can establish a few rules of probability in the search for formal relationships—that is, relations of form. A law can never be used to arrive at conclusions about individual cases. For the practice of scholarship this leads to another principle: If formal relations are found in a number of intellectual formations, it does not follow

6

that any other formation will exhibit these formal features merely because external criteria make this conclusion seem probable. And further: Even if the new object should turn out to be form-related, it is impossible to predict the particular variant the form will adopt. It is simply not possible to prophesy. But this last remark leads to methodological questions that will better be addressed in another context.

Although the practical rule about the marks of origin of every intellectual phenomenon might turn out to be valid in every individual instance, there are nevertheless, as noted, large groups of everyday details that do not lend themselves to formal analysis. Though they are insignificant, they are nevertheless symbols, and perhaps each of their formal details is just as genuine as the more obvious patterns, though they furnish too few points of reference for analysis. The research materials must be selected in such a way that they provide a rich and comprehensible articulation and the closest possible relationship with the form of the analysis itself. That is, if at all possible, they should make language the medium of expression, and among the various available linguistic patterns the language of theory seems especially suitable because it contains a greater number of rational elements than, for example, poetry. It is, of course, possible to some extent to discover the style of origin in works of music; German music, for example, exhibits a tendency to modulation and chromatics, whereas these are much less strongly marked in French and Italian music. But formal variations of this sort do not speak for themselves; we can point them out, but to express their meaning we have to translate them into the medium of language. Nor are all linguistic-theoretical phenomena of equal value; one category is preeminent, and par excellence may be called "self-expressive." Without extensive preparation it is not easy to say precisely what is meant by *self-expressive,* but a brief hint must suffice for the moment. The natural sciences speak not of themselves but of objects that essentially transcend the medium in which they are expressed, whereas philosophy, at least wherever it touches on dialectical problems, involves self-reflection about its subject matter—that is, about itself. Its subject matter is essentially immanent, and its medium—the epistemological process in its multifarious forms—is also the medium in which it is studied.

The materials chosen for the following investigation consist of self-expressive phenomena. In this way a common denominator is posited for a category of theoretical formations that, according to the traditional divisions of science, are assigned to a number of separate disciplines, such as philosophy, economic theory, theory of law, and political science. Accordingly, any claim that they treat related problems and are therefore closely connected in their structure cannot count on universal acceptance. The analyses in the following chapters must justify this claim. Here I will merely summarize some of the conclusions that are scattered through the text.

∽✦∾

The belief that the various scholarly disciplines just mentioned, which traditionally are treated separately, do not in fact have a closer relationship can be supported only on the grounds that each of them investigates a well-defined object differing from, and transcendent to, every other object. This belief is opposed to our thesis that the objects involved are neither well-defined nor transcendent but rather are immanent and that this immanence engenders a special epistemological difficulty that makes it highly questionable whether it makes any sense to characterize these intellectual formations as sciences at all. But what matters is not definitions but results. And they include the following: It is assumed that the particular forms of cognition, such as sense perception, are open to scientific, rational exploration through introspection or examination of their structure. The studies of perceptual concepts by Peirce, James, Hodgson, Brentano, and Santayana, however, demonstrate that each of these philosophers, though proceeding with unerring assurance, saw something different. It further proves beyond doubt that none of them actually saw any one thing; rather, each constructed a theory of perception according to specific laws that constitute the subject matter of our investigation. A similar situation obtains in the case of the Federal Reserve Board's policies and the theory of price stabilization. In fact, these theories had no relation to any knowledge of transcendent objects, but rather were constructed according to a stylistic law. The same holds true for analytic jurisprudence.

The study of form is thus not a methodological doctrine that establishes a system of a priori categories or forms of thought in various scientific fields. Insofar as theoretical formations are not sciences, this study merely points out formal similarities, to be specified more closely. The methodological means to this end can be grouped under different headings. As a beginning they may be divided roughly into personal and peripheral categories. The contrast of personal and peripheral suggests that the first type reflects formal features focused on the senses, whereas the peripheral type describes individual traits that become comprehensible only when they are combined with the personal.

One personal category, developed from the materials and from the interpretation of them, is the category of the open self. Found in analyses of the problems of time and existence in English and American philosophy, the open self describes the form given to the problem of dialectic in the United States. In contrast to projects such as Hegel's, in which the dialectic was made the core problem of philosophic thought, the efforts of Peirce and James sought to avoid dialectics and eliminate its various manifestations from philosophy. Projects that legitimize the dialectic, especially in its modification as a problem of self-consciousness, were universally assigned to the personal category of a closed self, while efforts to avoid it were given the name of open self.

This explanation sounds very dry, and by itself may not clarify why the problem of dialectics should have a personal quality as distinct from other forms. It is important to bear in mind that whatever genuinely pertains to dialectics necessarily touches upon the personal, whereas peripheral explanations have merely a didactic and illustrative value. Hume's skepticism, for example, demonstrates how his formulation of the dialectic is determined by his skeptical outlook on life—or, more precisely: not how the dialectic is determined but how the skeptical outlook, expressed in various ways, manifests itself in dialectical formulations as well, and thereby achieves its most complete and profound expression. It would not be difficult to construct a theory that shows precisely why every formulation of the dialectic has a personal quality; but I have no interest in doing so and prefer instead to try to present the purely empirical character of the applied categories. For that purpose the dialectic is exclusively a personal category, because it is the most emphatic expression of the outlook on life that lies at the heart of the material examined. The type of the closed self has been empirically introduced on the basis of empirical evidence, and a detailed analysis of the corresponding problem in James leads us just as empirically to develop the type of the open self. Hume's closedness has its origin in the experiences of skepticism and loneliness, while James's openness grew out of trust and sociability. The intimacy that James himself cites as the emotional motivation of his thoughts is in absolute opposition to the mortal sin of confidence for the closed personality.

Individual traits that enrich the somewhat vague meaning of the term *open self* are centered on the experience of intimacy. Here we may mention some minor topics that, as noted above, are in themselves insufficient to serve as material for an analysis of form. Though insufficient in themselves, they are nevertheless useful once a concrete meaning has been found that can interpret them. They can both substantiate this meaning and give it greater tangibility and probability. We may therefore be satisfied—and as far as rigorous analysis is concerned, we must be satisfied—to explain the open self according to James's dialectical formulations and to explain his motivation as a desire for warmth, for sociability, and for something concrete we can celebrate outside ourselves, as well as his dread of loneliness, death, and personal responsibility. But all these features take on new poignancy when an example is added, such as the following: A questionnaire sent out by Columbia University's Teachers College included a question on the respondent's number of friends and acquaintances. Among the responses were these: number of acquaintances, 2,000; number of friends, 500.

These data are brought to life by everyday details of American social life: the matter-of-fact way that everyone feels free to visit anyone else and feels confident of a cordial reception; the readiness with which information and every kind of help are given; the oppressive organized sociability in the form of clubs, committee meetings, communal meals, lectures, and the like; the easy way, always shocking to a European, the slightest acquaintances confide their most intimate affairs. One understands the strength of American openness and mania for intimacy when one considers the institution of early marriages—marrying at twenty-two or twenty-three is very common. The desire for intimacy is exemplified by the system of petting parties and sexual promiscuity, but also by the lack of an erotic culture and the naïve obscenities of burlesque, unrivaled by any European pleasure institutions. It can be seen as well in the standardized psychological categories of the American novel and its techniques, especially in the novels of Sinclair Lewis, which might be termed external documentation.

All these examples help to explain and provide richness, but all go beyond the personal form, extending into the area of the peripheral categories. The open self is no longer intended to describe only the form indicated by the dialectics of self-consciousness; all ramifications are meaningfully connected with the center, though they are clearly distinguishable and independent forms. The most important ones found here are the following:

1. *Social relations*. The open self illustrates the flight from the mystery of the self, dissolving loneliness in intimacy. When a majority of people exhibit these features in their intellectual forms, special forms of social relations arise, such as first appeared in the United States in pioneer communities. Chapter 5, on John R. Commons, analyzes this relationship in several of its manifestations: the problems of the labor movement, education in an egalitarian community, a new type of leadership, the organization of administrators, a theory of imperialism, the motivation of fiscal policies, and construction of the fundamental principles of social intercourse on the basis of social theories.

2. *The relationship to God*. The philosophies of Peirce and James furnish descriptive analyses to elucidate man's relation to God. The conception of God is fleshed out by the need for personal closeness, for communication, and for intimacy with a God who resembles man in every feature except that he is larger. He encompasses and protects, he fulfills a yearning for security and sheltering arms, since one's own person and one's own responsibility cannot provide support. The discussion of Jonathan Edwards (chapter 3) breaks through a surface description to touch on the historical dimension, showing how the forms of Puritan mysticism and Calvinist dogmatics are found again in modern theories of man's relation to God.

3. *Originality and objectivity*. When man experiences anxiety at being alone with himself and tries in the various forms of social and religious relations to diffuse himself outward, all those structures that have been created so as to allow man the enjoyment of being alone with himself are undermined. This formal feature is exemplified in American analytical jurisprudence, which claims no scientific-theoretical intentions, but claims merely to be following

practical ends. To the extent that theoretical objectivity—a typical value of solitude—is discounted in favor of practical work in the community with others, the significance attributed in other situations to the creation of theoretical constructs disappears. No great importance is assigned to being recognized as the author of a theory, and there is indifference to others' intellectual powers. When those aspects of the personality that are regarded as creating objective theoretical structures are not valued, outsiders' ideas are presented as if they were one's own because the sense of mine and thine is lacking. The chapter on jurisprudence will therefore contain discussions of originality and plagiarism.

Furthermore, if the objectivity of the theoretical model is held to be subordinate to its practical purposes, less care will be applied to perfecting it than would be taken if objectivity were the primary value. The treatment of theoretical problems is technically incomplete and bears traces of dilettantism. The final pages of the chapter on Commons contain several remarks on this problem, and the overall analysis of Peirce's theories brings together examples of technical inadequacies resulting from the inadequacies of the closed self.

4. *Intellectualism.* The intellectual forms will, in the course of the investigation, be frequently illustrated by reference to the concept of "concretion in discourse" in Santayana. The term is meant to refer to a mass of thought that is not amenable to analysis, that has been accumulated in the course of experience, and that has been elaborated into a theoretical structure on the basis of the initial experience but without further examination from subsequent experience. The larger or smaller framework of thought developed from the concretion is thus based on experience accumulated until it reaches its final point of concretion; thereafter it is intended to stand as a universal reality, without recourse to correction in response to contrary instances. It is quite possible that a theory elaborated through this method will be workable, but it is probable that in the course of its application it will deny reality and come into conflict with it. One can see a meaningful connection between this form and that of the open self on the one hand and originality and objectivity on the other. The devaluation of theoretical formations indicates not their destruction but merely the excessive emphasis given to their practical functions; theoretical models continue to

exist, but they are generated not for their truth value but for their ability to overcome external problems. They are treated mechanically, and the conviction that such intellectual machinery is an effective tool can be carried to the extreme of ethical and religious adoration on the basis of practical reasons, as happens in the case of theories concerning dollar stabilization. This particular theory, developed from a single topic, is not situated in any theoretical context and is incapable of developing further on its own. In fact, it can no more be developed further than we can turn a machine for manufacturing wire nails into one for packaging chocolate bars. The theory or the machine must be abandoned altogether and replaced with a new and appropriate one. Thus it is precisely the undervaluation of the theoretical formations that results in a radical intellectualism operating in a vacuum. Jurisprudence in particular furnishes an example. Further examples dealt with here are the anarchic theories of Josiah Warren and the theory of price stabilization in the policies of the Federal Reserve Board. Further instances are William James's analysis, in which the arguments for the justification of "pure experience" was used in a reversed sense to destroy the dialectics of identity. The same forms are found in Peirce's technique of argument, which consistently places an intellectual veil over the material without ever combining with it to form a consistent concept.

But the best indication of the reliability of this category is found in an area beyond the confines of this investigation: Edgar Allan Poe's intellectualism. In American intellectual life Poe's thinking has always been considered strange because other instances of empty intellectualism were overlooked. If the connection is not thoroughly explored, it seems unlikely that a pragmatic stance would be meaningfully linked to an intellectual one. The words *pragmatic* and *intellect* stand side by side, even though a superficial nominalism is prepared to claim that no connection can exist between them. But the concept of "concretion in discourse" indicates the point of contact: intellectual formations do not lie strung out along a plane of continuing development but exist as eruptions of understanding that spring up for an instant at the point of concretion, only to sink back again into the stream of action, making way for new eruptions unconnected to the earlier ones. If one link—that is, one concretion, with the intellectual web that has been spun from it—is excised from the chain of such eruptions, what results is the artistic form of Poe's detective stories. C. Auguste Dupin's brilliant performances typically take off from an obscure situation, to find the solution to the mystery through a process of thought and without need of further facts. Poe's detective stories may be an original American art form, rooted in the forms of the American mind. An extremely valuable contribution to further exploration of this problem would be a study of Poe's stories as historically perceived in France, from Baudelaire to *poésie pure;* presumably the result would be a history of misunderstanding.

The categories of *personal* and *peripheral* summarize the results of studies that are in essence historical. This work will clearly differentiate among three methods by which form has been shaped historically. The chapter on Santayana begins by examining the essential elements of form, so as to eliminate from the philosopher's formations anything that is not of a personal nature. The second section, on Santayana's poetry, initiates an analysis of an intellectual career in which all events appear to have been formed by their relation to the life of one person. The beginning commemorates the solipsistic experiences of youth; this experiential foundation is overlaid by subsequent experience; in the final stage, accumulated experiences are followed by old age. This is no simple sequence of more or less accidental events, which might just as easily be arranged in a different order. Rather, Santayana's solipsism, with its pallor, its uncertainty, its idealism, its romanticizing resignation, is tinged with the color of youth. Furthermore, the circumstance that Santayana, a foreigner, is isolated in the United States takes on significance in this context only because his isolation coincides with his youth. The accumulation of experience cannot precede youth; but there is evidence of a break between the original and subsequent experience, such that the accumulated mass of mature experience takes its form from the narrower basis of what was learned in youth; and only on another level does his mature experience become autonomous, and so can be accorded its own weight—though it never loses the stamp of youthful experiences altogether. Some forms found in the sonnets survive through subsequent variations into old age. Thus the first stage, youth, runs a simple course, while the following stages absorb all that went before; like the parts of a telescope, the earlier periods collapse into

later ones. Analysis must demonstrate that the earlier stages function in each later stage and are determinants, even though the later
periods—mature experience and old age—are autonomous.

Another form is used in the chapter on John R. Commons. What
is at issue is not the signature the life stages imprint on the intellectual expressions. Rather, in a neutral area of experience there
arises the description of a diversity of events, coming from the most
varied directions, that converge on a center of meaning. Each separate occurrence—Warren's incorporation of businesses into the atmosphere of the pioneer community; political corruption and the
demand for proportional representation; the economic theory of the
commonwealth; the life of Samuel Gompers; the commissions and
reports of the United States government and of private organizations; the establishment of index figures; banking policies; research
into the history of the labor movement—all these events appear
one after another in Commons' life. In *The Legal Foundations of
Capitalism* they coalesce into a meaningful whole that finally finds
the words to speak about itself. The individual life becomes the
collector and the expression of the history of a nation and of its
meaning. The person of Santayana, in contrast, was historically
neutral; such contemporary history as of necessity entered his work
is meaningful only to the extent that it formed his personality.
Commons the individual fades completely away; his life and work
is only one event among many, marked by the fact that unrelated
and silent matters found unity and a voice in him.

The person of Commons and his work combine with other events
into a hierarchy in which his philosophy, which gives meaningful
expression to the whole, occupies the highest place. In contrast to
the person of Santayana, which takes its meaning from the link to
man's biological unity, Commons' person is less clearly outlined.
It is open to a mass of accumulated historical details, and only in
that context can it be understood.

A third historical form is the anonymous history of an idea,
which I examine in discussing the concept of time in chapter 1.
The history is anonymous, though its sections may bear the names
of philosophers who have collaborated in developing the concept.
It does not matter which individual thinker did the work, since the
development of the concept has an immanent and meaningful connection that is only contingently related to the intellectual pro-

cesses of several people; it could just as easily have been developed in the work of a single thinker. The history of the concept of time is not a history of English doctrines about the problem of time; rather, it is necessary to discuss a specific concept of time to illustrate the typical contrast between it and the American concept. Historical documentation is subordinate to the efforts to show the line of development as clearly as possible.

The diversity of intellectual levels in the life of an idea or of a person calls for different methods of arranging the historical material. In the case of Santayana, for example, the chapter specifically devoted to him does not include every essential element that might be discussed; it merely depicts a section of the total person. The part of chapter 1 that deals with the English development of the concepts of time and existence serves as a preparation for the discussion of Santayana as much as it leads to the analyses of the works of Peirce and James, which are included in the first chapter. Santayana, too, operated with the accumulated apparatus of concepts from the English tradition; it is only by comparison with this apparatus that we can bring to light the new features added by his person and his social environment. But Santayana's case is far more complicated than those of Peirce and James because his philosophy develops forms of skepticism that continue the tradition of Hume, while with the other two the transformation of the problems—expressed through the open self—occurs without leaving behind remnants of skepticism. In spite of these contrasts, Santayana's thinking is formally related down to the smallest detail to Peirce's and James's ideas. The extent of this relationship of form does not become evident until the discussion of Puritan mysticism, which reveals the connections between the concepts of essence and pure experience, of chaos and God, of the development toward goodness and toward reason. To the extent that Santayana is a skeptic, he summarizes the English tradition—just as Commons completes the development of an idea in his work. To the extent that his thoughts reveal the forms of Calvinism and mysticism, they are variations on a theme, without any indication that there is an end in view. And to the extent that his work bears the forms of the stages his internal life—youth, mature experience, and old age—Santayana expresses a feeling of solitude, whose principal source is the isolation of the foreigner and the intellectual in America.

The discussion of John R. Commons' work does not stand alone. The sections that analyze his ideas on jurisprudence cannot be understood without the preceding chapters, which examine the history of English and American jurisprudence as they pertain to Commons' writings. The primary theme, social relations in their various forms, can be understood only in the context of the discussion of the open self in the analysis of William James. The development of the concept of time in political economy, which Commons applies to the concept of futurity, runs parallel to the development of the metaphysical concept of time presented in chapter 1; its full meaning depends on the discussion in that chapter.

If the study of a problem of form seems to take on the shape of an essay about an actual person, as in the cases of Santayana and Commons, these efforts do not necessarily detract from the overall coherence. Personal and anonymous processes complement each other, and if greater significance must be assigned to some, it is the personal ones. Because even if the thought of an impersonal movement of the mind can be grasped, its life is nevertheless empirically bound to that of man, which expresses itself and moves in a mental form. The form is not an inflexible boundary for a subject, causing its edges to be clearly delineated against the background; we may not even say that the form has incorporated animate movement, for that would imply a tangibility and stability by the use of which one can differentiate movements in contrast to substantial rest. Rather, all form is dissolved in the movement of the mind itself, and consequently the shadow can be caught for a moment only in the medium of history, which follows the movement. In arranging the categories, I have therefore deliberately omitted precise definitions, utilizing instead a broader description, fleshed out with specific examples. Because typical traits, elements, or forms are frequently cited, the reader may come to believe that listing the categories is an attempt at typifying. But they are not intended as type concepts, perhaps in the sense of Max Weber's ideal types. The ideal type is an auxiliary concept, used by historians to present fundamental points of view when describing any mass of material. The ideal type is added to the material from outside. It is constructed on the basis of a metaphysics of rationalism that intends to master and organize reality, rather than to observe it with a tinge of skepticism. A chance remark by Max Weber, to the effect that the choice of the historical topic must follow the fateful events of history itself, more nearly characterizes the life of history. Ponderous words are embarrassing, and what is really important may perhaps be said without invoking fate: The choice of topic must follow the choice made by history itself. Any cross section of life contains an infinite variety of possible continuations to the next point on the historical continuum. Of these only one is chosen—not by the historian, but by life itself. The historical line of meaning runs like a rope across the abyss into which everything that cannot stay on the rope plunges. Lines of meaning can be of varying length and varying universality. Some are short, lasting only a few minutes, hours, or days—such as a conversation, the events of a pleasant stroll, reading a book; and others—such as the history of the concept of time—span centuries. But the one attribute they all have in common is that each subsequent moment is a continuation of the preceding moment and is meaningfully connected with it. This is not to say that the history of mankind is a single continuum, with the present moment having accumulated the entire past. The lines of meaning do not combine into a single skein where not a single strand is lost: continuation and growth of meaning are just as evident as rupture and atrophy. Every day of life brings an end to thoughts through disappointments and forgetting, just as it brings expansion, fulfillment, and continuation. And if we tried to take hold of the confusion at any specific point, we could not know which of the lines will continue and grow into larger units and which will break off and be lost, perhaps as soon as the following day.

It does not seem useful to treat such a tangled web with short formulas and all-encompassing definitions. Setting up categories is intended merely as an introduction, to provide a few sketchy hints about a topic that can be fully developed only in the analyses themselves. The forms have been given such names as open self, intellectualism, and so on, but their significance is defined only in their history. Type concepts, a priori categories, and every other form of rational method are essentially ill suited to the adequate description of intellectual movements because they are atemporal. Each can be grasped by rearranging and reproducing the structure itself in such a way that the lines of meaning are revealed to be inherent in the material. In essence, interpretation must be limited to organizing and juxtaposing related and contrasting patterns, and all

18

summary expressions—such as our categories—are to be understood merely as aids that, though not in themselves autonomous,
fulfill their function by referring to the detailed discussions.

My method of investigation was determined by the nature of the
topic, which is designated as the form of the American mind—and
the words *form* and *mind* require a few explanatory remarks. The
easiest way to approach the problem of mind will be found in the
instances that have been presented with the greatest concern for
comparisons, such as the parallel concepts of sensory perception
elucidated by James, Hodgson, Brentano, and Santayana. Parallel
comparison is intended to distinguish between a structure common
to all cases and the thematic constructs that differ from case to
case. The fact that a necessary structure with variable themes can
be combined into an unbroken unity of an intellectual form presupposes that the structure itself contains a point of departure for
variability. Of necessity when the topic contains such a point, only
a variation can be described; it cannot be described "in itself." Thus
the only way to clarify its essence is precisely through comparison
of a number of these variations. Admittedly this method cannot
comprehensibly define the common element, but it can serve to
make an intellectual approach immediate and evident. The necessary structure proves to be an intangible that in various formations
determines dialectical versions that cannot be grasped rationally.
It is only because a lacuna of rationality becomes overt that the
structure can be modified in various ways. Structure and variable
themes meet in the intellectual form—and so it must not be mis-
understood as being solely one or the other. Rather, it is only when,
from one or another motive, a creative will is expressed in the irrational but clearly inevitable structure that the structuring of
mind occurs. Its birth out of a longing and an irrational inevitability
determines a uniqueness and a solitariness that precludes being
encompassed by catchphrases or universally valid laws. The shape
of the mind is never finalized and is never definitive. Its original
elements may permeate it to a greater or lesser degree, but they can
never be true or false. Empirically, the only criteria of magnitude
seem to lie in the depth and purity of the stimulation that has led
to the particular expression, as well as in its scope. Though they
are expressed through the form, it would be difficult to point to
precise signs. Language is always a reliable guide; great thoughts

may be expressed obscurely, but they are never found in everyday, impersonal, colorless language; conversely, the absence of precision in what has been said almost always corresponds to mediocrity and a lack of discipline in the expression. A more questionable criterion is that of scope: the extent to which a system uses a central thought to explain the problem may be an indicator of greatness. But other elements, such as the importance of the problems to be explained, are also involved. A conscientiously elaborated system of political economy of a thousand pages is not necessarily a more significant work than the hundred and fifty pages of Peirce's metaphysics, in which a creative will uses a fleeting touch to sketch a conception of the world in which death, chaos, love, God, and chance all have their places. The vagueness of the criteria of completeness corresponds to the fundamentally provisional nature of every intellectual form. Even when the object of a science is transcendent, as it is in the natural sciences, every separate point of the research can be provisional, and the end can be infinitely far away; but the goal is situated at the end of a road, and we move toward it in a sequence of rational steps. In the intellectual forms investigated here, however, such rational advances do not exist; rather, the same intellectual structures become the cause for ever new forms that either have no connection with each other or else express a heightened intensity and perfection. The intellectual form does not discover truths and does not determine facts; because it is self-referential, there is always an element of inadequacy, which stimulates thought processes to further attempts, which inevitably must equally be inadequate.

The case of sense perception represents the simplest intellectual form and is therefore best suited to a preliminary description. Most forms attain a higher stage of complexity through a process of accumulation. Santayana's concept of essence begins in the tradition of Hume with a penetration of the dialectically necessary structure by the event; this foundation is overlaid by a layer of experiential elements deriving from Calvinism (described in chapter 3); further determinants are the solipsism of youth and the loneliness of the foreigner; finally, aging and a sense of approaching death further transform the material. All these themes work in the same direction to bring about the concept of essence. Taking the concept as the point of departure does not, therefore, allow a clear-cut definition. The richness of the concept's intellectual content becomes evident only when it is dissected into the stages of its growth. Some of these stages, such as youth and old age, are closely tied to Santayana's life; others, such as the position of the foreigner in America, represent a concurrence of a personal disposition to solitariness with his external situation; still others, such as skepticism and Calvinism, belong to an accumulated intellectual tradition independent of Santayana. Thus the interpenetration of experience and structure is not simple; rather—especially in the superimposition of old age—a general intellectual form can be transformed into a structure that is penetrated by other experiences, though in a way that allows all earlier levels of structures and experiences to remain evident in the final formation.

I have distinguished between the personal and peripheral categories in such a way that the formulations that fall under each rubric, though substantively linked, are nevertheless given clearly different structures. When distinct but related personal-peripheral structures are penetrated by the same experiences, a relationship between them can be established that will be called "equivalence of style." The concepts of an equivalence of structure and of experience will be employed only as kind of verbal shorthand, for neither the structures nor the experiences are ever given in themselves, so that everything that could possibly be equivalent in them emerges only through the veil of forms that are themselves equivalent or not equivalent in style. The established categories may therefore be designated somewhat more precisely as categories of style, and these terms once again indicate that they are merely allusions to detailed investigations of style and do not of themselves furnish an exhaustive description. It would therefore not suffice simply to place the categories of dialectics and of social relations side by side, and claim that a significant relationship exists between them. Equivalence between the style of the concept of pure experience and, for example, the administration of a government agency can be seen only by an exposition of these forms themselves. The formations of the structures of self-consciousness in Peirce and James and the dialectic of the self-healing of social life in Commons are clearly style-related because the attempt to dissolve the dialectic in a naïve time series has its counterpart in Commons' rational although inconsistent assumptions that life's self-healing must be dissolved into a social process and cannot be an internal personal problem. The relationship of style is found in this parallel. If, further, the themes of intimacy and flight from solitude are mentioned, this reference has only an illustrative and didactic value, since a desire for social contact can often be found, without necessarily indicating patterns of the American type. Analysis must always proceed from formations to convey a real aura of interpreting words. It must never posit an arbitrary concept—such as time, space, or mass—to explain the form by reference to the concept.

Many expressions that cannot be encompassed in sketchy categories are found only in the realm of intellectual forms. The elements that penetrate the form are comparatively few and easily overlooked. Considered passively, these elements are structures. The word *structure* is appropriate, since it is meant to indicate not a material or an a priori content but a point of departure of a formulation that has its material nature in its relation to the formative will. It does not confront the formulation amorphously, but indicates the direction of its construction. The problems of self-consciousness, of social relations, of wealth, of economic valuation, and of religious relations are structures of this kind. All these problems have been expressed in terms that, though defined by the inevitable structure in such a way that a cursory examination might make them seem to be statements about specific subject matter, will prove on closer analysis to be irrational, self-referential, and repeated variations on the same theme.

The structures are few; and even when they do not exhaust the problem area, it is nevertheless clear that there cannot be very many of them. Any systematic search for additional structures— through further analyses of form—would easily lead us to a seeming completeness. Still more simple are the types of themes that have instigated such formulations. All are grouped around the most primitive and basic problems of life: the sorrows of loneliness, yearning for the company of others, for intimacy and love, the emotional adventures of youth, the disillusionment of old age, the expectation of death. These few structures and themes create the richness of form.

1

Time and Existence

I

Symbolic Being. The dualism by which we divide being in order to make its structure rationally intelligible does not seem to separate it neatly into two halves. Notwithstanding such divisions, the relations between the two poles remain and the elements that we were careful to separate in fact remain so tightly meshed that it becomes well-nigh impossible to speak of dualism. If, for example, we make the cut in such a way that all symbolic orders remain on one side while the other holds everything that is symbolized, we could establish the following categories: all sign systems in the strict sense (mathematics, natural sciences, humanities, language); the symbolic orders such as art, religion, and eroticism, the law, custom, and political actions; and finally, the less rigorously organized arrangements and orders of consciousness, right down to the simplest sense perception that, to the extent that it perceives, already points beyond itself to a being for which it is merely a symbol. Everything symbolized would belong to the other side, which—in order to contrast it decisively with the area of symbolic being—may be called existential being. But in fact neither symbol nor existence can be divided into realms in themselves; both transcend into the other to such an extent that it is more accurate to speak of a unity than of a duality. Because of their centrifugal function, the fact that symbols point beyond themselves means they are endowed with existence; whatever their objective or a priori content, this fact needs no further explanation. But conversely, existence is also endowed with symbolic being, since we possess no actual intrinsic reality over which a structure of nonreality rises. More precisely, *existence* is merely an expression for the transcendent nature of symbols, and to that extent it is just as unreal, just as much grounded outside itself. The relationship between the halves of being shifts restlessly back and forth. It allows one half to become the expression of the other and in this way enables one to imagine a point of rest in a single final expression. But this point is in fact no longer a fixed expression; it turns around dialectically from the apparently fixed point within the construction of irrealities and unveils this Archimedean point as being unintelligible as well, an x or a transcendent task, an object of belief, not of possession. Even this formula exaggerates the degree to which it is possible to divide being: the reciprocal relationship of the two parts removes any possibility of a rational separation of them. If we apply all the force of our tentative symbolic form to existence, it dissolves under the pressure of our imposition. Whatever we manage to wrest from it is, once again, merely symbolic, and again existence gradually dissolves into a darkening verge. We can push back this boundary; it is elastic and gives, but it never breaks to give us a glimpse of what is on the other side. Instead, it penetrates the symbols and lends them some of its weight, pulling them downward, tying them to a native ground, and giving them life, just as the sap rises to a tree's topmost branches, providing its sunlit crown with being, but during its growing and wilting never allowing us to forget that its flowering is grounded in the soil. We cannot cut being apart in such a way that all the symbols are piled up on one side while the other contains only existence. All being is symbolic—which is to say that it is imbued with the tension of a unity that our clumsy [*kantig*] words can express only as the duality of symbol and existence. To use language that comes as close as possible to this tension would require us to invent the category of singularity-in-duality. Such a formulation is not rationally intelligible; understanding, in fact, can come only from patient and careful examination of all the facts in depth and in detail.

Being is neither one nor two; as a whole it has no Archimedean point outside itself. Nor is it a closed rational system on the inside, for its transcendence into existence is an openness that essentially renders any closure into a system impossible. Thus, being is never an assured asset, an absolutely certain possession, but always a self-transcendent movement. But its objective is neither finite nor boundless; it must be understood only as a symbol of an immanent tension. We may believe in symbolic being, since it promises more

24

than it delivers; and we may doubt it, since it never quite gives what it promises; but we can never be sure.

Hume's Skepticism. The suspension between resigned skepticism and irresistible—but rationally unintelligible—belief took historical form in Hume's philosophical position. This position is important to American thought as both a contrast and a model. Hume's skepticism has its origin in a sense of life so foreign to Peirce's and James's that the cool doubt of the one can typically be contrasted with the warm trust of the other as evidence for two essentially different types of philosophizing. But the economic and cultural development of the United States, with its tendency to egalitarian democracy, has rendered the mind so homeless that such a significant thinker as Santayana, whose situation is further aggravated by his foreignness, finds himself adopting a solipsistic stance that comes very close to Hume's skepticism. But even in instances that include the experiences of foreignness and contradiction, modern thought adds to Hume's problem only in technical details. Accordingly, in a surprising stability of the tradition of the "world view of radical empiricism," as William James called it, modern thought introduces the basic concept of pure experience as a corrective to Hume's thoughts.

The core of Hume's philosophy is found in the monologue that concludes *An Enquiry Concerning Human Understanding.* In it, the dual-singular split in being takes the shape of a contrast between the human imagination and the judgments of "common life." Following an absolute and impenetrable necessity, nature has predisposed us to make judgments, just as it has chosen for us to breathe and feel; and we cannot escape the conflict into which this diversity of our capacities has thrown us. The rules according to which our reason operates may be certain and unerring, but in applying them, the inadequacy of our mental powers diverts us from the right way and leads us astray. The fact that we nevertheless do not despair of finding our way in the world and that our judgments are accurate must be ascribed to a special power of belief whose vital conviction refuses to be destroyed by the sober reflections of reason. When the philosopher abandons himself to the lure of his analyzing thoughts, he must despair of the existence of the outside world, the identity of its objects, the causal connection, the identity of his person, and finally of the truth of his own thinking. He falls prey to the darkest melancholy, akin to the mental state of the centipede who suddenly became unable to move any limb once it had thought about its form of locomotion. But just as nature drives out this negation of life, it heals the depression of the psyche by losing the entanglements of reason in an animal pleasure in play, in conversation with friends, and in diverse entertainments, so that the depressed state appears abstruse and ridiculous. Both powers rule our lives in the same way. Animal urges allow us to judge, act, feel, and suffer, while reason urges us to reflect on the foundations and principles of our actions. Neither has priority over the other, and if someone were prepared to question the legitimacy of existence, he would be acting as foolishly as someone who rejects philosophy because it casts him into the abyss of life-denying doubt. The true skeptic not only doubts his animal conviction but also undermines his doubt through new doubts and so is led back to belief. Skepticism is not a mistrust of nature, for nature as a whole does not confront us in such a way that a vote of confidence can be given or withheld. Rather, it is the inner tension that never arrives at a state of rest but is driven back and forth between the poles of animal ponderousness, indolence, and satiety on the one hand and reflective negation of life on the other.

Time and Existence. In Hume's writings and in those of subsequent philosophers, the interpretation and discussion of these problems is conveyed by the concepts of time and existence. Hume's concept of duration is still quite weak; it entirely lacks the richness and magnitude of such modern concepts of duration as Henri Bergson's. Duration has not yet taken on a reality of its own and is no more than the "mode" by which perceptions follow in sequence. Duration is not a quality of the perceptions themselves, nor does it exist independently of them. It is a dimension structured from nondimensional elements. Only in isolated instances—such as the treatment of time intervals and the concept of identity—do attempts begin to surface that lend substance to duration. But aside from such peripheral analyses without systematic significance, duration is the concept of a succession; it is a rationally reduced formulation. Despite its detachment from the external world, Hume does not systematically arrange the existential content of duration. His choice of terms indicates that his skepticism stretches between external existence and the data gained from introspection. He still

26

considers existence to be an autonomous part of the world, not a functional constituent element of every being; it is merely attached to the external world and is something "in which" we believe—an object of belief, not belief itself. The internal meaning of Hume's thought tends to dissolve the duality of the two-in-one relation, and in the monologue this tendency is fully expressed. But the treatment of the traditional materials dealing with this problem is so questionable that it is impossible to assign the correct weight to these intellectual themes. The conclusion that follows from Hume's critique—namely, that every statement about existence relativizes all nonexistential being into a symbol, thereby allowing it to participate in existence—was not in fact drawn by him. His attack concentrates principally on the transformation of existence from a God-given and divinely ordered being into a human setting.

The external world has not yet become a function of human thought; it confronts the stream of perceptions as an autonomous category. But the tendency to make it subjective becomes clear when we compare it with the conception of existence expressed in Locke and Berkeley. Both operate with the dogma of substance. Their questions about the existence of the external world are a quest for a rationally plausible account of the incontestable facts of two separate existences of self and world and of the relationship between them. Locke solves the problem by the attribution of "powers" to the external world and of their effect through the organization of the senses. Berkeley's solution involves the presumption of the existence of God and the assumption of spiritual activity. Hume, on the other hand, postulates the external world as the result of a human act, thus reducing it to an inner-worldly belief. This act abolishes the crucial distinction, though in his official terminology existence remains an external problem. The internal development of rational skepticism eventually leads Hume to refer all structural problems of being to the self and to develop a metaphysics of natural forces that encompasses all being. Nevertheless, he continues to express his view in the traditional conceptual language that refers to the construction of the external world. Hume dissolved the question of substance, replacing "faith" —in God and the Bible, as held by Locke and Berkeley—with an animalistic belief in the idea that the internal elasticity of the self is sufficient to create the world. The new belief inherits the function of faith in

27

God; and its counterpart, skepticism, is therefore more than an accidental attribute of Hume's character. It becomes the primary force of all thought that shuts up the world in itself, that replaces a divinely ordered universe with the loneliness of the self thrown back on itself.

The Dialectic of Skepticism. Great caution must be taken before a philosophical train of thought may be called a system, for strictly speaking, such a term presupposes that it is assembled in a space devoid of history, in a medium that allows units to be connected without a past into a timeless formulation. In fact, however, every attempt at system building operates with a historical mass of conceptual and verbal elements, with groups of problems, value judgments, and personal modifications of a tradition. All these are intended to be brought together into a more or less logically shaped cosmos—and in all probability that there will be great lacunae in the resulting construct. It would therefore be a great error to see Hume's conception of the world as a system or to recognize in the concept of skepticism a clear-cut formulation. It is characterized both by an open matter-of-factness and the cool detachment of the gentleman who never allows himself to be so deeply touched by things that they shake the basic equilibrium of his person. In spite of all its detachment, Hume's coolness is aware of a gravity of being that was expressed in later times by the formula: Life is too serious to be taken seriously. This stance—which would rather appear frivolous than give the impression that it might commit, much less celebrate, the shamelessness of a devotion to infernal powers—is expressed in a dialectical schema whose synthesis lies in the fatalistic acceptance that mythic nature, for unfathomable reasons, has condemned us both to skepticism and to belief. Its thesis: cognition of the stream of consciousness; its antithesis: belief in the external world along with doubt of it. The tension between thesis and antithesis is the so-called technical problem of skepticism. The third dialectical dimension also combines skepticism and belief, but this time they are of an entirely different sort: What for belief was a rift between fragments of being becomes in the metaphysics of nature an immanent quality of being, considered as a unit. All systems from Descartes' to Berkeley's were skeptical in the technical sense because they accepted the content of consciousness as a certainty and expressed more or less radical doubts of the world insofar as it is not-self. But it is only when the skeptical formula is in conjunction with a major skeptical personality that skepticism is revealed as more than a technical problem, as something that remains immanent in the world view even when the technical problem is solved.

Transformation of Skepticism. Though skepticism remains immanent to their view of the world, Hume's successors no longer deliberately turn it into the formational theme of their image of the world. Concepts are developed with a logic of which the philosophers themselves are unaware until, in Santayana's philosophy, it once more expresses the thought of a skeptical personality. Santayana can make good use of the conceptual refinements that a century and a half had brought about.

The internal development of this maturation can be summarized as follows: For Hume the only authentic object of knowledge was the succession of perceptions; the external world was an object of belief, not of knowledge. Thomas Reid's so-called common sense philosophy alters this basic skeptical schema by claiming equal certainty for every sort of object. It is precisely this certainty that grants the external world the same degree of reality that is assigned to the reality of the stream of the self. This reasoning almost seems a step backward, but in fact the reality of the world is grounded in "first principles," namely, the capacities of the self. The external world is again as fixed and certain as it was for Locke and Berkeley, but now, rather than being transcendent, its certainty is grounded in the capacity of knowledge. The world is increasingly subjectivized, and subjective capacities bestow existence as such on every form of reality.

Reid himself does not carry the argument further, but numerous details of his analysis indicate the direction in which it was developing. Among his "common sense" principles are "consciousness" and "memory"; both enjoy a specific relationship to duration. Consciousness is knowledge of the thoughts, hopes, and the like, with respect to one's self in the present, whereas memory places these same elements in the past. Time is not a form of intuition or a primordial and given dimension; it is derived from memory. Because we remember an event as "past," we conceive of a distance between the past event and the present moment, and we call this distance *duration.* According to this view, there is no "stream" of consciousness to be observed directly because the present is an in-

29

finitesimal dot on the borderline between past and future. If we "perceive" a succession or any other kind of motion, we are not "conscious" of it as Reid defines consciousness. Consciousness can merely provide still pictures of the moment we are remembering.

The image of consciousness as a chain of data along which we—marking the present point—march is totally inadequate. Time is turned into a relation of the contents of consciousness at the present moment because even memory is made out to be part of the present contents of consciousness. The concept of a present thus loses its meaning, since we possess only present moments, and everything we call the past is merely a particular structuring of such moments.

But Reid never arrived at this reflection and the conclusions that follow from it. He is content with the acceptance of consciousness and memory, their precise description, and the derivation of duration from memory. He does not consider the dialectical problem of constructing a self and a world, although his ideas lead him almost to the limit where the self becomes a freely suspended point, whose existence in time (in contrast to the perception of duration in the present moment) may reflexively be doubted.

The development of conceptual topics leads from the blending of the ordinary skepticism of everyday life with an epistemological problem within Enlightenment philosophy through Reid's isolation of the epistemological question to a third stage of skeptical thought. In this stage belief and doubt are stretched not from the succession of self to external existence but between the present moment of duration and the existence of the self and its world.

When defining identity, Hume already had occasion to consider duration as part of the internal structure of thinking. Subsequently it became, in principle, a dimension of the self. But since the self does not live in this dimension, whereas duration is an internal relation in the self understood as a present moment, this internal structure of the self suffers from a unique unreality and, so to speak, requires existence to give it enough weight to anchor it in the palpable materiality of the world.

Hume's epistemological skepticism was the vehicle for the ordinary skepticism of everyday life. Reid separated the two, but in establishing as certain every capacity for knowledge, he focused that certainty on the self much more sharply than did Hume; he therefore placed himself in a position where his existence along with all being becomes problematic. And in this way, along with the various changed meanings given to reason, skepticism, and time, the concept of existence was also altered. Hume strongly differentiated external being from the self. Reid reduces the antithetical concept of existence to its epistemological content and assigns to each individual the attribute of existence as an index. But then the totality of all the elements of being that are recognized as having existence (including the self) turns out to constitute a contrast with a new self, in which all attributes combine at a new point in the present. And from this present point in time we can raise skeptical questions regarding which attributes allow us to know that this point is more than a play of the imagination, and regarding what it is that makes us so confident that the series of snapshots are projections of real life. Santayana undertook the investigation of this highest stage of the concepts of time and existence.

Imbuing Duration with Existence. Between Reid's theory of knowledge and the highest form of skepticism lies the gradual imbuing of the stream of the self with substance. The new dialectical self—the self that contains all the attributes of knowledge and that confronts all existence, the self that initially grounds or justifies existence generally—this new self becomes the topic under investigation. To lay out this process in detail, I would have to recapitulate the history of British philosophy. A few names, with which the most significant elements are identified, must suffice here. Reid himself made the first attempts at a descriptive analysis of the stream of consciousness. Dugald Stewart extended Reid's fragmentary remarks into a complex system of ego structure by adding to Hume's principles of association. The categories of cause-effect, ends-means, and premise-conclusion were understood as subjective forms of association. Finally the totality of habits, the character of man as a principle of association, was established. Thomas Brown's theory of the coexistence of the contents of consciousness goes deeper; he demonstrated that the parts of the stream of consciousness do not neatly follow each other but interpenetrate and compose themselves into a concrete continuum. Finally, Sir William Hamilton's theory of memory introduced the dialectical problems of the present: according to Hamilton, memory is the function that joins into a continuum the otherwise isolated parts of the self—*in*

31

contrast to the perceived consequence and variation of its circumstances. Though his notion of the self is derived from a perception of the permanence and identity of the thinking subject, it is both a product of memory and an act of present consciousness. Memory and consciousness are thus intertwined into a complex that was subsequently analyzed by S. H. Hodgson.

Hodgson's Theory. In Hodgson's first major work (*Time and Space*, 1865) the vocabulary is still graphic; consciousness is described as a coherent chain that grows longer from moment to moment; like a plant from its seed, it grows from an earlier self and its content, so that the constituent elements of consciousness are not separate objects, appealing to each other according to laws of similarity or contrast, but "organic parts of a living whole." The association of thoughts, or their reintegration (a concept introduced by Hamilton), does not result from objective, mechanical connections (as it does, for example, in Hobbes's work) but according to the rules of association that are part of the organic whole of the mind. In his last great work, *The Metaphysics of Experience*, Hodgson's analysis of the interpenetration of consciousness and duration is rendered conceptually more precise through his use of the concepts of "thatness" and "whatness." The content of an act of perception is called the *whatness*, the fact of perceiving is called the *thatness* of perception. Neither of the two parts of experience exists independent of the other, and neither is the object of the other: the existence of the perceived content is not the object of the content, since the content alone is not a perception; and the content is not the object of perceiving but the "nature" of perceiving itself, by which it can be defined. The best description of the constituent elements of perception sees them as reciprocal "aspects" of each other and of the total perception; however, the perception (or experience) is not assumed to be a third, additional element, separate from the aspects. The inseparable union of constituent elements was claimed by Hodgson as the essential meaning of the statement *esse est percipi*. Perception in its simplest form is both process and content—that is, not a simple but a "compound thing," and this peculiarity is to be designated by the attribute "reflective." In this instance "reflection" means not retrospection—that is, looking back at something completed—but the immanent tension of experiences, reflection in itself. In fact, Hodgson explicitly refers to

Hegel's dialectic in explicating this tension. The dialectical construction of the stream explains the changes of meaning and variations in the concepts of consciousness and memory. If the focus is on the accumulation of the past—that is, on the process—then the turn toward self-reflection can be interpreted in psychological terms by reference to the function of memory. But if the accent falls more heavily on the present content, the interpretation stresses consciousness. Nevertheless, we must never forget that these psychological terms are used with a metaphysical meaning and that the dialectical analysis of the self has nothing to do with experimental psychology.

Effort and Shock. Though the self was now imbued with substance, nothing changed in the basic philosophical situation. Hodgson's concept of perception begins at precisely the point where Reid's analysis of "common sense" principles broke off: at the freely suspended point for which existential proof in a real world has not been offered. Hodgson's stream of experience does not yet contain a self, nor is the existence of a world guaranteed. He saw the separation of subject from object of perception as a supplemental division of a complicating nature, related to the problem of attention or effort. Hodgson provided an illustrative example: Suppose that the stream of perceptions flows spontaneously and that into this spontaneity a foreign noise intrudes; the stream is roiled, and we try to ascertain what has called forth this crisis; we listen hard in order to classify the disturbance according to its source and its kind, and this effort and attention to the changes also disrupts the simple stream, allowing a subject to emerge within it that itself listens for a future event that is meant to be understood, an objective world that can be understood. The experience of effort is the lowest discriminating mark for distinguishing conscious act of cognition from an object recognized in it. Attention devoted to the content of the changes must be described as a perception of discrepancy; when attention is devoted to the process, it lingers on in the discrepancy in the attempt to understand it more clearly. The activity itself cannot be seen without mediation; aside from content and process, assigned to every perception, the action is not transparent, it is not content but is a "real condition" for the experience of the activity, a breach on the part of reality that indicates that our life is not a dream but a reality—or, at least, reality *as well*.

In his last systematic work, *Scepticism and Animal Belief,* San-

33

tayana dealt with the same problem by calling it "shock." The flow of images in my consciousness may be a dream or an illusion. Only shock puts us in touch with existence. Only shock guarantees both the external world and the reality of our mental discourse. With this idea Santayana accommodates himself to the tradition of British philosophy at the same time that he completes the development of the problem of skepticism begun by Hume. Reid still conceived the stream of thought in terms of a vague description; Brown's idea of coexistence was the earliest formula for the problem of continuity; Hamilton recognized the memory of self as different from the recollection of individual contents of consciousness; Hodgson studied the self-penetration of the stream more carefully and brought it into relation with reality through the idea of effort. And Santayana took the final step by announcing the illusory character of the self. The movement concludes with the certainty of the self and the doubt of the external world replaced by the postulate of doubt of the self and the certainty of shock.

II

Santayana on American Thought. In the essay "Philosophical Opinion in America" (1918), George Santayana attempted to describe the changes philosophic thought in America had undergone:

> It seems, then, that the atmosphere of the new world has influenced philosophy in two ways. In the first place, it has accelerated and rendered fearless the disintegration of conventional categories; a disintegration on which modern philosophy has always been at work, and which has precipitated its successive phases. In the second place, the younger cosmopolitan America has favoured the impartial assemblage and mutual confrontation of all sorts of ideas. It has produced, in intellectual matters, a sort of happy watchfulness and insecurity. Never was the human mind master of so many facts and sure of so few principles. Will this suspense and fluidity of thought crystallize into some great new system? Positive gifts of imagination and moral heroism are requisite to make a great philosopher, gifts which must come from the gods and from circumstances. But if the genius should arise, this vast collection of suggestions and this radical analysis of presumptions which he will find in America may keep him from going astray. Nietzsche said that the earth has been a mad-house long enough. Without contradicting him, we might perhaps soften the expression,

34

and say that philosophy has been long enough an asylum for enthu-
siasts. It is time for it to become less solemn and more serious.[1]

These remarks are accurate insofar as they mention facts; they
are questionable insofar as they interpret. Conventional categories
were indeed, if not disintegrated, then killed by neglect. The cheerful
lack of respect with which an American professor of philosophy is
able to treat the ideas of "old Plato" and "that fellow Hegel, you
know" will arouse the ire or amusement—depending on one's tem-
perament—of any European. Likewise, attitudes toward the feasi-
bility of philosophical expression are highly impartial; philosophy
is treated more as an intellectual game than as something that demands active participation. But how these phenomena are to be interpreted cannot be stated with unequivocal certainty. Santayana
seems to believe that the detached acknowledgment and confrontation of European and Asian thought has brought about a wait-and-
see attitude that will eventually be resolved into a new large system.
And anyone familiar with the relatively nationalist isolation of the
European philosophies will not deny that the simultaneous arrangement by which they are organized for American intellectuals is an
advantage in that it can lead to skepticism and intellectual humility.
Nevertheless, it seems possible that, on the other hand, the Americans' detachment from the bulk of the philosophic tradition is based
on an intellectual attitude that is by no means indecisive but, on
the contrary, is very resolute and only slightly at a loss in the face
of matters that have no significance for them. Santayana, too, sees
this possibility whenever he merely observes without introducing
interpretive reflections. Speaking of the average professor of philosophy in an American university, he states:

His education has been more pretentious than thorough; his style is
deplorable; social pressure and his own great eagerness have condemned him to over-work, committee meetings, early marriage, pre-
mature authorship, and lecturing two or three times a day under
forced draught. He has no peace in himself, no window open to a calm
horizon, and in his heart perhaps little taste for mere scholarship or
pure speculation. Yet like the plain soldier staggering under his
clumsy equipment, he is cheerful; he keeps his faith in himself and
in his allotted work, puts up with being toasted on only one side,
remains open-minded, whole-hearted, appreciative, helpful, confident

1. George Santayana, *Philosophical Opinion in America* (London, 1918), 13.

35

of the future of goodness and of science. In a word, he is a cell in that teeming democratic body; he draws from its warm contagious activities the sanctions of his own life and, less consciously, the spirit of his philosophy.[2]

Indecisiveness in the face of the philosophical tradition simply goes hand in hand with an assured and robust attitude that comes from membership in the democratic community. The correctness of this stance will become evident in the study of John R. Commons' works; this chapter examines merely the general characteristics of the systemic form, leaving aside its historical foundations. Santayana therefore grants that the thinking of the average professional philosopher may be endowed with an original spirit, though he denies this same quality to American philosophy as a whole. In 1918 he believed that the United States had not yet produced a single thinker who had meaningfully articulated the American spirit in philosophy.

James on American Thought. But it is quite possible that Santayana's judgment—presumably shared by many Europeans—is based on a misunderstanding. American philosophy uses the language of English philosophy, and a continuity can be established unequivocally for the formulation of certain problems. But the thinking is not a continuation of the English practice; no intimate intellectual bond exists between the two, and we are unlikely to find more than superficial kinship in the treatment of problems. In spite of this break, the ideas that emerged through centuries of European development were studied and criticized by Americans, so that the impression is created that the bulk of acquired tradition, if only it is sufficiently worked through, must of necessity give birth to the new. However, a few thinkers—especially Peirce and James—stand aside from the effort of rehashing imported materials. Their work may appear raw and primitive to a European, and Santayana saw it as such, because it does not operate with European techniques. James especially was keenly aware of the contrast. In the first chapter of his *Pluralistic Universe* (1909) he wrote in detail about the European, and especially the German, technical apparatus of philosophy and about the disastrous influence German idealistic philosophy had on English thought. When the subject is phi-

2. *Ibid.*, 5.

losophy, he noted, it is "really fatal to lose connexion with the open air of human nature, and to think in terms of shop-tradition only."[3]

> In Germany the forms are so professionalized that anybody who has gained a teaching chair and written a book, however distorted or eccentric, has the legal right to figure forever in the history of the subject, like a fly in amber. All later comers have the duty of quoting him and measuring their opinions with his opinion. Such are the rules of the professorial game—they think and write from each other, for each other, and at each other exclusively. With this exclusion of the open air all true perspective gets lost, extremes and oddities count as much as sanities, and command the same attention; and if by chance anyone writes popularly and about results only, with his mind directly focussed on the subject, it is reckoned *oberflächliches Zeug* [superficial trash] and *ganz unwissenschaftlich* [completely unscientific]. . . . Great as technique is, results are greater. To teach philosophy so that the pupils' interest in technique exceeds that in results is surely a vicious aberration. . . . The english mind, thank heaven, and the french mind, are still kept, by their aversion to crude technique and barbarism, closer to truth's natural probabilities. Their literatures show fewer obvious falsities and monstrosities than that of Germany. . . .
> Let me repeat once more that a man's vision is the great fact about him. Who cares for Carlyle's reasons, or Schopenhauer's, or Spencer's? A philosophy is the expression of a man's intimate character . . . logic only finding reasons for the visions afterwards.[4]

James further notes that in the younger generation of American philosophers a profusion of technical jargon was becoming evident; he considered it a result of German influences and hoped it would soon disappear in favor of a return to the more humanistic forms of English empiricism.

James speaks of a contrast between German post-Kantian thinking and Western European and American philosophy. But precisely the fact that he must address his exhortation to return to a natural way of thinking to English philosophers (*A Pluralistic Universe* is based on lectures delivered at Manchester College, and they are particularly critical of the idealism of Green and Bradley) shows that the line between the two forms also separates the English type from the American. On the other hand, the remark that a more

---

3. William James, *A Pluralistic Universe* (New York and London, 1909), 17.
4. [*Ibid.*, 17–20, 176. Although this quotation is given as if it were more or less continuous in *Pluralistic Universe*, the last eight words in fact come from much later in the book. The lowercase *english* and *french* are as they appear in this edition of the James work.]

recent American generation was beginning to operate with European techniques is not very important, since the only philosopher after James who significantly advanced the American tradition is John Dewey; and his work shows the same peculiarities as does that of Peirce and James, so that the technique seems to appear only where vision is lacking.

But even admitting that between European and American philosophers there is a contrast of the sort James noted, it cannot easily be described clearly, even if all-encompassing definitions are forsworn. A preliminary approach is given by James's own remarks. In *A Pluralistic Universe* he repeatedly stressed the visionary nature of philosophizing, which turned the logical coherence of a system into a kind of supplementary afterword. But vision is the ground of all philosophy pure and simple—not only of American philosophy—so that the meaning of the word *vision* must be changed from a category of origin to one of expression if it is to be used to describe the American type. All philosophy worthy of the name has its origin in a vision, and every system uses a particular technique for its expression. Thus James does not deny the greatness of Hegel's vision, even though he disliked the technique of Hegel's system. If, therefore, the contrast is to be typified by emphasizing the characteristics of the vision, that word must designate the style in which philosophical thoughts are expressed. Understood in this way, James tried to conceive in a positive way what in his and Peirce's work Europeans usually see as a primitive and crude technique. It is not a defect in thinking but a reduction of the construction to simple strong lines, without subtle elaboration of details. Some few ideas are singled out—evolution, nature, self, God, death, reality—and in a few pages their sense and relationships are tersely indicated—more to reassure the reader that a meaning exists than to establish a rational framework for its own sake. The accent is not placed on the objectivity of thought; no attempt is made to pursue possibilities or detours, since no thought is really valuable enough in itself; rather, thought is merely a sign for a vision, to be expressed as concisely as possible and yet still be understandable. The most fleeting aphorism must on occasion serve to communicate. The burden of the European problematic is not entirely absent, but the arguments and quarrels of the various schools are merely external, seemingly more a badly adapted European habit than something inevitably connected with American thought. Philosophizing has—I explicitly avoid writing "still has" —the nature of prophecy; seekers of God report in sparse formulations what they have seen.

Peirce: The Principle of Contingency. This type of philosophy is spendidly represented in the work of Charles S. Peirce, William James's teacher. In six papers, altogether taking up fewer than 150 pages of large-size print, Peirce develops a philosophical system— or, it would be better to say, announces a vision of a world, since nowhere does Peirce attempt to follow up the consequences of his statements (uttered with oracular certainty) and examine them for their viability. He postulates three principles present in the structure of the cosmos and three tendencies visible in the development of the world: synechism, tychism, and agapism. Tychism is taken to stand for a set of problems treated in Europe under the name of contingency; synechism is the tendency of continuity; and agapism stands for a restorative love, which Peirce defines by referring to the Gospel of Saint John. He may have become interested in the first tendency, tychism, in the course of his extensive studies in mathematics and physics. (The bibliography of his writings on the theory and method of measurement comes to twenty-four papers, his works on logic and mathematics to twenty-three.)[5] In "The Doctrine of Necessity Examined" he finds that the observations normally cited in support of the doctrine of mechanical causality in nature no longer prove that nature contains an element of regularity, though this new view does not solve the problem of the specificity and universality of this regularity. Observations are even diametrically opposed to the claims of precision; at best, an attempt can be made to explain away inaccuracies by noting the lack of precision in measurement; and even this argument is not valid in the face of such phenomena as irregularity in the motion of gas molecules. To hold that natural laws are always exact would be arbitrary even when empirically it is not possible to point to contrary examples. Under any given circumstances, however, it is quite proper to postulate a theory of the essential contingency of natural law, since this thesis is better suited to the metaphysical

5. See Charles S. Peirce, *Chance, Love, and Logic: Philosphical Essays by the Late Charles S. Peirce, the Founder of Pragmatism*, ed. Morris R. Cohen (New York, 1923).

interpretation of the world than is that of universal precision: "Uniformities are precisely the sort of facts that need to be accounted for. That a pitched coin should sometimes turn heads up and sometimes tails calls for no particular explanation; but if it shows heads every time, we wish to know how this result had been brought about. Law is *par excellence* the thing that wants a reason."[6]

It seems that for Peirce the only possibility for understanding the phenomenon lies in his interpretation of it as the result of a prior development. Natural laws and the uniformities of the universe as a whole are late products of cosmic evolution. Interpretation allows the introduction into nature of an element of spontaneity. In this way the material of the universe is also determined; faced with the choice of explaining nature from mind or mind from nature, or finally of accepting the two principles independent of each other, Peirce decides according to the rule of Ockham's razor, which states that no more principles may be introduced than are absolutely necessary to the explanation. It is therefore impossible to accept independent principles, and to explain mind on the basis of the regularity of matter raises the problem of a justification for regularity. The explanation from mind is therefore the only possible interpretation. The only comprehensible theory of the universe must be that of objective idealism. Matter is exhausted mind. Worn-out habits become physical laws. The world is created as an unregulated chaos of unlimited possibilities and changes through the growth of habits and laws from nothing to an increasingly tangible reality. But the original nothingness is not a void; rather, it is full of an intensity of consciousness, compared with which all our current feelings appear like the convulsions of a molecule intent on shaking off the compulsion of a law of nature. Evolution can be understood only as the limitation of possibilities.

The Principle of Continuity. Why, we may ask, does chaos, bursting with life, change over from its condition of the highest intensity into other forms and begin to incorporate signs of death? And why, since it can avail itself of eternity, has the process of its dying not long ago been completed? We are caught in a net of pseudo-questions about, and pseudo-answers to, the problem of infinity, and it is almost regrettable that Peirce attempted to explain—imperfectly,

6. *Ibid.,* 162.

haltingly, and quite unnecessarily—the step from chaos into law. It is regrettable because, given the visionary nature and the complete inconsistency of his thoughts, and especially given the sparse hints at complications of the problem of continuity, the few crude and inadequate attempts at preserving the appearance of systematic connections appear petty and out of place. To arrive at habit and law from chaos requires a principle of habit formation that itself arose from the growth of regularity as the consequence of an infinitely improbable habit formation. Thus, after Peirce presented the brute fact of regularity as particularly in need of explanation, because it cannot be understood as the result of an accident, he allows habit formation to enter as the result of an infinitesimally small probability. The justifications of a philosopher's desire to see things as he sees them are always fraudulent. But in Europe, and especially in Germany, the intellectual apparatus is so extensive and the elaboration of the problems is carried to such lengths that it is easy to understand how a thinker concerned with arranging details of his work overlooks the large and crucial inconsistencies of his effort. But a situation that reveals in the smallest surveyable space the logical incompatibility of two linked thoughts in so remarkable a way, without scandalizing anyone, and without damaging the greatness of the philosophical vision, seems to be a specifically American phenomenon.

It is therefore impossible even here to provide an intelligible statement of Peirce's ideas on continuity, which are systemically linked to the justification of the formation of habits. The terminology is so vague that at best we can describe the emotional intention that has occasioned their use. The "law of mind," the analysis of which is the principal task of research on the problem of continuity, is formulated as follows: "Logical analysis applied to mental phenomena shows that there is but one law of mind, namely, that ideas tend to spread continuously and to affect certain others which stand to them in a peculiar relation of affectability. In this spreading they lose intensity, and especially the powers of affecting others, but gain generality and become welded with other ideas."[7]

Idea is here used with the very general meaning of "an event in an individual consciousness,"[8] and this definition determines the

7. *Ibid.*, 203–204.
8. *Ibid.*, 204.

direction of the analysis that follows. It is customary to speak of ideas as separate, in that we talk of sharing an idea with someone or recalling an idea; in fact, however, ideas are irrevocable and non-recurring, and past ones cannot be the current ones, nor can the ideas in another's stream of consciousness be mine. Thus, if past and present ideas can be compared, some kind of relationship must exist between them so that what seems to be past is in fact present, and this relationship is found in the continuity of the stream of consciousness. The present is not a point but is itself already an infinitesimal stretch of time that merges with others into a continuum without causing a breach that would facilitate the classification of one cluster of ideas as past, in contrast to another called the present. In the article "Architecture of Theories," Pierce established his claim to construct a philosophy using principles that have proven their worth in other sciences. He cites as examples principles in physics, mathematical thinking, biology, physiology, and psychology. In particular he supports his notion of continuity with detailed citations of the problems of continuity and infinity in mathematics. But it is easy to see that his description of the continuity of consciousness transcends the mathematical problem. He described the course of consciousness: "Let there be . . . a continuous flow of inference through a finite time; and the result will be a mediate objective consciousness of the whole time in the last moment. In this last moment, the whole series will be recognized, or known as known before, except only the last moment, which of course will be absolutely unrecognizable to itself. Indeed, even this last moment will be recognized like the rest, or, at least, will be just beginning to be so."[9]

These sentences develop a theory of the same structure as that of Hodgson, who distinguished between the subjective and objective aspects of perception, calling them "thatness" and "whatness," thus bringing the dialectical dimension of the depth of consciousness to the surface. Peirce gave the same description of unmediated objective perception of the object and an unmediated present event that is the wellspring of consciousness. The difference lies in their respective techniques: Hodgson gives an extensive and detailed analysis and goes to great pains to convey the difference among the

9. *Ibid.*, 207.

act and object of perception, the recording of objects in action in the present moment, and the description of the phenomenon of self-consciousness. Peirce is content to state that the present moment in itself is "absolutely" unrecognizable, while in the following sentence he claims the exact opposite—that the present, too, is recognized every bit as much as the past. A subordinate clause further restricts even this contradictory claim by noting that the present moment "at least" is conceptually prepared to be recognized. Thus he starts from the same view of the problem as did Hodgson, but he does not try to make it rational or to capture the various constituent elements of his analysis by naming them (thatness, whatness). In three lines he makes three statements that are mutually contradictory, without in any one of them using expressions that are fixed in their meaning. Nevertheless, his statements are not worthless; in spite of their irrationality, one understands what he means to say. But one also sees that it was not a passion for rational accomplishment that drove him to philosophize. A comparison of Hodgson's and Peirce's work immediately gives the impression that Peirce was the more original thinker and the more significant and philosophical mind. When we compare their theories individually, we do not find in Peirce a single statement formulated with a care for conceptual clarity comparable to what one finds in Hodgson's work. And beside these inadequacies in positive analysis, there are the incomprehensible comparisons with mathematical problems. Precisely these comparisons demonstrate that Peirce's vagueness of expression is not a conciseness caused by impatience; in fact, he saw the problems but lacked the concepts to express them properly. That is, his vocabulary stands in quite a different relation to his vision than did Hodgson's conceptual apparatus to his insights. Hodgson's concepts are the body of his thought; his thoughts have their life in the concepts and their very evolution. In Peirce's work, vision and verbal expression are separated; his meaning can be understood only if the words, sentences, images, and similes are read as suggestions without intrinsic value but that point away from and back to the apprehension of the philosophical object that has occasioned their use. If we pursue his language within its own realm, hoping to find a coherent thought by taking him literally, we are deceived and find only nonsense.

Spreading of Feelings. The connection that exists between these explanations of the nature of continuity and those that follow concerning the spread of feelings is not rational, but neither is it merely emotional. The term *feeling* is now used as the term *idea* was used earlier, without any apparent distinction in use and without any definition. To explain his thinking, Peirce cites the example of the spread of feelings in a simple organism, the amoeba. He claims that when such an organism's state of quiescence is disturbed in one place, the sensation spreads to other parts. The act of spreading takes place without unity or relation to a central organ and in an amorphous continuum. It is not a wave, advancing from one site to another; it does not move into a new area with the same speed with which it leaves the old. At the beginning it dies out rather more slowly than it spreads. The feeling has a substantial, subjective, spatial spread of the same scope as the irritated surface. "This is, no doubt," wrote Pierce, "a difficult idea to seize, for the reason that it is a subjective, not an objective, extension. It is not that we have a feeling of bigness; . . . . It is that the feeling, as a subject of inhesion, is big."[10] In one sentence the example of the amoeba is extended to the phenomenon of consciousness in general, without one word concerning the difficulties of the problem. The wordplay of subjective and objective spread conceals the fact that when extensions are subjective, they simply are not extensions. But in spite of the very superficial connection between the movement of language and the movement of philosophic thinking, the problem Peirce is addressing is clearly understood: namely, the inner continuity of mental process and the reciprocal penetration of states of consciousness, what in Brown's philosophy was called "coexistence." His objective idealism claims that the substance of the universe is mind, and in order to familiarize people with the substantiality, the palpable physicality of intellectual life, he uses organic and spatial images. In a rational description, the methods used to make the problem more comprehensible would have been technical. In his prophetic way of thinking, the methods involved are the symbols in which the force of his formations is exhausted. Rationally, the relationship between a thorough analysis of the dialectic of self-consciousness and duration would lead to a description of the phenomena of penetration and coexistence; in Peirce's work,

10. *Ibid.*, 222–23.

expression and vision are separate (since his thinking does not include a meeting of the two). No road leads from mathematical continuity to the amoeba's feelings. Rather, to try to understand them one must go behind the images and their expression, to their origin, to another position from which they arise.

Generalization. When ideas spread spatially and continuously, they are generalized. The simple idea becomes a general idea. Peirce's explanation of this statement is, once again, irrational; but there is one moment where it may be possible to see what he intended to say: "These general ideas are not mere words, nor do they consist in this, that certain concrete facts will every time happen under certain descriptions of conditions; but they are just as much, or rather far more, living realities than the feelings themselves out of which they are concreted. And to say that mental phenomena are governed by law does not mean merely that they are describable by a general formula; but that there is a living idea, a conscious continuum of feeling which pervades them, and to which they are docile."[11]

Nominalist interpretations of general ideas and attempts to give them a merely logical meaning were rejected. The general idea is made up of the same concrete stuff as the simple idea, the only distinction being the more comprehensive context of meaning found in the former.

Simple ideas are bound together by more than continuity; they follow each other not only without a gap but also meaningfully, and are merged in higher units of meaning that in turn encompass the details and determine their significance. The relationship between higher-order structures of meaning and elementary ones is not, however, the correlative of the whole and its parts; it is a phenomenon of logical genesis. Peirce uses the roundabout way of the example of an equilateral hyperbola to explain the connection between past and future and the foreshadowing of future elements of meaning through past and present generalized ideas of a higher order. All connections among the elements of consciousness are a process of connecting meanings. When an idea arises in the present moment, it has a connection of meaning to the past; it appears as a modification of the past idea, or—as Peirce claims in a leap—the new idea is tied to the past idea that suggested it, not *like* but *as* the logical predicate to its subject.[12]

11. *Ibid.*, 232.
12. *Ibid.*, 226.

*Personality.*The statement that "a person is only a particular kind of a general idea"[13] throws light on the intention of Peirce's philosophy. Everything he wrote about the relationship of a simple idea to the general idea—about their arrangement of meaning, the suggestion of the future immanent in the past, the concrete spatial extension of the substance of the idea—holds true for the description of the personality as a variant of the general idea. The personality, like any general idea, cannot be grasped in a brief act of understanding but must be lived through over time. The coordination of ideas in a personality is a teleological harmony, but not as simply a middle term in a steady movement toward a predetermined end. Rather, the person is structured in a developmental teleology: the present moment does not foresee everything that the future holds. "Were the ends of a person already explicit, there would be no room for development, for growth, for life; and consequently there would be no personality. The mere carrying out of predetermined purposes is mechanical."[14]

The Principle of Love. The margin of present uncertainty about the future within the present can be traced back to the ubiquitous principle of contingency. From the chaos of the most vital life, mind declines in expanding stages to death according to a natural law of exhaustion, in which contingency is only a little more effective and evident. This constellation of life and death contains the elements of a metaphysical tragedy. Peirce himself calls the primal chaos a nothing and mentions the growth of materiality along with the increase in regularity as opening perspectives on a relationship among meaning, finiteness, and death. But once again the thought does not move in the direction of conceptual precision; instead, the new vision searches for new expressions unconnected to previous ones. The growth into meaningfulness, which in the beginning (that is, spatially, on the first pages of Peirce's paper) is seen as a ripening toward death, has now become an expansion toward life that flourishes through love—the third principle of the cosmos:

> Suppose, for example, that I have an idea that interests me. It is my creation. It is my creature; . . . it is a little person. I love it; and I will sink myself in perfecting it. It is not by dealing out cold justice to the

13. *Ibid.*
14. *Ibid.*, 234.

46

circle of my ideas that I can make them grow but by cherishing and tending them as I would the flowers in my garden. The philosophy we draw from John's gospel is that this is how the mind develops; and as for the cosmos, only so far as it yet is mind, and so has life, is it capable of further evolution.[15]

The principles of life and death are contradictory in much the same way as contingency and lawfulness, discussed previously. The derivation of lawfulness from a game of chance, because its nonaccidental character can be indicated but not explained after the fact, is in keeping with the earlier claim that evolution culminates in life, following upon the dogmatic statement that evolution can end only in death. A gospel of love appears alongside contingency and continuity, without a systematic connection between the two: "Philosophy, when just escaping from its golden pupa-skin, mythology, proclaimed the great evolutionary agency of the universe to be Love. Or, since this pirate-lingo, English, is poor in such-like words, let us say Eros, the exuberance-love."[16] Love is excessive but not general or distant, directed not to abstractions but to persons; and not to unknown persons but to "our own dear ones"—the family, neighbors. The doctrine of the concreteness of general ideas and of personality is developed further to claim that love nurtures the concrete mind—once again irrationally, because if any consequence can be drawn from the facts of concreteness and substantiality of mind, it would first be to improve and develop what is truly nearest: oneself rather than others. That the doctrine of charity is preferable is based on historical reasons, to be discussed in greater detail in the analysis of Commons' philosophy; here only the general form of thinking will be described.

God. The substantiality and the personal character of mind lead to several religiophilosophical consequences, even though emotionally they might precede and determine the philosophy of objective idealism. If people are to love and understand one another, the medium of their communication must be of the same substance as themselves: "When an idea is transferred from one mind to another, it is by forms of combination of the divers elements of nature, say by some curious symmetry, or by some union of a tender color with a refined odor. To such forms the law of mechanical

15. *Ibid.,* 269–70.
16. *Ibid.,* 267.

47

energy has no application. If they are eternal, it is in the spirit they embody; and their origin cannot be accounted for by any mechanical necessity. They are embodied ideas; and only so can they convey ideas."[17]

The life of the mind is continuous throughout the universe, and without continuity communication would not be possible; even God lives within the mental continuum, and since all mind has a personal form, God, too, must have personality. Given the dogma of personality, together with the doctrine of communication through mental continuity, it follows that we are connected to the person of God and have an unmediated apprehension of it. But if that is the case—Peirce raises the question—how could the existence of God ever be doubted by anyone?

He replies that after long experience the most obvious, widely visible, and established facts are not always observed precisely because of their overwhelming self-evidence. He himself uses the doctrines of a personal God and of communication with him to explain the problem of divination: There are many ways for people to spread current ideas and many ways for doctrines to expand, but genuine innovation and original growth of the mind, the premonition of new things before we possess them, is possible only through lovingly submerging oneself in a richer person than the human one. The special ability of the genius to come upon new knowledge is properly called divination because the new material is found in the mind of God.

The Absence of Dialectic. The analysis of Peirce's dogmas, intended to indicate their "visionary" character, has made use of a method that, in achieving its purpose, partly negates it. For the philosopher's irrational statements were revealed as such by reference to corresponding rational formulations of problems, so that it might seem as if Peirce, though expressing himself obscurely, meant what the rational equivalents state. But interpretation by establishing parallels on the basis of equivalence is not intended to grasp more certainly and more completely what Peirce, perhaps through inadequacy, formulated less well. It is merely intended to direct us to the point where we can have an unmediated apprehension of the subject matter from which Peirce also took his depar-

17. *Ibid.,* 235.

ture, without claiming that the clearer form is therefore also the better one. Interpretation is not the reproduction of an original but merely a more or less weak means of making abstruse material more accessible. It is not an absolute system of coordination, in which the interpreted figures can be explicitly named, but is itself merely a variation on a theme that is always given only in its variations and never in its pure state. Now that we have clarified the distinctive features of Peirce's intellectual formation by using parallels—that is, by interpreting one thing by comparing it with another—the framework of interpretation must be dismantled in order to avoid being deceived about the main lines of the structure itself. If, for example, it is said that Peirce uses the image of the mathematical continuum and a few vague expressions to deal with a problem that appears to have been handled in a more rational way in Hodgson's analysis, it does not necessarily follow that Peirce "really" meant to address the problem of the dialectic of consciousness. On the contrary, such certainly was not his intention, or he would have said so. Instead, the comparison shows that material Hodgson used as a dialectical problem assumes a quite different form for Peirce. Mathematical continuity is a useful image for him precisely because the material does not appear to him in the form of dialectic.

If one took only a passing glance at Peirce's work, it would not be difficult to find grounds for this phenomenon: since his philosophy contains so little systematic connection, so little rational concentration, it enables one to presume that he did not penetrate to the problems of dialectic, that they fell through the cracks somewhere in the interstices of his incoherent theses; there is, therefore, a defect. But since one can hardly deny Peirce's genius as a philosopher, this assumption is highly questionable. It is most unlikely that he simply overlooked such a central problem while stressing less important things. It will therefore be more advisable to assume—and such an assumption is historically supported by William James's philosophy—that a new experience, essentially different from the European tradition of skepticism, displaces the accent of thinking in such a way that the dialectic is strongly affected and perhaps disappears altogether. The absence of connections between the problems of continuity and the stream of the self on the one hand and the gospel of brotherly love on the other indicates that the philosophy of the self does not carry the same all-absorbing meaning that it has in English thought. Familiarity with Peirce's work alone, of course, can scarcely confirm this conjecture or give it a fixed form. Only James's rationalization gives us a more precise grasp of this change.

Until now analyses of the visionary qualities in Peirce's philosophy treated it only as a problem of form; a prophetic will, it was said, and not the love of objectivity in the work, formed its statements. What the form itself manifests—the desire to communicate and a religious certainty—does not characterize the content, and several remarks about Peirce's principal theses are required. Peirce himself can only supply headings: the world-stuff, contingency, continuity, the idea of God. Their range and significance does not become evident until James elaborates and clarifies these themes.

Pure Experience. The task is rendered more difficult by the fact that in his own work James does not acknowledge a link with Peirce but derives his theories from the most diverse sources—from Hodgson, from Gustav Theodor Fechner, and to a large extent from Henri Bergson, George Berkeley, and Hume. It is precisely the reference to the English tradition that poses problems for a sociological method because, as noted earlier, it is in fact possible to characterize particular theories propounded by James in their technical content as a further elaboration of Hume's empiricism, modified only through the addition of "radical."

But just as in analyzing Hume we distinguish between the so-called technical problem of skepticism and ordinary everyday skepticism, we must also separate the details of James's handling of the problem, which are clearly a further development of Hume's thinking, from the completely different experiential background that confers new significance to them. The theory of the world-stuff, a theory of "pure experience" or "radical empiricism," attempts to set a pluralistic epistemology in place of traditional monistic or dualistic epistemologies. James answers the question of the relation between perception and object by stating that both—perception and object perceived—are made of the same substance and only subsequently were assigned to different areas. " 'Pure experience' is the name which I gave to the immediate flux of life which furnishes the material to our later reflection with its conceptual categories."[18] The term *immediate flux of life* is not meant as a vague description of the personal record of a self, but as the immediate field of the present. Only the present instant itself is pure experience, pure "thatness," without being characterized by its status in a realm, without its having a "whatness." Hodgson's categories are thus revived, but their meaning has changed. Hodgson used the terms to name the dualism of act and object; James recognizes neither one nor the other—"thatness" is the reference point of knowing, the origin; and only when "pure experience" has stopped being pure and has flowed over thatness back to the past and to reflection does it turn into whatness. But experience can contain more than whatness—that is, more than status in one realm only; it can be classified according to particular contexts: in one it can be called external reality, in another it can become perception and thought. To illustrate, James uses the image of the point at the intersection of two lines and therefore situated on both. The present moment, he continues, is the intersection of knowledge and the thing known, from which point the two separate and follow their own laws. If, for example, I am looking at a table, I can reflectively co-ordinate the neutral thatness of my optical perception either into my biography or into the history of the room. The two arrangements vary in their lawfulness: a "real" fire, for example, is surely extinguished by a sufficient quantity of "real" water, while a fire in my thoughts can have any amount of thought water poured on it without suffering in the least. It is only through lawfulnesses of this sort, through the relations between objects, that the realms are distinguished from each other, while in their substance they are identical. James answers the question regarding the composition of this substance by saying that it is made of the same material as the material we experience. It is not *a single* substance but a plural one, just as differentiated and individualized as the universe—or, better, the "multiverse"—itself; substance and experience fuse completely in their materiality. The pure experience of iron consists of iron, the pure experience of wood consists of wood, without our having to or needing to trace them back to a common material.

"Knower" and "Known." To Hodgson, the present moment has a dialectical dimension, whereas James clearly makes an effort to show its simplicity:

18. William James, *Essays in Radical Empiricism* (New York, 1912), 93.

As "subjective" we say that the experience represents; as "objective" it is represented. What represents and what is represented is here numerically the same; but we must remember that no dualism of being represented and representing resides in the experience per se. In its pure state, or when isolated, there is no self-splitting of it into consciousness and what the consciousness is "of." Its subjectivity and objectivity are functional attributes solely, realized only when the experience is "taken," i.e., talked-of, twice, considered along with its two differing contexts respectively, by a new retrospective experience, of which that whole past complication now forms the fresh content.[19]

In the act of perceiving as such, then, there is no division, and the historical problem of knowledge—to explain how it is possible to be conscious "of something"—is solved by saying that we are not conscious "of something" and that the relationship of knowledge to its object occurs outside the simple act in a subsequent reflection that presupposes a stretch of time. "Thinking" and "what is thought," or "the knower" and "the known," are two elements of pure experience that are joined together in the epistemological relation. The unfolding of the traditional problem of the single point at the intersection of two lines is indicated even more clearly than by the example of simple perception in the relation of a conception to its object. James cites as an example that he, sitting in his room, ten minutes away from a particular building, can conceive of this building, then make his way to the building and perceive it. The first conception and the second unmediated perception are two elements of pure experience that are perceptibly linked together in his consciousness through a series of transitions. The conception has the function of a "knower," the perception the function of a "known."

Reversal of the Problem of Knowledge. James's writing style has such an extraordinary clarity, simplicity, and sincerity that the critical points stand out starkly, and it takes no great skill to find them. Unfolding the act of knowing into a multiplicity of pure experiences in a temporal course leaves these pure experiences as the unexplained remainder. They cannot be recognized *ex definitione*, because as soon as they are recognized, they must be recognized as something, and their whatness is first a product of reflection outside of pure experience itself. To the extent that we try to investigate this experience,

19. *Ibid.*, 23.

it is a nothing, a boundary. With progressive reflection it proceeds into the future, and we cannot catch up with it, since anything we do catch up with is, by definition, already no longer pure experience; it has been modified by belonging to a realm of reality. But nowhere does James discuss how the realms of the self and the outside world can intersect in pure experience so that subsequently reflection can develop knowledge from it; nowhere does he discuss the most important knowledge, that of the existence of these realms themselves; nowhere, that is, does he discuss the traditional problem of knowledge, the traditional epistemological problem. The usual theoretical formulations begin with the realities of the external world and the self, in order to present the problem of their interaction in an act of knowing. James turns the pattern upside down and takes the point of intersection, pure experience, as the immediate given in order to show how reality is constructed by adjusting it to various functional contexts. The reversal, however, does not in fact alter the problem. James assigns to pure experience, which possesses no status in any reality, the same function as other theories of knowledge assign to the concept of a being, of an essence, of an opinion, of a meaning, or of an object, all of which are merely "valid," without being real. But what distinguishes James—like Peirce—from European, and especially English, philosophy is his determination to distance himself in the concrete realm of reflection from the mystery of the person, the disquieting secret of the person's growth into imagination, thoughts, evaluations, and images of every kind.

Altering the traditional movement of epistemology, which is toward the intersection of self and world, so that it moves in the opposite direction—that is, away from the intersection—is the symbol of this flight from the self. The concentration of all problems of the universe on the self and its present moment, which characterizes the theme of British philosophy, the crawling into the self, Hume's sorrows of solitude and skepticism—all these are abandoned. The point of origin, which otherwise would be the most central problem, becomes a barely noticed datum, and the emphasis of observation moves away from it to nonsecret, open, unskeptical areas of thought.

The Dimensionless Self. Mention has already been made that changes in the background of experience have generally taken place without a break with the traditions of the English intellectual apparatus. James refers to Locke's dual meanings of idea as thought and object in order to find the beginnings of a theory that he then refined into the dual function of pure experience. He then equates it with Berkeley's statement that what common sense calls reality is an idea to the philosopher. And to the extent that he proceeds only descriptively, all the elements that had gradually been introduced into English philosophy appear in his analysis of the stream of consciousness. He gives a graphic description of the coordination of a world from chaotic material by means of the individual personality: "The mind . . . works on the data it receives very much as a sculptor works on his block of stone. In a sense the statue stood there from eternity. But there were a thousand different ones beside it, and the sculptor alone is to be thanked for having extricated this from the rest. Just so the world of each of us, howsoever different our several views of it may be, all lay embedded in the primordial chaos of sensations, which gave the mere *matter* to the thought of all of us indifferently."[20]

The personality and its individually chosen activities are recognized here and carefully observed. In another section we even find much of Hume's "magic" of association, as when James speaks of "this magical imponderable streaming," of the romanticism of the fleeting moment, and occasionally of the explication of transitive facts:

> There is not a conjunction or a preposition, and hardly an adverbial phrase, syntactic form, or inflection of voice, in human speech, that does not express some shading or other of relation which we at some moment actually feel to exist between the larger objects of our thought.[21]

And again in a description:

> The rush of our thought forward through its fringes is the everlasting peculiarity of its life. We realize this life as something always off its balance, something in transition, something that shoots out of a darkness through a dawn into a brightness that we feel to be the dawn fulfilled.[22]

But as soon as these looser, more illustrative digressions are gathered up again into a rigorous conceptual statement, the association

20. William James, *The Principles of Psychology* (2 vols.; New York, 1890), I, 288.
21. *Ibid.*, 245.
22. James, *Pluralistic Universe*, 283.

with other thinkers disappears, and the dominant traits of James's philosophy come to the fore. The concept of "thought" may serve as an example. In James's work, too, the word is highlighted with a capitalized initial in order to distinguish its systematic meaning from ordinary usage. In essence "Thought" is the same as pure experience, the present immediate moment of life. It is a "vehicle of choice as well as of cognition."[23] The more open description of the person who, like a sculptor, carves an image of the world out of the indifferent material of the sensations becomes refined into the concept of a colorless vehicle to which is entrusted the necessary functions of choice and knowledge. "But the Thought never is an object in its own hands."[24] It never recognizes or denies itself. "It appropriates *to* itself, it is the actual focus of accretion, the hook from which the chain of past selves dangles, planted firmly in the Present which alone passes for real, and thus keeping the chain from being a purely ideal thing. . . . The present moment of consciousness is thus, as Mr. Hodgson says, the darkest in the whole series."[25]

James, however, comes to this conclusion for quite different reasons. For Hodgson, thought has its object in the present moment of consciousness, but in such a mysterious way that the moment is called "dark" with some justification. For James, on the other hand, it is dark because this consciousness is absent. James goes even further in the process of stripping the present and knowledge of their mysteries: he identifies "Thought" with "Self." Each such "Thought" in the present destroys its predecessors, and in the act of destruction it incorporates the previous moment, acknowledges its heritage, and is in each case the final possessor of all that may be called *self*. There is no extensive stream of the self, but only the present moment. And James counters the statement that at least in this present moment of life we are conscious of ourselves, that at least here we recognize our thoughts as a stream of life flowing in us:

> My answer to it is my last word, and I'm very much afraid that it will sound materialistic to many. But I cannot help that, for I have my intuitions and must obey them. Whatever the case for others, I am as convinced as anything that the stream of thinking (which I emphatically recognize as a phenomenon) is merely a carelessly bestowed

23. James, *Principles of Psychology*, I, 340.
24. *Ibid.*
25. *Ibid.*, 340–41.

name for something that on closer examination turns out to be in the main consisting of the stream of my breath. . . . I am convinced that breath is the essence out of which philosophers construct the entity they know as consciousness. *This entity is fictive, while concrete thoughts have total reality.*[26]

Peirce's work still leaves a doubt whether his indefinite formulations of the problem of the present moment were intended as a dialectical description or whether his use of the image of a mathematical continuum was a sign for the theory of a dimensionless present. There can be no doubt that James's work intends to move away from the dialectic, even though the inevitable structure of the problem makes such distancing impossible. In this respect James's work demonstrates the correctness of his statement that the grounds for a philosophic vision can be found only in retrospect and are not essential. To explain pure experience and its reflective distribution to various realms of reality, he employs a form of argumentation that in another structurally related case serves to make the opposite intelligible. This second case is connected with the theory of "radical empiricism" or pluralism.

Radical Empiricism. The "world view of radical empiricism" is constructed in contrast to the rationalist systems. Rationalism stresses universals and, with respect to being, gives precedence to the whole over the parts. Conversely, empiricism explains the universe by stressing the parts, the elements, the individual, treating the whole as a collection and the universalities as abstractions. Therefore empiricism is fundamentally "a mosaic philosophy," a philosophy of plural facts "as those of Hume and his followers." The facts are referred back neither to substances in which they inhere nor to an absolute mind that creates them as its objects. But James goes further than Hume: he "radicalizes" his empiricism by adding to the objects of experience a class neglected or expressly excluded from earlier forms of empiricism: the relations of all classes of experience. "The relations that connect experiences must themselves be experienced relations, and any kind of relation experienced must be accounted as 'real' as anything else in the system."[27]

The exclusion of relations of experience in earlier forms of empiricism resulted in rationalist attempts to supplement the world

26. James, *Radical Empiricism,* 37.
27. *Ibid.,* 42.

image and its lack of connections with a realm of a priori categories and transcendental experience; radical empiricism renders these artificial superstructures unnecessary. As examples for such experiential relations James cites the series "with, near, next, like, from, towards, against, because, for, through, my," roughly arranged in a scale of ascending intimacy. "With" is the most general relation, without which a coherent universe cannot be constructed, whereas a universe without "nextness" or "likeness" does not appear possible. One of the most intimate relations is "the co-conscious transition"[28] through which one experience merges with another when both belong to the same self. Experience of "mine" and "yours" are in different ways "together," but "mine" goes into "mine" and "yours" into "yours" in such a way that "mine" and "yours" never merge. The history of a self is a process of change over time, "and the change itself is one of the things immediately experienced."[29] The continuity of experience is thus a special case within the broader category of immediately experienced relations between things.

Structure of the Universe. James applies the narrower theory of radical empiricism to the structure of the universe in general; and on the occasion of this expansion he repeats the arguments for "pure experience" in reverse. The advantages of a pluralistic world view as against idealistic monistic systems—especially those of Hegel, Lotze, and Bradley—were indicated, and James attempts to find the weakness of identity philosophy at a single, easily comprehended point from which he can strike at the center of the system. He therefore gives the following picture of the dogma he intends to attack: Monism does not take the world to be a collection of separate things but sees it as an all-encompassing datum, nothing existing outside it. This datum is presented as an absolute mind that creates the parts by thinking them, much as we invent the content of our dreams or the characters in a novel. The finite parts "are" as objects for the absolute; and the absolute "is" as the thinking of the parts. The absolute and the parts are identical in content; the absolute is the knowledge of things, things are what is known of the absolute. James objects to this view, and one must pay careful attention to his formulation of it:

28. *Ibid.*, 47.
29. *Ibid.*, 48.

But one as we are in this material sense with the absolute substance, that being only the whole of us, and we only the parts of it, yet in a formal sense something like a pluralism breaks out. When we speak of the absolute we *take* the one universal known material collectively or integrally; when we speak of its objects, of our finite selves, etc., we *take* that same identical material distributively and separately. But what is the use of a thing's *being* only once if it can be *taken* twice over, and if being taken in different ways makes different things true of it? ... Ignorance breeds mistake, curiosity, misfortune, pain, for me; I suffer those consequences. The absolute knows of those things, of course, for it knows me and my suffering, but it doesn't itself suffer. ...

Things true of the world in its finite aspects, then, are not true of it in its infinite capacity. *Qua* finite and plural its accounts of itself to itself are different from what its accounts to itself *qua* infinite and one must be.[30]

This may be compared with the argument in favor of pure experience:

If the "pure experience" of the room [cited as an example] were a place of intersection of two processes, which connected it with different groups of associates respectively, it could be counted twice over, as belonging to either group, and spoken of loosely as existing in two places, although it would remain all the time a numerically single thing. ... The one self-identical thing has so many relations to the rest of experience that you can take it in disparate systems of association, and treat it as belonging with opposite contexts.[31]

Abstracting, then, from percepts altogether, what I maintain is, that any single non-perceptual experience tends to get counted twice over, just as a perceptual experience does, figuring in one context as an object or field of objects, in another as a state of mind: and all this without the least internal self-diremption on its own part into consciousness and content. It is all consciousness in one taking; and, in the other, all content.[32]

Almost the same words are used to give the argument for and the argument against the identity of a phenomenon in different orders. But the motive is the same in both cases: the concept of pure and internally unbroken experience is meant to remove the dialectical mystery from epistemology by denying its existence and creating the various realms of reality out of the neutral pre-real experience

30. James, *Pluralistic Universe*, 38–40.
31. James, *Radical Empiricism*, 12–13.
32. *Ibid.*, 17–18.

by the trick of "taking twice over." In his criticism of identity philosophy James demolished the mystery by presenting the trick of "taking twice over" as illicit and stating that the two realities (the absolute and the limited) were independent. In one case the identity of the differences in the act of knowing is replaced with the double function of the identical. In the other, only the identity is questioned and the different is allowed to remain different. The dialectical concept of identity is eliminated in both cases.

Intimacy. The structure and intention of James's thinking is thus clarified, rendering a rational justification impossible. But an attempt can be made to uncover his emotional motive, though difficulties will present themselves, since James never wished to discuss this matter in detail and remained faithful to the fiction of a rational justification of his philosophy. But other remarks on his motivation can be found, and James himself provides the concepts for his own interpretation. He likes nothing better than to replace the rational concepts of monism and pluralism with the emotional ones of alienness and intimacy, thus opening perspectives on social and political institutions. The "most alien" conception of the universe and its parts in relation to a greater whole on which it depends is that of the world and God as its external creator—the traditional Christian doctrine. Referring to this, James wrote: "The vaster vistas which scientific evolutionism has opened, and the rising tide of social democratic ideals, have changed the type of our imagination, and the older monarchical theism is obsolete or obsolescent. The place of the divine in the world must be more organic and intimate. An external creator and his institutions may still be verbally confessed at church in formulas that linger by their mere inertia, but the life is out of them, we avoid dwelling on them, the sincere heart of us is elsewhere."[33] Every form of pantheism is superior to theistic dualism because the former, in the communion of God and world, confers an intimacy that theism can never achieve. And James assures the reader that it is "normal to be sympathetic. . . . Not to demand intimate relations with the universe, and not to wish them satisfactory, should be accounted signs of something wrong."[34]

But the various "intimate" systems are not of equal worth. Some

33. James, *Pluralistic Universe*, 30.
34. *Ibid.*, 33.

of them are still too alien to satisfy all the requirements for personal closeness and warmth. The system of idealistic monism, in spite of the essential identity of the absolute and the world, considers this identity under very different aspects. The finiteness of the one and the infinity of the other raise such contrasts between them that true intimacy is impossible. We are ignorant, but the absolute cannot be ignorant, since it supplies an answer for every question it poses. It cannot be patient: because it encompasses everything at the same time, there is nothing it has to wait for. It can never be surprised; it can never be guilty. No predicate connected with duration can be connected to it because it is all time all the time—that is, it is timeless. The concept of the absolute gives rise to alienation in the world because we are not of its kind. We cannot be confident, much as we may want to be; we must be ever vigilant. We are dealing with a social problem, "for after all, the common *socius* of us all is the great universe whose children we are."[35]

A pluralistic stance achieves the highest degree of intimacy with the world. It contains no absolute, all-encompassing form, no "all-forms" but only "each-forms." The universe is not rationally connected in all its parts; it is not a closed organism that, round as a ball, floats in metaphysical nothingness; rather, wherever we may wander in it, we will find an "environment," an all-encompassing warm landscape. We never stand on the edge of the world, shivering and gazing into vagueness. Always other finite matter is close and is continuously linked, and we make our way in this: "Everything you can think of, however vast or inclusive, has on the pluralistic view a genuinely 'external' environment of some sort or amount. Things are 'with' one another in many ways, but nothing includes everything, or dominates over everything. The word 'and' trails along after every sentence."[36]

"The pluralistic world is thus more like a federal republic than like an empire or kingdom. However much may be collected, however much may report itself as present at any effective centre of consciousness or action, something else is self-governed and absent and unreduced to unity."[37] We find God *within* the universe of our experience, not outside or all-encompassing. The criticism of ab-

35. *Ibid.*, 31.
36. *Ibid.*, 321.
37. *Ibid.*, 321–22.

solutism has not destroyed the possibility of a higher entity, it has merely made room for a conception of God that James calls the idea of the "common man." "The God of our popular Christianity is but one member of a pluralistic system. He and we stand outside of each other, just as the devil, the saints, and the angels outside of both of us."[38]

The God of David or Isaiah is a finite entity; the cosmos does not reside in him; rather, he resides within the world. The finite God, as depicted in the Bible, is logically possible, and when contrasted with the philosophy of absolute mind, the biblical God is the more likely hypothesis. Because of the assumption of a finite God, who is identical only with what is good in the world, we are protected from the insoluble problems of evil and theodicy. God as a finite entity also exists in time, and has his own environment and a history.

The Material of Experience. A system of radical empiricism cannot advance such a hypothesis simply because it is possible and probable. James cites the experiences that permit the assumption of God. These are the experiences of death and resurrection and communion with God. What is meant is not physical death but the deathlike end of certain mental processes within the experience of an individual: moral collapse, despair, and a new life following on moments of self-surrender: "The believer finds that the tenderer parts of his personal life are continuous with a *more* of the same quality which is operative in the universe outside of him and which he can keep in working touch with, and in a fashion get on board of and save himself, when all his lower being has gone to pieces in the wreck. In a word, the believer is continuous, to his own consciousness, at any rate, with a wider self from which saving experiences flow in."[39]

Religious congregations harbor an ideal something that in part is ourselves and in another part transcends us and flows into our lives, animating our energies; this ideal has regenerative powers that cannot be reached in any other way.[40] No general statements can be made concerning the nature of the something that transcends us;

38. *Ibid.*, 110–11.
39. *Ibid.*, 307.
40. William James, *The Varieties of Religious Experience: A Study in Human Nature* (New York, 1902), 523.

such statements would be superfluous in any case; for all practical purposes it is enough to know that a higher power, existing above humankind and continuously connected with it, is kindly disposed toward it. It is enough that the power is (1) different from and (2) greater than ourselves. James here develops a principle of the "next step," which is of the greatest significance for the total philosophy of democracy in the United States (see the chapter on Commons): "Anything larger will do, if only it be large enough to trust for the next step."[41] It need not be infinite or solitary. It is enough for it to be a greater, godlike self. It may perhaps be one among many such greater "somethings," varying in size, and polytheism is one possible hypothesis in the pluralistic world view.

The Open Self. The philosophy of radical empiricism frankly abandons the attempt to structure a rational image of the world. All intellectual rigor has dissolved, leaving the soul in a landscape of infinite security. It is not solitary; beyond it there are friendly powers in diverse gradations of size and generality, with never an end in sight. Beyond the farthest reach there are ever more remote and greater ones. The wanderer never comes up against a boundary where the embracing security stops. The involution of the universe and humankind expressed in the dialectic is dissolved and unfolded into naïvely structured historical courses in a finite time. God himself has such a history—and the human being is not alone but is open to him and continuously approaching him. The demonic nature of individualism, the suffering of loneliness and skepticism, which lead us to plumb the depths of the present moment, have all dissolved. Knowledge has itself changed from an act that in mysterious ways brings together the self and the world into a nonmysterious, finite, temporal process of pure experience. Here we recognize the completed form of Peirce's ideas: contingency has become the irrational in the pluralistic world; the tendency of continuity has been more precisely specified; communication with God has evolved from a short remark into the center of a system; and the motive of intimacy has become explicit. The gospel of love and increased goodness and meaning is preserved in the hope that God or the gods are the principle of the good and assist us in overcoming evil. And all these themes together tend toward a philos-

41. *Ibid.*, 525.

ophy of personality in contrast to the European (exemplified in the English) school, with its dialectic. If we conceive the European tradition, with its mania for conceptualizing the mystery of the person rationally, as a doctrine of a *closed* self, the philosophy of the type of Peirce's and James's can be called the doctrine of the *open* self. The contraction of time and existence to the present moment of the self and the problem of the origin of the world no longer have much meaning. Even in the section where James restricts the self to the immediately perceived present, so that time would at this point be an illusion, the opportunity to probe the problem of duration and the past more deeply is lost. And in another section the self is again seen in its real temporal extension, with no indication of how duration comes into existence. The structural difference between the philosophy of the open self and that of the closed self is clearly intelligible. The chapter devoted to John R. Commons will deal with the political and social demands that James himself brought into conjunction with it.

2

On George Santayana

I

If philosophy is taken to mean a type of knowledge that, though distinguished by object and method from the experimental sciences, is nevertheless coordinated in its nature as a science, the objection can be raised that philosophical investigation continues to this day to deal with the same problems as it did at the beginning of its history in the West, without noticeably coming any closer to definitive solutions. Georg Simmel countered this conception of the scientific nature of philosophy and the possible accusation of its lack of success with his impatient formula to the effect that problems are not made to be solved.

He was expressing an attitude concerning the proper subject of philosophy that may have been held to a greater or lesser degree by every thinker from time immemorial. But its deliberate relativizing of the distance between the subject and the philosopher himself seems particularly characteristic of the present age. The paradoxical tone of the formula is based on a play on words: a noun that by convention means "a question raised for inquiry, consideration, or solution" is used to designate circumstances that are in no way intrinsically problematic but become problematic only when we direct our thoughts along the lines of this formulation. The denial that the meaning of a problem lies in the solution to it merely makes use of a form of speech to deny the possibility that philosophical problems can be solved. Behind the attitude toward the nature of problems dealt with by philosophy that contemptuously dismisses as arrogant any attempts to solve the riddles of the world lies a devotion to a form of life and to the changes of life that is so overwhelmed by visible phenomena that comparatively modest interpretations are considered to be petty and ridiculous.

In an essay on Lucretius, Santayana expressed a philosophic experience similar to Simmel's. He wrote: "If the ideas embodied in a philosophy represent a comprehensive survey of the facts, and a mature sentiment in the presence of them, any new ideas adopted instead will have to acquire the same values, and nothing will be changed morally except the language or euphony of the mind."[1]

Here the clash between the philosopher and his subject matter is expressed with more restraint than is found in Simmel's outburst, which indicates the entanglement of philosophers and their thoughts. The world of things and the mature mind are phenomena independent of each other in an all-embracing cosmos. The cool, distanced statement, to the effect that the ideas of a philosophy are representative of both things and the mind in their reciprocal present, ascribes this temporal conjunction to the powers of accident and fate. Philosophical thinking does not in this case appear under the activist image of the subject's attack on the object. Egocentric epistemology (which alone admits problems and solutions) is replaced by a metaphysical contemplation in which worlds and thinkers must assert themselves with equal impersonality so as to give birth to the idea. The consequences of these births cannot add to factual knowledge. Just as the infinite individuation of a single kind of object determines that the same substance can take new shapes, so wisdom clothes the same truths in new cosmic parables, determined by the irrational accidents of language, society, education, and individual fate. Philosophical doctrines—so Santayana explicates his statement—contradict one another when they cling to the word and try helplessly to catch the unknown. But they agree and supplement one another when they are symbols, thoughts wrung from the experiences of the hearts of poets. Then all philosophies are equal, and all of them are merely ways to report on a stream of things, to share in the same good and evil that all generations encounter.

꧁꧂

The same stream of things is the subject matter of all philosophical discourse, but in each it appears in another guise, and never without mediation. Interpreting Santayana's mental universe by relating it

1. George Santayana, *Three Philosophical Poets: Lucretius, Dante, and Goethe* (Cambridge, Mass., 1910), 68.

to an absolute standpoint is therefore impossible in principle. Only indications comparing it with object-related symbols can narrow the shared ground of intuition and indicate and define reciprocal differences in formulation. In Santayana's view no realm of being has been assigned to philosophical method as its special field of investigation. Like art, philosophy can use all things for its material. It is the function of philosophy to compare things in form and value and to give the mind speculative mastery over them, just as mathematics does this for the form and diversity of the material world. Every subject matter for philosophical discourse—an artistic or religious experience, a statement in logic or the mathematical sciences of nature—can therefore be a possible starting point for analysis. But in Santayana's system one particular subject stands out for the simplicity of its structure: the concept of essence. Essence is won by descriptive analysis of the elementary processes of consciousness, superbly exemplified in physical perception. It may be crudely and provisionally described as the residue of an act of conceiving minus the spatial-temporal object, the person who does the conceiving, and the stream of consciousness. To understand the symbolic contents of this residue, two quite similar types of introspective analysis of material perception may be cited here: the analyses carried out by Franz Brentano and Shadworth Hodgson.

In analyzing the conception of a single musical tone, Brentano believes that "the inner experience undoubtedly seems to show" that at least two conceptions are present concurrently: the primary conception of the musical tone and a secondary conception of the conceptions of the tone, but without there being two separate acts of consciousness, as is true in the case of a memory directed to a past psychic phenomenon. The secondary conception, which has as its object the first one—the one that is immediately directed to the note—has accompanied the first act, but in such a way, namely as being dependent on the first, that this first one, so long as it endures, "at the same time inwardly contributes to the existence of the other." The complete psychic act thus has as its object not only the physical phenomenon but also and simultaneously, in a parallel conception, itself. Furthermore, if a parallel element of independent action accompanies the primary conception, the parallel conception would have to be a tertiary object for a fourth one, and so on ad infinitum. But introspection discloses no such regression.

66

The chain of events in which each overrides the other in fact concludes with the relation of the psychic act to the conception of the tone as secondary object. "The psychic act of hearing, aside from the fact that it conceives of the physical phenomenon of the tone, becomes at once, according to its tonality, object and content for itself." Thus the primary object of hearing is the tone, but the secondary object is not only the perception of the tone but also the secondary relation per se.

This description of psychic activity leads Brentano to the claim that it results from a careful analysis of inner experience. In his work *Von der Klassifikation der psychischen Phänomene*, however, one passage is phrased in such a way that—at least on this point—the method of his psychology is not descriptive analysis; speculative elements at least *also* affect the formulation of his concepts. In the second appendix to this work, entitled "On the Psychic Relation to Secondary Objects," he wrote:

> However, for the secondary object of mental activity one does not have to think of any particular one of these references, as for example the reference to the primary object. It is easy to see that this would lead to an infinite regress, for there would have to be a third reference, which would have the secondary reference as object, a fourth, which would have the additional third one as object, and so on. The secondary object is not a reference but a mental activity, or, more strictly speaking, the mentally active subject, in which the secondary reference is included along with the primary one.[2]

The overall phenomenon of psychic perception is called "that which is psychically active," and it serves to distinguish the relations to the object. The primary relation is with the tone, but the secondary "relation" is not to the primary but to the completed act, which encompasses the primary relation as well as itself. But to assure the reader that his description of this state of affairs was correct, Brentano did not cite a plain and simple reference, which is the only methodological instrument of descriptive psychology; instead he developed an argument about the *necessity of the assumption*. If the secondary relation did not have itself for an object, the only alternative would be a system of infinite interconnections,

2. Franz Brentano, *Von der Klassifikation der psychischen Phänomene* (1911; rpr. Hamburg, 1959), 138–39, Vol. II of Brentano, *Psychologie vom Empirischen Standpunkt*.

and Brentano was not inclined to adopt such a system because of its complexity.

Direct description has been replaced by an argument for constructive convenience because the material presents certain difficulties that might not have been resolved any other way. The point of departure for analysis in the framework of quotidian experience, the raw material, is the fact that sense perceptions are not simply conscious; they are self-conscious. The machine does not hear: I am the one who hears, and I am aware of hearing. The difficulty in Brentano's argument stems from his belief that he must, or that he was able to, resolve this state of affairs by using the terminology of "object" and "act" or "relation." That the musical tone is the object of the psychic act seems beyond doubt, but so does the fact that this object and the assumption of a simple act directed to it does not adequately describe self-conscious hearing. The next step would be the assumption of a second act, directed to the first, but this description does not suffice, because it would collapse the memory into internal perception, and these two phenomena are clearly different from each other. It is therefore advisable to speak of only *one* act and to distinguish the relations it contains. In order to restore this divided act to a kind of unity, its two relations must be distinguished descriptively but in such a way that while the primary one has an object external to itself, the secondary one has as its object both the external (the first relation) and itself.

Brentano presented this particularity as a difference of objects, but it is at least as much one of relations. If we assume that an act has an object simply because act and object are different and are distinguishable elements of psychic phenomena, it is possible to speak of an act that has itself as an object only because language is tolerant. It might possibly make sense if we were to assume that the equality of act and object were meant as a logical identity, but this assumption would not help the psychological description, which specifically requires nonidentity in order to confer meaning on the psychic act-object relation. We therefore find ourselves compelled to decide that this talk of an act that has itself for an object is meaningless in psychological terminology and that Brentano never became aware of the situation. The only way out of this logical-psychological absurdity is to assume a special type of relation that permits its terms to coincide without becoming logically identical; this is what is traditionally called dialectic relation. This relation is not a possible subject matter of psychological description or logical understanding; it is exclusively a topic of dialectic speculation. As such it can be encompassed by the other levels of observation only negatively, as the relation that permits a coincidence of its terms without their becoming logically identical and in which an "act" can be its own "object," because psychologically these words have no meaning. It is the self-enclosed relation from which the form of the terms cannot be removed; rather, the terms are at the same time the form of the relation. And Brentano used this dialectical construction to deal with a situation that is not a possible subject matter for description.

A presentation of Hodgson's analysis of sense perception in his *Metaphysic of Experience* requires some explication of terminology. Hodgson examines the perception of a musical tone, calling this perception *experience*, a concept corresponding to Brentano's impersonal *hearing*. The act and object are distinguished as the *thatness* and *whatness* of perception, or as *perceiving* and *content*, and finally, in a third contrasting pair, as *existence* and *quality*. Within the context of these concepts Hodgson attempts to present a certain conception of the dialectical relation of hearing:

> Calling the content the *whatness* of the perception or experience, we may call the fact that it is perceived its *thatness* or existence as at present known. Neither of these two parts of the total experience exists apart from the other; they are distinguishable, inseparable, and commensurate. Yet neither is the *object* of the other. The existence of the content perceived is not the object of the content, for the content alone is not a perceiving. And again the quality or the content of the perceiving is not its object, but is the nature of the perceiving itself, the nature by which alone it is definable. That the perceiving is not the object of the content, is almost too obvious to be remarked. The *whatness* and the *thatness* are thus best characterized as opposite *aspects* of each other and of the experience, yet without taking the experience as a third thing, or anything but their inseparable union.[3]

The psychological termini of object and act (content, perceiving) are used only as auxiliary concepts, roughly to mark the places intended to indicate the meanings of the dialectical concepts of thatness and whatness, because in the dialectical relation there are

3. Shadworth H. Hodgson, *The Metaphysic of Experience* (4 vols.; London, 1898), I, 60–61.

no psychological relations, and the attempts to describe the relation of the two "aspects" becomes exhausted in the negation that neither is the object of the other and that both together are certainly not the object either.

Hodgson, however, was not content to leave it at this expression of helplessness. Instead he attempted to explain how the phenomenon arises and how the conceptual pair of existence and quality is used to serve this explanation. *Existence* characterizes the duration of the perception through an empirical stretch of time, while *quality* characterizes its objective qualification in the same period of time. To explain dialectic through duration, Hodgson examines the phenomenon of two tonal perceptions following one after the other, "hearing C" and "hearing D." When two or more tonal perceptions follow in time intervals that are not too far apart, as for example the striking of a clock, what we perceive is not one tone as "one," followed by another "one." Instead, the later perception flows into the earlier one as memory, so that we hear not the striking of "one" followed by "one" and so on but, for example, "seven." The entirety of the note sequence rises above its elements, and this ordering element is made possible by memory. For the purpose of analysis, let us take the short sequence of tones C and D. The experience that contains the perception of the tone D also includes the memory of tone C. The perception of C and D converges in a single act that, with the appearance of D, is led back to C and becomes memory. At the actual moment when this tone is perceived, D is a presentation, while C is already a representation. Whereas in the actual perception of C this same C was the "whatness" element of perception, now, simultaneously with perception D, C in both its aspects has become an "object." The content of perception C, in a continuous psychic act, has been transformed with its existence into the "object" in the present moment of perception D. The *single* perception that D presents at the actual moment of perception represents at the same time a preceding part of itself together with its content.

Hodgson returned from the analysis of two perceptions in quick succession to simple perception, claiming that no essential difference exists between the two. Both, including simple perceptions, are representative, he believed, though this circumstance is more clearly intelligible in the phenomenon of two successive perceptions, since every state of consciousness leads back to the past from the first moment of its existence. These experiences are called "simple" only because our experience cannot perceive a simultaneous or successive segmentation. "Perception as a process consists in the conversion of *content* into *object*, simply in consequence of its character as a reflective process."[4]

The process of perception reflects by existing, and it exists in its own reflection. As reflection it is part of knowledge; as existence it is part of being. The same stream of consciousness is both knowledge and existence. Similarly as in Brentano's writings, description and construction intersect. Brentano used dialectic to explain away the disquieting circumstance that a state of consciousness includes parts that have something to do with objects and acts without being objects or acts; Hodgson did so by employing the concepts of time and reflection. Starting from a psychological-descriptive concept of reflection and its relation to the past as object, Hodgson minimizes the distance between the points in time of reflection and its objects, first by reducing it to a proximity that can no longer be grasped as distance in empirical description and then by allowing the two points to converge constructively, much as Brentano turned the secondary relation into its own object. The displacement of reflection from its original psychological meaning into a denatured constructed meaning takes precisely the same place in the explication of the problem as does the denaturing of the concept of the act in Brentano's work. Both times this trick makes it possible to speak in terms that seem valid both descriptively and logically. The difference in the two solutions is found in the technique by which the act is completed. Brentano was intent on distinguishing between an internal perception and a memory; since it was a matter not of a simple reflection on a different act but of an immanent division of a *single* act, closing this rift required a dialectical turn. Hodgson, on the other hand, used precisely the structure of reflection to construct the simultaneity of the object and the reflecting consciousness by crossing a boundary. He needed no dialectic closure because his two acts were kept apart from each other through a fictive time, so that the problem of infinite regress could not arise. Both thinkers deal with the same situation, the structure of which is traditionally

4. *Ibid.,* 80.

called dialectic, but they employ different means in their constructed formations. One created a dialectic between the concepts of act and object, the other worked with the concept of time, so that the elementary process of consciousness, sense perception, is not a simple observed situation, such as the green color of a leaf, but is erected in a structural space—and a very complicated one—of the dialectic.

⊷❊⊶

The analyses of the act that is not an act and of the reflection that is not a reflection were carried out in such a way that the methodological meaning of Santayana's statement about the essence of philosophy becomes fully clear. The juxtaposition reveals the differently constructed content of the concepts and indicates that both refer to shared material that is doubtlessly brought home to every thinker through the "stream of things." Thus the philosopher does not "describe"—at least not in this case—situations communicated to him by inner experience. Rather, he surrounds himself with a speculative scaffolding, and the material for his speculation seems hardly more than a disquieting occasion for idealized formations. It is in these formations, not in the materials used (which are always the same), that Santayana places the value and essence of philosophy; and one can sense already in the minute analyzed fragments of his philosophic systems the worlds they represent. Brentano's self-reflective act represents German identity philosophy, whereas Hodgson's concept of reflection is derived from the English metaphysics of time in the form of the Scottish school. These two examples are especially valuable because in the minimum of philosophical subject matter—the elementary content of consciousness—they reveal the relation of specific large social forces with specific worlds of ideas, and they open up possibilities for an exact sociological study of thought.

⊷❊⊶

The inquiries that in Santayana's system correspond to the German and British examples I have cited are grouped around the concept of essence. The meaning of this concept is discussed at length in various of Santayana's writings. A clear, fairly long definition, however, is found only in the essay "Three Proofs of Realism" in *Essays in Critical Reason*, where Santayana gives the following explanation:

By "essence" I understand a universal, of any degree of complexity and definition, which may be given immediately, whether to sense or to thought. Only universals have logical or aesthetic individuality, or can be given directly, clearly, and all at once. When Aristotle said that the senses gave the particular, he doubtless meant by the senses the complete fighting sensibility of animals, with the reactive instinct and sagacity which posits a material object and places it in its external relations, here, now, and in such a quarter. But the senses as understood by modern idealism suggest rather a passive consciousness of some aesthetic datum, and this (which I call intuition) can never find anything but an ideal individual, which being individuated only by its intrinsic quality, not by any external or dynamic relations (since none are given), is also a universal. This object of pure sense or pure thought, with no belief superadded, an object inwardly complete and individual, but without external relations or physical status, is what I call an essence.[5]

The form of these speculative approaches to the same material is so different from Brentano's and Hodgson's methods that these two types of dialectic, though worlds apart, come to seem almost identical, since both took their point of departure from the concrete content of consciousness, a sector of the stream of consciousness, and from the difficulties of providing a rational account of this experience, whereas the concept of essence focuses attention on part of the total act, the immanent subject matter. In place of the mutually overlapping act and dependent objects, there appear the clear unities of essence and intuition, whose reciprocal relationships need not be legitimated by pseudo-psychological concepts because from the outset no attempt was made to locate the "material"—that is, the phenomenon of self-consciousness—in the intellectual space of psychology. Since Santayana did not insist on clarifying a complex situation by citing a few obviously futile psychological terms, he had much greater freedom of movement in his speculative formulation; the difficulties in construction encountered by Brentano and Hodgson disappear because Santayana did not attempt to set up a construction in the wrong locale. The essentially unproblematic circumstance became a problem for Brentano because he became involved with psychological concepts. Brentano's primary object was the spatiotemporal musical tone, and the secondary one was the perception of the tone, whereas Santayana

5. George Santayana, "Three Proofs of Realism," in Santayana, *Essays in Critical Realism* (New York, 1920), 168n.

showed absolutely no interest in the transcendent object as part of the perception and focused his attention only on the essence—that is, roughly speaking, on Brentano's secondary object. This essence alone is the counterpoint to intuition, and the problems of the divided act, of infinite regress, and of closure do not arise because Santayana constructs the immanent object of a perception—the essence—not as "consciousness of something," because he considered essence not as an act, as Brentano did, but as an object [*Gegenstand*]. Hodgson came much closer to this view, since he, too, invested no significance in the transcendent object. His "content" corresponds to Santayana's essence, and his "existence" to intuition, except that he believed that he must find a connection between the two so as to make duration part of the overall structuring of "experience." Santayana's essence seems to acquire duration only when it becomes the subject matter of intuition, a temporal process that by nature almost seems to belong to a realm without space and time. In Santayana's philosophy transcendent object, essence, and intuition stand adjacent to but separate from each other, as if the dynamic of an act had never fused them into a unity. The objects [*Gegenstände*] of perception, the essences, reside in themselves, passive and purified, as if for aesthetic contemplation or mathematical intuition. The words of the definition cited above suggest these peculiarities: essence is spoken of as "given immediately," as an "ideal individual," as "aesthetic datum." And the manner of comprehending these data is called "passive consciousness" directed "at an object inwardly complete and individual, but without external relations or physical status."

In the essay "Three Proofs of Realism" the intellectual space in which the essence resides is not a psychological description but an epistemology—the theory of critical realism. This term is to be understood at a minimum as an acknowledgment that there is such a thing as knowledge—that is, that perceptions and concepts relate to objects that are not determined in the act of perception or conception, whereas at a maximum, realism would be the assumption that all that has been perceived or conceived actually exists—that is, that perception and conception always communicate the truth without mediation, without the possibility of error. For the epistemology of realism, therefore, a gap exists between the realms of substance and appearance; this gap is bridged by the transcendence

74

of knowledge, by the relation of knowledge to an object outside itself. "Truth" therefore becomes possible through the fact that the two reciprocally contradictory elements of the two realms overlap. But this overlap does not mean a coincidence of the existences of substance and appearance. It is not that the psychic process overlaps with a piece of the external world. Instead, when the knowledge is "true," both contain identical essences. It is not that the act of knowledge is adequate to its object but that the essence given in intuition is recognized as identical with the essence of the object. The object embodies the essence, whereas it resides in intuition only as a datum—for example, the various essences, pea-greenness, sphericalness, likeness, and twoness are given to me and at the same time can be embodied in two peas. This exchange between the material status of essence as form of the objects and its ideal status as a datum of intuition defines it decisively and separates it from the world of acts and facts. The act of knowing and the objects known have their determined existence, origin, datum, place, substance, function, and duration independent of each other. Essence, on the other hand, can recur endlessly without losing its identity.

The problems Brentano and Hodgson had to deal with arose in their constructions, not in the topics they addressed, although the fact that they were led into speculations of this kind at all was because they had to provide a speculative shape to the material. Santayana's reserved, epistemological formulations of the concept avoided the dialectic of self-consciousness for a time, but an epicyclical and devious explanation was required to divert attention away from unresolved matters that had caused the difficulties in the systems of the other two philosophers. The difference between their concept formations and Santayana's lies in the aesthetic-logical nature of essence on the one hand and the intimate fusion of Brentano's tone perception with Hodgson's content of the process of consciousness on the other. This internal connection of immanent objects [Gegenstände] with the act in its quality of process was the root of the problems inherent in the concepts of act and reflection, and even though they can be avoided by relating the material to other ordinates of the construction, a disturbing remnant seems nevertheless to linger. The essence is the spaceless and timeless object [Gegenstand] passively grasped by a vision. Questions of the correctness of the things seen cannot arise in such a simple act, since whatever the observed object [*Gegenstand*] may be, it is precisely what it is, having no relation to objects [*Gegenstände*] outside itself.

The first element of doubt is introduced into this unproblematic vision when it comes to relating the identity of essence in various contexts to different intuitions. What is meant is not an analytic identity but a problematic one; it is not the identity of the essence with itself that is in question but the recurrence of the identical essence in a variety of acts. In the course of the argument, however, Santayana, like Hodgson, moved from the plurality of acts back to a single enduring intuition, finding in it the same relation of identity as in the case of recurrence.

Identity thus understood presupposes two commonsense principles: time and memory. The assumption that essence is identical in acts separated by time as well as in acts that simply endure over time postulates the medium of time in which timeless essences can be repeated or endure as objects [*Gegenstände*] of intention. I can remember an earlier intuition or one in the immediate past along with its essence, and I can see that the currently given essence is identical with the earlier one. In this way identity is rooted in the assumption of structures that have been removed from the "stream" of being but, because of this timelessness, continuously dip into time and can become an object [*Objekt*] in it, as can the principles of time and memory.

In this confrontation of timeless and unrelated essence with temporal intuitions, however, the world seems to disintegrate into just as many unrelated elements as there are essences. In the perception of a tree, for example, because essences are timeless and therefore no change can occur within them, every change in the light, my position as related to the tree, small differences in how I hold my head—all would mean a new essence. Thus, infinitesimal variation in the datum under the flash of the intuition directed at it would seem to resemble an infinitesimal splintering of the world, in which case the principle of memory and the relation of identity based on it would have hardly any meaning in view of the extraordinary improbability that, in fact, the same essence occurs twice within the same stream of consciousness. When Santayana wrote about the recurrence of an essence and the possibility of turning his attention to acts of the same essence separated in time, when he made statements about the same essence in subsequent discourses, the word *essence* is clearly used with two different meanings: the ever-recurring essence must differ in nature from the infinitesimally changeable stream of essence unrolling with the stream of consciousness.

In his *Ideen zu einer reinen Phänomenologie und phänomenologischen Philosophie,* Edmund Husserl called these two different meanings of "essence" *noema* and *hyle.* The object [*Gegenstand*] of perception in his phenomenological reduction is the *noema,* which is balanced by the components of real experience, the hyletic moments. Using the example of a tree, Husserl postulated that one and the same noematic color of the tree attracts our awareness in the continuous unity of a changeable perceptive consciousness *as* an identical, unalterable color per se, and this one noematic color shades in a continuing manifoldness from the perceived colors (hyletic constituent elements of color). The hyletic constituent elements are evidently given, and evidently in the same way we effect the coordination of them to the corresponding constituent elements of the object [*Gegenstandsmomenten*], along with the coordination of a continuum with its discontinuous unity. But there can be no doubt that unity and manifoldness belong to different realms. Everything that is hyletic belongs to concrete experience as an enduring part of reality, whereas noema includes all the "representativeness" and "shading" in the manifoldness. This assignment to separate realms is related to a deep-seated difference in being, since to be the real components of the experience means that these hyletic constituent elements are not perceived, are not grasped objectively [*gegenständlich*]. It is the noema alone that is the object [*Gegenstand*], and the material components, in conjunction with the noeses that inspired them, have merely a representational function: "That which is '*transcendentally constituted*' 'on the ground of' the material [*stofflich*] experiences 'by' the noetic functions is, to be sure, a 'given'; and, if in pure intuition we faithfully describe this experience and its noematic object intended to [*sein noematisch Bewusstes*], it is *evidently* given; but it belongs to the experience in a sense entirely different from the sense in which the really inherent and therefore proper constituents belong to the mental process."[6]

6. Edmund Husserl, *Ideen zu einer reinen Phänomenologie und phänomenologischen Philosophie* (Halle, 1913), 204.

The distinctions made among noematic, hyletic, and noetic components are superior as analysis to Brentano's, Hodgson's, and Santayana's constructs. But precisely on this crucial point of consistency as construction, Husserl offered nothing new. He did formulate his concepts of object [*Gegenstand*] and "pure sphere of
experience," the source of all object constitution [*Gegenstands-
konstitution*], but he did not address the ensuing problem of how
noesis works so that the hyletic constituent elements are constituted as the noema. In this way he bypasses the domain of philosophical speculation altogether. Nevertheless, his analysis also il-
luminated the meaning of the constructions. The stream of
experience with its formal and material components is the primary
element in psychic actions. This is a given that both Brentano and
Hodgson rely on. The conscious division into object [*Gegenstand*]
(Brentano's primary relation and Hodgson's content) and knowing—that is, the stream components (secondary relation and existence)—is the structure all attempts share, making it necessary to
bring the timeless object [*Gegenstand*] and the temporal process
together in a rational relation grounded in the foundations of dialectical constructions. In the stream, form and material embody
their temporality; in the object [*Gegenstand*] the noemas have become solidified into a rational structure of meaning or significance,
the essence. And this metaphysical movement from the stream in
its formations and their rootedness in it is the material of speculation. The equivocal use of the term *essence* in Santayana's writing, however, is of a simple, nonspeculative nature. The double
meaning does not spirit the contradiction out of existence, as happens in the concepts of act and reflection given in the other examples. The intermingling is purely the result of Santayana's honesty as a thinker. The meaning of *object* [*Gegenstand*] was assigned
to essence. The problem of establishing an object [*Gegenstand*] in
enduring or repeated conscious acts through the noetic continuum
is therefore so similar to other noematic continuums and other
noematic structures that the slightest inattention must extend the
meaning of essence to the hyletic constituent elements. Precisely
this accidental extension, in contrast to the conscious widening of
the construction as found in Brentano's and Hodgson's thinking,
shows that the speculative focus cannot be found in this shift—
which has a strong structural resemblance to the speculative equiv-

78

ocation of the others; rather, a logical-aesthetic datum is outlined in other dimensions of concept formation, as is indicated by the primary meaning of essence as a timeless object [*Gegenstand*].

The essence is reached by way of an analysis that may be called *skeptical reduction* to distinguish it from Husserl's phenomenological reduction. Working in the tradition of Descartes and Hume, Santayana carried the idea of radical skepticism further to destroy the last systematic assumptions contained in the basic attitudes of these philosophers—thoughts for Descartes, the stream of ideas for Hume. To understand a manner of thinking, a philosophical discourse, or a temporal sequence of the process of consciousness requires the assumptions of time and memory, and perhaps of a self as well. All these principles are present in establishing a realm that can only be the object [*Gegenstand*] of belief and of animal faith. The existence of the external world, the self, the stream of consciousness, the connection of a chain of ideas are "knowns"—that is, they are opposed to me, something outside the scope of my knowledge, not immediate givens. Skepticism must be carried to the point where it abolishes all the existential qualities in the objects [*Gegenstände*] of my intuition. Only when they are not seen as having some significance that points beyond them, as the appearances of a substance, as mental processes, or as events in a world, but are taken for what they are in themselves, is a point reached that can no longer be treated as relative by radical skepticism. These essences differ from the Platonic ideas in their lack of metaphysical and ethical meaning. An essence is not a model or prototype of existence, nor does it exert any metaphysical control such that the things of the external world can conform to it, imitate it, or occupy a relatively lower rung with respect to it. Turning attention to one object [*Objekt*] and preferring it over the other express selective principles, but these clearly belong to the realm of existence, not essence. The realm of existence contains essences for both good and evil and for every nuance, every continuum of shading around an object; it contains essences for all attention that can be paid to all existences that ever occurred, for all those that never occurred, and even for essences for which no existence can be found (for example, geometries without an empirical scope of application). In this sense it is more extensive than existence, so that compared to the background of this realm the given universe seems accidental when we consider that it has infinite possibilities for being other than it is. In an unusual reversal of the mythological space of philosophy, in which chaos commonly lies below, here it seems to become the final skeptical residuum, raised high above the "stream of things," shifted to the realm of possible essences.

Neither the metaphysical rank nor the value of the Platonic idea is preserved here, but merely the function within Socratic epistemology, in which the essences are indispensable terms for the transcendence of knowledge and for the possibility of recognizing facts. Much as Brentano—using careless turns of phrase—revealed the apparent results of his inner experience to be speculative necessities, so Santayana spoke with consciously constructed intention about the skeptical analysis of the constructed content of essence in statements of hypothetical necessity: "If" there were no ideal characters for intuition—which belongs neither to the psyche nor to the external world, in spite of being a given for the existential process—nothing further could be imagined, much less acknowledged as true. Every cognitive act (falsely thought to be an epistemological act) would be a piece of the stream of consciousness without an object, or a part of existence without relation to a mind. Only essence that is itself nonexistent is a possible medium of knowledge and a sign for an object whose existence is intended by the knowing mind. The residuum of skepticism, which can "no longer be relativized," is thus a speculatively necessary term in any philosophical discourse that takes self-consciousness (here in the form of epistemological transcendence) for its topic. If an operation of consciousness is not to be simply enclosed in the self but is meant to point to a world beyond itself, a medium for this transcendence must be assumed, and such a medium can be described only through the negation of all existential qualities. The method of skeptical reduction, the removal of all forms of existence (of the external world, of the self, of the stream of consciousness), is the preferred instrument for assigning essence to its philosophical place, namely that of the residual with negative predicates but a necessary function, much as an astronomer can use his observations to calculate the position of a star though his instruments never show its existence. The emergence of the timeless essence from the temporal stream is not described or explained. The concept is formulated speculatively, since it is not possible either to explain or describe it. Essence has no other signification than that of speculative lawfulness. It is a boundary concept, an indispensable operational sign for rational discourse about the materials of self-consciousness and transcendence—beyond which, however, nothing is real. Therefore, if essence and intuition, content and existence, noema and noesis, primary and secondary relation, are all treated as parallel phenomena, then psychological, epistemological, logical or phenomenological hypostases of dialectical functions seem to appear. The temporal process and the dialectic function cannot be put into parallel positions. Rather, to indulge in imagery, the nonexistent boundary concept may be compared to the tip of a pyramid over the foundation formed by process. The references to constructing the noema through real constituent elements of experience, the transcendental constitution, or the givenness of the essence for an intuition are merely figures of speech, as are Brentano's "act" and Hodgson's "reflection"—harmless as long as they are intended as imagery.

If essence is understood in this way—in its speculative (nonexistent) mode of being—its relation to the hyletic constituent elements, with which it seems to converge at a specific place, is clarified. Santayana's essences need not be concrete elements; they can be formulations of whatever complexity is desired. A whole philosophical system can even be designated as an essence, so as to create relations between parts of an essence that are situated next to each other or above one another. If this internal constitution of the essence is penetrated to the final elements, we approach a boundary where concrete constituent elements—noematic constituent elements, to use Husserl's language—no longer exist but where the object [Gegenstand] is dissolved into the constituent elements of the real experience that "construct" it. Since these constituent elements lie in the continuum of the process, crossing over the border leads naturally into a different and no longer concrete realm, and we can no longer distinguish any organization in them. The contrast of hyletic and noematic constituent elements does not result in concepts of the internal experience of various discovered objects [Gegenstände]. Rather, the hyle is a sign for the operation of crossing the border from essence into process, just as essence was the sign for a speculative operation. The dovetailing and parallel course of essence and intuition, of content and existence, and the nexus between the identity of the essence—that is, the object [Gegenstand]—with duration are thus grounded in the form of the speculative process, because even if the contrast between essence and intuition is made with discretion, with the transition to an infinitely small constituent element of formed material, the essence can nevertheless seemingly be dissolved in that medium where the distinction of form and material no longer has any meaning, since neither prevails over the other as object [Gegenstand].

⊷⊱⊰

Santayana's remark about philosophic method refers to a stream of things that always carries the same material and to symbolic formulations in which the concepts have equal value when they refer to the same material in various systems. The task of analysis was therefore prescribed as determining the material in a given symbolic formulation and disclosing the particular symbolic constituent elements. Since such an unmediated presentation is impossible, the material must be made tangible through comparison with related formations and through the comparative loosening of the systematic links. Then it is seen as the ideal intersection of various lines of construction, as with the formulations of Brentano, Hodgson, Husserl, and Santayana. The material showed itself to be a prespeculative world—a world in which we naïvely know about things, are confused, are aware of knowing, confront things, and distinguish ourselves from them. But as soon as this material is to be shaped into rational concepts, difficulties arise. Brentano and Hodgson dealt with these by setting up a dialectic of concepts belonging to other realms, whereas Santayana introduced the concept of essence to overcome them. Thanks to this accommodating treatment of the material, the structure of the formulation becomes significantly clearer and is revealed to be the naming of philosophical loci discovered according to a law of speculative necessity. Prespeculative material and the shaping of it into the form of speculation combine in the structure of the object [Gegenstand]. The next task would be to investigate the symbolic content of this object [Gegenstand] in Santayana's system, since in spite of its ephemeral, nonexistent nature, essence becomes the expression and the representative of a view of the world. This trait arises as early as its methodological function for philosophy, since the constitution that we have just discussed in terms of the penetration of material and form was for Santayana the dialectical evolution of an essence. He considered the science of dialectic as starting from a "concretion in discourse" and an "intent" directed to the evolution of the concretion. This concretion in discourse, or essence, is the very complex structure that serves a philosopher as the point of departure for his speculation; its sense is clarified and unfolded in the process of discourse. The philosophical system, appearing to the thinker as the vague outlines of a whole, would be the essence he gradually explicates in the process of philosophizing. The discourse differs from all natural scientific research in that the initial essence, once given, requires no additional perception. All predicates accrue to the subject as answers to questions that arise concerning the given topic. The subject itself is fixed through the point of departure and the intention directed to clarification, so that the verification is carried out by regression and comparison with the result in the reconsideration of the same topic. The purpose is to understand the original datum, not to find new data. In this sense dialectic is "synthetically a priori," since constancy of intention and progress in the clarification of what begins as a given are the only two principles of a compelling dialectical deduction. That the dialectic method so described was in fact utilized is shown by analysis of cases, since Brentano's, Hodgson's, and Santayana's speculations were all attempts to start from a point determined by historical accident to be just so and not otherwise and to maintain consistency in the results of the speculation—thus giving rise to the further question of how concretions come about and what position the concretion occupies in a wider philosophical space. To answer these questions and thus to explicate the symbolic content of essence requires a descent into the genesis of Santayana's world.

II

In 1923 Santayana published a new edition of his early poems, most of them dating from the period 1880–1900. In a preface he explained and justified his action: When a philosopher is mentioned, the image of a logician or a psychologist is usually falsely conjured up, a man whose profession it is to weigh arguments and toil to solve complex problems. "I see no reason why a philosopher should be puzzled. What he sees he sees; of the rest he is ignorant; and his sense of this vast ignorance (which is his natural and inevitable condition) is a chief part of his knowledge and of his emotions."[7] Philosophy is not a topic that engages Santayana only on occasion; it is a necessity of life, his daily answer to everything he encounters. He lives by thinking, and he is constantly amazed at the oddness of this world and of his person in it. All his thoughts and expressions in literature, science, and criticism therefore become essential parts of his philosophy; the verses of a philosopher are epigrams like those of the Greek sages, who turn the drama into a morality play, whether of a personal passion or of an expanded outlook on nature.

Santayana is Spanish by birth, and though he mastered the English language so completely that, together with Joseph Conrad, a Pole, he is considered a modern master of English prose, he still feels like a stranger in it. Its roots do not quite reach his center. He lacks the memories of early childhood, of fairy tales and nursery songs, and he lacks the firm grasp of landscape and society. Communion with nature and a sensitive love for rural life, so deeply embedded in English literature, do not echo in Santayana's work. Landscape is made the background for a scene among the gods or the symbol for human fate, as it was used in antiquity, and human beings are a subject for reflection. Even his urbane and cultured erudition does not enter deeply into the byways of life and the thickets of destiny. Santayana's road to poetry is a literary one, and his work does not exhibit the magic that words assume when a true poet illuminates their meaning, as if they were being expressed for the first time. Santayana's prose and his verse, practiced masterfully, nevertheless remain an instrument that seems wielded by the artist's hands, only to return to silence. What stands out is the pallor of the language that envelops the thoughts like a precious cover but never meshes with them to create a powerful, indelible symbol. Critics, whether disparaging or admiring, have remarked on the sureness of Santayana's control over his ideas, his critical sense. His wit and irony draw them into his world; but later, released from their thrall, they cannot remember what they have heard or read. His language, skimming the surface of things, never

7. George Santayana, Preface to Santayana, *Poems* (1923; rpr. New York, 1946).

84

fully reveals the world, coming to a stop before a veil that lets us only guess at final things. What Santayana wrote about a realm beyond could apply to his language:

> We catch the broken prelude and suggestion
> Of things unuttered, needing to be sung;
> We know the burden of them, and their question
> Lies heavy on the heart, nor finds a tongue.
>
> Till haply, lightning through the storm of ages,
> Our sullen secret flash from sky to sky,
> Glowing in some diviner poet's pages
> And swelling into rapture from this sigh.[8]

The melancholy of these lines completely expresses the weak power that language exerts over thought; their resignation and aesthetic distance, the gentle exhaustion and deep loneliness of the monologue are the medium of Santayana's early and decisive experiences. In the poem entitled "Solipsism" the world turns into a dream; the passion of the scene and its painful coloration come from the poet's soul; the sufferings of this world, which no god can have wanted to be real, are only cruel dreams. Here, in lonely solitude, the poet stakes out a precinct where the foreign, friendless man can stand firmly, where he finds his gods and his mystical redemption. In spite of Santayana's hesitation to take a firm grip on things, this is the area that confers on his language—which otherwise would be empty rhetoric—its passion and tension, namely, the mourning and resignation of his early work and, later, the irony of his final attitude. In his explanatory preface Santayana can therefore ask double forgiveness for his poems. Verses are part of a literary tradition, and a "man of letters," he feels, cannot avoid occasionally expressing his thoughts in verse. It is as impossible to render the term *man of letters* into German as it is to translate the word *gentleman*. At best we could compare the rank of the latter in society with that of the former in the realm of the mind. *Literat* would be to diminish the concept, *Dichter* would be going too far. To connect the term with *Geisteskultur* is too reminiscent of shirt-sleeve professionalism; *Bildung*, of the academic. All these terms touch on essential traits of the "man of letters" without hitting his essence. For Santayana broad knowledge is indispensable, as is the

8. *Ibid.*, xiv.

philosophic stance. But both are used not to teach or persuade but to communicate, "addressed only to those whose ear it may strike sympathetically and who, crossing the same dark wood on their own errands, may pause for a moment to listen gladly."[9] Devotion to the work, fanaticism in creation must never blind us to perfection, form, calm. The objective must not be lost along the way. Straying in the forest of questions must never be placed above revelation of what is seen. And poetry has its justification in the service of revelation; poetic diction always remains linked with holy, archaic experiences, and the verse form raises and supports the clear logic of the words over itself; the poems bestow the pomp of a religious procession, without which many of the poets' intuitions would lose their magic and their dignity, and there is no other expression for tragic finality than poetry.

The right to use verse as a form supports the passion in the primal experience of the solitary self: "A Muse—not exactly an English Muse—actually visited me in my isolation; the same or a ghost of the same, that visited Boethius or Alfred de Musset or Leopardi. It was literally impossible for me then not to re-echo her eloquence."[10] The compulsion and the breathlessness of this period demand a poem, and only after the painful birth of wisdom and denial is completed can the clarity of prose, based on greater knowledge, bear witness to a world that has come into being with greater freedom and cheerfulness. Santayana calls his poems "my philosophy in the making."[11] Its consecration still lies over the later systems, erected on the mountainous mass of historical culture and radiating to the ends of a universe. The poems contain the same system, still lacking the fullness of the material, closer to the origins of person and fate, hieratical signs for the world.

※

The twenty sonnets of the "First Series" document a path away from youthfully doting admiration and pious acceptance of Christian dogma. The secret of the Catholic rites, passionate piety, and change in the love of God are understood and measured in the yearning for beauty and adoration in lucid reason:

9. *Ibid.*, xi.
10. *Ibid.*, xii.
11. *Ibid.*

> I sought on earth a garden of delight
>
> . . . .
>
> Where gentle music were accounted prayer,
> And reason, veiled, performed the happy rite.[12]

This divine service must shudder before the picture of the crucified Jesus, whose wounds forbid the happiness and beauty of life, and guided by his reason alone, it seeks new serenity with the Eternal Mother—tortured in the abandonment of inner doubts, return to the old faith, and lack of trust in the new light of knowledge that illuminates only a few steps of the solitary journey.[13] After this prelude the series is strictly constructed in four times four sonnets. The first group deals with the prison and the suffering of the self: consciousness and history have robbed us of the innocence of natural life, with its cheerful joy in happiness and the brief mourning, passing as rapidly as clouds;[14] self-consciously doubting, the self finds itself banished inside itself, unable to know what is a dream and what is truth and reality,[15] so that only love for the "eternal Whole" overcomes the disappointments of the dream of self;[16] but it, too, cannot lead to forgetfulness, and it is the spirit that leads above the self, is chained in its prison, condemned to bear witness to suffering.[17] The doctrine of the four sufferings of the self—consciousness, dream, love, and spirit—is followed by the doctrine of the four mitigating virtues: for the individual self is merely a part of the suffering world and adapts to the justice that allots to it its share in the sorrow of the tormented world spirit,[18] and it can bear its share patiently because death ends all pain; this life is only a short vigil between the slumber before birth and subsequent eternity;[19] it would therefore be presumptuous to expect satisfaction or rewards for the small self in the great struggle of the world—"the covenant God gave us is a task,"[20] and if its glitter and its mercy do not shine, its holiness is therefore no less worthy of adoration.[21]

12. *Ibid.,* Sonnet I, p. 3.
13. *Ibid.,* Sonnets I–III, pp. 3–5.
14. *Ibid.,* Sonnet IV, p. 6.
15. *Ibid.,* Sonnet V, p. 7.
16. *Ibid.,* Sonnet VI, p. 8.
17. *Ibid.,* Sonnet VII, p. 9.
18. *Ibid.,* Sonnet VIII, p. 10.
19. *Ibid.,* Sonnet IX, p. 11.
20. *Ibid.,* Sonnet X, p. 12.
21. *Ibid.,* Sonnet XI, p. 13.

The virtues of devotion, patience, renunciation, and adoration still the rebellion of the spirit against the law of the world and allow it to seek peace and humble fortune in nature. Sonnets XII–XV loosen somewhat the rigidity of the dispensation; the sincere acceptance of fate is expressed in lighter reflections and simple symbols. In the overall course of the world the self is only a humble episode, preceded by greater matters and followed by weightier events. The river flowing through the plain, cascading down the mountains, calm, slowly coursing toward the ocean and its own end, is the appropriate image.[22] The poet describes the lightness and sweetness of the days when, without hope and ambition, we follow life's labyrinthine paths, without impatience at delays, without aimless curiosity or longing for a destination.[23] Chaos may live on, but it does not roil the small cosmos of the self; what once was pain, the self's enchainment to the dream, now becomes joy and the source of happiness. The self creates a paradise, encapsulated in its nature, without concerning itself with macrocosmic events. Images of the deity cannot be threatening if eyes are closed before them, thus chasing them away; the storm does not hurt the flake that flutters before it.[24] In the communion with nature, in the peacefulness of the planets' course, the self finds its peace.[25]

When we contemplate these, however, their beauty takes on life; nature is full of gods beyond the blue of the sky, in every tree and every spring, and Eros leads the self further away from the adoration of these separate beauties to the love of the one beauty beyond all things; it is a serious love, departing further from the glow of what is worldly and penetrating to the one inconceivable godhead, the world-creating one, that all things love by being and resting in the beauty of their being, and to whom the world pays homage with every birth and every death. God and beauty, world-creating Eros, and primordial truth flow together toward the one destination of adoring longing, the last home of the self:

> Above the battlements of heaven rise
> The glittering domes of the gods' golden dwelling,
> Whence, like a constellation, passion-quelling,

22. *Ibid.*, Sonnet XII, p. 14.
23. *Ibid.*, Sonnet XIII, p. 15.
24. *Ibid.*, Sonnet XIV, p. 16.
25. *Ibid.*, Sonnet XV, p. 17.

The truth of all things feeds immortal eyes.
There all forgotten dreams of paradise
From the deep caves of memory upwelling,
All tender joys beyond our dim foretelling
Are ever bright beneath the flooded skies.
There we live o'er, amid angelic powers,
Our lives without remorse, as if not ours,
And others' lives with love, as if our own;
For we behold, from those eternal towers,
The deathless beauty of all wingèd hours,
And have our being in their truth alone.[26]

The way from the sorrows of self and world, through renunciation into the finiteness of nature, and rising from nature through Eros to the idea—this path leads not through a free space, through no reality; the journey is from beginning to end an adventure of the self in the self; the way leads not through a completed universe; this world is created only as we walk through it. In a process of the self's unfolding, the self places the world outside itself, limits itself, and lifts itself up to an idea while always remaining the same self. Through all the stations it bears the burden of melancholy, dreams, and solitude; the goal is not liberation but a dim reflection that the soul need not be a stranger on the earth because its roots lie in a place beyond; for it, too, is a part of the "holy air," omnipresent, and devoted to God. That is why the poet places on the altar of the great Mother a crown of thorns, though it bears blossoms.[27] The expansion of the self into the world, nature, and Eros is not a real extension; just as an individual in a hall of distorting mirrors can fill the world of illusion that surrounds him with images of himself, so does the self see itself in numerous refractions, at ever-different sites, but basically always in its own company, trapped in its hall of mirrors. The connection is not experience but the unreal thread of solipsistic, parthenogenetic speculation, fated to break down at the first clash with a reality outside the self.

The "Second Series" of sonnets, this time with no hall of mirrors, deals with clash and collapse through the power of Eros. As with the first series, there is evidence of a strict construction. But this time the structure is slightly more complex; the series contains two sets, equal to the first in their spiritual power. If the first series can

26. *Ibid.*, Sonnet XIX, p. 21.
27. *Ibid.*, Sonnet XX, p. 22.

be described as the journey of the self into itself, the first part of
the second series can be called the mortal way and the second part
the divine way of the self on the way to transfiguration. In the first
journey the poet gains the form of the world; in the second and
third he becomes nature and spirit, thus realizing the form of the
first. The life schema is fulfilled.

The first and second sonnets act as an introduction, much like
the first three sonnets of the adventures of the self.[28] The labori-
ously gained serenity and mastery over the unstable balance in the
self-world is now in jeopardy, just as traditional faith was earlier.
Instead of reason it is now Eros that guides the self's destiny:

> 'Tis love that moveth the celestial spheres
> In endless yearning for the Changeless One,
> And the stars sing together, as they run
> To number the innumerable years.
>
> . . . .
>
> And the same hand that reined the flying hours
> And chained the whirling earth to Phoebus' throne,
> In love's eternal orbit keeps the soul.[29]

The lament and the account of the shock are followed by the story
of a love fated from the outset to hopelessness because nothing new
occurs, there are no new actors to perform a new life in a new
setting. The old self, with its primordial solitude, travels through
the next ring on the road to redemption. Moments of youthful forgetfulness and glimpses of happiness alternate with consciousness
of a final unsatisfied being, an insurmountable separation of souls
in the most intimate contact. The lines express the torment of an
indecision that knows the outcome has already been decided but
that even in the act of submission is still reluctant to acquiesce in
thoughts of death.[30] Sleep surrounds the soul at the edge of despair,
and a serene sense, of being open once again to the world outside
itself, draws the strength to live from the sight and is able to gather
itself to new resolution:

> Strengthen me, Heaven, and attune my lay
> Unto my better angel's clear refrain.
>
> . . . .

28. *Ibid.*, Sonnets XXI, XXII, pp. 25–26.
29. *Ibid.*, Sonnet XXII, p. 26.
30. *Ibid.*, Sonnet XXVI, p. 30.

Slowly, saith he, the April buds are growing
In the chill core of twigs all leafless now;
Gently, beneath the weight of last night's snowing,
Patient of winter's hand, the branches bow.
Each buried seed lacks light as much as thou.
Wait for the spring, brave heart; there is no knowing.[31]

The springtime hope of nature is linked to reminiscences of Petrarch's love of God and the classical belief in a superhuman fate and idea, until the soul is ready for the renunciation in a threefold love: the love of a brother, who has no choice who his sister is; the love of a lover for his beloved, but without doubts or expectation of love in return; the love of the saint, but without ecstatic visions.

Thus in my love all loves are reconciled
That purest be. . . .[32]

The self has risen through the torments and consolations of the soul to the stage of spirit. Physical separation through accidents and convention mean nothing when confronted with the loving, solitary contact at this high level, which requires no concrete mediation.[33] Even an admission of love would be superfluous here, where the worldly form of the beloved is merely a vessel of divine grace, its body the transubstantiation of the spirit's beauty:

And might I kiss her once, asleep or dead,
Upon the forehead or the globèd eyes,
Or where the gold is parted on her head,
That kiss would help me on to paradise
As if I kissed the consecrated bread
In which the buried soul of Jesus lies.[34]

The soul finds more than consolation in the ray of the beauty of this image. Turmoil and despair are extinguished in the new realm where the gods are once more alive and guiding their worshipers.[35] The stars, the beauties of the earth, and silent worship serve the goddess by their existence. Confession, which had seemed superfluous, would now be appropriate. The divinity does not bend down to mortals; rather, the spirit can only rise toward her in eternal

31. *Ibid.,* Sonnet XXVII, p. 31.
32. *Ibid.,* Sonnet XXXI, p. 35.
33. *Ibid.,* Sonnet XXXII, p. 36.
34. *Ibid.,* Sonnet XXXIX, p. 43.
35. *Ibid.,* Sonnets XLIII, XLIV, pp. 47–48.

prayer, give proof of its devotion to her image at every crossroad of its thought, and praise her goodness. Love enters completely into reflection:

> When I survey the harvest of the year
> And from time's threshing garner up the grain,
> What profit have I of forgotten pain,
> What comfort, heart-locked, for the winter's cheer?
> The season's yield is this, that thou art dear,
> And that I love thee, that is all my gain;
> The rest was chaff, blown from the weary brain
> Where now thy treasured image lieth clear.[36]

The beloved has become nameless, she stands before the spirit as a shadow of divinity, as the eternal one that in all loves is the only one intended.[37] In the last three sonnets (XLVIII–L), at last the mind becomes the idea and is redeemed in the idea. Number XLVIII uses the image of the legend of Helen's brothers, the one mortal, the other immortal. When death approached one, the other gave him half his immortality so as to alternate in living and in dying. But Zeus transformed both into stars, both of them seeming immortal. The poet claims that the death of his heart was similarly approaching when the youth of his beloved inspired him with light and new warmth, so that now he lives in her beauty and truth, and having become one with her, he can enter into the divinity of the idea.[38] A great love has carried him to eternal rest and to peace with all things. Chaos and worldly commotion have lost their terror, since the spirit has seen the reality of what is greatest and has been dissolved in it:

> The flame that quickeneth the world entire
> Leaps in my breast, with cruel death to cope.
>
> . . . .
>
> Is not the comfort of these singing hours,
> Full of thy perfectness, enough for me?
> They are not evil, then, those hidden powers:
> One love sufficeth an eternity.[39]

Analysis of the sequence of ideas—which, since Santayana is a genuine philosopher, is a journey through life—and the passages

36. *Ibid.*, Sonnet XLVI, p. 50.
37. *Ibid.*, Sonnet XLVII, p. 51.
38. *Ibid.*, Sonnet XLVIII, p. 52.
39. *Ibid.* Sonnet L, p. 54.

from the poems show the attitude more clearly than interpretive language is often able to. Sonnet XIX, quoted in its entirety, is, more than the others, a symbol of the deep separation between the poet's person and thoughts and his choice of words. Olympian recollections of a golden temple, Oriental dreams of paradise, Christian heavenly powers, the caves of memory, charity, repentance, Platonic ideas and love, all become intertwined, all are equally emptied of their substance, all are equally aesthetic images for the spirit that could say: There is no god, but Mary is his mother! Here we look in vain for the magic of language, in which one word will lead to the next, for the penetration of meaning radiating outward from a center. The culturally formed, previously completed images are used as aesthetic aids in the service of signification; the beauty of phrase and the music of words stand like walls around the meaning, and the word becomes flesh in only a few passages, which embody without mediation the experience of solitude. One such passage is found in another sonnet's sestina:

> For some are born to be beatified
> By anguish, and by grievous penance done;
> And some, to furnish forth the age's pride
> And to be praised of men beneath the sun;
> And some are born to stand perplexed aside
> From so much sorrow—of whom I am one.[40]

The wandering of the self from its origins to its redemption is an ascetic adventure far removed from the sensuousness of words and reality. The metamorphosis of primordial suffering and capitulation through the torments of the soul to renunciation of the spirit and the transfiguration in the idea moves forward from the self in the narrowest space, almost anxious about bumping into realities at any point—as shown most clearly where the strongest invasion of the reality of Eros is from the outset muffled, denatured, and toned down until it is raised to the level of renunciation. Such fanatical renunciation can hardly be derived from historical relationships, for Platonic denial rests on the firm ground of the adoration of secular reality as the incorporation of the idea, and the ascent to it is merely the final goal of philosophical speculation, whereas Santayana's will to renounce dominates his thinking and is a part

40. *Ibid.*, Sonnet XI, p. 13.

of all that he contemplates, so that it is precisely erotic experience that appears as no more than an exception to renunciation; the suggestions of Platonism, much as they affect the choice of images and words on the basis of historic knowledge, have nothing in common with the classical spirit. It is easier to detect in their fervent longing for something above us a remnant of early Catholic devotion. Even fewer similarities appear between the dominant but wan power of Santayana's Eros and the wave of erotica and sexuality expressed at the turn of the century in the works of Zola, Strindberg, Wedekind, Freud, Wilde, and Weiniger [sic, but perhaps Otto Weininger]; Santayana's is too weak and distanced from reality. In spite of the shift from the journey of the self to reality that occurs at the beginning of the second series of sonnets, the self remains self-enclosed, seemingly using the world only as the occasion for expressing its earlier solitariness more emphatically. The transition from the world of mirrors to the real world has not freed the self; it has merely given new opportunities for renunciation. Nor can we appeal to the model of Dante, because Santayana deliberately distances himself by his disbelief in the separation of this world from the beyond and the strictness of the directing will. His renunciation is never a moral judgment on the world, but rather a flight from the quandary.

In spite of its pervasive eroticism, the overall image of Santayana's world leaves no legitimate place for the female. The first chapter in the second volume of The Life of Reason, "Love," deals only impersonally with relations between the sexes and their function in structuring the world, with their sublimations, with the transition to everyday life—and the partners in the relationship might just as easily be of the same sex as of opposite ones. It is not until we come to the chapter on friendship that we find some general remarks about spiritual differences between the sexes and the resulting impossibility of genuine friendship between them. In this chapter Santayana states that a man and a woman agree only in their conclusions; their reasons are always different. Intellectual harmony between them is easily possible, but its allure and fascination do not lie in mutual understanding; it is a covert convergence of alien essences, somewhat like a kiss in the dark. "The human race, in its intellectual life, is organised like the bees; the masculine soul is a worker, sexually atrophied, and essentially dedicated to impersonal and universal arts; the feminine is a queen, infinitely fertile, omnipresent in its brooding industry, but passive and abounding in intuitions without method and passions without justice."[41] Therefore friendship with a woman will always be more or less than friendship: less because of the intellectual imbalance; more because there is always something mysterious and oracular surrounding a woman's spirit, which inspires instinctive reverence and renders evaluation of her statements by male standards impossible: "She has a kind of sybilline intuition and the right to be irrationally *à propos*. . . . There is a gallantry of the mind which pervades all conversation with a lady, as there is a natural courtesy toward children and mystics; but such a habit of respectful concession, marking as it does an intellectual alienation as profound as that which separates us from the dumb animals, is radically incompatible with friendship."[42]

This statement, concluding the list of differences, encapsulates the remoteness and external approach evident throughout the passage. The description indulges thoroughly in symptoms without ever penetrating to the essence; the occasion when the differences become significant, the conversation, is thus merely an occasion, unrelated to the experiential center of the person. Accordingly, the contrast between the erotic philosophy and the woman's insignificance could not be revealed in more astonishing ways.

Stripped of the worlds of culture and action, the sonnets at heart retain only the fervor and pure will to live of a self that avoids entanglements and pettinesses precisely through its lack of feeling of reality and relations to external events. Horace M. Kallen has captured this impression of Santayana's personality in an essay, "America and the Life of Reason"—not by analyzing the work, but by forming an opinion of the human being—and his statements must be repeated here for their documentary value:

> Those who remember him [Santayana] in the class-room will remember his as a spirit solemn, and sweet and withdrawn; whose Johannine face by a Renaissance painter held an abstracted eye and a hieratic smile, half mischief, half content; whose rich voice flowed evenly, in cadences smooth and balanced as a liturgy; whose periods

41. George Santayana, *Reason in Society* (1905; rpr. New York, 1948), 149, Vol. II of Santayana, *The Life of Reason; or, The Phases of Human Progress,* 5 vols.
42. *Ibid.*

had the intricate perfection of a poem and the import of a prophecy;
who spoke somehow for his hearers and not to them, stirring in the
depths of their natures and troubling their minds, as an oracle might,
to whom pertained mystery and reverence, so compact of remoteness
and fascination did he seem, so moving, and so unmoved. Between
him and them was a bar for which I know no similitude save that
which is suggested sometimes by a Chinese painting of the tranquil
Enlightened One, the irresistible magnet of his sedulous devotees, fill-
ing their vision and drawing them on as he sits, inscrutably smiling,
above them. This detachment, which often seemed to have a tinge of
sadness and insufficiency in it, is a quality of all of Mr. Santayana's
works and endows them with something of the passionate impersonality of great music.[43]

III

The title of one of Santayana's books is *Character and Opinion in
the United States*.[44] It is a confrontation between a living character—one who is still philosophically inarticulate—and a philosophical view, the "genteel tradition," which has nothing in common
with the character, above whose material life it is elevated. In this
situation Santayana sees the current condition of the American
mind: its nature is, in his view, still alien, a luxury in the American
world, adapted and cultivated from foreign conventions. It cannot
derive its strength from a destiny that has only just begun. Santayana represents the strongest expression of the foreignness of the
mind to American society. He, himself a foreigner, was more sensitive to the separation and more inclined to draw the consequences
than was Emerson, the preacher, the member of the community,
whose transcendental stature grew out of mild alarm at the unsatisfactory state of affairs rather than fervor and uncompromising
dedication. Precisely his foreignness, both as an intellectual and as
a human being, which enabled an advanced and substantial society
to be seen only as a curiosity, an aesthetic phenomenon, has a valid
place in the American intellectual world. The isolation of the mind
in a world of purposeless material success, the isolation of the vir-

43. Horace M. Kallan, "America and the Life of Reason," in Kallan, *Culture and
Democracy in the United States: Studies in the Group Psychology of the American
Peoples* (New York, 1924). The quotation is from pp. 258–59.
44. George Santayana, *Character and Opinion in the United States* (New York,
1920).

tue of an optimism that sees the justification of gainful employment in such success and draws from it new faith to undertake new
efforts and achieve renewed success—the isolation in this world
has in the extreme case driven out solipsistic experience as the
basis of thought.

If we try to describe rationally what is meant by "experiential
basis," it appears that in the organization of a personal world at
least one element, possibly several, must occur doubly. In Santayana's poems the sequential stratification of the solitary self, the
soul, the mind, and the idea was accompanied by an element of
experience that is identical with the first world element, the "solitary self," but is given a special coloration of activity or will because of which we conventionally designate it as experience. But
only as companion to the first world element does it carry out a
"normal" function, since it is only here, in the first series of sonnets, that it overlaps with practicality; with the incursion of reality
in eroticism—new practical material—however, the experiential
basis does not extend farther. Rather, the new life appears, broken,
in the old experience. It is "broken" not only as an optical image;
the falling apart of practicality and experience actually breaks the
fullness of life into halves and generates that wanness and weakness earlier noted as characteristic of Santayana's vocabulary. It
was on this dual organization of the person—most clearly visible
when, as here, the two sets diverge—that Santayana established a
principle of philosophical criticism. Every system contains practical experiences, introduced by the "stream of life," penetrated by
the energy of "mature sentiment," of personal experiences. Thus,
Santayana is able to provide a certain degree of dialectical clarification through arguments in the categories of "conversation." But
the essential content of philosophical thought, its experience, is not
a possible subject matter of theoretical argument; it is never false
because will cannot be disproved, only destroyed. Therefore all
philosophical discussion of a noninterpretive sort is superfluous
and meaningless. "The age of controversy has passed; that of interpretation has succeeded." That he himself did not live according to
this demand—the result of his basic philosophical stance—but often indulged in misunderstandings and derogative value judgments
is simply additional proof of the "break."

If the analysis of the essence as it reaches a new level is to be understood, it now demands a technique different from that employed earlier. The parallel placement of Brentano's, Hodgson's, Husserl's, and Santayana's concepts eliminated the common element as, considered naïvely, indifferent background material. A form of speculative formation common to all then emerges. This latter leads either to treating psychological concepts dialectically or—as with Santayana and Husserl—to the frank acceptance of nonexistential realms of being. An examination of the speculative form makes possible value judgments about "good" and "bad" constructions on the basis of a standard of value that, for each point reached in the course of a speculative operation, requires the introduction of special signs or names. It is therefore permitted to say that Brentano's construction was worse than Hodgson's because the latter introduced the dialectical concepts of thatness and whatness; and Santayana's theory was superior to both because the introduction of the concept of essence completely avoided the dialectical treatment of concepts from other realms. Husserl's formulation would be the best because the hyletic constituent elements are set against the noematic ones; but because an underlying speculative will is absent, his analysis can hardly be listed with the others. The dimensions of material and speculative reason are joined by solipsistic experience in the course of constructing the essence. In the poetic world of the sonnets the rational concept of essence corresponds to the sphere of the idea, raised from the self's primordial suffering through renunciation, spirit, and love, and through the transformation of practical emotional and intellectual experiences. It is a poetry with an imagery burdened by reminiscences of the Platonic ideal, the glow of Olympian deities, and the self's yearning for a home. A thorough philosophic-conceptual study of essence leaves no room for the metaphysics of the suffering of the world. Its place is taken by skeptical reduction; and Platonism is eliminated to make room for the systematic effort of the idea in Socratic epistemology. What remains, however, is the strangely chaotic function of the realm of essences; it is strange because the system does not require it. The essence stands revealed as a hypothetically necessary concept in the epistemology of critical realism, stating no more than the fact that for everything that ever arose as existence for a consciousness, or will arise, or can arise, there is an essence that must be found, because, by definition, without such an essence there can be no existence for a consciousness. Essence and existence together are thus metaphysically real and speculatively constructed correlative entities or concepts, and the potentially infinite diversity of the triad self-essence-existence derives these potentials not from one of the two realms but from a third one.

The introduction of the concept of infinity into the realm of essences is a leap similar to the transition from noema to hyle. Just as a subject matter was dissolved from within into the minimum of constructed elements, until it disappeared into the process, so here all of the concrete world is minimized by appearing as one of an infinite number of elements, each different from the others, all together forming the totality of chaos. It differs from process in that process is the primordial medium of the given world and only of the given world; whereas in chaos my actual world, together with its engendering process, is merely such a borderline case as the real experiential constituent elements are for the transcendentally constituted noema. The idea of chaos is not confined within the problematic nature of self-consciousness and the transcendence of cognition in the previously treated speculative stage; it transcends this area of speculation as a whole, and in this transcendence it generates precisely the idea of an infinity of possible worlds. Self-consciousness, up to this point the material for speculative formation, now emerges as an active process of formation: The phenomenon of apparent duration and real identity of an essence, grounded in the commonsense principles of time and memory that alone make knowledge possible, becomes—to use, for the moment, a dialectical phrase—directed at itself. The essential structure of the relation between existence and essence, remains recognizably one of opposition, and this turning away from the formation of the concept of essence in the speculative process of skeptical reduction to its treatment as object leads to the concept of chaos. The turn to the new level of process also reveals the nature of the "speculative form." The transcendence of knowledge, customarily understood as the relation of meaning or psychic process to a real object lying beyond (for example, in the antithesis of existence-essence), has the general function of a relation with the beyond altogether. Even the given material—the self, the environment, error, perceived truth—as the point of departure for a speculative formulation is not "pure" material; it is possible only as a naïve experience of transcendence of a world beyond my person, so that the speculative "form"—seemingly brought to the material from outside—adds nothing that was not previously present. On the contrary, it begins by artificial reduction to an immanent construction. Only after completion is it possible to speak again of essence, existence, and process as "objects" that can be transcended in the direction of chaos; thus, *after* the formulation it creates a situation that displays great similarity with that of the "material" *before* the formulation. The clear speculative stage beyond which the road leads to chaos is obviously given as a practical experience or as material before every speculative process, so that the process is circular. The "form" is of the same matter as the "material," and the ultimate concept, which does not disintegrate into others through such circles, seems to be "transcendence" with its correlative concepts of time and memory.

The philosophic space is thus bisected into a material-form sphere of the first order and a secondary transcendence, which sees the first from outside. It is this transcendence, coming systematically later but preceding in experience, that makes the first sphere possible as a whole. In this circumstance, assigning chaos to a single element of the first sphere, the essence, seems arbitrary. The idea of an infinity of worlds is not an independent concept. It arises as a correlative to the givenness of the *one* world, which—precisely because it is *one*—could just as easily be another one. Chaos is merely one of the points that must be attained in the progressive process of thinking if transcendence is to be conferred on the basic constituent facts involved in thinking (as its material and the principle of its formation). In this interdependent system of form-material relations and the necessity of process, a purely analytic scheme—the shift of chaos to the realm of essence—results in a nonrational juncture. The background of the sonnets explains its genesis. The flight from worldly suffering came to rest in a realm of ideal immortality. Its essential being was not a concept of philosophical necessity, nor was eternity a technical term but a religious deliverance and transfiguration. This beyond of the immortal spirit is the home of the suffering self, but it is also the metaphysical ground of all worldly being, in a sense not far distant from the Platonic view. Though the philosophical conceptualization rationalized the image of such a beyond, the irrational coincidence of essence and chaos in the system evidences traces of the primordial experience.

The idea of "concretion in discourse" is thus given greater philosophical significance. If the "circumstance" of a material means that a transcendent object has been established and is to be understood as a speculative necessity or interpretative formulation of what has been established, the Kantian contrast of form and material becomes superfluous. It was of didactic value to our presentation because "material" was a practical sign for what is "shared" in the various speculations. But the questionable nature even of a didactic value became evident as soon as it became impossible to predicate differences in the speculative form and as soon as all differences in construction clearly had their origin in the point of departure for the speculation. Only the introduction of the level of experience provides a term that is at least helpful in rising above the dead center and legitimately allows the use of new terms. We can, for example, speak of the "diversity" of speculative constructions. "Material" is a hypostatic identity for the observation that somehow equivalencies in the various systems shine through, that under the various aspects something invariably the same can nevertheless be detected. "Form" means the decoding of the total object under examination into its constituent parts. And, finally, "experience" provides the basis for the differences in the aspects of equivalent materials that are disclosed in the speculative process.

Thus we must seek the decisive content of philosophical speculation in the experience, the level that can only be interpreted. And since the ontological center of Santayana's solipsistic experience is the longing for an ideal spiritual being in the beyond, his doctrine of death and immortality contains the core of his philosophy.

In his first major work, *The Life of Reason* (in five volumes), this doctrine is placed at the center, the conclusion of the third volume (philosophy of religion). The chapter "Ideal Immortality" singles out the layers of dreams of immortality—Olympian eternity, survival in the species, individual triumph over death in animalistic values and in the values of reason. The Olympian ideal—man as earthly, individual, elevated in all his vital functions, provided with eternal youth—is the primitive mythic expression of the desire for immortality. But nature does not permit this dream to be realized; the will of the individual passes away with his physical death, and if any part endures, it can only be through procreation. The life of the individual takes on the permanent form of his will; but the material substance changes until it decays. In the life of generations the form is overtly destroyed again and again, but the living substance is imperceptibly preserved. The metaphysics of a universal will [*Weltwille*] would thus feel that death has been vanquished, but the individual, the conscious vessel of the will, is not safe from the death of his person, and the procreative instinct is just as much a death wish as a will to live.

This inevitable defeat becomes bearable through the birth of values—altruism, parental love, loyalty. They bloom directly out of the ruins of any hope for personal immortality; the individual's death and the life of the species assert themselves in engendering a new dimension of being: values. This constellation of death and life intertwined and the creation of values by the pressure of death on life are the driving thoughts in Santayana's speculation. The meaning of existence as such, he believes, is not the completion of a particular purpose but the indefinite drive to continue in existence. The fundamental law of will, like the first law of matter, is to persevere in the beginning stage. The essence of vitality is therefore inertia, and an external force, opposed to life, must intervene to determine the direction of the existing organization of inclinations and instincts and to change them, just as an external force is needed to stop a star in its orbit and redirect it.

Even the process of nourishment is such an enforced activity. Hunger is the beginning of weakness and agony, which ends in death unless the appropriate satisfaction can keep life going. The animalistic values of the hunt, of love, of action, which arise from animal needs, exist on a higher level than that achieved by an *anima vegetativa*, which knows only spontaneous reactions and whose value is limited to being. The felicity of actions in the sphere of freedom overcomes death at the same time that the two are related, since such actions have their roots in animality. Finally, "the life of reason" is raised above animal life, having gained a new sphere of freedom in reason. Nevertheless, this elevation does not relieve it from the natural foundation; rather, it finds its meaning in rational control.

The rational sphere is the realm of human, ideal immortality. Ongoing physical existence in subsequent generations does not vanquish death, since it does not fulfill the primary desire for personal survival, and even the reproductive drive is defeated by the possibility of complete annihilation of life or of an evolutionary change. There are no grounds for assuming that the engendering substance—whatever it might be—that brought forth life as we know it has exhausted its powers in the process. It is possible that, were life to be completely destroyed, after a long interval other life forms might come into being in other corners of the universe. Natural death is an insurmountable fact, and in our struggle with it the feeling of defeat will always win out. It is in no way problematic, and we need not wait for the experience of our own death to be persuaded of its reality. At every moment of our life death celebrates its predecessors, and memory, through whose representation we somehow survive the past for the moment, delivers immediate proof that in reality we will die. *Everything* moves in the midst of death, because it moves; but only reason can view time, so that a shadow of what is past remains, and this shadow neutralizes the existence of what has been lost. The more we reflect and the more we live in memories and ideas, the more we become saturated with the experience of death. We overcome death precisely by granting it the status of an idea.

On this high plane of experience and reflection, death and time, immortality and memory dissolve into each other. The pathos of life is grounded in accepting fate as an opportunity to live in the idea. Just as the exigencies of life bring out the animal satisfactions and thus attach value to the threat of death, memory, with its clear knowledge of death, provides the opportunity to recognize and understand its nature in a realm of ideal being beyond existential transitoriness. From the simplest perception that, reaching into the past, intrudes on my consciousness up to the highest systematic concepts, which encompass large segments of reality simultaneously, there extends a web of essential meanings, untouched and untouchable by death. But the clear gradation of metaphysical vigor in the vegetable, animal, and human form, culminating in the idea of deathlessness, only seems to overcome its own principle of change and decay because ideal immortality is not a separate existence, independent of its base in nature. Eternity, timeless itself, is a vision in time, and we observe it only as such. Only when we confront time and death are we immortal in the sight of them. This immortality, however, is not fulfilled at a final moment; every real stretch of time is imbued with our death; and even in the tender emotions or the heartrending storms during which we, almost as otherworldly creatures, are overwhelmed by the passing and flowing of time, we remain beings of this world—no more than creatures living in the vision of death.

Thus *life* seems to be a word that, on the human level, designates the development of belonging to the deepest experience. To the mortal and immortal, the victor and the vanquished, both death and eternity can be merely destiny, its joys and sorrows to be endured. But Santayana's thinking is prejudiced in favor of immortality and essence. Even the fact that the only chapter that deals with both death and immortality is called "Ideal Immortality" points to an irrational tendency. In spite of the clearest analysis of the intertwining of experience and commonsense principles, this attitude assigns to essence, as the bearer of eternal being, a higher rung on the ladder than is given to the animal basis and the tendency to decline. The concept of essence was formulated as the residue when the positive existential predicates have been subtracted. If we speak of a separate realm of essence, a way of being different from existential being, the phrase has merely a graphic analogical meaning. Just as essence is not real, it cannot be the site of immortal or eternal life. In a subsequent work, *Scepticism and Animal Faith*, Santayana himself defined "immortality" more precisely as "whatever, having once arisen, never perishes."[45] He added to the definition his opinion that nothing exists that is immortal. He specifically rejects the essential yearning to believe in immortality, the opinion that, once born, the creature continues to live on forever, and that "eternal" being is thus related to something that has come into being. But if the essences are "eternal"— that is, never having at any time become—they merely exercise the ephemeral function of providing a vision of time *in* life and can never raise this life in a *real* way above itself into a sphere of deathlessness. In spite of the harshness of this analysis and comprehension, there remains the "ideal immortality." Just as experience invades speculation with the irrationality of identifying chaos and essence, so, in spite of a clearer understanding during lucid moments, longing coerces us toward *real* deliverance, toward awe and

45. George Santayana, *Scepticism and Animal Faith* (New York, 1923), 271.

a break with reality; for without death and time, not even our deliverance on earth would be possible.

The will to live at any cost, if only in an unreal state, leads to a doctrine of immortality in a *communitas spirituum*. Things indicated to be good in light of the ideal do not take their value from a transcendent realm; the reverse holds true: The ideals are formed on account of the necessities of their natural basis. In love, sexuality is idealized; in economic and political organizations, the necessities of physical preservation emerge; in friendship, a herd instinct appears; in art, a drive to activity (industrialism) manifests itself. Therefore the doctrine of good things cannot in fact provide everyone with a valid system of values and a prescription for action; nevertheless, it can demonstrate the natural tie between our longing and the origin of our wishes, so that rational control of our lives becomes possible. Since the values consist of natural objectives with a natural foundation, all attempts to lead a harmonious life share some points of reference and therefore serve as reciprocal examples. The closer an individual comes to realizing the natural ideals of his life, the more he serves as an example to those who come after him. He conquers time not only by his own rationality in his personal life; rather, to the extent that his perfection contributes to that of others, his life endures longer in a realm of reason, actualized in all those who are of the same mind. "By becoming the spectator and confessor of his own death and of universal mutation, he will have identified himself with what is spiritual in all spirits and masterful in all apprehensions; and so conceiving himself, he may truly feel and know that he is eternal."[46] Concerning this identification of the complete person with its most evanescent aspect, the mind—which we would do well to call "self-disembodiment," since the realm of essences is not an independent other beyond—the same objection can be raised that Santayana himself raises concerning the identification of personal life with the life of the species and the conquest of death with physical continuation in subsequent generations. Just as the individual self has to die, even if it puts up a brave front of species survival in the face of the deplorable business of personal death, so the self here is just

46. George Santayana, *Reason in Religion* (New York, 1905), 273, Vol. III of Santayana, *The Life of Reason*, 5 vols.

as much compelled to die, because in a realm of absolute reason, other minds take it up as a model. In the *Symposium* Plato developed a similar doctrine of procreation in beauty and its propagation as an analogy to natural engendering. His parallelism illuminates more clearly than does Santayana's philosophy the root of the concept of a community of saints and a belief in the reality of a duration of the timeless spirit, in the search for actual immortality in flight from the ephemeral nature of human life.

The idea of a *communitas spirituum* and collaboration in achieving the other's perfection contains a broader idea that, like chaos and ideal immortality, grows out of a bias in favor of eternity. The subtitle of *The Life of Reason* is *The Phases of Human Progress*. This concept, referring to a systematic evolution of the mind, was, in its general outlines, inspired by Hegel's phenomenology. In Santayana's system, however, this internal evolution strictly follows the construction of the sonnets, with their tripartite division into the journey of the self, the invasion of Eros by reality, and the turn toward the idea. The first volume corresponds to the first part, with its description of commonsense principles, the elementary structure of the self. The second opens with a chapter on love and a description of its function in the organization of a personal universe before broadening the discussion to include the problems of society's economic and political structure. It contains chapters on free (friendly) and ideal associations. The last three volumes deal with the world of religious, artistic, and scientific ideas. The development of the structure of the mind, however, has a meaning that goes beyond a systematic inventory of principles; it also sees in the sequence of layers the way to perfection, as exemplified by the doctrine of immortality. The stages of Olympian faith, survival in the species, and ideal immortality are sequentially ascending forms of such a belief in rational perfection. The refinement of the human mind to a stage of perfect rationality, where it is conscious of its natural conditions and finds in its harmonious ascendancy the joy of life, is cultivated throughout Santayana's thought, from his early mysticism and tendency to Platonic thinking to the rational ideas of essence and immortality. The community of the mind is also more than a group of coordinated individual perfections. It holds a place of special pathos in the system because the help the other receives from our actions means an increase of rationality in an objective realm of reason, an increasingly pure elevation in the mind, an overcoming of the animal basis of mind.

IV

Perhaps it is permissible to distinguish two phases in Santayana's thinking, since he, the preeminent observer of his own person, noted and remarked on them. They appear in temporal sequence, but not so as to replace one cluster of thoughts with another. The contrast is most appropriately described as a gentle, almost imperceptible shift in balancing thoughts present from the outset. The dominant idea remains to the end in the realm of essence, but its relationship to its basis undergoes changes. In the sonnets the journey to the realm of ideas takes off from the self as the only unmediated reality; the external world is incorporated into this world only with difficulty. It remains a subject matter of reflection and an occasion for internal growth rather than something in which the writer can immerse himself without embarrassment and of which he can become a part.

Ten years later, in *The Life of Reason*, reality has assumed enough weight to prevent it from leading to essence by the circuitous route of sublimation through a solipsistic self. Instead, in the second of the five volumes, *Reason in Society*, the self is seen as part of nature in its natural environment. The self and its environment, its sphere of action, have fused into the natural basis of the life of reason; therefore a new ground for the choice of values emerges. But even now no more metaphysical attention is paid to nature than is necessary to determine its function as the basis of reason. The actual philosophical analysis deals only with its shapes, its development, and its possible objectives. Nature is the point of departure; it can safely be neglected as soon as it has fulfilled its work of supplying the phases of the life of reason with the possibility of existence. The power resides in the developing movement through the sequence of increasingly pure formations, in a youthful joy at overcoming old forms in favor of new ones, when the stress is on overcoming rather than on the objective. Even in the realm of reason proper the movement of education through the *communitas spirituum* and the stream of higher culture through the model continues to predominate. The "life" of reason appears to be its romantic "adventure."

The later works in no way detract from the outline of this system, but they do not add to it. Nevertheless, they assign new proportions to its parts. The fervor of the early, painful experiences pales as the events retreat into the past. The ardor of the moment disappears, and what remains is "practical experience," growing heavier with the passage of time, sinking deeper into the person, no longer actual in daily emotional and intellectual experiences. Between the sonnets and *The Life of Reason* lies the first stage of the process of concentration—required by the extension of historical knowledge. In the study of ancient philosophy the conceptual elements join to form the foundation for the rational expression of "practical experience." Heraclitus represents the unmediated formless stream of things, the concept of eternal flow. Democritus' atomic theory adds the form and the ideal of universal comprehensibility. The Socratic art of the dialogue destroys any dogmatism and establishes the autonomy of the mind. The Platonic system, finally, completes the philosophy of ideal entities. Beyond these elements, Santayana held, there were no later additions to a philosophy of reason. Aristotle merely improved on the details and imparted consistency and precision to the parts of the system. The rest of classical philosophy represented a steady decline.

Among the modern thinkers, Santayana feels an affinity only with Spinoza, because he was the only philosopher among all those who wrote on philosophic topics. Schopenhauer seems to arouse Santayana's sympathy at least; occasionally Santayana calls him the only gentleman among German philosophers.

In the serene spheres of knowledge, individual figures are not ranked on principle, and what early experiences could not bring about—an unmediated, universally uniform acceptance of reality— becomes possible in the contemplative realm of culture. The self is increasingly drawn out of its isolation and learns to see the totality of the universe in its proper proportions, so that in *The Life of Reason*—if, for the moment, we overlook the decisive formation of the basic concepts through the solipsistic experience—the image of the self appears in the colors of movement and development only as a reflection of earlier partisanship. With the disappearance of this aftermath of experience, the amassed practical experience and culture is left to its own devices, and the elements are ordered according to their own weight.

In the 1922 edition of *The Life of Reason* Santayana reflected on this change in his philosophical stance. Only the attitude had changed, he explained, not the content of his doctrine. He had come to prefer other perspectives, in which the same objects appear with reverse distribution. What before was kept in the background—nature—had moved to the fore, and the life of reason had to cede its place at center stage. The interest in the change of intellectual stances had faded; the life of reason now appeared episodic, polyglot, interrupted, and uncertain. Not all phases of art, religion, and philosophy could be taken seriously simply because they took themselves seriously. Today they seem a little tragic as much as immature and, in that respect, comic; and he, Santayana, was less intent on choosing among them and judging them as if only one among them could be correct. None of this decline in intensity took possession of the mind absolutely, and the best that they could offer was not themselves but the way to the voice that speaks through them.

In *The Life of Reason* the figures nature and mind were real only as transformation; life was seen as steadily moving on from one to another. As the profusion of expressions loses its meaning, the two poles of development, with their intrinsic value, are more clearly perceived. Neither the one nor the other figure is of special importance; rather, the fundamental metaphysical relationship—by which the mind, in order to be real at all, cannot remain isolated but must become allied—continues to be the only subject matter worthy of attention. As faith in the final validity of any expression wanes, new values of reality are revealed. The position of tragic seriousness—suffering with the world—is replaced by irony. None of the formulations in philosophy, art, and religion has the right to assert its own absoluteness, and for this reason their struggles and demands are never completely real; they merely pretend, and the greatest attraction of life is the possibility it offers us of taking part in the game with dignity, conscious of its seriousness even while we enjoy the freedom that comes from knowing that the form in which it occurs is accidental and obligates us to nothing at all.

It is impossible to cite a precise date when Santayana's philosophical stance changed—especially since the change is not one of dogmatics but a shift of perspective that develops gradually and internally. I noted above that, left to its own devices, the bulk of practical experience and culture in Santayana's thought is driven to the new status through internal logic; but that description was not complete. Though the later form derives from the tradition of the earlier one and was intended to promote what is inherent in it, nevertheless, of all possible reformulations—for example, those that might dissolve the irrational conjunctions at the center of the constitution of concepts—he chose this one in particular, which leads from romantic sympathy and renunciation to irony. And that choice was determined by Santayana's character. The shaping influences of solipsism could not be eliminated, since they formed the deepest and most decisive level of the personality; training in history had explicated as much as was in its power. The only thing that could lead further was age. (Here analysis becomes difficult because the ordinary histories of philosophy at best show how doctrines replace each other within a philosopher's lifetime and how periods develop in a logical process; and modern psychological movements seem to have forgotten all about age in their concern with the special emotional complications of youth. For these reasons the expression must remain uncertain, leaving more to conjecture than to assertion.) The most tangible symptom of age was just mentioned—the elimination of the significance of the intermediate realm of figures and the simplification of the configured system into the dualism of nature and essence. But the changes that cannot be described exactly are of greater importance. Santayana's later works (*Winds of Doctrine; Scepticism and Animal Faith; Dialogues in Limbo*) suggest that whatever the younger man considered important was being discarded piecemeal. The disappearance of the realm of figures and its classification as "adventure" and "romance" are merely the outward signs of the process of disillusionment. The color and profusion of the world grow increasingly unreal when confronted by the simple lines of metaphysical reality that unfold in its diversity. The thinker who earlier lived on the surface sinks back into himself to the same degree as his life moves into the past. For the outsider this gradual retreat from experiences, practices, and culture into a ground that contains them all but lets them appear in the new guise of an ominous smile and earnestness—this process we call age—confers new dignity on an old doctrine, making it resemble a natural event that can merely be understood, no longer examined critically. Respect for the nature in which the thinker lives, and at the same time the irony with which he confronts this life, do not constitute a theory; rather, they have grown out of the intensely increasing reality of death. And the fortuitousness of the appearance of life grows increasingly pallid by comparison. The overwhelming reality of the natural dissolution of the self penetrates the shape of the mind as slowly it withdraws from the struggles of the living by presenting more clearly the senselessness of the fight in view of the inevitability of fate.

Though it is impossible to settle on a date, some symptoms point to the beginning of the process. *Dialogues in Limbo* contains the following passage:

> I confess that my own spirit is not very romantic, and yet at times it would gladly dehumanize itself and be merged now in infinitely fertile matter, now in clear and unruffled mind; and I am inclined to identify my being even now with these elements, in which I shall soon be lost, rather than with that odd creature which I call man, or that odder one which I call myself. Nothing can reconcile me to my personality save the knowledge that it is an absurd accident, that things pleasanter to think of exist in plenty, and that I may always retire from it into pure spirit with its impartial smile.[47]

A similar passage is found in *Three Philosophical Poets*: "Nationality being an irrational accident, like sex or complexion, a man's allegiance to his country must be conditional, at least if he is a philosopher."[48] This sentence, written in 1910, is already phrased in dualism and rejects the accidents of historical position, race, or sex as meaningless when compared with intellectual reality. But the grounds for this comparison is rational knowledge—the weight of the arguments has persuaded the philosopher to make this statement, whereas in 1925 the weight of life causes man to say what he sees, without arguments. The same thought, logically springing from the same dualistic construction of nature-mind, has on the one occasion its driving force in the thinker's intellectual will, and on the other in the unmediated experience of the coming dissolution in which all responsibilities disappear. The earlier passage may therefore be taken as representative for the transition from the area

47. George Santayana, *Dialogues in Limbo* (London, 1925), 154.
48. Santayana, *Three Philosophical Poets,* 85.

of learning to that of old age: the outlines of the later system are already noticeable, while the center of gravity of thinking still lies at the level of rational argument. That the idea of dualism does not appear here accidentally, without a systematic connection, is shown by the structure of the work that contains the passage. The book deals with three interpretations, of Lucretius, Dante, and Goethe —with the intention of showing three types of poets: Goethe as the poet of the unmediated profusion of life without limits; Lucretius as possessed of an insight into nature and the limits of human life; and Dante as exercising an intellectual mastery of the universe, judging the good and the bad, far removed from their natural foundations. To these forms of philosophical writing, each of which solves merely one part of the aesthetic problem, Santayana opposes his ideal of art as a form of human activity above the foundation of natural life, but freeing himself of his misery in his playful mastery. "Life has a margin of play which might grow broader, if the sustaining nucleus were more firmly established in the world." At present man has not yet overcome all the problems of physical survival, and not before the art of the "good work" can the art the art of "good play" arise.[49] "To play with nature and make it decorative, to play with the overtones of life and make them delightful, is a sort of art. It is the ultimate, the most artistic sort of art, but it will never be practiced successfully so long as the other sort of art is in a backward state; for if we do not know our environment, we shall mistake our dreams for a part of it, and so spoil our scene by making it fantastic, and our dreams by making them obligatory."[50] Both elements of the later philosophy are found together here; the dualism of a nature bound by laws and an uncommitted play is shown by the simple line of rational construction and the background of the double experience of necessity and intellectual freedom. Respect for reality and irony, both of which in combination describe his attitude toward reality, are here separated into two autonomous realms of mastery and use of the laws and of artistic play.

Three years later this transition has become fully conscious and completed. In a poem dated December, 1913, Santayana welcomed old age with its magic of greater distance from the petty cares of life and greater closeness to life's reality:

49. *Ibid.*, 214.
50. *Ibid.*

A Minuet
On Reaching the Age of Fifty

I.

Old Age, on tiptoe, lays her jewelled hand
Lightly in mine.—Come, tread a stately measure,
Most gracious partner, nobly poised and bland.
　　Ours be no boisterous pleasure,
But smiling conversation, with quick glance
And memories dancing lightlier than we dance,
　　Friends who a thousand joys
Divide and double, save one joy supreme
　　Which many a pang alloys.
　　Let wanton girls and boys
Cry over lovers' woes and broken toys.
Our waking life is sweeter than their dream.

II.

Dame Nature, with unwitting hand,
Has sparsely strewn the black abyss with lights
Minute, remote, and numberless. We stand
　　Measuring far depths and heights,
　　Arched over by a loving heaven,
Intangible and never to be scaled.
If we confess our sins, they are forgiven.
　　We triumph, if we know we failed.

. . . .

IV.

　　Hasten not; the feast will wait.
This is a master-night without a morrow.
No chill and haggard dawn, with after-sorrow,
　　Will snuff the spluttering candle out,
Or blanch the revellers homeward straggling late.
　　Before the rout
Wearies or wanes, will come a calmer trance.
Lulled by the poppied fragrance of this bower,
　　We'll cheat the lapsing hour,
And close our eyes, still smiling, on the dance.[51]

The same year—1913—saw publication of the volume *Winds of Doctrine,* a collection of six essays, not tightly enough interrelated but nevertheless with sufficient unity to be called an account of the questions of the day, from the newly won standpoint. The first essay, "The Intellectual Temper of the Age," gives an overview of

51. Santayana, *Poems,* 130–32.

these questions, while the following ones—"Modernism and Christianity"; three discussions of Bergson, Bertrand Russell, and Shelley
respectively; and the concluding lecture, "The Genteel Tradition
in American Philosophy"—elaborate the ideas enunciated in the
opening essay by pursuing concrete ramifications.

Santayana sees the essential attribute of the age in its "moral
confusion": Christian civilization has not yet disappeared, but another one has begun to take its place. We still understand the values
of religion; we are still educated in the tradition of our architecture,
of our sculpture, painting, literature, and music; we still have an
inclination for monarchies and aristocracies, for the order of our
local institutions, for class privilege, and for the authority of the
family. On the other hand, the all-encompassing dogmatism of
Christianity has been broken; the culture of the East, the pagan
past, the industrial socialism of the future raise their voices with
equal demands to be heard. Our whole life is saturated with the
slowly rising spirit of an emancipated, atheistic, international democracy. Other epochs, Santayana continues, had gone through
similar confusions, but the contrasts were represented by groups of
people who stood on one side or the other with their whole being.
Uniquely in our time—alongside such groups—confusion has permeated individuals also, causing the special conciliatory compro-
mising developments of the present. During the Reformation, religious affiliation compelled a clear position, while the religious
modernism of the present day is not clearly related to any dogma
and perhaps is altogether unrelated to Christianity. "A bishop may
be a modernist, a chemist may be a mystical theologian, a psychologist may be a believer in ghosts."[52] The students of natural
science are helplessly facing their own scientific machinery, unable
to judge the limits of their powers. Political liberalism leads to demands for social control over working hours, wages, and private
property. Philanthropic movements lead to the individual's absolute submission of body and mind to majority instincts. The maxim
of the "greatest good for the greatest number" is perverted into the
"greatest idleness of the largest possible population."[53] Internationalism and the idea of the brotherhood of man in practice grind to a

52. George Santayana, *Winds of Doctrine: Studies in Contemporary Opinion*
(1913; 2d ed. New York, 1926), 4.
53. *Ibid.*, 5.

halt before differences in skin color, and the political advocates of this conviction preach it only until a wave of national emotion sweeps them to act against both internationalism and human brotherhood.

This conflict can be attributed to the fact that the human mind is not an integrated organism that determines our actions; the reverse is true: only slowly do we become conscious of the philosophies that underlie our deeds, "so that (to speak geologically) our practice may be historic, our manners glacial, and our religion paleozoic. The ideals of the nineteenth century may be said to have been all belated; the age still yearned with Rousseau or speculated with Kant, while it moved with Darwin, Bismarck, and Nietzsche."[54] Past levels stretch into the present, and only occasional signs point to the future: such as the new love of nature, the importance of physical education, the new woman, and a position of amicable understanding regarding all the passions.

But philosophy seems still to be in complete disarray, without any signs that integration is beginning. Modern subjectivism began with Berkeley's and Hume's theory, according to which practical experience is not a discovery of transcendental things but is itself the only subject matter of knowledge. Kant developed this theory of knowledge further to the constitution of practical experience through the subjective transcendental categories. And the modern philosophical movement, in William James and Henri Bergson, transformed the necessary antecedents of practical experience into pieces of themselves and deprived ideas of any certainty and categorical necessity. For Bergson truth is given only in the duration of intuition; the slightest transcendence—for example, through memory—is already an illusion beyond the immediately felt reality, so that the last stage of epistemological subjectivism would be its decline into solipsism without any knowledge at all. But at this point the mysticism of intuitionism coincides with the commercial cult of vitality; what can raise intuition out of the immediate into the realm of infinite thought are conceptions of reality in the categories of change, growth, activity, creation. The movement of the immediate particular is seen (of course only as the result of inadequate analysis of the problem), while comprehensive unities disappear

54. *Ibid.,* 7.

from sight as unreal. William James destroyed the concept of consciousness in his essay "Does Consciousness Exist?" The individual mind must be removed from any epistemology that allows perception to arise from the object [*Gegenstand*]. Modern psychology submerges such feelings as anger and love in functions of the organism in the same way that ideas become fragments of material reality. This theoretical entwining of idea and matter, called pragmatism, sees science as an aid to industrialism and philosophy as a manner of thinking that explains away the differences between science and religious faith and thus serves life. The mind is touted as an unpatented lubricant, enabling the machine that is the human body to perform twice as well. But it would be unkind to ask this philosopher what is the value of industrialism and of life.

Santayana counters the philosophy of submergence in the stream of life with "ideal passion," situated at the center of the mind, whence it determines its own attitude and measures life by the "moral essences" beyond the immediate stream. Devotion to life at any price is somewhat degrading; any self-respecting mind is unwilling to live if it cannot do so according to its own rules. And if the mind has acquired some wisdom, it will in no case be too eagerly focused on life. Devotion to individual life, without direction or form, lacks the passion of the person, and consequently the directing seriousness and the cool sight for what is real are equally lacking, as is the willingness to cast off life because—aside from its form—it has no value. That is why today there are no great men. A great man, according to Santayana, need not distinguish himself by special virtue or by the correctness of his views; but he requires a steadfast mind and a decisive, clear character. If he is to dominate, something in him must be dominant. We sense his greatness in the clarity with which he expresses things potentially present in all of us but to which we cannot give shape. Greatness is spontaneous; simplicity, trust in one clear instinct are essential to it. In our time, in which no one has trust in himself or in reason, in which the word *dogmatic* is a reproach, great men cannot therefore flourish. Whatever ideal passion lives in the thinkers of our day, it is forced aside into the realms of nonexistence, of essence, and seeks satisfaction in unquestionable conquests in this area—Shelley's poetry, ideal anarchy without reality, is a type of remoteness from existence; Bertrand Russell's mathematical passion is another. Santayana characterizes his own stance in general through the feeling "that the sphere of what happens to exist is too alien and accidental to absorb all the play of a free mind, whose function, after it has come to clearness and made its peace with things, is to touch them with its own moral and intellectual light, and to exist for its own sake."[55]

In this last passage the motifs of Santayana's thinking merge: he began with the contemporary situation of the mind, characterized the period as a transition to new integration, and closed with the idea of the homelessness of the spirit in our time, just as earlier he had discovered his personal alienation and the alienation of the spirit in general in American society and in the sonnets the metaphysical homelessness of mind in this world. Homelessness in our time he sees here as congruent with the earliest experiences of primordial loneliness and the practical experience of growing older, since the quoted passage no longer refers exclusively to the contemporary situation but formulates the principle of "the spirit for its own sake" as an absolute; under no circumstance can the accident of existence completely occupy the mind, and the stance of contemplative distance will always be the most appropriate to the function of mind in the world. The late schema of the system—the polarities of existence and essence—completely dominates his thinking, and its absoluteness has absorbed the life of the homeless mind. The contrast between nature and reason becomes more rigid, and in his last systematic work (*Scepticism and Animal Faith*, 1923) Santayana's discourse removes his new attitude about the life of reason so far from its basis that the separate movement of mind stands at the center of attention, without reference to the origin of the movement. A chapter entitled "Literary Psychology" discusses "this impossible thing, the science of thought," which has taken the place of the art of thinking. Thought can be discovered only as animated. In the process of thinking I can always appeal to practical experience as corrective, but in no way can this experience or this thinking become the object [*Gegenstand*] of study: "It is invisible, past, nowhere. I can only surmise what it might have been, and rehearse it imaginatively in my own fancy. It is an object of literary psychology. The whole of British and German philosophy is merely

55. *Ibid.*, 24.

literature."[56] In its deepest significance it appeals to what a man tells himself when he looks over his adventures, repeats his perspectives, analyzes his thoughts, and raises assumptions about their origin:

> The universe is a novel, of which the ego is the hero. . . . The composition is perhaps pedantic, or jejune, or overloaded; but on the other hand it is sometimes most honest and appealing, like the autobiography of a saint; and taken as the confessions of a romantic scepticism trying to shake itself loose from the harness of convention and of words, it may have a great dramatic interest and profundity. But not one term, not one conclusion in it has the least scientific value, and it is only when this philosophy is good literature that it is good for anything.[57]

The final consequences are here drawn from the view of the nature of philosophy with which this discussion opened; if philosophy grows out of the convergence of the stream of things and a mature mind, and if all philosophers, speaking of the same object, see it only in different temperaments, languages, historical and social situations—then all these qualities are of special significance for an understanding of a particular philosophy, whereas material and speculative form in general are due indifferently to all philosophies. The rational level in them—necessary to logical construction—is least important for an understanding, so that rational criticism never touches what is the peculiar nature of any one philosophy. The transition from one system to another, the movement in philosophical thinking, therefore takes place not by logical analysis, though such an analysis might present itself externally as the form of the movement; rather, the dramatic unity of a philosophy, which is its ultimate basis but is never completely consistent, is broken down into elements in order to build new entities out of these elements, though the new units are no more rational than the old ones:

> But here, as elsewhere, myth is at work. We make a romance of our incoherence, and compose new unities in the effort to disentangle those we are accustomed to, and find their elements. Discourse is not a chemical compound; its past formations are not embedded in its present one. It is a life with much iteration in it, much recapitulation, as well as much hopeless loss and forgetfulness. . . . It is a living, a perpetual creation; and the very fatality that forces me, in conceiving

56. Santayana, *Scepticism and Animal Faith*, 254.
57. *Ibid.*

my own past or future, or the animation of nature at large, to imagine that object afresh, with my present vital resources and on the scale and in the style of my present discourse—this very fatality, I say, reveals to me the nature of discourse everywhere, that it is poetry.[58]

The history of philosophic thought is here divested of everything concerned, properly speaking, with its development, rationality, and history, and what remains is devotion to the pure movement in new notions of philosophical entities, to the conflict between the feeling of joy in constructing and pain at the inevitable loss of what has been won—devotion to life in the moment of transition. Philosophy as poetry continues to be "poetry of facts," but it is so independent of them that the philosopher finds movement in the realm of mind for its own sake more important than reference to facts. For the last time the infiltration of solipsistic experience places the weight of its irrational wisdom on the scale to tilt it in favor of the pole of essence.

What Santayana means here with the word *movement* becomes clearer when it is compared with his 1905 statements on philosophic method. At that time he considered that the point of departure for philosophizing was the "concretion in discourse," an essence that at its core contains the totality of the philosophical system, which totality releases itself by means of logical prediction but without any relation to new practical experiences. How such a "concretion" comes about was not clearly described, but since an entire philosophical system can be derived from it, it is sure to contain everything later found in it: the material, the speculative form, the personal experiences.

What was unique to this view was the break between the natural process, in which the concretion must have arisen, and the realm of essence into which it was suddenly transferred; from this point on, it only developed systematically out of itself what had accumulated in it during its past life. Various reasons could be adduced for the rigidity of the thought: the influence of Platonic studies and the indeterminate conception of a firm, tangible structure of the system; the coordination of mathematical objects [*Gegenstände*] and Platonic concepts in the realm of essence; rationalist belief that closed systems are actually possible. All these influences may have

58. *Ibid.*, 261.

been at work, and perhaps more than any of the others, a youthful will to system in response to the fear of chaos—a fear that becomes familiar only in later life, thus losing its terrors. It is surely true that philosophical systems contain structures that can be roughly described by the idea of concretion and its rational evolution; but in a large system the rigidity of logical coherence is no more than a line of order drawn through a field of points, where each point could as easily fit along another line. The elements in one system could be elements in another and still retain the aura of possibilities no matter where they are organized at the moment. And the concept of concretion does not do justice to even the rational structural component, since the concept ignores the situation where *several* construction lines may run parallel in *one* system or may cross each other, depending on the different systematic tendencies in the particular philosopher's thought. The total construction may be loosened by the variety of order it contains and by the essentially amorphous nature of the elements to such an extent that what becomes more important than a specific, clearly outlined thought is the total relationship of the strivings for order to the entirety of the chaos. The philosophy of "literary psychology" stands roughly on this level of the profusion of thought. This philosophy is connected to the theory of concretion through the circumstance that the movement of thought occurs in the same sphere as, previously, the evolution of the essence. But it goes far beyond the earlier inflexibility by absorbing the process in the realm of mind as the opposite pole to nature. The introduction of the concept of "dramatic unity" and the reshaping of such unities dissolves the firmness of the systematic connection in the fabric of tensions between the various centers for the construction of such unities. Thinking is no longer merely thinking "about something" but is primarily a reality with its own lawfulness, full of unexpected possibilities, a mystical wilderness whose path leads to God without requiring the mediation of the world of which this thinking speaks. Mind retains its position as the pole opposite to nature, the medium of knowledge, but at the same time its function is dialectical, and it is precisely the nature it confronts that has brought it out as part of itself, so that the mind's value is not exclusively in its transcendence but just as much in its being-in-itself.

The dialogue form in Santayana's last work, *Dialogues in Limbo*, is therefore more than a whim. It came about through more than mere pleasure in aesthetic perfection. These dialogues are supported by a vision of a world of thought in which every figure is only a station on the infinite journey of mind that pours itself into ever-new forms, hallowing each by its presence, coming to a final rest in none. Every attempt at ordering the world is backed by a person's will and is irrefutable as a natural event; no attempt is binding on any other. The lawfulness of seeing the world precisely in this way and in no other at the same time frees me of the obligation to accept other forms than my own. Since the world of a philosophic system is not a closed unity but is varied, the rays of order within it crossing and recrossing, with any choice among them being neither possible nor desirable, that world receives its best expression in the conversation of a multiplicity of people. But Santayana did not mean a conversation in a society in which—the ideal case—everyone is equally entitled to take part in constructing the conversation and everyone asserts his person only so far as is necessary to maintain a balance. Santayana excludes this possibility by moving his conversations to the underworld, where each speaker permanently has the form he attained at the apex of his earthly life—Democritus the wisdom of age, Alcibiades the abundance of youth—and can give expression to no other form. The technique of the Platonic dialogue is also assumed only superficially, in Dialogues 6–8, where Socrates is the principal speaker, because Santayana's dialogues are not intended to instruct; their purpose is just the opposite: to demonstrate that at heart "teaching" is not possible, since there is no such reality as *one* opinion, but that the realm of thought, in its profusion, heavy with chaos, contains many possibilities of world formation. The structure of his conversations is therefore precisely the reverse of instruction: Santayana himself, as the "stranger"—descending to the underworld from the realm of the living—confronts the principal speakers (Democritus, Socrates, Avicenna). But the dialogue is not persuasive; it merely demonstrates how far the speakers agree. The arguments as such do not engage one another on the basis of their rational weight alone; they are always tied to the center of the speaker's person, so that in spite of lively repartee back and forth, the persons touch each other only externally, never penetrating beneath the skin, and at the end of the dialogue they move apart again into separate loneliness. But their persons are not completely isolated from one another; the "stranger" is not a shade and therefore does not share the trait of inflexibility in his own person: he is the only one among them whose thinking is alive and has internal tension. He, the counterpart in each of the dialogues, holds the others together: the shades are only links in the life of his thinking, and as one after the other slides back into the isolation of his mind after the conversation with him, the "stranger" leaves behind possibilities of his own thinking—and yet he does not leave them entirely behind, since all of them interact in the cosmos of his thinking, representing the diversity of beginnings toward achieving a world order that meet inside him.

The ideas expressed in the *Dialogues* introduce nothing that was not contained in earlier works, if they are systematically examined. Even the construction follows the schema of the sonnets and *The Life of Reason:* nature (self), Dialogues 1–5; society, 6–8; mind, 9–10. What is new is the mythic vividness and the formulation of the basic thoughts. Some quotations will illustrate this most clearly.

The disillusion of old age (mentioned above) is made identical with the disillusion of Democritus' philosophy of nature:

> If there were no appearance there could be no opinion and no knowledge of truth; and true science in discounting appearance does not dismiss appearance, but sees substance through it; for the face of truth cannot be unveiled to mortals by any novelty or exchange of images, but only when in some deep and contrite moment of understanding the mask of ancient illusion becomes transparent altogether, loses its magic without losing its form, and turns into disillusion.[59]

> Reason draws upon mortals only in the last thought of all, when seeing that nothing is real save the atoms and the void (not as fancy may picture them but as they truly are), the mind crowns itself for the supreme sacrifice, and lays down all its flowering illusions upon the altar of the truth.[60]

On the philosophy of nothingness:

> The void is no less real than the atoms, and larger: it does not resist them, and while by their sport they diversify it, it does not change. So let your ship have an anchor laid deep in nothingness: on that anchor you may ride any storm without too much anxiety.[61]

59. Santayana, *Dialogues in Limbo,* 16.
60. *Ibid.,* 16.
61. *Ibid.,* 63.

The liturgy of the Autologos, the god of appearances:

> *Work, O work within me, divine Autologos, the miracle of mad-*
> *ness, that what exists not in nature may arise in thought.*
> *From the abyss of nothingness, draw what dream thou wilt.*
> *May it be a pure dream, perfect and entire. Why should one nothing*
> *devour another nothing in fear and hate?*
> *Suffer each day's sun to set in peace: slowly, after the pause of*
> *night, another will rise to lighten the morrow.*
> *As all suns pass before the face of darkness, and hide it awhile with*
> *their splendour, so on many-coloured wings thought flies through the*
> *silence, but the silence endures.*
> *Blessed be thy coming, Autologos, and more blessed thy going.*[62]

Though in these dialogues thinking relinquishes not the slightest amount of sharpness and at no time does the conceptual formula become imprecise, another world shines through the language. That world is the world of the origin of rational expression, but its order is determined through mythic images of space and color. There was occasion to note that the realm of the essences, equivalent to chaos, was moved to the top through the solipsistic experience and early training in Platonic images; it continues to occupy this place, but as concretion in discourse begins to dissolve, giving up its rigidity and absorbing the movement of thinking, the presentation of chaos becomes softer and darker, the less distinct field of forms spreads out side by side as the unstructured mass in the background. It becomes the abyss, the bottom of the ocean, an undefinable stream that carries away the thoughts of the words, an unquiet darkness before which the sparks of our thinking appear to be truth, a dark lap to which we return when we are dying, a symbol of the threatening disintegration that always reminds us that we lead a life with the blessing of nothingness.

The figures of life appear in doubtful distortion, as masks, before this darkness that, though emitting motion, is itself unmoving. One of the soliloquies mentions the "mask of the philosopher"; as long as the system continues to live tangibly in the mind of the creator, it seems to be nature itself; but when the work is completed and the expression firmly fixed, and other people can see it, it becomes a mask. Every slightest trait of the soul is immortalized, the same old passion and the same deaf thought speaks from the dis-

62. *Ibid.,* 64.

torted lips. The thinker himself finds it strange, as the verses of his youth might appear to an old man, or like the reflection in a mirror that, at first sight, one takes to be the image of a stranger.

More and more the ray of thinking focuses on the experience of "being foreign"; youthful solipsism was a dream, but the solitude of the soul in the misery of the world changes only its level of reality; the assimilation of practical experience through education, through isolation in a foreign language, through the special isolation of the mind in American society (Santayana speaks of "the vacuum which is created in America around distinction, and which keeps the national character there so true to type, so much on one lively level"),[63] through the experience of aging and the isolation of the mind in nature—none of these manages to destroy the fundamental attitude of the "stranger," and even as late as the writing of the *Dialogues* Santayana introduces himself as the "stranger" in the realm of the mind. Though this outsider contains many possibilities and therefore can feel affinities with many others and can understand them, finally he remains alone with himself. The volume of "soliloquies" closes with a piece on "Hermes, the All-Understanding," the "Figaro of Olympus," the widely traveled god, with lies and riddles in profusion, the lover of illusion, friend of all opportunities to play a trick on reality and to bare the questionability of its claims. Santayana speaks of him in this way:

> Here is a kindly god indeed, humane though superhuman, friendly though inviolate, who does not preach, who does not threaten, who does not lay new, absurd, or morose commands on our befuddled souls, but who unravels, who relieves, who shows us the innocence of the things we hated and the clearness of the things we frowned on or denied. He interprets us to the gods, and they accept us; he interprets us to one another, and we perceive that the foreigner, too, spoke a plain language: happy he if he was wise in his own tongue. It is for the divine herald alone to catch the meaning of all, without subduing his merry voice to any dialect of mortals. He mocks our stammerings and forgives them; and when we say anything to the purpose, and reach any goal which, however wantonly, we had proposed to ourselves, he applauds and immensely enjoys our little achievement; for it is inspired by him and like his own. May he be my guide: and not in this world only, in which the way before me seems to descend gently, quite straight and clear, towards an unruffled sea; but at the

63. George Santayana, *Soliloquies in England, and Later Soliloquies* (New York, 1922), 53.

frontiers of eternity let him receive my spirit, reconciling it, by his gracious greeting, to what had been its destiny. For he is the friend of the shades also, and makes the greatest interpretation of all, that of life into truth, translating the swift words of time into the painted language of eternity. That is for the dead; but for living men, whose feet must move forward whilst their eyes see only backward, he interprets the past to the future, for its guidance and ornament. Often, too, he bears news to his father and brothers in Olympus, concerning any joyful or beautiful thing that is done on earth, lest they should despise or forget it. In that fair inventory and chronicle of happiness let my love of him be remembered.[64]

64. *Ibid.*, 263–64.

3

A Formal Relationship
with Puritan Mysticism

Santayana's work presents greater difficulties to the interpreter
than do the philosophies of Peirce and James because Santayana's
person stands at the frontier where the European and the American
mind abut. The breadth of his education, the quality of his technique, and his skeptical stance bring him so close to the European
tradition that one may well interpret his system of the final form
(in *Scepticism and Animal Faith*) as a continuation of Hume's
skepticism in the intellectual landscape of the present. But the
same elements are open to a variety of interpretations. It is precisely the skepticism that might share Hume's coloration that
takes on a different sense when it is understood as arising from the
loneliness of the stranger in a society that differs from his in both
language and mind; it is a loneliness that is essentially much more
significant for the United States than for any European nation. In
Europe the "stranger" is an exceptional phenomenon, a curiosity;
until limits were set for immigration, the United States consisted
virtually entirely of strangers; the formation of the national character continued, but until the end of the nineteenth century, with
the huge waves of immigration from eastern and southern Europe,
America was more than a "country" in the European sense of a
geographic region, because the newly arrived masses, the strangers,
had no less influence on the formation of political institutions than
did the previously settled, assimilated population. In the United
States, the "foreigner" is a typical phenomenon, and standing-at-
the-border is every bit as much an American problem as is unquestioned membership in an older tradition. Horace Kallen says of Santayana, "If during his forty years in the United States he did not
become an American, he certainly ceased to be a European."[1]

1. Horace M. Kallen, *Culture and Democracy in the United States: Studies in
the Group Psychology of the American Peoples* (New York, 1924), 258.

In the conjunction of these partial perspectives it seems important to find a structure of thought that unites Peirce, James, and Santayana with one another and links all of them to an older form of Puritan mysticism. The kinship becomes obvious in the concepts of pure experience and essence. In earlier chapters the two were treated separately and connected only by the fact that Hodgson's theory of perception served as a comparative example for both. As against the constructive efforts of Brentano and Hodgson, who see the problem of dialectic and apparently rationalize it, Santayana's and James's attempts belong to a different type because both avoid dialectic. One of them, James, does so by giving the name of *pure experience* to the critical point of convergence between self and world without in any way explaining it. The other recognized the problem of convergence but, by naming it *essence*, overlooked the epistemological inconsistencies and turned to the metaphysical content of this concept. Both make it possible to disintegrate dialectic by the claim that both self and world are made of the same substance: essence is both the form of external reality and the subject matter of an intuition; pure experience is ordered in various functional connections that, though they are subject to different laws, otherwise consist of the same material. The two derive their intellectual genealogy from different sources. Santayana refers to Plato and Socrates; James to Locke, Berkeley, and Hume. But it is possible that the origins of both are to be found in Puritan mysticism. It is not difficult to find evidence in James's case. His book *Varieties of Religious Experience*, the whole of *The Will to Believe*, and pieces of religiophilosophic content scattered through all his work indicate his familiarity with the special forms of American religiosity, and always they serve him as the material, the "experience," on which his theory, and especially construction of the pluralistic world image, is based. For Santayana the influence of this tradition is given by his education at Harvard under James and Royce and later as their colleague.

The formal affinity exists unmediatedly between the theories of substantive unity of the self and the world in Peirce, James, and Santayana, and Puritan mysticism as espoused by Jonathan Edwards. Using this Puritanism as an intermediary, we can reconstruct a larger connection with the Calvinist-Puritan dogma. Dogma and mysticism meet in Puritanism in such a way that the dogmas of the calling and choice become the occasion for the mystical submersion and communion with God. The orthodox Puritan image of God assumes a rigid separation of God and world. God is "most absolute, working all things according to the counsel of his own immutable and most righteous will, for his own glory, . . . most just and terrible in his judgments, hating all sin, and who will by no means clean the guilty."[2] He is self-sufficient, independent of his creation; he does not derive his grandeur from it, but merely manifests it "in, by, unto, and upon them."[3] The image of God is the same as the image of the English king, the "dread sovereign Lord King James" of the Mayflower Compact, enthroned over his subjects and guiding the world according to his will and his mercy, without consideration of those over whom he rules and without their having rights of any kind whatsoever. Through his inscrutable ways, to vouchsafe his splendor, this God has preordained some people and some angels to receive eternal life, while others are destined to eternal death.[4] Their number is fixed and cannot be changed.[5] The choice of who is blessed is made according to God's eternal and unchangeable design, according to his mysterious ways and according to the pleasure of his will, from freely given mercy and love, without any effort by his creature or any power to move God through faith or good works or any other condition.[6] "The rest of mankind, God was pleased, according to the inscrutable counsel of his own will, whereby he extendeth or withholdeth mercy, as he pleaseth, for the glory of his Sovereign Power over his creatures, to pass by, and to ordain them to dishonour and wrath for their sin, to the praise of his glorious justice."[7]

The dogma of predestination in this strict form may well have introduced difficulties in the practice of religious life, because wherever it is mentioned, the dogma is accompanied by a highly inconsistent psychological excursus intended to wipe out the dis-

2. *Boston Platform* [*A Confession of Faith; Owned and Consented to by the Elders and Messengers of the Churches, Assembled at Boston in New-England, May 12, 1680*], quoted in Cotton Mather, *Magnalia Christi Americana; or, the Ecclesiastical History of New England, from its First Planting, in the year 1620, unto the Year of Our Lord 1696* (1702; rpr. 2 vols., Hartford, 1853), II, 184.
3. *Ibid.*, 184.
4. *Ibid.*, 185.
5. *Ibid.*
6. *Ibid.*
7. *Ibid.*

mal impression on the soul of anyone who takes it seriously.[8] The dogma alone could lead to the following reflection: Being one of the chosen or one of the damned is irrevocably predetermined; conduct in this life does not influence divine providence; therefore one can arrange one's conduct without regard to the future. But the *Boston Platform* prevents such reflections with the commandment: "The doctrine of this high mystery of predestination, must be handled with special prudence and care, that men attending the will of God revealed in his word, and yielding obedience thereunto, may from certainty of their effectual vocation be assured of their eternal election."[9] The doctrine of effective calling is inserted between the dogma of predestination and indifference to an unalterable destiny. Calvin saw indifference—or its opposite, corrosive doubt—as the work of the devil. The most dangerous temptation Satan brings to the faithful is doubt about election; it leads a wretched mortal to wish to penetrate the mysteries of divine wisdom; the calling—together with illumination, the inner calling—is the guarantee of salvation, which cannot deceive.[10] Calvin expressed a principle in this passage, as did the quoted paragraph of the *Boston Platform*. He mentions only temptation, and tersely names illumination as the pledge of being chosen. The practice of spiritual caution becomes broader and begins to indulge in longer comforts and persuasions intended to help the individual to overcome the unhappy condition of doubt. For example:

> When you look upon, and are terrified with all those amazing miseries which are lying upon all mankind in the curse, and see how woefully you yourselves are involved in it, and are thereupon beginning to sink into despondency, and be filled with a fearful expectation of this vengeance falling upon you; and begin to say: if the case be so, our hope is gone, and we are cut off for our part; now look forward, and see what good news the Gospel hath brought to a company of forlorn perishing sinners: See here, that there is a possibility of your escaping the damnation of hell, nay that there is a fair probability of it, since there is a new and living way opened, and discovered to you: say, that for all that hath befallen me, I may yet be saved; this is the hope that is set before you, labour to run into it. . . . Hope is the very life of endeavour; what men despair of they will never attempt to compass;

8. Based on passages in Rom. 8:24, 28–30.
9. *Boston Platform*, quoted in Mather, *Magnalia Christi Americana*, II, 185.
10. John Calvin, *Institutes of the Christian Religion*, ed. John Allen (1536; rpr. 2 vols., Philadelphia, 1921), II, 217–41.

but where there are any sparklings of hope, they will push men on to seek their help: and hope can gather spirits from the appearance of a meer [sic] possibility, a *Who knows?*[11]

Using the same probability calculation, James later defended his pluralistic universe; common sense—that is, the thinking and feeling of the average man—is less radical than philosophy and tolerates the idea that the world is not thoroughly rational and saved but that some part is lost; all that practical life requires is the chance of bliss. "No fact in human nature is more characteristic than its willingness to live on a chance. The existence of the chance makes the difference, as Edmund Gurney says, between a life of which the keynote is resignation and a life of which the keynote is hope."[12] If life's chances are turned into "live hypotheses," they affect human action, and the discontinuity of the expected contributes to his gain: to advancement, advantages, good positions. The phrases of the Puritan exhortation remain unchanged when they are applied to more worldly objectives instead of eternal salvation: a man's faith helps him to attain his goal. "His faith acts on the powers above him as a claim, and creates its own verification"[13]—no matter whether the verification is God's choice or the successful marketing of a new brand of car. The calling and its accompanying illumination lead man beyond himself and beyond worldly doubts to an immediate connection with Christ and to the assurance that flows from communion with the divine Being. Christ gave us communion with him when he was preaching the gospel and thus proved that God gave him to us to be one of us with all his good deeds.[14] Whosoever believes in him has passed from death to life (John 5:24). Salvation is "a mystical and spiritual union" of Christ and the believer that binds them most intimately.[15]

The movement of the Puritan soul typically runs from belief in the dogma of predestination through doubt about being one of the elect to the exhortations and persuasions of the probability calcu-

11. Samuel Willard, *A Compleat Body of Divinity* (Boston, 1726 [written 1687–1707]), 249.
12. William James, *The Varieties of Religious Experience: A Study in Human Nature* (New York, 1902), 526–27.
13. William James, *The Will to Believe, and Other Essays in Popular Philosophy* (New York, 1898), 24.
14. Calvin, *Institutes of the Christian Religion*, 182.
15. Willard, *Compleat Body of Divinity*, 428.

lation, to end in communion with Christ and the assurance of bliss. But the movement never deviates from orthodox belief; the personal relationship with Christ is only one constituent element of the total religious life that rests on predestination. In the first half of the eighteenth century, in the person of Jonathan Edwards, the separation of dogma from mysticism begins in the United States. According to the dogma God is an arbitrary, threatening, absolute Person who deals with believers as a king deals with his subjects, who can claim no rights. In mysticism the perilous superiority disappears, and the religious life is dissolved in the immediate relationship to divinity, in a sequence of ecstasies that do not require dogma. It seems, Edwards said, that intellectual understanding should not be sought in the new doctrinal knowledge or in unheard and indecipherable new ideas, since clearly the increase of knowledge in new, tangible thoughts is far different "from giving the Mind a new Taste or Relish of Beauty and Sweetness."[16] Mystical communion frees the individual from the pressure of uncertainty about his fate, for man does not confront God as a stranger, as a different kind of being; his intimate touch, the overflow of a greater Being that is nevertheless of the same kind, creates the warmth and serenity of life. James mentions the same contrast in speaking of the intimacy as opposed to the "foreignness" of theistic and idealistic philosophies. The dogma of predestination does not entirely disappear, but it shifts from the area of religion into a doctrine of national election. The Constitution of the United States, with the religious faith it demands of its citizens, has a function related to the earlier dogma, but the circle of the chosen is no longer indifferently taken from among all of humanity; here there can be no doubt that American citizens are the elect, definably belonging to a race distinct from the rest of humankind.[17] Within the community so described, however, no difference is made between the elect and the damned. The change from the political and religious ideology of absolutism to the democratic community of equals occurs in the eighteenth century and is completed in the religious move-

16. Jonathan Edwards, *A Treatise Concerning Religious Affections, in Three Parts* (Boston, 1746). [Voegelin provides no page number. However, the quoted passage can be found in *Religious Affections*, ed. John E. Smith (New Haven, 1959), 278, Vol. II of *The Works of Jonathan Edwards*, 9 vols. to date.]

17. On the dogma of national imperialism, see the chapter on John R. Commons herein.

ment of Congregationalism and Unitarianism in the early nine-teenth century. It begins with Edwards in the separation of mystical experiences from strict faith in the church, so that it was possible to say of his first philosophical efforts: "They mark also the begin-nings of constructive philosophy in America. To search the intel-lectual history of Edwards is to ask, not merely for the antecedents of a great thinker, but for the genealogy of a new race."[18]

In Edwards' works and his life, dogma and mysticism were sep-arated only in practice, not in principle. His sermons are the best-known example of the excesses in which the Puritan imagination indulged when painting the torments of hell and eternal damna-tion, endlessly dwelling on doubt about the certainty of elected-ness. His ministry and his official statements are replete with the strictest dogma. Compared to these, his mystical and philosophical works are so unconnected that it is almost impossible to use Cal-vinism to understand the philosophy or the philosophy to under-stand the dogma unless we note that the intensity of the mysticism, addicted to redemption, parallels the force of the doubt about being one of the elect. F. J. E. Woodbridge believes that Edwards would have completed the separation openly and consciously had he not died before he could do so.[19] His posthumous works "Concerning the End for which God Created the World" and "The Nature of True Virtue" carry mystical pantheism so far that the break with dogma cannot possibly be ignored. Woodbridge believes that they were not published during their author's lifetime because Edwards saw himself compelled to revise his whole life. It is Woodbridge's opinion that these last works should be considered not as the final formulation of Edwards' early theories, as is usually done, but rather as "works of promise."[20] This view has much to recommend it, but it calls for an elaboration that is more precise. When set

18. John H. MacCracken, "The Sources of Jonathan Edwards' Idealism," *Philo-sophical Review*, XI (1902), 26.

19. F. J .E. Woodbridge, "Jonathan Edwards," *Philosophical Review*, XIII (1904), 400.

20. On dualism, see Frank B. Sandborn, "The Puritanic Philosophy and Jonathan Edwards," *Journal of Speculative Philosophy*, XVII (1883) 410. "The surprising fact is, that, with these remarkable powers of analysis and reasoning, which would have made Edwards a match for Hume on his own ground, and with this demand of his age to be fed on that sort of food, the Puritan minister yet stood resolutely by his chosen task of preaching Christianity as he understood it to the poor Indians of Stockbridge, and the anxious saints and sinners of New England wherever he en-countered them."

against the works that immediately preceded them, these last two works very nearly assume a clarity of language and come close to finding the form of a dogma that cannot be reconciled with Calvinism. But conceptually they are less clear than Edwards' youthful writings, where he postulated a similar pantheism, and their tone is far less resolute. Systematically, the last writings are far less "works of promise" than the first. If they nevertheless seem weightier—by sketching the beginnings of a new dogma and theology—than the early works, which are expressed in a much more traditional philosophical terminology, the reason can be found in a change of Edwards' intellectual stance, whose principle has been indicated above. In the early works the mystical experiences and the philosophy based on them are kept within the bounds of typical movement from belief in predestination to the personal assurance of being one of the elect. In the late works this connection seems to have been severed: the pantheistic mysticism has become independent and is no longer a constituent element in the Puritan's life of the soul. Rather, he has given up the core of Calvinist dogma (though not its words) and finds the center of religious life in the connection to God. It is no longer Christ who mediates the certainty of divine election; rather, an indivisible God himself radiates to the world and enfolds us as part of himself. Mysticism, which was a partial phenomenon in the total structure of Calvinist theology, has separated from this context and has become the source of a new religiosity independent of the European forms.

The connection with strict faith and at the same time the occasions to mysticism can be seen most clearly in Edwards' middle works. His treatise on the religious affections, written in 1746, opens with an explication of the important question that is posed to humanity and each individual: "Wherein do lie the distinguishing notes of that virtue and holiness, that is acceptable in the sight of God?"[21] The question is based on the uncertainty of election, but the very next sentence indicates Edwards' independence of dogma because the question is declared to be equivalent to another: What is the nature of true religion? Such a question is entirely independent of dogmatics. Whatever form the question takes, everyone's efforts must deal with clearly understanding and with dis-

21. Edwards, *Treatise Concerning Religious Affections,* in *Religious Affections,* ed. Smith, 84 ("Preface").

tinguishing "in what true religion consists."[22] And the treatise is the attempt at an empirical and very careful description of the symptoms that accompany a mystical experience—based on Edwards' personal experiences and occurrences during the revivals that had taken place a short time earlier in New England. He assures his readers, for example, that a feeling of grace is not heat without light; rather, illumination gives the faithful a better understanding of divine things, which lasts past the moment.[23] He describes the bodily sensations during an affection: the soul can be aroused in such a lively and strong way that the circulation of the blood and "the animal spirits" change noticeably; often physical sensations arise, especially around the heart and the internal organs, because of which the heart is generally declared to be the seat of the emotions. There is a detailed description of the techniques of prayer, song, sacraments, and sermons, intended to achieve a "conformity" of the human soul and God.[24] But in spite of this empirical mysticism, there are also reservations, which establish the connection with dogma. Occasionally, in discussing the spiritual communion of saints with God, for example, Edwards writes:

> So the Saints are said to live by Christ living in them. . . . The light of the Sun of Righteousness don't [sic] only shine upon them, but is so communicated to them that they shine also, and become little images of that sun which shines upon them; the sap of the true vine is not only conveyed into them, as the sap of a tree may be conveyed into a vessel, but is conveyed as sap is from a tree into one of its living branches, where it becomes a principle of life. The Spirit of God being thus communicated and united to the saints, they are from thence properly denominated from it, and are called spiritual.[25]

But the attempt to describe as fervently as possible God's union with the saints is followed by the reservation that the saints nevertheless do not participate in God's essence because they are not deified with God or christed with Christ, as the revolting and blasphemous language of some heretics claims; the saints merely take part in God's fullness in the sense of Eph. 3:17–19 and John 1:16.[26]

22. *Ibid.*, 99 ("Preface").
23. *Ibid.*, 343.
24. *Ibid.*, 114–16.
25. *Ibid.*, 200–201.
26. *Ibid.*, 203. Eph. 3:17–19: "That Christ may dwell in your hearts by faith; that ye, being rooted and grounded in love, / May be able to comprehend with all saints what *is* the breadth, and length, and depth, and height; / And to know the love of

And yet on the next page we find the statement that God makes "the Creature Partaker of the divine Nature."[27]

The passages I have cited show that the experiences of the community with God had their origin in Calvinist problems and that Edwards does not want to lose the connection with the dogma. But they also show the tendency of the mystical experiences to establish a self-sufficient "true religion" without regard to any official theology. This tendency is most evident in Edwards' diary.[28] It details the history of his certainty of a vocation and thus also begins with the dogma of predestination:

> From my childhood up, my mind had been full of objections against the doctrine of God's sovereignty, in choosing whom he would to eternal life; and rejecting whom he pleased. . . . It used to appear like a horrible doctrine to me. But I remember the time very well when I seemed to be convinced, and fully satisfied, as to this sovereignty of God, and his justice in thus eternally disposing of men, according to his sovereign pleasure. But I never could give an account how, or by what means, I was thus convinced, not in the least imagining at the time, nor a long time after, that there was any extraordinary influence of God's Spirit in it.[29]

The first occasion when the soul was filled with "inward, sweet delight in God and divine things" resulted from reading a scriptural passage (1 Tim. 1:17): "As I read these words, there came into my soul and was as it were diffused through it, a sense of the glory of the Divine Being."[30] Experiences of this sort repeated themselves, became more intense, and shed their glow over his entire life and the world:

> After this, my sense of divine things gradually increased, and became more and more lively, and had more of that inward sweetness. The appearance of every thing was altered; there seemed to be, as it were, a calm, sweet cast or appearance of divine glory, in almost every thing. God's excellency, his wisdom, his purity, and love, seemed to appear in every thing; in the sun, moon, and stars; in the clouds and

---

Christ, which passeth knowledge, that ye might be filled with all the fulness of God." John 1:16: "And of his fulness have all we received, and grace for grace."

27. Edwards, *Treatise Concerning Religious Affections,* in *Religious Affections,* ed. Smith, 203.

28. Sereno E. Dwight, ed., *Memoirs of Jonathan Edwards, A.M.: The Works of Jonathan Edwards in Two Volumes* (London, 1840).

29. *Ibid.,* I, liv.

30. *Ibid.,* lv.

blue sky; in the grass, flowers, and trees; in the water and all nature; which used greatly to fix my mind. I often used to sit and view the moon for a long time; and in the day, spent much time in viewing the clouds and sky, to behold the sweet glory of God in these things; in the mean time singing forth, with a low voice, my contemplations of the Creator and Redeemer. . . . I had vehement longings of soul after God and Christ, and after more holiness, wherewith my heart seemed to be full, and ready to break.[31]

The dogma is forgotten here, and the narration turns into the story of the community's experience of God, expressed in the terms of a naïve, unreflecting pantheism that sees the glory of God in all worldly phenomena. It leads on to the experience of holiness and a most fervent longing for God:

Holiness, as I then wrote down some of my contemplations on it, appeared to me to be of a sweet, pleasant, charming, serene, calm nature; which brought an inexpressible purity, brightness, peacefulness, and ravishment to the soul. In other words, that it made the soul like a field or garden of God, with all manner of pleasant flowers; all pleasant, delightful, and undisturbed; enjoying a sweet calm, and the gently vivifying beams of the sun. The soul of a true Christian, as I then wrote my meditations, appeared like such a little white flower as we see in the spring of the year; low, and humble on the ground, opening its bosom, to receive the pleasant beams of the sun's glory; rejoicing, as it were, in a calm rapture; diffusing around a sweet fragrancy; standing peacefully and lovingly, in the midst of other flowers round about; all in like manner opening their bosoms, to drink in the light of the sun. There was no part of creature-holiness, that I had so great a sense of its loveliness, as humility, brokenness of heart, and poverty of spirit; and there was nothing that I so earnestly longed for. My heart panted after this—to lie low before God, as in the dust; that I might be nothing, and that God might be *all*, that I might become as a little child.[32]

It would be extremely hard to decide just how far such a report of the emotion of mystical experiences may be translated into concepts from which conclusions regarding any systematic connections can be drawn. And it is only with the reservation of very possible error that we may dare to interpret more closely some of the images in Edwards' expression and to point to their probable intellectual links with systematic thought. The first experience Ed-

31. *Ibid.*
32. *Ibid.*, lvi.

wards discusses occurred without his becoming properly conscious that something extraordinary had happened. But its content, submission to God's sovereignty, nevertheless seems to have determined his later religious life, since he repeatedly—most especially in the last description—seeks out images meant to express his complete submission, his obliteration, his being-a-child; and it is possible that the dogma of predestination, with its idea of a powerful, strict God, continues into the symbolism of ecstasy that is no longer connected to the dogma as such. It is juxtaposed to observations of a pantheistic nature, which see the glory of God everywhere in nature, and the image of the modest flower among others, which with its calm peace of rapture in community is no longer even slightly reminiscent of the threat of election and the possibility of damnation. This new area of religious life, which reveals traces of its origins only dimly in a few images, the mysticism that allows the opportunity for structuring a world view independent of orthodox belief—these might be the ground in which to find the beginnings of a philosophical system that has been captured only in short essays, sketches, and notes. The most significant coherent piece is contained in "Natural Philosophy" under the title "On Being."[33] Without any additional introduction it begins with the

33. For the dating of the early writings, see H. Norman Gardiner, *Selected Sermons of Jonathan Edwards* (New York, 1904), viii:

He [Edwards] entered the Collegiate School of Connecticut in Saybrook—afterwards Yale College—at thirteen, and in 1720, shortly before his seventeenth birthday, graduated at New Haven with the valedictory. In his sophomore year he made the acquaintance of Locke's *Essay Concerning Human Understanding*—a work which left a permanent impress on his thinking. . . . Under its influence he began a series of *Notes on the Mind*, with a view to writing a comprehensive treatise on mental philosophy. He also began, possibly somewhat later, a series of notes on natural science, with reference to a similar work on natural philosophy. It is in these early writings that we find the outlines of an idealistic theory which resembles, but was probably not at all derived from, that of Berkeley, and seems to have remained a determining factor in his speculations to the last.

Parts of "Notes on the Mind" and "On Natural Science" are reprinted in Dwight's biography. But Dwight allowed himself changes in sentence structure, spelling, punctuation, and even words, so that the original is severely distorted. No critical edition of Edwards' works exists. Individual writings, especially the important "On Being," are found in a critical new edition in a dissertation by Egbert C. Smyth, "Some Early Writings on Jonathan Edwards, A.D. 1714–1716," *Proceedings of the American Antiquarian Society*, October, 1895, new series, X (1896) [?—Eds.], 212–47. The treatise includes, in facsimile, sections of "The Soul" and "On Being," and reprints of the manuscripts with exact versions of spellings. By comparison of manuscripts, the date of 1717 or 1718 is assigned to "On Being." Because the dissertation

assurance that something must be eternal—a something that besides being eternal is also infinite and omnipresent, because there is nothing the mind cannot imagine. Edwards further assures the reader that the infinite and omnipresent Something cannot be solid. The necessary eternal Something must be space, since that is the only thing that cannot be ignored by mental experiments: "It is self-evident, I believe, to every man, that space is necessary, eternal, infinite, and omnipresent. But I had as good speak plain: I have already said as much as that space is God."[34] The surprising identification seems very natural to Edwards, since it goes against reason to think that something that is eternal might exist without anyone's being conscious of it. It is even impossible that anything should exist without someone thinking about it, for nothing exists except in a fashioned or unfashioned consciousness.[35] If a space were closed off in such a way that no one could see inside, its content, as not-perceived, would lose its existence unless it continued to live in God's consciousness. From this it follows that conscious beings are the only ones that have true being and actual substance, since the existence of all other things depends on them.

This is as far as "On Being" goes. It does not develop the thoughts

is not readily available, I refer to the reissue of "On Being" in I. Woodbridge Riley, *American Philosophy: The Early Schools* (New York, 1907), 130ff.

There is another fragmentary edition of Edwards' early writings, *"Selections from the Unpublished Writings of Jonathan Edwards, of America.* Edited from the original MSS., with Facsimiles and an Introduction, by the Rev. Alexander B. Grossart, Kinross. Three hundred copies. Printed for private circulation (1865)." There are said to be two copies in the United States; I was never able to see one.

[The manuscript "Natural Philosophy" contains the essay "Of Being" and several other essays, notes, and propositions. "Of Being" can be found in Jonathan Edwards, *Scientific and Philosophical Writings,* ed. Wallace E. Anderson (New Haven, 1980), 202–207, Vol. VI of *The Works of Jonathan Edwards,* 9 vols. to date. For unknown reasons—perhaps following Smyth or Riley—Voegelin consistently gives the essay's title as "On Being."]

34. [Jonathan Edwards, "Of Being," in Edwards, *Scientific and Philosophical Writings,* ed. Anderson, 203.]

35. This, at least, is how I read the text: "Yea it is really impossible it should be that Anything should bee and nothing know it then you'll say if it be so it is because nothing has Any existence any where else but in consciousness no certainly no certainly no where else but either in Created or uncreated Consciousness." [This quotation is rendered *ibid.,* 204, as "Yea, it is really impossible it should be, that anything should be, and nothing know of it. Then you'll say, if it be so, it is because nothing has any existence anywhere else but in consciousness. No, certainly, nowhere else, but either in created or uncreated consciouness." The repetition of *no certainly* in the German edition occurs at the end of one line and the beginning of the next and probably represents a printer's error.]

into a system; it is satisfied with setting up the thesis, in a tone of certainty resembling Peirce's later writing. The content concerns itself with the same problem as other American essays: the identity of the materials of thought and being.

All Edwards' further comments and notes serve merely to solidify and explain some of the points touched on in "On Being." One extensive passage of this sort is found in "Notes on the Mind."[36] Edwards wishes to protect himself against misunderstandings that might arise from his statement that the world exists only in consciousness. The statement does not intend to situate the world physically in a brain, because the human body and the brain itself are merely conceptions; spatial extension itself is not a reality, it is a quality of imagery. All things we perceive are therefore really in the place where they seem to be, not because the place has its own reality, independent of consciousness, but because spatial relations are relations within our perceptual consciousness. Our consciousness cannot thus be located in a specific place in the world. Instead, our perceptions are the things themselves, to which we give existence through our consciousness. Our consciousness of things is congruent with them, being equally extended in space and of the same material—just as Peirce's and James's theories claim concerning the "subjective extension" of feelings and the material identity of consciousness and world. The theory of knowledge therefore concludes that truth is the consistency and agreement of our ideas with God's ideas.[37] "Hence we see in how strict a sense it may be said, that God is truth itself."[38] If we, as humans, still harbor any doubts, and if we require arguments in order to ascertain the truth, that is only because of the narrow field of vision of our knowledge. If we could see all ideas at the same time, there would be no error and no questions. For God, therefore, everything is evident.

We can see the kinship of this idealism with that of Peirce and with James's radical empiricism. Because the problems were interrelated, even the details of the theory led to the same solutions. Remembering Peirce's divination theory, we can compare it with the following passage by Edwards:

36. Jonathan Edwards, "Notes on the Mind," in Edwards, *Scientific and Philosophical Writings*, ed. Anderson, 368–69.
37. *Ibid.*, 341–42.
38. [*Ibid.*, 342.]

The mere exertion of a new thought is a certain proof of a God; for certainly there is something that immediately produces and upholds that thought. There is a new thing, and there is a necessity of a cause. It is not antecedent thoughts, for they are vanished and gone; they are past; and what is past is not. Do we say, It is the substance of the soul; if we mean that there is some substance besides that thought, that brings that thought forth; if it be God, I acknowledge it; but if there be meant something else that has no properties, it seems to me absurd.[39]

It is hard to imagine a more complete agreement between two philosophers. The passage demonstrates more trenchantly than any other the independence of the American history of ideas from that of Europe. Jonathan Edwards' ideas are so close to Berkeley's that for a long time it was believed that plagiarism was at work,[40] but

39. Quoted in a MS by Egbert C. Smyth, "Jonathan Edwards' Idealism," *American Journal of Theology*, I (1897), 957.

40. For the kinship between Berkeley's and Edwards' philosophies, see H. N. Gardiner, "The Early Idealism of Jonathan Edwards," *Philosophical Review*, IX (1900), 589:

Berkeley's early doctrine is . . . that the esse of material things consists in their percipi. Now it is no doubt true that in urging this doctrine his main interest was to enforce the truth of the divine being and action, and the substantiality and causality of spirit. That spirit is alone substantial and causal is indeed the real Berkeleyan idealism. But the relation of things sensible to spirits and especially to the mind of God is hardly considered by Berkeley in his early writings; he contents himself with the thought that God imprints the ideas of material things on our senses in a fixed order. To the objection that material things when not actually perceived by us must be nonexistent, he can only reply "that there may be some other spirit that perceives them though we do not" (*Principles*, § 48). The esse of things is thus their percipi. Later in life Berkeley went beyond this, and taught that the esse of things is not their percipi, but their concipi, that the world in its deepest truth is a divine order eternally existing in the mind of God. But it is this doctrine which, along with the phenomenalism which he shares with Berkeley, is the characteristic doctrine of Jonathan Edwards. It is implied in his conception of the real, as distinguished from the nominal, essence, and in his conception of truth as the agreement of our ideas with the ideas of God, and it is definitely expressed in various passages, best perhaps in his formulation of his idealism . . . : "That which truly is the substance of all bodies is the infinitely exact and precise and stable Idea in God's mind, together with the stable Will that the same shall be gradually communicated to us and to other minds according to certain fixed and established methods and laws." The phenomenalism in Edwards is relatively subordinate. But similar ideas appear at all prominently in Berkeley only in *Siris*, which was not published till 1744.

Discussing possible influences on Edwards, Gardiner suggests Descartes, *Meditations*; John Norris, *Theory of the Ideal or Intelligible World*; Collier, *Clavis Universalis*.

Egbert C. Smyth has virtually established the fact that Edwards was not familiar with Berkeley's work when he wrote his philosophical fragments. See Smyth, "The

Berkeley's ideas were picked up and posthumously given meaning in Hume's skepticism and were a preliminary stage toward the closed self. The elaboration of this idea became the work of English philosophy following Reid and the Scottish school. In the United States the same ideas did not follow any skeptical tradition but worked with the "openness" of the self; the naïve juxtaposition of God and man remains intact. The theory of knowledge does not suffer from dialectics; but for Edwards the problems are exhausted in the agreement of thinking with the ideas of God; nor is it much more complicated for Santayana. The reservoir of new ideas is called God by Peirce and James; Santayana calls it chaos and places in it all the essences that might possibly be both the subject matter of intuition and the form of reality in each case.

The systematic structural relationship is indisputable. With some reservations, on the other hand, a claim was raised concerning the relation between philosophical idealism and Edwards' mystic ecstasies. To support this position, a few further passages from the posthumous dissertation, dealing with the purpose of the creation of the world, will be cited here. This work does not use philosophic terminology, so foreign to the style of the diary, so that it is difficult to see the connection; instead, it points backward to theological debates that combine a precise conceptual language with a pantheistic mysticism to such an extent that no doubt can remain concerning the unity of meaning of the diaries and idealist philosophy and the body of Edwards' work. The theology of the dissertation takes the form of a theory of creation by emanation.[41]

'New Philosophy' Against Which Students at Yale College Were Warned in 1714," *Proceedings of the American Antiquarian Society*, n.s., XI (1898), 176, 251–52. The "new philosophy," which had been assumed to be Berkeley's, was in fact that of Descartes, Bayle, Locke, and Newton.

41. Jonathan Edwards, "Dissertation on the End for Which God Created the World," in Edwards, *Ethical Writings*, ed. Paul Ramsey (New Haven, 1989), vol. VIII of *The Works of Jonathan Edwards*, 9 vols. to date.

On pantheistic elements in Edwards' work, see Alexander V. G. Allen, *Jonathan Edwards* (Boston and New York, 1889), 12:

In his treatment of excellence Edwards appears as in agreement with Plato's conception of God as the idea of the good. There is also in his tone a still stronger reminder of Spinoza,—the doctrine of the one substance, of which the universe is the manifestation. In some respects also he approximates in these "Notes on the Mind" to the famous doctrine of Malebranche that we see all things in God; as when it is emphatically asserted that "the universe exists only in the mind of God." Of the inspiration which prophets had, it is remarked it was in a sense intuitive. "The prophet, in the thing which he sees, has a

Since God is imbued with an infinite profusion of the possible good, of perfection and happiness, it appears valuable that this profusion pours outward and flows into the world. "Such an emanation of good is, in some sense, a *multiplication* of it. So far as the stream may be looked upon as any thing besides the fountain, so far it may be looked on as an *increase* of good."[42] It therefore seems appropriate that the infinite source of holiness, moral excellency, and beauty would open and communicate its sanctity; that its profusion of bliss and happiness would pour out in a rich stream like the rays of a sun. It may therefore be assumed that God's purpose in creating the world was the glorious emanation of this abundance on the good. But it would be unseemly to assume that God wished to communicate himself to the creation, because such an assumption would presuppose an existence different from his own. Thus, God's tendency to emanation was not a tendency toward a world that had already been in existence but a tendency to himself as something widespread.[43] But the tendency to himself is not a limited selfishness, such as might be opposed to altruistic benevolence. The divine being is being in general, encompassing universal existence. In his benevolence toward his creation, God cannot stretch out his heart in such a way that creatures originally outside it may be gathered in. Rather, he broadens himself, as it were, and instead of finding objects for his benevolence, he creates them. He does not take into himself anything that is foreign, but by pouring out himself and expressing himself in the creatures of the world, he himself is blessed within them.[44] The goal of world history is an ever more perfect emanation of God in the world, by his making it ever more like himself. "The heart is drawn nearer and nearer to God, and the union with him becomes more firm and close: and, at the same time, the creature comes more and more *conformed* to God."[45]

Here we find several contradictory elements. The efforts to let the entire world appear as emanations of the godhead lead to di-

clear view of its perfect agreement with the excellencies of the divine nature. All the Deity appears in the thing, and in everything pertaining to it. . . . He perceives as immediately that God is there as we perceive one another's presence when we are talking face to face."
42. Edwards, *Works*, III, 20.
43. *Ibid.*
44. *Ibid.*, 38.
45. *Ibid.*, 26.

alectical formulations that are hardly distinguishable from the theory of a world spirit who is conscious of himself. But Edwards draws no systematic conclusions from these thoughts. On the contrary, when on occasion he remarks that "those elect creatures" must be seen as the purpose of the entire creation, for they are truly one with God, he is looking for a way back to the doctrine of predestination. Thus the emanation does not encompass the whole world; in the theology of pantheism the forms of the orthodox dogma recur in a paler form, and for Edwards a remnant of imperfection and evil remains in the world. And it is only from a historical process that we may expect adaptation to God and the victory of the good: but that is in every feature the pluralistic universe James constructed and Peirce sketched out with his principle of evolutionary love. And even Santayana's philosophy believes in the historical growth of reason in the world, so that the original Calvinist dogma is preserved in these pale forms of rational skepticism. In all these worlds a remnant of evil remains, and it can be conquered only in a temporal flow through cultivation of what is good or reasonable, with the help of the treasure buried in God or chaos.

4

Anglo-American Analytic Jurisprudence

I. English Analytic Jurisprudence

It took until the 1870s and 1880s for the history of analytical jurisprudence in England to take on sufficient weight to allow a wide
range of problems to become clear. The long intervals between the
analytic efforts of Hobbes, Jeremy Bentham, and John Austin were
followed by the Supreme Court of Judicature Act of 1875 and the
abolition of the civil rights doctrines in common law, which conflicted with the jurisdiction of the Courts of Equity; at long last
there was an opportunity to deal more directly with what might be
the systematic and fundamental characteristics of the law—though
no explicit idea of the nature of such characteristics or principles
existed. Because of the lack of clarity, discussion of a wide range of
problems and the tradition of handling them must also be specified
in some detail. It is not so much a conscious growth of clearly
outlined questions into an internal logic as it is a series of attempts
to highlight a mass of problems from ever-new and immediate
standpoints, without these problems ever being mastered to the
point where a detached overview would become possible. This particular form of scholarly development may explain why later works
ignore or completely overwhelm the early brilliant analyses—analyses that in their detail exhibit such superior acumen that they are
the equals of the best modern analytic schools. These efforts, fairly
independent of each other, do not, however, diverge completely
because (1) the identity of the subject matter compels a certain
uniformity of statements concerning it and (2) the schema and
model of Austin's treatment of the problems informs them all.

Austin's lectures on jurisprudence bear the subtitle "The Philosophy of Positive Law,"[1] by which he states the two basic problems treated in the work: the definition of "positive law" and the "philosophical" methods used in the treatment of it. Speaking of method, Austin described "general jurisprudence" as a science concerned with describing those principles, concepts, and distinctions that are common to all legal systems; and this definition refers only to those legal systems that are more mature, more thoroughly worked out, because this maturity and thoroughness renders them especially well suited for instruction.[2] The examples of common necessary concepts Austin cites are: duty, right, liberty, injustice, punishment, reparation, and their relationship to the concepts of a legal system, sovereignty, and independent political organizations; further, the differences between the written and the unwritten law, *jus in rem* and *jus in personam*, private and public offenses, and the like. The enumerated descriptive examples of the concepts are followed a few pages later by a formal generalization: Jurisprudence should concern itself with the subject matter and purposes of law that are common to all systems, as well as with the kinship of various systems that are rooted in common human nature or are the result of similar social situations.[3]

At its core this program contains a methodological difficulty to which Austin and his followers in England and the United States barely addressed themselves and one that has also not found an adequate solution in German jurisprudence. At the beginning of the twelfth lecture Austin writes: "Through an analysis of the first six lectures, which define the area of jurisprudence and determine the strictest meaning of the legal system, I partially arrived at the objective that I called necessary in the preceding lectures, that is, the objective of determining in detailed analysis the meaning of the concepts we employ in our science."[4] The most exigent demands

1. "Positive law" adopted from Hugo. See John Austin, *Lectures on Jurisprudence*, ed. Robert Campbell (2 vols.; New York, 1875), I, 211.

["Hugo" was Gustave Hugo (1764–1844), of whom, in regard to the term *positive law*, Austin says: "I have borrowed the expression from Hugo, a celebrated professor of jurisprudence in the University of Göttingen, and the author of an excellent history of Roman Law." *Ibid.* (5th ed.; 2 vols.; London, 1885), I, 32. The 5th edition of Austin's *Lectures* is the earliest that the translator and editors have found, and it was this edition against which quotations were checked. The page locations of various passages differ considerably from those given by Voegelin for the 1875 edition, presumably the first, and are given in brackets.]

2. *Ibid.*, 213 [5th ed., II, 1073].
3. *Ibid.*, 216 [5th ed., II, 1077].
4. *Ibid.*, 228. [*Cf.* 5th ed., I, 343, where at the beginning of the twelfth lecture

145

of modern logic were met by this immanent definition of a scholarly area by means of his basic concepts. But at the same time the defining concepts that fundamentally determine the subject matter of jurisprudence, the legal structure, are meant to be concepts that serve within various legal systems to designate substantially equal empirical legal situations. This methodologically impossible demand cannot be satisfied on a practical level, and analytic jurisprudence as a whole is laced with the problem of the incompatibility of the structural concept of the problem of "law" and those concepts that describe substantially stable traits of social reality equivalent to the problem of "right."

Austin carries out the demarcation of the positive idea of law in two stages. In the first, basic normative concepts are reciprocally defined; the second adds criteria that determine which norms are, strictly speaking, legal norms. The correlative basic concepts of command, duty, and sanction are expressed in three formulas:

1. "If you express or intimate a wish that I shall do or forbear from some act, and if you will visit me with an evil in case I comply not with your wish, the *expression* or *intimation* of your wish is a *command*."

2. "Being liable to evil from you if I comply not with a wish which you signify, I am *bound* or *obliged* by your command, or I lie under a *duty* to obey it."

3. "The evil which will probably be incurred in case a command be disobeyed or (to use an equivalent expression) in case a duty be broken, is frequently called a *sanction,* or an *enforcement of obedience.* Or (varying the phrase) the command or the duty is said to be *sanctioned* or *enforced* by the chance of incurring the evil."[5]

The behavior that is commanded, the sanction, and the obligatory effect of the sanction on the behavior are reciprocally correlative; they are "inseparably connected terms"; each of them "implies" the others and "presupposes" them; each "embraces the same ideas as the others" but denotes them "in a peculiar order or series." Each of them "signifies the same notion" but "denotes" only a certain part of it, while "connoting" the rest.[6] The variety

nothing very like Voegelin's quotation of Austin can be found. Possibly Austin revised his comments between the 1875 edition and this one.]

5. *Ibid.,* 13 [5th ed., I, 89].

6. *Ibid.,* 15 [5th ed., I, 91–92].

of these expressions and their frequent repetition in the lectures show how clearly Austin kept in mind the necessity of providing internal connections for his basic concepts. But he did not therefore mean relations in a realm of pure logic. The relationship of meanings is embedded in social reality; it is not a meaning in itself but the necessary structure of meaning as vouchsafed in the actual behavior of empirical persons. The two first formulas do not reveal this intention so clearly, but the third explicitly mentions the "probable" creation of the evil and the "chance" of sanctions—a vocabulary, that is, that was made popular in Germany by Max Weber's sociology.

This way of embedding meaning in social reality becomes clearer in a second group, which supplements and completes the schema of legal concepts. One concept in this group is of little significance: the norms must apply to a number of activities by one or more persons. Subsequent studies[7] overlook this characteristic, and in the fully developed American formulation of the problems,[8] the judicial decisions Austin excluded from his statements become the central focus of his definition of law. The others, however, become typical for the structure of the theory of law: a general command is a positive law only when it is established by a sovereign person or a sovereign group of persons and is directed to a member or several members of the independent political society in which this person or group of persons is sovereign. Just as is true of the first group of concepts, here, too, logical correlation and the meaning of reality merge. Alongside the assurance that the concept of sovereignty is "correlative" to the concept of submissiveness and both are "inseparably connected" to the concept of an independent political society,[9] we find the following definitions: If (1) the bulk of a given society habitually obeys a particular and common authority, whether this authority is a single person or a group of persons; if (2) this authority does not habitually obey another particular human authority; then (3) the authority is sovereign in this society, and the society (including the authority) is political and independent.

The six concepts—in groups of three correlatives—define the

7. Herbert T. Terry, *Some Leading Principles of Anglo-American Law, Expounded with a View to Its Arrangement and Codification* (Philadelphia, 1884), 11. [Although Voegelin mentions "studies," plural, this is the only one cited.]

8. John Chipman Gray, *The Nature and Sources of Law* (New York, 1909).

9. Austin, *Lectures*, I, 116 [5th ed., I, 335–36].

area of a general science of the law or a general jurisprudence and at the same time are its fundamental concepts. In the following efforts to add further concepts to the original ones, the intellectual focus shifts from jurisprudence to the sphere of positive law. To explain the essence of a "right," Austin employs it in relation to the fundamental concepts. By this method he can point to its rightful place in a pure theory of law. A "right" must be considered in its relation to law, duty, and sanction. Even if not every law creates a right, it is true that every right is the creature of a law. Nor does every duty and sanction imply a right; but every right implies a duty and sanction.[10] The concept of subjective right is apparently intended to be derived from the fundamental concepts; but the stricter definitions that immediately follow no longer describe "right" as a derivative relationship but take it as a center in order to determine from it what further legal concepts are required. This way is used to introduce the concepts of person, thing, action, and prohibition, because rights reside in persons and refer to persons, and so forth, as their subject matter. The concept of injustice is no longer derived immediately from duty; rather, Austin states: just as rights imply duties and sanctions, so do duties or sanctions imply possible wrongdoing.[11] This statement intends to claim that wrongdoings are connected with right by way of duties and sanctions, which are implied by law; similarly, wrongdoing can also be derived from law. But the statement is false, since law is to duty as concept is to fundamental concept, and duty is to wrongdoing as fundamental concept is to derived concept. This statement, which sets up a false equation, may be the most precise expression of the shifting and doubling of an intellectual focus in analytic jurisprudence.

Quite clearly the formation of concepts is directed to the second focus by classifying duties independent of their correlation with sanction and commanded behavior.[12] Duties are distinguished as relative or absolute. A relative duty is imposed on one party and corresponds to the right of the other; no right corresponds to an absolute duty. This situation caused Austin to conclude that the definition of an absolute duty is purely negative and must therefore systematically follow the treatment of subjective law. He comes to

10. *Ibid.*, 229 [5th ed., I, 344].
11. *Ibid.*
12. *Ibid.*, 231 [5th ed., I, 346].

this conclusion although on the previous page he explicitly stated that by its sanction, every command creates a duty for the person at whom it is directed; and although the chapter on absolute duties defined them as deriving from the sovereign's command and derived their nature as duties from the concept of sanction.[13] But this positive definition is immediately interrupted by the second focus in an attempt to depict absolute duties as well as duties against specific persons, who therefore have a right to the duties' being met. For, notes Austin, in their more long-range objectives even these duties (for example, not to get drunk, not to commit suicide, not to torture animals) are owed to persons, because they have been established with a view to society's needs.[14]

The interrelationship of the lines of thought shown by this example is typical for the overall development of the theory. In what follows, further examples will be cited only to the extent that they are essential to demonstrate new systematic situations.

A recognition of the two foci of the system and the attempt to connect them rationally involves division into primary and secondary rights and duties.[15] Rights and duties can arise from offenses and are called secondary, or they arise without infringing upon other rights and duties, in which case they are called primary rights. Between the two there is a relationship of purpose; the secondary, or sanctioning, rights are intended to prevent breaches of primary rights. The difference can therefore also be determined as law, the observance of which is directly enforced by the courts, and right, whose observance is indirectly enforced. The bulk of the law based on sanctioned rights and duties is constituted by criminal and civil law. The center of gravity in this lies in secondary right, since it alone is "absolutely necessary." The primary rights and duties owe their existence exclusively to the sanctioned prohibition of particular actions or omissions. "In strictness, my own terms, 'primary and secondary rights and duties,' do not represent a logical distinction. For a primary right or duty is not of itself a right or duty, without the secondary right or duty by which it is sustained; and *e converso.*"[16]

13. *Ibid.*, 278 [5th ed., I, 400–401].
14. *Ibid.*, 279 [5th ed., I, 403].
15. *Ibid.*, 179–80 [5th ed., II, 762–63].
16. *Ibid.*, 185 [5th ed., II, 768].

Every secondary right represents an essentially inseparable entity with its matching primary one, and the habit of describing rights and duties, offenses and punishments separately is useful only for purposes of technical description. The same process of punishment or restitution is applied to various classes of primary right, and the repetitions would be cumbersome. The supremacy of sanctioning rights is so effective that for large areas of the law (for example, absolute duties) primary right is not presented as such but is implied in the description of activities threatened with punishment. Thus the entire area of law depends on the sanctioning process— its structure is comprised of the six fundamental concepts—and seen from this point of view, the subdivision of primary rights appears as a systematically nonindependent description of activities that, when committed, are punishable. The fact that the subsection can at the same time appear, from the viewpoint of an order of human behavior (without consideration of the compelling nature of the order), independently and ethically more important than the legal process is what causes the methodological complexities of the system.

The immediate occasion for Austin's lectures was the inauguration of London University in 1826. Austin was appointed professor of jurisprudence, and in the winter of 1827–1828 he traveled to Bonn to familiarize himself more thoroughly with German philosophy of law. In the spring of 1828 he began his lectures in London, with great success. But the following year the number of students dropped so sharply (for lack of interest) that it became financially impossible to maintain the chair. In June, 1832, he delivered the last of his lectures. In 1834 the Society of the Inner Temple tried again to establish a course in jurisprudence, but the undertaking failed for similar reasons.

After Austin's fragmentary lectures it took until 1880, when Thomas Erskine Holland's *Elements of Jurisprudence* was published, before analytic jurisprudence was presented in systematic form.[17] Around this time there were two methods for the systematic treatment of law. One is represented by casebooks; the most significant one in Holland's time was Smith's *Leading Cases*, which was adapted for American use by John Indermaur in *Epitome*

17. Thomas Erskine Holland, *The Elements of Jurisprudence* (1880; 8th ed. Oxford, Eng., 1896).

of Leading Common Law Cases (1883). These collections of decisions dealt primarily with legal obligations and torts by presenting leading cases and, in the form of additional decisions, grouping related material around them. The manuals are more comprehensive in detail and set up in the form of a legal code.[18] These works essentially cover the same ground as the casebooks but supplement it with a more precise description of some rules of evidence for civil proceedings.

The second type is represented by Herbert Broom's *Selection of Legal Maxims*.[19] The work is a collection of standardized maxims that from time to time can be applied to legal theory. Maxim 147, for example, reads, "Ubi jus ibi remedium." This is explained in the commentary: "*remedium* may be defined to be the right of action, or the means given by law, for the recovery or assertion of a right. According to this elementary maxim, whenever the common law gives a right or prohibits an injury, it also gives a remedy: lex semper dabit remedium. . . . It is a vain thing to imagine a right without a remedy, for want of right and want of remedy are reciprocal."[20] But theoretical formulations of this sort are isolated and are not elaborated into a coherent system; the cited maxim, for example, occurs under the rubric "Fundamental Legal Principles" and alongside such statements as "In jura non remota causa sed proxima spectatur," "Actus dei nemini facit injuriam," "Lex non cogit ad impossibilia," "Volenti non fit injuria," "Nemo debet bis vexari pro una et eadem causa," and so on. Another group, concerning rules of public policy, cites "Salus populi suprema lex," "Dies dominicus non est juridicus," and so forth. Still another chapter, dealing with the crown, includes "Rex nunquam moritur," "Rex non potest peccare," "Roy n'est lié par ascun statute, si il ne soit expressement nosmé." These groupings of general principles are followed by other statements dealing with civil law, contracts and property, and rules of evidence.

The spirit that inspires this collection of maxims is given conscious expression in Broom's *Philosophy of Law*.[21] It is introduced

18. A typical manual is Josiah W. Smith, *A Manual of Common Law* (2d American ed.; [?], 1881).

19. Herbert Broom, *A Selection of Legal Maxims: Classified and Illustrated*, (1845; 4th ed. Philadelphia, 1854).

20. [*Ibid.*, 153–54.]

21. Herbert Broom, *The Philosophy of Law: Being Notes of Lectures Delivered During Twenty-Three Years (1852–1875)* (Cambridge, Eng., 1876).

by Lord Mansfield's definition of jurisprudence as a rational science based on universal principles of justice, though modified by custom and authority. What he means by principles of justice are the fundamental features of the material of civil law, and Broom therefore divides the field of jurisprudence into (1) theory of the principles and (2) theory of legal proceedings.[22] But he makes the distinction not in order to connect the two by a theory such as Austin's of primary and secondary rights. Rather, lacking any desire for a system, he calls the study of legal proceedings less "attractive" than the study of principles. Further, he notes that the form by which knowledge of the legal process is acquired cannot be made attractive. And that is the reason, he continues, why his philosophy of law is limited to an exposition of the legal principles and excludes the problem of the legal process (except for a few rules for giving evidence). It is precisely the same purposive link between sanctioning and primary statements that caused Austin to claim the inseparability that Broom sees as a reason to neglect the legal process;[23] he feels that civil proceedings are in large measure only "ancillary" to the protection of private rights and that criminal proceedings basically serve the same purpose.

Austin's comparatively rigid order of legal concepts concerning sanctions and proceedings is resolved in a more or less serviceable outline establishing the body of jurisprudence, and the place of his fundamental concepts has been taken by natural-law principles. The complete loss of the previously attained systematic heights is opposed by isolated attempts to carry the analysis of legal concepts to an extraordinary completion. Monahan's *Method of Law*[24] takes as its basic problem the arrangement of an order of conduct under appropriate symbols. Every body of laws contains an order of conduct that constitutes the meaning of its existence, and this order should conform to the conduct of those affected by it.[25] Such an order can be imagined without a legal system, whereas in the reverse case, the purpose of a legal system would be only to compel order. But even if a legal order can be imagined without a compulsory apparatus, it becomes a legal standard only through the actual

22. *Ibid.*, 7.
23. *Ibid.*, 9.
24. James H. Monahan, *The Method of Law: An Essay on the Statement and Arrangement of the Legal Standard of Conduct* (London, 1878).
25. *Ibid.*, 27.

or potential intervention of the courts.[26] Austin's arrangement of the system has been restored, but the internal connection among the concepts has been simplified: The arrangement of two times three correlative concepts is replaced by a simpler standard concept, from which the definitions are derived. Legal principles are expressions for common characteristics of lawful conduct. "Duty," for example, means that action "should" conform to the norm, without regard to a sanction. The legal sanction determines the common duty closer to the legal obligation. "Injustice" is conduct that does not conform to the norm. If the discussion is to be about the conduct of all persons except one particular person, or if one or more persons are to be excluded from the conduct of a class of person, the word *duty* becomes awkward and the symbol *law* proves to be more practical.[27] The fact that a person has a right means that the conduct of all other persons violating that right is illegal. The ideal would be a legal order so arranged that it would be possible in every case to say whether a person's conduct does or does not conform to a simple norm. And when this simple relation becomes difficult or impossible for linguistic reasons, *duty* and *right* are useful symbols. "But we do not see a rhetorical balance of rights and obligations; nor do we see what advantages a classification of rights would have."[28] In this way Monahan destroys the bulk of the problems connected with philosophy of law that make up the greater part of all books on jurisprudence before and after him. Precisely the classification of rights, the balance of rights and duties in "jural relation," and the belief in a legal order in the sense of natural law do not disappear from analytic jurisprudence, which may well be the source of the energy that drives it to ever-new efforts.

Monahan's jural method works in a sphere of symbols; all actions that enter the area of law can be reduced to the element of conformity to an order, and if this element is seen as the only real one, all complex concepts in relation to it seem to be appropriate symbols, though they are not essential to law but are meaningful only on a linguistic level. There is no consideration of the possibility

26. *Ibid.*
27. *Ibid.*, 55.
28. *Ibid.*, 59. [The quotation here is a back-translation from Voegelin's German; the editors were unable to find a copy of the Monahan volume and ascertain the original English wording.]

that social reality, which requires symbols because of its diversity, when considered in another light may be not a complex element but an irreducible one. The connection of the social content of reality with the jural form of conduct is the special problem of Hearn's jurisprudence.[29] He, too, derives the general outline of the system from Austin, but he revises Austin's doubling of intellectual foci by deriving legal concepts from the concept of subjective rights.[30] Once again command, sanction, and duty are correlated— at least so Hearn claims, referring to Austin's theory.[31] In fact, however, his analysis of the fundamental concepts is more precise; he dissects the concept of command into seven elements: (1) the person from whom it emanates (in the case of a state regulation, the state person [Staatsperson]); (2) the person to whom the command is addressed; (3) the desire of the person who issues the command; (4) the behavior or its omission that is demanded in the desire; (5) the "notification"; (6) a "menace"; (7) assumption of the presence of power to coerce the conduct.[32] A law is "the intimation of the will of the State to its subjects concerning their conduct, an intimation usually expressed through certain appropriate organs, and enforced by other organs."[33]

This more rigorous analysis, which concentrates into one concept of command all of Austin's fundamental principles, allows a more precise description between the elements and their arrangements. The command issued by the state persons to the person addressed constitutes the legal duty. When legal misconduct is performed, duty (rather than any right) is breached.[34] The wrong puts the person in a new relation to the sanctioned organs, the relation of "liability" through the sanction.[35] The relation of rights exists

29. William Edward Hearn, *The Theory of Legal Duties and Rights: An Introduction to Analytic Jurisprudence* (Melbourne and London, 1883).
30. "Their [absolute duties'] importance has been obscured by two circumstances. In the first place, Austin's system was based upon the consideration of rights, and he was consequently embarrassed by a class of duties which did not correlate rights, and for which he could therefore find no fitting place. In the second place, in the minds of the administrators of the criminal law, the breach of the duty has practically smothered the duty itself." *Ibid.*, 58.
31. *Ibid.*, 53.
32. *Ibid.*, 5. [Hearn actually lists six, not seven, "elements in a command," giving the first element simply as "the two parties," which Voegelin divides into the person commanding and the one commanded.]
33. *Ibid.*, 6.
34. "A wrong is not the violation of a right, but the violation of a duty." *Ibid.*, 153.
35. *Ibid.*, 53.

among three persons: if a command demands the fulfillment of a duty in such a way that the fulfillment benefits a particular person or group of persons, and this particular person has a right to petition in case of noncompliance—then there exists not only the duty relation between the state person and the ordinary addressee, but also a relation between him and the third party, and the state person participates in this through sanction on the claim of the third party.[36] Some secondary meanings of natural law that define the word *rights* are explicitly rejected; a right has nothing to do with conformity to an ethical "standard." It means exclusively a positive legal relation, independent of moral norms or principles of abstract right. "It is in the fullest sense the creature of law."[37] It is created by positive right, and controlled by it while it exists, and is extinguished according to its rules.[38]

Monahan's and Hearn's discussions are the high point of analytical jurisprudence. Holland's and Salmond's systems and Terry's American work all situate jurisprudence on a broader base and attempt (in Holland's case) to encompass the entire legal system theoretically. But the analysis sacrifices precision; we can do little more than furnish examples of the instances of blurring and indicate the new configuration of problems that arise.[39]

Holland's *Elements of Jurisprudence* opens with a section on "Law and Rights." This is followed by three sections on, respectively, private rights, public rights, and the rights of nations. It closes with discussions on the application of rights (interpretation and the like). The dual title of the first part indicates that no attempt is made toward a unified theory: the problem of proceedings (law) is separated from the question of legal rights, and the juxtaposition of two autonomous areas under one title, jurisprudence, becomes the typical trait in further scholarly developments. The

---

36. *Ibid.*, 141.

37. *Ibid.*, 143.

38. See also *ibid.*, 153: "A right has no independent existence. It denotes merely a certain course of proceedings taken by its donee upon the breach of a certain species of duty."

39. Some other works are of less historical significance: [Sheldon] Amos, *A Systematic View of the Science of Jurisprudence* (London, 1872); Amos, *The Science of Law* (5th ed.; London, 1881). (The first was written for legal specialists, the second for the general public.) Amos links his principal features to Austin. Sir W. H. Rattigan, *The Science of Jurisprudence; Chiefly Intended for Indian Students* (London, 1888), is a textbook for Indian students and is based on Holland and Austin.

methodological approach to the problem is similar to Austin's, except that Austin's assumption of the fixed correlative connection of meaning in every legal system is destroyed by the contradictory assumption that general jurisprudence is a "progressive" science, whose concepts must adapt to changes in positive systems.[40] Although Holland stresses the fact that the more general of these concepts would undoubtedly remain stable, the consequences of Austin's syncretism of legal structure and legal content—which he applied only tacitly, and which he defused in part by the acuteness of his understanding—now come into effect and dissolve jurisprudence into a collection of empirical concepts described in the various systems as accidental situations.

The definition of the legal precept varies slightly from Austin's; it is "a general rule of human action, taking cognizance only of external acts, enforced by a determinate authority."[41] But Holland draws no conclusion from this definition itself. Instead, systematically quite independent, jurisprudence is defined as a science that deals with the means by which the law attains its ethical purposes (which lie outside consideration), and these means are the creation and protection of legal rights,[42] a definition that is systematically independent of the first definition of a legal statement. A legal right is "a capacity residing in one man of controlling, with the assent and assistance of the State, the actions of others."[43] The validity of the right is derived from state sanction, and it is this that establishes the connection with the definition of the legal precept. But this connection is purely instrumental, not logically systematic; between the idea of controlling someone's actions and the idea of violating a duty there exists no connection in the area of procedure itself; only through the interpolation of social or individual purpose can the idea of controlling actions be connected with the concept of the law. The importance of this formula becomes evident when it is compared with Hearn's introduction of the concept of right: Hearn starts from the relation of duty and adds to the concept of

40. Holland, *Elements of Jurisprudence*, 9.
41. *Ibid.*, 37. [11th ed. (Oxford, Eng., 1910), 41. The translator and editors consulted various editions of Holland, but the 8th (1896), used by Voegelin, was not available. The direct quotations here and notes 43, 47, 48, and 50 below were checked against the 11th edition, page references for which are given in brackets.]
42. *Ibid.*, 70.
43. *Ibid.*, 72, 75. [11th ed., 82.]

the conduct of the duty-bound person the stricter definition of use for a third person, connected to the third's right to bring suit; the thought process ranges from the concept of duty through the introduction of new elements to the concept of right. Holland begins with the legal concept and claims explicitly that in theory it does not matter whether a system of laws begins with a consideration of rights or of duties, since the two are correlative with each other.[44] As a result, illegal conduct seems to be conduct less undutiful than unlawful.[45] The problem of duties without corresponding rights is solved by presuming the state to be the exponent of legal rights. The body of criminal law is arranged according to this assumption of rights and duties.[46] In fact, however, Holland goes beyond his assumed correlation of duty and right and turns the legal concept into the intellectual focus because the definition of duty is: "Every right, whether moral or legal, implies the active or passive furtherance by others of the wishes of the party having the right. Wherever any one is entitled to such furtherance on the part of others, such furtherance on their part is said to be their duty."[47] The turn from the structure of the concept of the legal process to social purposes is so complete that the purposive relation between the sanctioned and the primary area of law is once more brought to the fore; if all went well, according to Holland, there would be only a primary right; the totality of sanctioned right is merely "added because of transgressions."[48] This sentence also abandons the essential linkage of the two types of right retained by Austin and places the center of gravity once more in the doctrine of the principles of legal rights.[49]

The phrase "rights at rest and in motion" must be highlighted in

44. *Ibid.*, 76.
45. *Ibid.*, 285.
46. *Ibid.*, 117.
47. *Ibid.*, 75. [11th ed., 86.]
48. *Ibid.*, 130. [11th ed., 145.]
49. For a comparison of the two types of jurisprudence, see Charles Malcolm Platt, "The Character and Scope of Analytical Jurisprudence," *American Law Review*, XXIV (1890), 603–15. Platt distinguishes two groups in the object of jurisprudence:

To the first belongs positive law in general,—that is, taken quite independently of any special purposes to be effected by means of it. . . . Whether a law be one of ownership or of contract there are equally involved in the distinct apprehension of it and its workings such notions as those of state, sovereign, command, duty and sanction. The first great department of analytical jurisprudence is conversant with these and other similarly implicated conceptions, defining them and exhibiting their mutual relation. The second portion of the

the treatment of legal rights because vital problems of American jurisprudence are based on this dualism. What is meant by *right at rest* is the "nature and extent" of a right, whereas *right in motion* refers to the "form of its creation and its extinction."[50]

Holland's *Elements* created a condition of disintegration; Terry's *Principles*[51] represents its lowest point. The title alone indicates that the chief interest is placed not in the theoretical unity of the legal concepts but in arranging the material into a body of laws. For this reason, too, Terry does not attempt to derive his concepts from one center; rather, the most diverse topics break into the body of material in order to point it in just as many different directions. Several attempts to improve Austin's conception were attempted on the basis of the cluster of concepts dealing with process. The place of the sovereign—a particular group of persons that issues the command—is taken by the "state," an indeterminate "postulate" that precedes jurisprudence and cannot be investigated by it.[52] This "state" has little in common with Austin's sovereign or even the independent political society, though it is impossible to say precisely what meaning in fact attaches to it, since Terry's terminology is extremely vague. In one place he seems inclined to let the concepts of sovereign, state, and law flow into one another, so that all these words would signify no more than the unity of the legal system.[53] This assumption is made plausible by Terry's explicit efforts to incorporate the common law in the legal system following Austin's model.[54] As stages of the positive creation of law Austin listed (1) the immediate exercise of legislative or judicial power through the sovereign; (2) the exercise by subjects of these explic-

---

science includes certain special phases of positive law, namely, such as are requisite to make it correlate with one or another of the broad human needs that have found legal embodiment. This division is occupied with the features which positive law has received from the large general principles upon which it has been moulded, the features upon which its adaptation to those purposes depends.

50. Holland, *Elements of Jurisprudence*, 132. [11th ed., 147.]
51. Terry, *Some Leading Principles of Anglo-American Law, Expounded with a View to Its Arrangement and Codification.*
52. "I assume that the nature of State or 'independent political society' is sufficiently well known to the reader. The explanation of this does not belong to the science of law, but is taken as one of its postulates." *Ibid.*, 5.
53. See *ibid.*, 11: "Instead of using the word 'sovereign,' we commonly say the 'State,' . . . or the 'law' in such expressions as 'the law intends.' "
54. *Ibid.*, 12.

itly or tacitly transferred functions.[55] The common law can become positive law in a state when it is integrated in the law courts' system of sanctions. Both Austin and Terry refer to Hobbes's statement according to which the lawgiver is not the person or organ that enacted the law but the person under whose authority it continues to be the law—a definition that divests the idea of *lawgiver* of its empirical meaning and turns it into a standard function of the legal system. Another attempt to preserve the unity of the legal connections consists in the description of "legal facts."[56] These are not arbitrary empirical events as such, but merely such facts as are developed in a legal proceeding according to the rules of evidence.

The concept of duty is derived from command. Legal duty is the condition of a person who is commanded or prohibited by law to engage in a particular conduct.[57] Every duty is owed to another person; all duties are owed the sovereign—and those that correspond to a legal right are also owed the interested third party. But Terry has no specific systematic view of this point, since he considers it merely a question of terminology whether this last mentioned duty is owed *only* to a private person or to the sovereign as well.[58]

Along with rights that correspond to duties, the concept of law introduces a new type of rights that are far removed from any connection with the concepts of duty and command. This new type combines both the elements found in Holland's stressing of the social utility of rights and others that have something in common with Monahan's symbolism.[59] Beside the corresponding rights there are protected rights (for example, the right to own property). Terry argues[60] that if one wished to express them in the terminology of corresponding rights, one would have to see them as complex groups of such rights. But this view would not correspond to the needs of the science of law. It would be extremely awkward, in some cases impossible, to define duties without first describing the right that is to be protected. In the case of rights to property, for example, there was no general duty "not to interfere with things."[61]

---

55. Austin, *Lectures*, II, 23 [5th ed., II, 534].
56. Terry, *Principles*, 50.
57. *Ibid.*, 84.
58. *Ibid.*
59. *Ibid.*, 94.
60. *Ibid.*, 91.
61. *Ibid.*, 94.

This claim of the utility of legal terminology broadens to include its justifications through specific empirical social situations. A protected right is a person's specific situation, which the state protects by imposing corresponding duties on other persons. The substance of this duty consists in actions or omissions of actions that, if carried out, would jeopardize the protected position.[62] This confusion of protected rights differs from corresponding rights, even though they have corresponding duties, and even though they had been described as convenient symbols, so that in fact they are not rights at all. This passage becomes somewhat hopeless, but it is characteristic of the complete dissolution of systematic thinking.

A reorganization of the body of problems clustering around the pole of conduct and right is begun in Salmond's *Jurisprudence* under the concept of the "Administration of Justice" and the legal forms of social reality.[63]

For Salmond, the law consists of the rules of law recognized and sanctioned by the courts.[64] Recognition and sanction make up the form by which the state function of administering justice is carried out: maintaining the legal condition in a polity through the power of the state,[65] protecting legal rights, and making reparations and punishing injustice. The right in itself is of a secondary nature—accidental and insignificant; it exists in the fixed principles according to which this state function is exercised. Justice is the purpose of this function, whereas laws are merely a means, and the means must be defined by its relation to its purpose.[66] In Salmond's view an administration of justice without laws is perfectly thinkable. The analysis of legal precepts as a sanctioned state command is inadequate because it lacks the relation of rights and justice. It is not that legal precepts are free of an element of coercion—this "central fact" of basing laws on physical force is not disputed here[67]—but the total concept of law also includes the idea of justice. And though positive law empirically deviates from the demands of jus-

---

62. *Ibid.*, 97.
63. John W. Salmond, *Jurisprudence; or, The Theory of the Law* (London, 1902). An earlier work, *The First Principles of Jurisprudence* (London, 1893), was subsumed in the later publication.
64. *Ibid.*, 11.
65. *Ibid.*, 14.
66. *Ibid.*, 17.
67. *Ibid.*, 53.

tice, they are nevertheless one in idea.[68] Salmond supplies no justification for his view; instead he indicates the consequences that
would result if it were rejected. They appear to him sufficiently
absurd to make the correctness of his theory persuasive. For if we
were to deny existence of a natural law, we would also have to deny
natural and moral duties. Rights and duties are essentially correlative, and if a creditor had no natural right to repayment of the
debt, the debtor would not have a natural duty to repay the debt. If
we deny the existence of natural laws, we must go further and
doubt the existence of natural justice as well. We would have to
use Greek skepticism to claim that the difference between justice
and injustice does not reside in the nature of things but is instead
an element of human institutions. If natural justice is not to be an
illusion, natural laws must be assumed.[69] Thus right is more than
might, as the imperative theory claims, but it is not simply justice,
either; it is justice speaking to people in the voice of the state.[70]

Salmond's jurisprudence is not entirely in accord with these explanations, but it consistently follows a train of thought that began
with the idea of the administration of justice and continues through
the precept of law as the union of justice and coercion, going on to
claim the existence of large classes of laws that do not include an
element of coercion.[71] The first group of this kind consists of "sanctioning laws," such as a declaratory rule that damage resulting from
competition is not grounds for bringing suit.[72] The second group—
the only important one—includes all procedural law. Its rules are
observed by court officials in the administration of justice—they
are not sanctioned commands to the subjects. The idea of the administration of justice becomes the borderline that separates the

68. *Ibid.*, 55, 52.
69. *Ibid.*, 222.
70. *Ibid.*, 55–56.
71. *Ibid.*, 57–58.
72. The case of "permitted rules of law" is a simple example of a trait of theory
formation in general. It would be unjustified to "deal with" Salmond's classification
as "false" because sanctioning laws are only elements of laws made necessary by
language or social position and only seem autonomous. What matters in the interpretation is to present clearly the leading rational theme (in this case, the theme of
the administration of justice) and to demonstrate how it absorbs rationally unconnected problems. The rational categories of "true" and "false" can be replaced with
the concept of "appropriateness" to designate this form of thinking. This procedure
does not prevent evaluation of styles of thought according to the degree of rationality
they allow in systematic development.

rules of law (as sanctions) for the administration of justice in the social community from procedural rules. The jurisdiction over relations between members of the community is distinct from the instrument of its forcible control and order.

The order of social reality is encompassed in a group of systematically related concepts. The point of departure is the purpose of the administration of justice: to protect rights and punish their violation.[73] A right is an interest recognized and protected by a rule of law. Its observance is a duty, its violation a wrong.[74] Every jural right or wrong conduct—as well as every just and unjust action—takes its legal or moral character from its relation to human interests: life, liberty, health, reputation, use of material objects. Not all de facto interests are also de jure interests; the administration of justice selects from among all the conflicting interests some to be protected and others to be rejected.[75] The social reality is organized legally from the point of view of protecting interests, and the concept of right determines the semantic import of the other legal concepts. Right in the strictest sense (the correlative to duty) contains as its essential element the relation to a specific other person on whom is imposed a specific conduct or omission (duty) in favor of the first person.[76] Legal right in the wider sense, however, can be understood generally as an advantageous position or as advantage created by rules of law in favor of a person.[77] This class of rights in the broader sense encompasses right (in the narrow sense), liberty, power, and immunity.

Jural liberties are the advantages that arise from the absence of legal duties; they encompass all things a person may do without being prevented by law. The legal sphere is a sphere of duties and coercions, the sphere of liberty is one of free will. Salmond uses two phrases to distinguish between them: "things which others *ought* to do for me"; "things which I *may* do for myself."[78]

The concept of power is circumscribed by examples. I have the

73. Salmond, *Jurisprudence*, 217.
74. *Ibid.*, 219. It is difficult to include the concept of injustice systematically. On p. 218 injustice is called the correlative to duty. But a few pages later, justice is called the necessary correlative to duty (p. 223). The concept of natural law here collides with the problems of the legal structure.
75. *Ibid.*, 220.
76. *Ibid.*, 225.
77. *Ibid.*, 231.
78. *Ibid.*, 231–32.

legal power to make a will, to marry, to bring suit; judges have the power to exercise their function. This type of right differs from right in the strictest sense by the lack of corresponding duties; it differs from liberty by the feature of legal consequence. A power is "that which I *can* do effectively." "I use my liberties with the acquiescence of the law; I use my powers with its active assistance; . . . I enjoy my rights through the control exercised by it over the acts of others on my behalf."[79]

The situation of immunity is given when the law, ruling in my favor, refuses to give another person a power over me. An example cited is the advantage a debtor can gain through the statute of limitations; the advantage is not a right in the strictest sense, since the creditor is placed under no obligation; it is not a liberty, since the debt and the duty to pay up remain; nor is it a power. It is an immunity, consisting of the abolition of the creditor's right to sue for this particular debt. The formula of immunity states, "What others *cannot* do against me."[80]

The burdens of corresponding persons match the four advantages or protected interests. The law is matched by the duty of obeying it, freedom by the liability of the other person because of my actions (for example, violent ejection of a burglar). Power is matched by the danger of the legal consequences of execution and punishment (but also pleasant consequences, such as inheritance). Immunity corresponds to the disability of another to use legal means to affect the position of the first person in his position.

The concepts can be arranged in the following table of correlatives:[81]

Right	Liberty	Power	Immunity
Duty	Liability	Liability	Disability
others *must*	I *may*	I *can*	others *cannot*

When the first line of concepts is arranged with its negatives, the following table results:

Right	Liberty	Power	Immunity
Liability	Duty	Disability	Liability

79. *Ibid.*, 233–34.
80. *Ibid.*, 235–36.
81. *Ibid.*, 237.

Two different concepts must be designated by the same term, *liability,* because the common law does not have enough symbols for the different situations.[82]

The table of correlatives is arranged according to two principles. The first group of four (right, duty, liberty, liability) contrasts with the second group as a group of conditions in contrast to the concepts of movement. Holland's division of "rights at rest and in motion" is here elaborated into possible legal situations. The first group designates the existence or nonexistence of a static relation; the second group designates the possibility or nonpossibility of entering upon or of ending such a relationship. Both groups, therefore, contain time as the essential element of meaning—in the first, as duration of the relation; in the second, as organization of the duration through initiating and abolishing the relation. The second constructive principle opposes the pair right-power (with its correlatives) to the pair liberty-immunity (with its correlatives). The first of these groups refers to social reality insofar as it is positively affected by rules of law. The second deals with the social reality insofar as it is free of legal regulations. Thus the structuring of concepts is not sustained by the theory of law, where concepts such as liberty and immunity cannot be arrived at from the legal process. These situations are more adequately characterized by the fact that they have *no* relation to the concept of legal proceedings but are related to the structuring of social reality itself insofar as it is or is not affected by the function of the law.

The legal concepts immediately connected with the idea of procedure can be arranged in two formulas: the sanction S of the state organization becomes operative when the person A behaves in the manner C.

(1) $S \ldots A \ldots C.$

This group of concepts establishes the duty of A, given sanctions, to behave in the manner non-C. Secondly, a person B has the right to sue (R) in the case that A behaves in the manner C.

(2) $B \ldots R \ldots C_A.$

This group of concepts constitutes B's legal right to non-C conduct by the person A. Hearn came very close to such a schema;

82. *Ibid.,* 236.

where his theory fell short was in burdening it with a number of ethical conceptions. "Duty" is an empirical situation in which person A happens to find himself compelled to see his conduct C followed by the sanction S. Every secondary meaning, to the effect that conduct C and sanction S be omitted, and A *should* behave in the manner of non-C, thus acting according to a standard—called *law*—goes beyond the procedural relations into the area of ethical demands. Basing the legitimacy of duty on command contains elements of natural law that muddy the purity of the situation. When the concept of duty based in natural law is relinquished, the problem of injustice as a negation of duty falls away. A conceptual schema that requires A to engage in conduct C and, in case of unjust conduct—non-C—threatens sanction S, encroaches on the sphere of natural law. Unjust conduct—non-C when regarded from the standpoint of the conduct required by the system—is a positive conduct. It is the only conduct relevant to the process and the sanction. In the same way, defining turns of phrase must be excluded from the second group of concepts, such as "B has the right to sue in case A does not fulfill his duty." B retains his right to sue for the case of C conduct that is positively determined by the chance of sanctions if it should occur. The "right" is the situation in which B finds himself by the chance that his intervention causes conduct C_A, followed by sanction S. If "right" and "duty" in this sense, and their determinants S, A, C, B, R, are all legal concepts, we must find a different word for the concepts established by Salmond; inherent in them is the reference to situations that are understood by interpretation on the basis of a social-ethical scale of values. We will retain the designation *legal concepts* for Salmond's tables and distinguish between them and *procedural concepts* to indicate that the legal concept of right or duty is only nominally related to the procedural concepts of right and duty.

All structural elements of the legal problem that occur in the English analytic school are found again in the (American) Hohfeld school: the idea of positive, state-sanctioned rights; the problem of the concepts of legal process and right; Salmond's schema, with its two structuring principles; legal problems as questions of the empirical social situation and the implication of the concept of time. But all are reshaped and arranged in new intellectual contexts that distinguish them sharply from the way they appear in the English formulations.

Apart from the English tradition, the significant structural materials are influences from the doctrine of natural law and the sovereignty of the Supreme Court as examples of an order of legal proceedings. Their presentation must precede the analysis of the Hohfeld school.

II. American Analytic Jurisprudence

The Americanization of English analytic jurisprudence becomes obvious in George H. Smith's *Elements of Right and of the Law*.[83] The author justifies his attempt to establish a philosophy of law by referring to the significance and dignity of his subject matter, since the concept of law involves every claim a person can make to personal liberty and security, to the acquisition and use of property, to family and life—that therefore the law expresses the sum total of all man's deepest interests. Unfortunately, however, he points out, the science of law was in decline in England and America—in America because of a general lack of interest in philosophical subjects, in England because of the dominance of a false theory that, starting with Bentham, came to possess the British mind completely. This theory—the theory of analytic jurisprudence— "poisons the wells of all science of law" by its claim that the law was merely an expression of the will of the state and was not based on the necessary principle of natural law. Smith does not feel that use of the phrase "poisons the wells" is excessive, nor is the radical condemnation of a generally acknowledged theory, because this theory ran counter to humanity's deepest convictions in general, and specifically to those of jurists and philosophers of all times and nations except for England and America, and even to those of English jurists before Bentham appeared on the scene.[84]

Smith recognizes three elements of the law: statutes, customs, and common sense. From these three elements legal definitions can be derived, though each in itself is insufficient. A legalistic definition would claim that all right is legal right [*das alles Recht Gesetzrecht ist*] (Smith refers to law as *statute* and ignores the meaning

83. George H. Smith, *Elements of Right and of the Law* (2d ed.; Chicago, 1887). (Almost the entire first edition was destroyed by a fire in the publishing house. The second edition does not give a date for the first edition.) Terry's *Principles* do not yet show any obvious Americanisms in the structure of his theory.
84. George H. Smith, *Elements of Right*, "Preface," iv–v.

of the concept of law understood as the concept of individual laws in the English school). The historical definition of law is derived from legal customs. The philosophical definition sees in the law a science of natural justice. Smith feels that the legalistic, analytic definition is totally untenable, whereas the two others, though incomplete when taken separately, mutually supplement each other to lead to the proper concept of law. The historical concept defines law as the jural (as opposed to legal) principles found in the manners and customs of a people, without seeking further justification except the fact of their empirical existence. The philosophical concept goes further to claim that the empirical legal principles are more or less precise expressions of necessary truths that can be proved scientifically. The historical theory is not false, but it is incomplete because it refuses to recognize the "necessary truths." In fact, according to Smith, the historical theory is included in the philosophic theory, since the *practical* standard to which conceptions of law refer are the "general consciousness" or the "unanimous moral convictions of a people." Both schools consider this the legitimate and, in practical terms, the only possible standard, but the philosophical jurist is intent on subjecting the traditional ideas of law to scientific scrutiny so that, should they prove to be untrue, they can gradually be amended.[85]

It is possible to leave the terms *legalistic-jural* (*historical-philosophical*) out of account and find that an empirical system of rules of law is set opposite a standard of its modification—whatever this standard may be. The legalistic view seems so insignificant in this context because it derives from the group of legal theorists who stress procedure, and the problem of the substance of law and its changes is essentially foreign to it. Smith, even before Salmond, fully developed the concept of legal scope in contrast to procedure, just as Salmond subsequently made the concept of the administration of justice the center of his considerations. But in his work the idea is stated more acutely, and especially with more historical significance, because of the commanding meaning accorded to the position of rights in the American system. His book therefore opens with the sentence, "The principal end of government is to act as judge, or umpire, in the controversies which arise between men as

85. *Ibid.*, §§ 368–75.

to their mutual claims and demands upon each other."[86] Starting with this function, the scope of the theory or law is outlined as the science of "right"—that is, of liberty and power, to act unhampered with reference to the subject matter of particular rights.[87] The scope of "administrative" legislation therefore is already outside the subject matter of the theory of law. Administration is concerned with achieving effective state administration and with a concern for the general welfare, whereas jural legislation is limited to ordering legal relations between individuals. The technique of this order is the legal system and the right to sue granted to legitimate claimants. But in contrast to the value-free theory of procedures, the concept of legal action is linked to the moral concept of law. Corresponding to the maxim "Ubi jus ibi remedium," every moral right is subject to legal action, and conversely, every legal action corresponds to a right. But since imperfections are inherently a part of the empirical administration of justice, there are times when an action is brought for claims that are "false" according to natural law, and it then becomes necessary to distinguish between just and unjust actions, depending on whether or not there are rights that correspond to them.[88] The claim of natural-law principles goes beyond their scientific examination and, as politics, strongly influences the formulations of the positive legal system.

It cannot be claimed that the idea of the administration of justice originated in the United States; it was part of the common property of the natural-right doctrine of the eighteenth century. In his *Essays* Hume notes: "Man, born in a family, is compelled to maintain society from necessity, from natural inclination, and from habit. The same creature, in his farther progress, is engaged to establish political society, in order to administer justice, without which there can be no peace among them, nor safety, nor mutual intercourse. We are, therefore, to look upon all the vast apparatus of our government, as having ultimately no other object or purpose but the distribution of justice."[89] The Declaration of Independence and the Preamble to the Constitution indicate that the purpose of founding a state is to guarantee human rights and to establish a system to

86. *Ibid.*, § 1.
87. *Ibid.*, § 21.
88. *Ibid.*, §§ 240, 241.
89. [David Hume, "Of the Origin of Government," in Hume, *Essays: Moral, Political, and Literary* (2 vols.; London, 1875), I, 113.]

secure justice. What is important to the history of American philosophy of law is merely the process of energetically reviving the natural-law theory, as is suggested by the fact that when it came to formulating postive law according to principles of natural law, legal rights were relegated to the background in favor of the judiciary represented by the Supreme Court.

Edward L. Campbell brings out these conditions excellently in his work on natural-law philosophy published the same year as Smith's *Elements*.[90] Like Smith, Campbell limits the concept of "law" to a specific jural one, as opposed to other laws, and only this law in the strictest sense is the subject matter of legal theory. Jural law overlaps only in very general outlines with the lex non scripta of the common law, whereas statutory law contains a number of ancillary laws that must be understood in light of principles of utility or economy or as having arisen arbitrarily and then become codified because it is necessary to have a regulation (for example, to regulate traffic).[91] Statute law (including rules of the court and procedural law) is not capable of deriving from scientific principles, while the unwritten law is the unalterable part of any legal system that can become the subject matter of a science. The doctrine of jural law is the doctrine of law itself, in contrast to the instruments to maintain and sanction it.

It is not by accident that the unwritten law coincides with jural law. Because it is unalterable and part of "universal consciousness,"[92] it does not require detailed codification; it is absorbed in the positive legal system through implication or brief references. The Bills of Rights in the American state and federal constitutions are such inclusions of natural-law principles in the positive system. It could even be claimed that the simple act of establishing a constitution is sufficient to serve as formal adoption, since the Constitution was established "to secure these rights" and the purpose implies the means.[93] Knowledge of rights is communicated through

90. Edward L. Campbell, *The Science of Law, According to the American Theory of Government* (Jersey City, N.J., 1887).

91. For the contrast of lex scripta and non scripta, see also James C. Carter, "The Provinces of the Written and Unwritten Law," *American Law Review*, XXIV (1890), 1–24. Carter rejects codification because the written law cannot be held valid for new cases and only new cases are important for development of law. The principles for deciding new cases cannot be taken from the law code, thus contradicting the sense of the instrument.

92. Campbell, *Science of Law*, 12–13.

93. *Ibid.*, 13.

acts of intuition: concepts of rights are axioms of the human mind; they arise spontaneously and of necessity from the organization of our mind, allowing us to make sound judgments concerning right and wrong whenever we find ourselves in some empirical situation that requires a judgment. They are intuitively perceived like any other truth of the metaphysical sciences. More important than this theoretical content of intuitive method—adopted from Scottish common sense philosophy—is its religious justification. The unalterable principles are given us by God; it is he who has furnished us with "rights" and given us the ability to know them unmediatedly and without thought. They are the single, sufficient, and authoritative source of law. Rules of conduct ordered and sanctioned by the state are human rights, in contrast to divine ones, from which they derive their validity. Without the divine authority of the principles, no theory of the state would be possible; human law would be "a nebulous and amorphous mass of empyric dogmas," and human government a mass of political functions without assignable boundaries or limitations.[94]

To deduce certain rights by intuition requires some principles to be assumed; these are the principles on which Commons explicitly based his philosophy of law and economics. They are the principles of time and finiteness, contained in the rights of liberty and property. Smith defines a right generally as "the liberty or power of acting freely with reference to the object of the right."[95] The fundamental right is the right of personal liberty in the broadest sense of physical freedom, reputation, and disposal over material goods. Without the use of "material things that naturally exist around us"—air, water, land, nourishment, shelter, fuel—humans cannot live; more than the quantity essential for bare survival is required to live healthily and with some comfort and to exercise and develop one's faculties. To the extent that man is deprived of the goods he requires, he is robbed of liberty. The only limits to his legitimate needs are set from the outside, by others' rights to liberty that collide with those of the first person. Such collisions are inevitable, since whatever a person appropriates for his own use is therefore withheld from all others. In some cases—such as using the ocean

94. *Ibid.*, 23; *cf.* 73.
95. George H. Smith, *Elements of Right*, § 21.

for navigation—this collision is not dangerous because the ocean is large enough to accommodate any number of boats. In other cases—such as the appropriation of goods in short supply—many can be permanently deprived of what the few possess. Since such a deprivation affects *everyone*, no single person has the right to rob another of his appropriated goods. Only the intervention of the state can regulate distribution. Only in cases of absolute necessity, when physical survival is at risk, does the individual have the right to make use of another's goods, and even then only if in so doing he does not jeopardize the other's physical existence.[96]

The elementary structure of the relations between man and nature requires rights to be awarded or withheld. The human person as the organizing center creates, as it were, an eddy in the stream of nature that otherwise flows smoothly, none of its parts being owned by other parts, needing them, or being in a position to be deprived of them. Man as the center steps out of this river and creates a new timeline in which the maintenance, construction, and development of his person run their course. "Liberty" and "development of faculties" are merely other names for the organization of the world around centers that stand in opposition to the inarticulate stream. Smith sees this construction as something in relation to which a right must be defined. Such a question would be nonsensical if a single individual were confronting nature. But it does take on meaning when several individuals compete for the appropriation of the same sections of nature—that is, for the relations of a society with nature. Nature appears as a quantity of things that can be appropriated and for which therefore there is no problem of rights so long as they exist in unlimited quantities. Only when the relationship of demand and supply turns into scarcity does the question of fair distribution arise. Limitation thus enters the man-nature relation from the side of nature. The condition of limitation, the assimilation through the process of human life, comes from the human side.

Campbell shifts the point of view slightly. His analysis of property stresses the fact that the object that has become property by this transition from its previous condition remains unchanged in its essence as a physical object. Therefore its character as property

96. *Ibid.*, §§ 116–31.

must rest on a special relation, originating in the person. To understand this relation, he cites the example of a man who made his own pocket watch. He postulates that the owner himself dug the needed raw materials out of the earth. He then asks: when and how, given this assumption, does the watch become "property"? "All will agree that the instant he had reclaimed the material from the unappropriated stores of nature they became 'his own'; that as fast as the work of construction progressed, the fruits of his labor became 'his own'; and that the instant it was completed it was his watch."[97]

Dissecting "property" into the process of its production through personal work isolates the individual in his relation to nature, removing it from its connection with society. Here it is not the group confronting a limited quantity of goods, with each entitled to an equal share; instead, property is seen as "acquired"—or, more precisely, as "to be found in the process of acquisition." The idea of rights is not introduced by the roundabout route of competing persons and scarcity of goods. Instead, the "limitation" that leads to rights now comes from the person himself as the limitation of his ability to work or, in the last resort, as the limitation of his life, which by advancing upon nature appropriates parts of it to itself. Both elements—the organizing will and the limitation of its effect—are united in the person as the origin of the phenomenon of property.

Within the doctrine of natural law, here are the beginnings of a structural analysis of the jural-economic action that Commons carried to a systematic conclusion.

A theory of sociological practice runs parallel to natural law and its investigation of individual legal relations and takes its direction from the institution of the sovereignty of the Supreme Court. John Chipman Gray simplifies the procedural problem of English analytic theory by returning to the contrast of the "nature" of the law and its "sources."[98] Positive law is state-sanctioned law in the lit-

97. Campbell, *Science of Law*, 26.
98. Gray, *Nature and Sources of the Law* (New York, 1909) (2d ed.; from the Author's Notes by Roland Gray, New York, 1921). [In citing thus, Voegelin may simply be calling readers' attention to the existence of a second edition, since the page references in the following notes accord entirely with the 1st (1909) edition, not the 2d.] See also Gray, "Some Definitions and Questions in Jurisprudence," *Harvard Law Review*, VI, 21–35.

eral sense: "The Law of the State or of any organized body of men is composed of the rules which the courts, that is, the judicial organs of that body, lay down for the determination of legal rights and duties."[99] Only the regulations of the law courts are rights inhering in the state; all other so-called rights are "sources of right," especially statute law. It is therefore false to say that the sale of wine, for example, is subject to penalties; the proper phrasing would say that if a man sells wine and is found guilty by a jury of this offense, he should be punished.[100] "The shape in which a statute is imposed on the community as a guide for conduct is that statute as interpreted by the courts."[101]

The critique of the state embodied as a person initiated by Terry is continued—on the one hand by submerging it entirely in a methodological category, on the other hand by considering it a necessary hypostasis to explain social life. The state, according to Gray, is an artificial person, created so that, its entity being accepted, its organs are given a unity of operation. The idea of the state, he continues, is a device to persuade particular persons—kings, governors, voters, judges, tax officials, hangmen—to engage in cooperative action to benefit all human beings.[102] The notion that the state could be a value, separate from the lives of the men and women who are and will be its constituents, Gray considers a superstition.[103] The state is an abstraction; its concrete organs are ordered in a very worldly way by the "true rulers" of society.[104]

The disappearance of the personalized state with the acceptance of unified procedure, however, does not leave the legal system hanging in midair. Behind legal declarations, and requiring their unification, stands the idea of society. Discussing Austin's concept of sovereignty, Gray argues that within a society such as England, the sovereign in Austin's sense is not an agglomerate of individuals who happen to be king, peers, and members of Parliament—that is, an unorganized horde—but is the king and the two houses, acting separately according to very complicated rules. A state reality *underlies* the rules that create the sovereign. The law of any society

99. Gray, *Nature and Sources of the Law*, 82.
100. *Ibid.*, 104.
101. *Ibid.*, 119–20.
102. *Ibid.*, 63.
103. *Ibid.*, 67.
104. *Ibid.*, 68.

assumes the existence of a society; to deny it would be suicide. "This personification of an abstraction, the naming of it,—family, village, tribe, city, state,—and the giving to it human beings as organs, seems a necessity of human existence."[105]

Smith's and Campbell's natural-law doctrine is significant in American development not because of its novelty but because of its antianalytic stance—for the present still philosophically either entirely without conscious support, as for Smith, or deriving its authority from commonsense intuitionism, laced with theism, as for Campbell—that twenty years later came to fruition in a consciously pragmatic doctrine arising from a typically American situation.[106] Nor does Gray's philosophy of law add many new ideas; it merely sharpens the contrast of "nature" and "sources" of law through realistic observation of the American legal system. The passage just cited dealing with the "true rulers" of society, who appoint the jural organs and through these control the definition of justice, applies directly to the naming of the members of the Supreme Court by the president—that is, by the party and business interests he represents. Considering this germ of Gray's theory, it seems possible that here too the analytic quality refers back not to a scientific-rational culture that suddenly arose out of nothing, but to a shrewd empirical view.

Around 1910 a movement began, instigated by the Association of American Law Schools, with motives similar to the school that arose in England in the 1880s. In England uniform legislation called attention to the problems of legal principles and codification; in America the ominous growth of legal material in court decisions, the inadequacy of procedural law, the splitting of civil rights into fifty systems sometimes considerably at variance with one another, led to suggestions and measures to manage the chaos that was not merely possible but existing in fact. A quantitative illustration of the problem is given in Edwin M. Borchard's table of the number of articles in various systems of civil law:[107]

105. *Ibid.*, 67.
106. For natural-law doctrine in Rousseau's sense, see also James de Witt Andrews, *A Commentary on the Jurisprudence, Constitution, and Law of the United States* (2d ed.; 2 vols.; Chicago, 1908), I, §§ 103–104, 112.
107. Edwin M. Borchard, "Some Lessons from the Civil Law," *University of Pennsylvania Law Review*, LXIV (1915–16), 577–78 (abridged). [The count of "fifty" different systems is Voegelin's, although there were forty-eight states at the time.]

Argentina	961	California	2,104
Austria	602	Georgia	1,040
Belgium	1,042	Idaho	2,343
Italy	950	Iowa	1,299
Brazil	806	Louisiana	1,161
Chile	1,100	Montana	1,855
France	1,042	New York	3,384
Germany	1,048	North Carolina	542
Switzerland	203	Ohio	2,154
Hungary	729	Oklahoma	962
Paraguay	774	South Carolina	942
Venezuela	777	Tennessee	1,991

All the European and South American states keep the number below 1,200, except for Peru with 1,824 and Spain with 2,182. The American states, however, require a considerably greater number of technically very complicated paragraphs.

Another table, concerning legal decisions and the statutes, was compiled by the librarian of the Association of the Bar of the City of New York:[108]

English reports, total number of volumes		2,431
Current yearly additions		16
American state reports	7,370 vols.	
American federal reports	1,050 vols.	
Total number of volumes		8,420
Yearly additions		214
English public statutes, total no. of vols.		160
Yearly additions		1
American statutes, total no. of vols.		3,164
Yearly additions		32

This table was published in 1914. Only two years later Borchard mentions 9,000 volumes of decisions and a yearly increase of 300 to 400.[109] The outcome is the current chaotic state of the law and

108. Cited in John Basset Moore, "The Passion for Uniformity," *ibid.*, LXII (1913–14), 538.

109. Borchard, "Some Lessons from the Civil Law," 572. The latest figures cited in the *Proceedings of the American Law Institute*, I (1923), 71:

A computation in 1917 showed 17,000 volumes of American reports and 7,000 volumes of British reports. Each year witnesses large additions to this mass of

the complete inadequacy of legal decisions. The situation came about as a result of the retention of the system of precedents, the federal constitution, and the inadequate training of jurists.

The system of precedents results in the mass production of reports of decisions. Their publication is not competently regulated; it is merely a sideline of specific publishers. The decisions of every court are reported to a central collection point, which indiscriminately sends them out for publication. Significant decisions stand cheek by jowl with trivial ones, cases of purely local interest are slipped in with others of national importance, decisions of the higher courts are lumped in with those from lower courts and with others still on appeal. The sheer bulk of cases makes it impossible for practicing attorneys thoroughly to research them and find legal principles, so that in exercising his profession the lawyer must rely on a few cleverly selected cases. And this situation in turn increases the tendency to attribute undue authority to isolated cases, thereby increasing the demand for them. A single volume of decisions can hold references to 5,000 and more precedents. Rigid observation of precedents is connected with a decline in the quality of textbooks. Today it is almost impossible to write a text on any aspect of the law in a form that develops the principles of the field, because the jurists insist on complete citations of all decisions. Therefore the labor of composing a textbook has become another sideline of the decision-publishing industry; its level barely rises above that of a detailed listing.[110]

The federal organization of the states prevents national control of decisions as is common in England. The homogeneous English judicial hierarchy allows the courts and barristers to collaborate, so that the Council of Law Reporting eliminates from the Law Reports all cases that have no value as precedent—though the *Law Times* does publish all cases not included in the official collection.[111]

The third crucial factor in the unsatisfactory situation is the in-

---

cases. During the year 1914–1915 it was estimated that 175,000 pages of American reports and 5,000 pages of British reports had been published.

Furthermore to this monstrous and ever increasing record of judicial precedent is being added each year not only the record of the opinions of the chief law officers of each state on questions of public law, but also the decisions of public service commissions and other administrative boards.

110. Moore, "Passion for Uniformity," 539.

111. Borchard, "Some Lessons from the Civil Law," 575.

adequate training of jurists. Even in law schools they are taught by the case method, in order to prepare them for practicing. On this topic Borchard notes, "The system of case citation as the guiding rule of our legal method in reality caters to the incompetent judge, for, with the power to rely upon previous decisions, it enables a judge so inclined to avoid the necessity for independent thinking."[112] Only a very few law schools pay even the slightest attention to the history and philosophy of law. "How few of our students acquire any familiarity with the contributions of such jurists as Amos, Maitland, and Gray, not to mention von Jhering, Gierke, and Duguit. . . . The work of such leaders of thought as Wigmore and Pound receives far too little appreciation from our bar and our courts."[113] The lack of familiarity with history of law, theory of law, and especially the details of such legal systems as Roman law demotes juridical studies and practice to the technique of referring to previous decisions, without theoretical understanding of the material.

The standardization and codification of legal materials is intended to help this situation. But the device lacks the precondition of the existence of a group of jurists who might undertake the work. The lack of systematic training because of inadequate schooling and the inability to read foreign languages, in which the most important relevant works are published, are the chief obstacles to the creation of such a group.[114]

112. *Ibid.*, 576.
113. *Ibid.*
114. The first attempt to provide an overview of the mass of American law and to simplify it is being undertaken by the American Law Institute. The beginnings of this effort go back to 1914, when Hohfeld's treatise "A Vital School of Jurisprudence and Law" (see below) stressed the duty of the universities to collaborate in the work of improving American legal institutions. The war interrupted these first steps toward organizing to this purpose, and it was not until 1921 that the Committee on the Establishment of a Juristic Center was named at the annual meeting of the Association of American Law Schools. This committee completed the necessary preliminary work, and on February 23, 1923, the Institute was founded with financial support from the Carnegie Corporation ($1,075,000). The task of the Institute was defined: "The particular business and objects of the society are educational, and are to promote the classification and simplification of the law and its better adaptation to social needs, to secure the better administration of justice, and to encourage and carry on scholarly and scientific legal work" (*Proceedings*, Vol. I, Pt. 2, p. 21).
   At first the work of the Institute was limited to a "Restatement" of existing law. It was to be presented so as to formulate and stress "legal principles" and to follow these principles with analyses of the pertinent judicial problems and with reference material. The principles were to have the clarity and precision required

During the session of August, 1909, the Association of American Law Schools therefore named a committee to select the most important works in history of law on the Continent. These were to be translated and issued as a series of volumes to represent a compendium of Continental history of law for American jurists. The memorandum that led to the establishment of the committee states the following purpose:

> The recent spread of interest in Comparative Law in general is notable. The Comparative Law Bureau of the American Bar Association; the Pan-American Scientific Congress; the American Institute of Criminal Law and Criminology; the Civic Federation Conference on Uniform Legislation; the International Congress of History; the libraries' accessions in foreign law,—the work of these and other movements touches at various points. . . . The present-day movements for codification, and for the reconstruction of many departments of the law, make it highly desirable that our profession should be well informed as to the history of the nineteenth century.[115]

---

for classification; however, the language common to classification was not always chosen. The "Restatement" is specifically not meant for classification, because to have done so would have introduced into the American legal system a rigidity that is happily avoided in the flexible common law. The influence of the "Restatement" was to be exerted through practical application by lawyers and judges, not through legislative recognition. To guarantee this influence, the membership of the Institute and the commission is structured in such a way that all interests are represented and it can be taken for granted that the members will observe their own work. The membership includes among others: the chief justice and two other justices of the Supreme Court, a number of judges of the higher federal courts and the highest state courts, representatives of the state bar associations, representatives of the National Conference of Commissioners on Uniform State Laws, the deans of the law schools that are members of the Association of American Law Schools, the members of the organizing committee, and a great many invited jurists and professors. Elihu Root was named honorary president; [George] Wickersham held the presidency, with Benjamin N. Cardozo as vice president. So far, the work of the Institute is of a preliminary nature; a "restatement" of any of the areas is not yet available. The first works will deal with legal conflicts (between the federal courts and the state courts) and torts.

115. From the Introduction to the series, serving as Preface to each volume. The following works, selected and translated, were issued in the Continental Legal History Series (p. xii):

1. Various authors, *A General Survey of Events, Sources, Persons, and Movements in Continental Legal History.* (This volume includes papers by Maitland, Carlo Calisse, Jean Brissaud, Heinrich Brunner, von Stintzing, R. Schröder, H. Seigel, Otto Stobbe, H. Zöpfel, Joost Andrian van Hamel, Eugen Huber, Ebbe Hertzberg, and Rafael Altamira.)
2. Various authors, *Great Jurists of the World from Papinian to Von Jhering.*
3. Jean Brissaud, *A History of French Private Law.*
4. Rudolf Hübner, *A History of Germanic Private Law.*
5. Adhemar Esmein, *A History of Continental Criminal Procedure, with Spe-*

Justice Holmes expressed the significance of this monumental work of translation in an introduction to the first volume:

> I can but envy the felicity of the generation to whom it is made so easy to see their subject as a whole. When I began, the law presented itself as a ragbag of details. The best approach that I found to general views on the historical side was the first volume of Spence's Equitable Jurisdiction, and, on the practical, Walker's American Law. The only philosophy within reach was Austin's Jurisprudence. It was not without anguish that one asked oneself whether the subject was worthy of the interest of an intelligent man. One saw people whom one respected and admired leaving the study because they thought it narrowed the mind; for which they had the authority of Burke. . . . The works of foreign scholarship were then inaccessible. One had to spend long days of groping, with the inward fear that if one only knew where to look, one would find that one's difficulties and questions were fifty years behind the times. Now, a man can start with the knowledge that he starts fair—that the best results of Europe, as well as of this country and England, are before him. And those results are so illuminating that diligence alone is enough to give him an understanding of how the law came to be what it is, of its broadest generalizations, and (so far as any one yet can state them) of the reasons to be offered for continuing it in its present form or for desiring a change.[116]

The following year—in August, 1910—a committee was appointed to oversee the Modern Legal Philosophy Series (consisting of M. R. Cohen, Drake, Kocourek, Lorenzen, Mechem, Pound, Spenser, and Wigmore). The memorandum explains the undertaking:

> We are on the threshold of a long period of constructive readjustment and restatement of our law in almost every department. We come to the task, as a profession, almost wholly untrained in the technique of legal analysis and legal science in general. Neither we, nor any community, could expect anything but crude results without thorough

---

cial Reference to France.
6. Carl Ludwig von Bar, *A History of Continental Criminal Law.*
7. Arthur Engelmann et al., *A History of Continental Civil Procedure.*
8. Carlo Calisse, *A History of Italian Law.*
9. Jean Brissaud, *A History of French Public Law.*
10. Paul Huvelin, *A History of Continental Commercial Law.*
11. A. Alvarez et al., *The Progress of Continental Law in the Nineteenth Century.*

[This list and the one in note 118 below are presented essentially as Voegelin gives them. Authors' first names have been added. Both series were reprinted by A. M. Kelley Publishers, New York, 1968–69.]

116. Oliver Wendell Holmes, "Introduction," in Various Authors, *A General Survey of Events . . .* , ed. Ernst Freund et al. (Boston, 1912), xlviii.

preparation. Many teachers, and scores of students and practitioners, must first have become thoroughly familiar with the world's methods of juristic thought. As a first preparation for the coming years of that kind of activity, it is the part of wisdom first to familiarize ourselves with what has been done by the great modern thinkers abroad—to catch up with the general state of learning on the subject. After a season of this, we shall breed a family of well-equipped and original thinkers of our own. Our own law must, of course, be worked out ultimately by our own thinkers; but they must first be equipped with the state of learning in the world to date.[117]

The memorandum suggests a process of adoption similar to the one the English analytic school instituted when it incorporated the German theory of law from digests and from Jhering's and Bierling's work. But whereas in England such adoption was the private work of several scholars and the selection was determined by their personal choice of theoretical problems, in the United States awareness of an unsatisfactory situation led to cooperative, bold translation of European works into English, although no individual scholars adopted them and included them in the system of their own understanding.[118]

What was "bold" in the undertaking is expressed in the "General Introduction" to the series. First, it reassured practical jurists who might take offense at an excess of training in philosophy. The introduction asserted that it would be ridiculous to claim that philosophers must become lawyers or lawyers turn into philosophers in order to achieve perfection in American jurisprudence.[119] It was

117. *Report of the 33d Annual Meeting of the American Bar Association* (1910), 963.
118. The following works appeared in the series:

1. Karl von Gareis, *The Science of Law.*
2. Fritz Berolzheimer, *The World's Legal Philosophies.*
3. Luigi Miraglia, *Comparative Legal Philosophy.*
4. Nikolai Mikhailovich Korkunov, *General Theory of Law.*
5. Rudolf von Jhering, *Law as a Means to an End.*
6. [?] Vanni, *The Positive Philosophy of Law.*
7. Alfred Jules Emile Fouillé *et al., Modern French Legal Philosophy.*
8. Rudolf Stammler, *The Theory of Justice.*
9. Ernest Bruncken *et al., The Science of Legal Method.*
10. Giorgio Del Vecchio, *The Formal Basis of Law.*
11. Various Authors, *The Scientific Basis of Legal Justice.*
12. Josef Kohler, *The Philosophy of Law.*
13. Pierre de Tourtoulon, *Philosophy in the Development of Law.*

119. Morris R. Cohen *et al.,* eds., *Rational Basis of Legal Institutions,* Modern Legal Philosophy Series (New York, 1923), vii.

enough, the essay continued, that the current generation of legal progress be supported and guided by philosophy. There seemed no doubt that it would progress in a pleasing manner in view of the American character as Tocqueville described it: In most operations of the understanding the American relies on his individual judgment, and there is no other country in the world that values philosophy less than the United States. On the other hand, Americans tend far more to generalizations than do the English and value them far more highly. From this peculiarity of the American mind, the introduction concludes, since philosophy is, after all, only the science of general concepts—the analysis, new formulation, and reconstruction of "concrete experience"—"we may well trust that (if ever we do go at it with a will) we shall discover in ourselves a taste and high capacity for it, and shall direct our powers as fruitfully upon law as we have done upon other fields."[120]

Philosophy of law is understood as the doctrine of the principles of the substance of law, or of the social order. A theory of the purpose of law, the introduction continues, is unavoidable as the basis of action in legislation and judges' interpretation. Absence of principles can end only in anarchy. The social institutions would be thrown back on blind opinion by natural forces instead of being guided by intelligent free will. Even the phenomenon of experimental legislation, characteristic of the Anglo-American countries, could not succeed without social aims.[121]

The necessity of preliminary training in theory for any reformation of the legal system, the elements of natural law, and the tradition of English theory converge in the analytic theory of law developed by Hohfeld and his followers. To understand it as typically American, we will arrange its crucial features under the headings of (1) pragmatism, (2) originality, and (3) intellectualism.

1. *Pragmatism*

In his 1914 address "A Vital School of Jurisprudence and Law: Have American Universities Awakened to the Enlarged Opportunities of the Present Day?" Hohfeld himself incorporated the movement described just above.[122] The speech develops a program for a law-

120. *Ibid.*, viii.
121. *Ibid.*, ix.
122. Reprinted in Wesley Newcomb Hohfeld, *Fundamental Legal Conceptions*

school curriculum; a significant innovation is the introduction of thorough training in history and theory of law. In remarks commenting on "analytic jurisprudence" as a course of study, Hohfeld refers to his own analysis of fundamental legal concepts, which had been published the previous year.[123]

The outline of the fundamental concepts of law is presented in two tables of jural correlatives and opposites.[124] The first table reads:

| Right | Privilege | Power | Immunity |
| Duty | No-right | Liability | Disability |

The table of opposites is arranged as follows:

| Right | Privilege | Power | Immunity |
| No-right | Duty | Disability | Liability |

These lists differ from Salmond's tables by substituting the word *privilege* for *liberty* and *no-right* for *liability* (the correlative of *liberty* in Salmond's tables). The meaning of the words remains unchanged. But in developing his views, Hohfeld does not start with a theory of protected interests in order to evolve the possible situation by reference to legal protection or by the absence of reference to legal proceedings or to the contrast of rights at rest and rights in motion. Instead he argues that fundamental jural relations in the strictest sense are sui generis and that therefore any attempts at formal definition must always be unsatisfactory if not completely useless.[125] When he calls concepts sui generis, Hohfeld is not trying to justify the necessity of reciprocal definition of concepts, as Austin did. Rather than defining them "formally," he points out the contrast with his method of interpretation through examples. The fundamental legal concepts (or better, the eight words) are used in both tables. Then their significance and application are to be more closely determined by testing them on concrete cases. In twenty-seven pages (pages 36–63) Hohfeld therefore refers to an abundance of English and American decisions and citations from other au-

---

as Applied in Judicial Reasoning and Other Legal Essays, ed. Walter Wheeler Cook (New Haven, 1923).

123. *Ibid.,* 349.

124. *Yale Law Journal,* XXIII (1913–14), 36. The essay was first published *ibid.,* 16–19. A second essay followed, *ibid.,* XXVI (1916–17), 710–70.

125. *Ibid.,* 36.

thors' commentaries to lend historical authority to the use to which he puts his concepts and to their meaning as found in historical usage. Since historically there are several meanings, the task Hohfeld sets himself is impossible. Nevertheless, there are some results, because in the course of the investigation its conditions tacitly change and a priori principles are introduced, making it possible to interpret and select the material in the desired sense. The assumption is made that a duty must always correspond to a right, so that the existence of a legal situation without duties results in the group of privilege–no-right. In the same way that authority is assumed to be an ability to change legal situations, so it can be used to find legal situations not subject to such authority—in other words, "immune." Corbin explicitly mentions this constructive law of concepts, which Hohfeld only suggests implicitly.[126] Corbin points out that judicial and popular language largely agree on the meaning of the concepts *duty* and *authority,* so that the whole table can be easily constructed by proceeding from these two concepts to determine the negatives and correlatives. Thus the a priori scheme is not even found as the form of the materials from the examples themselves. It is prestructured on the basis of two firm concepts and enlarged through formal relations of the correlatives and negatives. And yet the idea of this scheme in an area of logical being in itself carries no weight in the intellectual world of American theorists. They recognize no contrast between the variety of materials and a firm structure within it. Instead, concretion in discourse, in Santayana's sense, is the point of departure for concept formation in regard to subsequent practical application. The fact that no more and no less than eight concepts result, of which two pairs each are linked through the category of negation, and that this grouping of concepts indicates an elementary social form regardless of its content, does not appear methodologically significant. Instead, Hohfeld explicitly states that these concepts seem to be the "lowest common denominators of the law"[127]—that is, the smallest shared substantial elements, from which the more complex arrangements are structured. Corbin further declares that they are fundamental because they furnish the various combinations that

126. Arthur L. Corbin, "Jural Relations and Their Classification," *Yale Law Journal*, XXX (1920–21), 230.
127. Hohfeld, *Fundamental Legal Conceptions,* 64.

make up the concepts of property, trust, easement, and the like.[128] But to say that these formal elements are understood as the least possible substance is already going too far, for what is characteristic of pragmatic logic is the substitution of "concretion" for the dualism of form-content. The concrete event is felt as a mass that can be rationalized, not according to logical rules, but as needed. The fact that rationalization is possible at all is to be taken as given; the question concerning the laws of rational structure is never posed. The world is an anarchic manifold organized in mere fragments in order to help negotiate the difficulties of the next moment.

The experiential background of fragmentary organization of the world produces subsidiary methodological comments that are understandable only given the background. In presenting the concepts of authority and liability, Hohfeld refrains from excessive fundamental analysis by noting: "Too close an analysis might seem metaphysical rather than useful; so that what is here presented is intended only as an approximate explanation, sufficient for all practical purposes."[129] In some of his work Kocourek takes the analysis further; for that reason Corbin vigorously rejects Kocourek's view, remarking that, in weighing ordinary language against analysis, Hohfeld had achieved a compromise at a "convenient and serviceable" point. Corbin goes on to argue that Hohfeld carefully followed linguistic usage in order to have the "average lawyer" understand him, whereas Kocourek "detrimentally" constructed a terminology "of unnecessary complexity," far removed from ordinary language; this procedure "made thinking and expression more difficult"—"it cannot be crammed into unwilling mouths." In order to limit the permissible analysis, these statements contain a number of concepts that are not aimed at the truth content of the theory of law but subordinate it to certain practical demands of legal application and to the average lawyer's intellectual capacity. What is remarkable is the phrase that complicated terminology "cannot be crammed into unwilling mouths," which means that the correctness of a theory would be determined by the more or less willing brains—or mouths—of lawyers. Equally important is Hohfeld's idea that analysis that goes beyond a certain degree of preci-

128. Corbin, "Jural Relations," 229.
129. Hohfeld, *Fundamental Legal Conceptions*, 50.

sion is "metaphysical." The adjective is used here as the pejorative for everything that does not follow the immediately obvious practical purpose.[130]

The definition Hohfeld uses to summarize the result of his historical investigation is extremely terse: "A right is one's affirmative claim against another, and a privilege is one's freedom from the right or claim of another. Similarly, a power is one's affirmative 'control' over a given legal relation as against another; whereas an immunity is one's freedom from the legal power or 'control' of another as regards some legal relation."[131] In two articles of 1919 and 1920, Corbin more closely determined the meaning of the crucial words *claim* and *control* by introducing into the definition the encompassing concept of "jural relation."[132] One of these papers—"Legal Analysis and Terminology"—contains a number of definitions of legal concepts to be used in teaching at the Yale Law School. The students, who were just beginning their study of law, were to be supplied with a stock of exact concepts that would enable them to analyze and understand cases more easily. It is assumed that the students had no scholarly interest in these concepts but that they would use them as instruments, since they were available. The form of the presentation is therefore purely dogmatic; no attempt is made at critical justification. The fundamental concept, which also precedes Hohfeld's, is that of "legal relation." It is not understood to be methodologically pure; prescriptive law and natural law are intrinsically tied to it. "Law" is a regulation concerning human conduct, starting with the legislative organs of an organized society. (By this definition, courts are also legislative organs.) The definition is followed by the cryptic statement, "When a rule of law has been reduced to words, it is a statement of the legal effect of operative facts."[133] What constitutes a rule of law if it is not reduced

130. See also the discussion in *Proceedings of the American Law Institute,* I (1923), 68–69. "The difficulty in obtaining an exact legal terminology is enhanced by two circumstances. First the language of the law must not be too recondite for general understanding. A philosophical terminology, though exact, may be so difficult to learn or to understand or to apply as to be undesirable. . . . Changes can be made and must be made where exactness of expression imperatively requires them, but such changes must be gradual, and there is a limit beyond which they can never go lest the language of the law cease to be plain English."

131. Hohfeld, *Fundamental Legal Conceptions,* 60.

132. Arthur L. Corbin, "Legal Analysis and Terminology," *Yale Law Journal,* XXIX (1919–20), 163–73; Corbin, "Jural Relations," 226–38.

133. Corbin, "Legal Analysis and Terminology," 164.

to language (quite aside from the fact that it is a matter not of words but of meaning) remains unclear. In any case Corbin's use of this phrase allows him to gloss over the transition from the sphere of norms into another, which he calls the sphere of natural law. Reduced to words, the rule states: Certain circumstances will generally be followed by immediate or remote legal consequences in the form of action or nonaction on the part of the legislative and executive organs of society. When legally relevant circumstances exist that lead to particular legal consequences, then the persons affected by them stand in a "legal relation" to each other. The statement that between A and B there exists a legal relation is a prediction concerning the behavior of social organs. The pragmatic nature of these "laws" is brought out in the second article.[134] Here the jurist's task of discovering what the law is in a particular case is reduced to the question, "What will our organized society, acting through its appointed agents, do?"[135] To come up with an answer, a "rule of law" has to be applied; it is in agreement with a natural law in enabling us to "predict physical consequences and to regulate our actions accordingly." The entire complex of the problem of norms and of the analysis of commands is pushed into the background by the single question: "The essential fact is the existence of societal force—when and how that force will be applied."[136]

The element of command is no longer included in the separate legal concepts. "When we say that society 'commands,' we do not

134. Corbin, "Jural Relations," 226–27.
135. *Ibid.*, 226.
136. *Ibid.*, 227. Corbin was not the first to introduce the idea of "prediction" in American jurisprudence. See Oliver Wendell Holmes, "The Path of the Law," *Harvard Law Review*, X (1897), 475, rpr. in Holmes, *Collected Legal Papers* (New York, 1920), 167–202. On the subject of the science of law, Holmes argued:
"People want to know under what circumstances and how far they will run the risk of coming against what is so much stronger than themselves, and hence it becomes a business to find out when this danger is to be feared. The object of our study, then, is prediction, the prediction of the incidence of the public force through the instrumentality of the court" (p. 167).
"The primary rights and duties with which jurisprudence busies itself are nothing but prophecies" (p. 168).
"A legal duty so called is nothing but a prediction that if a man does or omits certain things he will be made to suffer in this or that way by judgment of the court; and so of a legal right" (p. 169).
". . . this body of dogma or systematized prediction which we call law" (p. 169).
"The prophecies of what the courts will do in fact, and nothing more pretentious, are what I mean by law" (p. 173).
Corbin does not mention Holmes's essay.

mean that someone is shouting hortatory words at B from a house-top or from a throne, although there may be such an actual shout (as when the traffic policeman says 'Stop' or 'Move on'). We mean generally no more than that there is in some degree a uniformity of societal action and that unless B conducts himself in a certain manner this societal action will be detrimental to B."[137] All that remains of the English and German tradition is the idea of government sanction as an essential element of the law and the concept of rights as a protected interest. Four formulas cover the possible legal relations:

1. What *may* A do without the threat of punishment in favor of the other person?
2. What *must* A do under threat of punishment in favor of the other person?
3. What *can* A do to change existing legal relations with the other person?
4. What *can* A *not* do to change existing legal relations with the other person?[138]

Arranged differently, the following outline results:

> May . . . permission . . . privilege—no right
> Must (may not) . . . coercion . . . right—duty
> Can . . . danger (new relation) . . . power—liability
> Cannot . . . security (against new relation) . . . immunity—disability.[139]

The theory of the nature of the state is decidedly affected by limiting individual interests that state authority is empowered to protect or not and by eliminating the problems of commands or norms. Limiting law to court decisions, Gray dissolved the state into a fiction. Corbin goes somewhat further and finds that the concept of legal relation, which can exist only between two persons, destroys once and for all the "juristic nonsense" of corporate "entities," the rights of states, social interests, and other fictions—"cherished among ourselves as well as among our quondam friends

---

137. Corbin, "Rights and Duties," *Yale Law Journal*, XXXIII (1923–24), 503.
138. Corbin, "Legal Analysis and Terminology," 166. [Corbin actually enumerates only the first three relations given here. Voegelin draws the fourth from Corbin's further analysis following the numbered list.]
139. *Ibid.*

in Prussia."[140] Actions, inclination and disinclination, feelings, and wishes, he continues, are always individual. Legal rules are made for individuals. And social welfare is, in the final analysis, always individual welfare. It is not "labor" that is in conflict with "capital"; rather, a laborer without capital may fight another who has capital. "Interests of the person" do not clash with "interests of property," since only persons have actual or legal interests. A state, a jural person, an association can act only through individuals. "Social" development is possible only through individuals. Every form of socialism is at heart merely another form of individualism. The basic substance, coming from natural law, of the "legal relation"— that it must be a relation between two human beings—here similarly destroys collectivist problems as Böhm-Bawerk, with his concept of goods, destroyed the "rights and relations" as special classes of goods. The legal relation, which in fact is a formal element of the social structure (a more detailed analysis follows below), is misunderstood as a material element and treated as the smallest unit of complex institutions. Rights in rem and in personam, for example, are lost in relations between two persons, so that a legal relation in rem exists between A and B whenever an indeterminate number of relations of the same sort occur between A and other persons. This form of law is called "multital." A right in personam is called "unitales" when it is directed against only one person and "paucitales" when several specific persons are involved.[141] In the same way Böhm-Bawerk broke down complex rights and relations into the values of individual goods. Both forms of breaking down social reality into the full variety of its institutions were abolished in Commons' theory of law and economics; in it the legal relation is given its position as the basis of all institutions, thus permitting the discipline of descriptive institutionalism. But what remains is the pragmatic element, which allows for an understanding of the relation of law and economics in which it is not a meaning in a realm of logical being but is elaborated using the language of expectations of concrete behavior. What remains to be discussed is

140. Corbin, "Jural Relations," 227n2.
141. Hohfeld, *Fundamental Legal Conceptions*, 65–67 (first published in *Yale Law Journal*, XXVI [1916–17], 710–66); Corbin, "Legal Analysis and Terminology," 170–71; Albert Kocourek, "Plurality of Advantage and Disadvantage in Jural Relations,"*Michigan Law Review*, XIX (1921) 47–61 [Voegelin erroneously cites the title of this essay as "Rights in Rem," here corrected].

the background of experience, before which formal elements do not appear as firm structures but must be found through the examples taken concretely from the history of law.[142]

2. *Originality*

The pragmatic approach of Hohfeld's theory of law is expressed in his attitude toward the authorship of the concepts. He did not invent the table of the eight fundamental concepts: it had been set up the same way by Salmond; Hohfeld merely changed the names of two concepts. And Salmond's table, in turn, had its precursors in the tradition of the English analytic school and in German jurisprudence. Theoretically, Hohfeld's development of the same concepts can even be called a major step backward, since he did not propose them as essential concepts but determined them from historical usage as average meanings. Like Corbin, he is quite unconscious of their systematic value and sees their determinants not in the logical structure of the theory of law but in their "utility" and in the capabilities of average jurists. But neither Hohfeld's nor Corbin's work provides any indication that the whole theoretical achievement in developing the concepts was not initiated by them. Anyone unfamiliar with the works of their precursors must assume, when reading Hohfeld's and Corbin's papers alone, that they were the ones to discover these schemata of legal concepts. Annexing the theoretical productions of others is not considered dishonorable because it does not appear as a value in the pragmatic world view.[143] It is a way to step out of the river of action for a moment

142. For the analysis of complex formations in elements, see Wesley Newcomb Hohfeld: "The Nature of Stockholders' Individual Liability for Corporation Debts," *Columbia Law Review*, IX (1909), 285–320; "The Individual Liability of Stockholders and the Conflict of Laws," Pt. 1, *ibid.*, 492–522, Pts. 2 and 3, *ibid.*, X (1910), 283–326 and 520–49; "The Relations Between Equity and Law," *Michigan Law Review*, XI (1913), 537–71; "The Need of Remedial Legislation in the California Law of Trusts and Perpetuities," *California Law Review*, I (1913), 305–35; and "Supplemental Note on the Conflict of Equity and Law" and "Faulty Analysis in Easement and License Cases," both *Yale Law Journal*, XXVI (1916–17), 767–70. The papers on equity and law demonstrate that there are not two legal systems operating side by side and fighting against each other but that it is merely the vocabulary that makes a contrast appear. "Rights" and "equity" relations can be reduced to "legal relations" in *one* system.

143. To illustrate this claim: In Professor Commons' seminar I gave a lecture on the development of American problems in theory of law. On that occasion it turned out that neither Professor Commons nor the members of the seminar were aware of the origin of Hohfeld's system in British jurisprudence and that they did not feel that adopting the system without giving credit violated the standard of honesty in

in order to find a more effective mechanism to deal with reality. But the thought that theoretical values exist for their own sake and go through an evolution in their own sphere remains alien.

In Hohfeld's case, however, such plagiarism seems unusual even by American standards. In an article subsequently prefaced to Hohfeld's published work, W. W. Cook finds it necessary to make some clarifying and apologetic remarks on this problem.[144] The apology is carefully structured in a number of general phrases: that no single person—neither in the natural sciences nor in the science of law—can be the originator of large segments of new perception. The most that can be expected is the addition of several stones to the ever-growing structure of science and scholarship; whatever one person writes must therefore consist in large part of reformulations of others' thoughts. Any scholar would have reason to feel proud if he could merely arrange the facts accumulated by others in such a way as to cast a new light on the subject—"a light which will serve to illuminate the pathway of those who come after us and so enables them to make still further progress."[145] After this description of the scholar's lot, full of self-denial, Cook contrasts its hard work and little success and then goes into greater detail to explain that the fundamental concepts, with one exception (no-right) are not new; that they can be found in common law and that other writers on jurisprudence, especially Terry and Salmond, had a great deal to say about them. But unlike all preceding investigations, Hohfeld's statement of the concepts was far more precise; they became systematically linked through negation and correlation; and most important, Hohfeld was the first to demonstrate their practical importance in the analysis of legal institutions (especially in the law-equity problem).[146]

It is true that this apologia is stimulated by a feeling that Hohfeld's discoveries need to be defended; in order to make a striking

---

scholarship. It seemed to me that a scholarly result is seen only as an instrument available for use by all and sundry. The sphere of "use" lies completely outside the sphere of scholarship. Even the word *outside* is to say too much; the scholarly sphere itself is in no way recognized. Only the separate result is seen as a point of passage to practical evaluation.

144. Walter Wheeler Cook, "Hohfeld's Contributions to the Science of Law," *Yale Law Journal*, XXVIII (1918–19), 721–38.

145. Walter Wheeler Cook, "Introduction," in Hohfeld, *Fundamental Legal Conceptions*, 5.

146. *Ibid.*, 16–20.

point, it even goes so far as to claim that Hohfeld had added new concepts, which is not true; and that his definitions are more precise than those of his predecessors, although Hohfeld specifically rejects setting up formal definitions. But on the whole they do not just happen to be casual in form, but are meant to be casual. For Cook opens his essay with the observation that the English and American jurists have regarded analytic jurisprudence as an "academic" discipline, "without practical value"; and he finds this opinion justified by the facts. Almost all writers on the subject, he argues, are followers of the erroneous theory that their task was complete when they had furnished a critical justification and definition of legal concepts. "These writers" saw only very dimly or not at all that an analysis of legal concepts is not an end in itself, except for intellectual amusement. They do not demonstrate the usefulness of analysis for practicing lawyers and judges in solving their problems, and even less do they show the usefulness by practical application to concrete examples. Hohfeld's "great merit" is to see that though analytic jurisprudence may be "interesting" when pursued for its own sake, its principal value lies in facilitating and improving the solution of legal problems. In this regard it is no different from any other pure science. So as not to be unfair to the memory of Hohfeld and to arouse the belief that he had seen it as more than a useful tool, it had to be explicitly added that for him practical solutions had been the chief problem, and analytic theory of law merely one instrument among others, such as comparative law and history of law.

Cook's effort to rescue Hohfeld's honor—which no longer apologizes for plagiarism but makes an effort to show that Hohfeld was not interested in analysis as such and was merely forced to deal with it in order to solve practical problems, even if he ran the danger of acquiring the reputation of an impractical theoretician—introduces a term that shows the spirit of the attempt in a new guise: the word is *message*. Cook notes that one of the greatest messages Hohfeld gave to the profession of law was that an adequately analytic jurisprudence was among the indispensable tools of a properly trained lawyer or judge. The concept *message* entered ordinary language from religion. Today it can be used in its original meaning in the revivals of the Salvation Army, when converts are called upon to tell the story of their conversion and to bring to their listeners the message of salvation. In a wider sense, the word is very frequently used in the extended area of popular education and in particular the lectures arranged by women's clubs. Whether the speaker is discussing the political situation in China, expressionist painting, or Prohibition—he delivers a "message." The idea of education in general is religiously saturated by the belief that the greatest possible contact with the greatest possible number of people and with the aid of a quantitatively large accumulation of unrelated bits of knowledge (therefore the extraordinarily voluminous lecture business in America) will result in "progress." Those who promote this form of educational system do not see the fragments as unrelated—because they are unconnected to any discipline—but only as tools for the immediate stimulation of intellectual activity, which results in a feeling of participation in the stream of civilization and in part has the purpose and effect of an opiate (a flight from reality).

Three types of persons who convey messages are especially closely linked with the business of university education: the president, the "noted educator," and the football coach. The functions of president and "noted educator" are often combined in one person. The president's function is primarily for public show, and his message, which appears in the form of magazine articles or—if the president has an important post, like Nicholas Murray Butler at Columbia University—in the New York *Times*, must maintain the link with public opinion and preserve the favor of financial supporters of the institution.[147] The "noted educator" has a message of a more technical nature, and under certain circumstances—often

147. The July 7, 1926, issue of *The Nation* printed the following item:

"What is a College President? The regents of the University of Oregon are ready to tell us. The official statement of their investigating committee which nominated Dr. Hall gives the reasons for their choice:

Dr. Hall as president of the University of Oregon will prove to be a very popular man. He is very easy to meet, has a pleasant smile, and one is immediately impressed by his unbounded energy. He is not only a real college executive but has had business experience as well in connection with one of the banks in Madison, Wisconsin. Dr. Hall is a very able public speaker, and his services undoubtedly will be in great demand throughout the State. We are very enthusiastic about the new president.

"Possibly Dr. Hall has other qualities besides those which led to his selection, but at any rate he has a voice and a pleasant smile and has been connected with a bank. Is anything more needed?"

he engages entirely in banalities—is responsible for a concrete experiment of the kind A. Meiklejohn is currently attempting to carry out in Wisconsin: a selected group of students will study the history, literature, philosophy, science, and art of one culture—for example, that of ancient Greece—for one year, in order to gain an overall view of a culture. That this message is more complete in religious than scientific terms is shown by the telling detail that knowledge of Greek is not a prerequisite. Finally, the football coach brings the message of physical training, perhaps on occasion voluntarily issuing statements on the value of compulsory military education in college, and introduces students to the technical aspects of sexual life insofar as this is necessary and not covered by older colleagues.

By way of the idea of connecting with the community and with individual intellectual and physical education, the essence of the message forces its way directly into scholarly life, and even scholars of the highest rank—such as the Nobel Prize recipient [Robert] Millikan—become restless under the pressure of public opinion and feel compelled to publish selected platitudes on the connection and agreement of science and religion. Only a few scholars—for example, the biologist [Thomas Hunt] Morgan—earn a reputation for avoiding mixing science and education and offering no message.

With his program of reforming law schools and theory of law in the service of restructuring American law, Hohfeld is placed at the center of this socially optimistic religious movement. This effort is aimed at adopting the techniques of European cultural achievements (the purpose of translating European works) in order to remove the superficial flaws in American intellectual life and establish superiority with the same vigor that led to preeminence in the economic sphere. Fanaticism has no patience with slow absorption and intellectual growth. The translations of European jurisprudence have so far had little effect and are read hardly at all.[148] The energy expended in organizing the work of translation evidently satisfies the immediate purpose—the feeling that something is being done—and there is no desire actually to assimilate the works. Hohfeld's theory of law is an attempt of a similar sort. He, Corbin,

148. See Borchard, "Some Lessons from the Civil Law," 576. The same complaint—that American jurists do not read the translations of European works—was voiced by Professor Page of the University of Wisconsin (interview).

and Cook earnestly rejected the current understanding of theoretical problems, and the intent of the work was directed to a "message"—practical help that must not be problematic but gives advice in clear, terse dogmas and, in the case of Corbin's dogmatic collection of definitions for students, ends in the total abolition of theory.

The work is seen as "outside," centered not in the person but in collaboration in a common purpose, as the construct of an impersonal subject matter transcending individual achievement. That is why Cook uses a second word to describe Hohfeld's work. This word, which has as much typical meaning for American life as does *message,* is *contribution.* "Contribution" expresses an attitude toward intellectual endeavor that does not see such an achievement as the work of the person, the expression of personal philosophical stature; rather, it democratically reduces the individual to a number in the mass of cooperating minds. "Contribution" has a primary cultural-philosophical significance as the relation in which history stands to the civilization of the present. Greece, Rome, the Middle Ages, Europe, all are seen from the aspect of their "contribution" to the height of American civilization. [If the writer believes in gestures of humility, he will reverse the relationship and speak of "our debt to Greece and Rome."] One of the highest forms of critical recognition for a scientific or scholarly work is the formula that it is "a real contribution" to the discipline in question. Starting with the linear rational development of modern natural science and taking its bearings from the evolution from amoeba to Abraham Lincoln, in happy innocence of all cultural-morphological problems, every form of human endeavor appears especially as an "activity" that, whatever it produces, can do so only in a forward and upward direction, so that the individual may have only a modest part in progress but is assured of this small part. The subject matter on which the labor of progress is practiced is impersonal but lacks the compactness of a philosophical system or a work of art. Structures are not dropped into it from above; the substance of the problem, and with it the methodology, arise anew out of every concrete situation, so that in spite of shared work and gradual accretion, the process has neither tradition nor purpose. "Progress" is accepted as somehow structuring itself, while the "messages" and "contributions" come from no place or time and seek their progressive position in the process according to an unknown law. The ahistorical nature of message and contribution is characteristic of the strong feeling of connection and incorporation in the metaphysical progress of the world process. As a result, forms of cooperation, the feeling that "we're all in the same boat," emerge; the experience is one of a shared attack on an irrational and undefined enemy—chaos is vanquished over and over by progress. This attitude eliminates the problems of adopting a tradition, of originality, of theoretical connection, and of the growth of a culture.

3. *Intellectualism*

The nature of a direct attack on a "concrete" problem, without the roundabout route of traditional treatment of the subject matter, is expressed in outbursts of the intellect unlinked to the structure of the subject matter. "Concretion" as a starting point is generally a fragment of little weight. Santayana's idea of concretion as the origin of an all-encompassing philosophical system represents a rare case. Now, if a fragmentary concretion furnishes the sole material for the construction of a system intended to be applicable to other cases, a rift ensues between the subject of the material that has issued in the theory and the rational web that is spun from it. Kocourek's work in the theory of law is one case of such an empty construction. The constructive principles that enter Hohfeld's "tables" are the rights "at rest and in motion," the sanction, and the idea of "legal relation." From the standpoint of a doctrine of legal procedure, this schema might give rise to the objection that certain of the concepts it contains have no jural meaning. Roscoe Pound claimed as much for the concepts of liability, disability, and no-right, though his criticism was not based on the principal substance of the problem.[149] Kocourek went into greater detail; he found the correlative pairs of right-duty and power-liability constructed properly, but neither of them seemed to him either correlative or of jural importance. "Privilege" he found equivalent with "liberty" in applying to an absolute situation that has no specific correlative. "No-right" he saw as no more correlative than "no-power." In the same way, "immunity" meant lack of relation, the situation of noncorrelation to any action on the part of other persons.[150] The table of

149. Roscoe Pound, "Legal Rights," *International Journal of Ethics*, XXVI (1916), 97.
150. Albert Kocourek, "The Hohfeld System of Fundamental Legal Concepts,"

correlatives, he argued, would therefore have to be restructured as follows:[151]

Jural Concepts		Nonjural Concepts	
Right	Power	Liberty	Immunity
Duty	Liability	None	None

Accordingly, the table of negative concepts is altered to read:

Jural Concepts		Nonjural Concepts	
Right	Power	Liberty	Immunity
No-right	Disability	No-liberty	No-immunity

The decision as to whether a concept is "jural" or "nonjural" is made according to the criterion of the threat of sanction. Where this threat is absent, there is no legal relation. The concept of legal procedure is opposed to the social concept, which Corbin and Cook advocate. On the occasion of criticizing a decision, Cook formulated the position for the advocates of the social concept of law:

> Those who would deny that a privilege is a jural relation would, if they were logical, have to say that a decision for the defendant involves a determination of a mere question of fact and not of the jural relations of the parties. Surely, this cannot be so. When courts determine that certain facts give a witness a privilege not to testify, or that certain other facts make defamatory remarks about one's neighbor "privileged" and so not actionable, they are determining the jural relations of the parties, just as much as if they were to find against the privileges claimed and thereby to recognize the existence of rights. Whichever way a new problem is decided, therefore, the court establishes for the first time what legal relations result from the state of facts in question. If the decision is for the plaintiff, a *right* and correlative *duty* are recognized; if the defendant wins, his *privilege* and the correlative *no-right* of the plaintiff are recognized.[152]

The principle of the problem can be presented free of juristic terminology by a schematic presentation of the auxiliary verbs:

Illinois Law Review, XV (1920–21), 24–39. See also Kocourek, "What Is Liberty?" *ibid.,* 347–49.

151. Kocourek, "Hohfeld System," 39.

152. Walter Wheeler Cook, "Comments," *Yale Law Journal,* XXVIII (1918–19), 391.

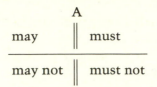

The schema represents the various actions open to the person A, with the diagonal group of *may–must not* expressing the desired conduct, while *must–may not* stands for undesired behavior. The *must* group indicates behavior under sanction. The *may* group describes the sphere of liberty. From the viewpoint of conduct, only the *must* group is material to a legal relation; when the individual's total situation is considered, both groups are equally essential to the construction of reality.

This schema is the cross section of expectations of sanction or nonsanction at a single point. If two or more cross sections were to be connected with each other, a new verb would have to be introduced to express the possibilities of the change. Every conduct in time changes the cross section of expectations: for example, I may consume or sell an object that belongs to me. If I consume it, I cannot sell it; if I sell it, I cannot consume it; in each case my cross section is altered. The changing concept of "can" can be presented in a simple diagram with the concepts of "may" and "must" if the positive words are accompanied by the negative meanings, so that *may* indicates *must not* as well, and *must* points to *may not*. The schema would then look as follows:

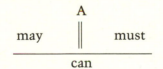

The concepts above the horizontal line indicate the point of the cross section, divided according to sphere of liberty and coercion; *can* indicates the dimension of change.

The introduction of a second person does not affect this diagram. Even if the behavior of person A takes its bearings from that of person B, the possibilities of conduct break into a *may* against B and a *must* against B, and nothing more. The dimension of change remains unaltered in their structure, even if *can* refers to social behavior—testifying, delivering, offering, accusing. The second person, B, and his possibilities of conduct as well as the attitude toward him appear only as a contextual determination in the schema, changing nothing in its form.

After this analysis the full magnitude of the problem of concretion can be understood. None of the American jurists undertook the analysis we have just carried out; the theory begins at a point that is already complicated by all three levels of the problem. The concepts of right and duty do not coincide with the basic situation of *may* and *must* because they are not seen from the perspective of *one* person. The correlation between them comes about because the duty of A and the right of B are opposed to each other. That A's duty is congruent with "A must" seems obvious, but if we were to search for B's right in a contemporaneous cross section of B, it would not be found either in "must" or in "may," for according to the definition of a right as the control over the behavior of another person—that is, the right to bring suit and get a judgment against A—the behavior that brings about the correlation—B's suit against A—clearly lies in a different cross section. The concept pair right-duty thus goes beyond the fundamental structure by (1) assimilating person B—thus assimilating a contextual determinant; and (2) introducing a time difference into the concept of law. The concept of power is arrived at through hypostasis of the dimension of change; "can" is the dimension that links the cross sections; that is, it is not behaviors of "can" that are juxtaposed to those of "may" and "must"; rather, "can" is the quality of all behavior aimed at changing the legal situation. Every "may" and "must" behavior is at the same time a "can" behavior, so that there are actually no such entities as "powers."

"Liability" once again refers to the second person and any future behavior he may engage in that will change the legal situation.

All behaviors of right and duty are by definition powers because they bring about a change in the legal situation. Furthermore, power spills over into Hohfeld's privilege and Kocourek's liberty, for privilege and liberty encompass the entire sphere of "may," with which the powers, insofar as they are a matter of "can," coincide, since "can" is merely a dimension of the sphere of liberty. Insofar as "power" is meant as behavior against another person, it is a relevant section, more specifically determined, of the "may" sphere. The same complication is characteristic of the other concepts in the schemas.

Concretion, which is Hohfeld's point of departure, encompasses three levels of meaning, among which one is dominant in general. The principal dominant factor is furnished by a particular content of the "may" and "must" spheres: the interest of A, which is protected from another person B, and the behavior of A, which is coerced to protect B's interests. Within American theory, criticism must therefore follow fixed tracks: it may not destroy the basic concept of the legal relation between two persons. Criticism can therefore never be directed at principles but must always address the examples used by one or another writer. Kocourek's criticism of Corbin, Hohfeld, and Cook, as well as any countercriticism, is therefore most valuable for the proofs that an example cited to illustrate power can also serve to illustrate privilege, liberty, right, and immunity. These proofs are worthwhile because they show that Hohfeld's diagram of legal concepts and those forms subsequently derived from it are worthless. But since they work only on examples, not on principles, they are of no further significance.

Concepts of such high and unequal complexity cannot be used to construct a simple system through correlation and negation. That the attempt is nevertheless undertaken leads to that peculiar phenomenon of discrepancy between construction and material that we call "intellectualism." Kocourek begins his attempts at construction with the firm claim: "In legal analysis the starting point is jural (legal) relation."[153] A legal relation is a "situation" in which one person—to be called "dominus" of the relation—can control his behavior toward another person—here called "servus"—with assistance from the law. Depending on whether the dominus controls his own behavior or that of the servus, two types of legal relations emerge. These are subdivided into "principal" and "lower" types. The principal types are power and claim; the lower types are privilege and immunity. Privilege is a kind of power; immunity is a kind of claim. No systematic reasons are given for these subdivisions. Kocourek believes it would be "uncomfortable" to say that one has the privilege to refuse the negative act of establishing no defaming statements in the testimony of a witness at a

153. Kocourek, "Plurality of Advantage and Disadvantage," 48. See also Kocourek, "Various Definitions of Jural Relation," *Columbia Law Review* (1920), 394–412.

trial; and that it would be too "emphatic" to speak of a "power" to the defaming claim; the refusing aspect (privilege) of the behavior was therefore combined with the positive aspect of action in the phrase "privilege to do the act." Thus "privilege" describes an "exceptional" situation, a nonessential trait of reality that cannot be systematically incorporated. The fact that this concept is included in the diagram while another one, such as representation, is excluded has no justification based on the structure of the subject matter; it can be explained only by an irrational predilection for the number eight, which, though it does not logically allow limitation of the diagram of concepts, makes the form of a geometrical diagram possible. Kocourek arranges the concepts into a table:[154]

Dominus ||		Servus
Advantage ||	Correlatives	||	Disadvantage
Power	→		Liability
Privilege	] →		Inability
Immunity	] ←		Disability
Claim	←		Duty

In this diagram privilege and immunity do not have the 1907same meaning as in Hohfeld's table. For Hohfeld they designate the sanction-free sphere, whereas here they are pinpointed as special forms of power and claim.

Alongside these jural relations in the narrow sense (nexal relations) Kocourek places quasi-jural relations. They are similar to the nexal ones, but the person who claims their advantage is unable to realize it through judicial assistance. Typical cases of quasi-jural relations are wrongdoings not covered by government sanction, as well as immunity against transferring one's own title, verbal promises of gifts without delivering, and the like. The addition of bodily harm would therefore also be quasi power, on the same level as an offer that is unsupported by sanction. The common element in these examples seems to be the second person's absence of commitment, so that behaviors are set that may be built into legal procedures in some way

154. Kocourek, "Plurality of Advantage and Disadvantage," 49.

or other but that at present do not (or ever will) establish a legal relation with another person. If, for example, the gift were delivered, Kocourek would speak of the power of person A and liability of the person B. As long as the action is incomplete, only a quasi relation exists, which gives B a quasi claim, not a nexal claim, to the gift. If the examples are applied to the may-must schema, the wrongdoing, for example, falls under "must" and, as "not-may," does not constitute a positive relation to another person. Kocourek does not see the fact that A's wrongdoing eventuates in B's right to sue as positive, since it grows out of A's interest and the disturbance of the interest— even though criminal—destroys the relation.

The offer comes under the heading of "may"; since acceptance cannot be immediately coerced, and since the act of acceptance is not a "must" for B but the full relation of the contract with sanction follows only upon B's acceptance, the relation is merely quasi-jural.

The introduction of quasi-jural relations can be considered Kocourek's criticism against himself, since in actual fact he breaks down the idea of the legal relation between two persons with the absolutely correct observation that such a relation does not exist; rather, the elements are the behaviors of individual persons, which appear as a relation only through a very complex combination. But Kocourek overlooks this problem in principle, which leads to the postulation of quasi relations; he is content to set this type of relation alongside nexal relations and to add to the table of principal relations another showing secondary relations.[155]

The internal structure of nexal relations is shown in the following table:[156]

Jural Opposition

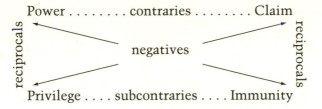

155. See also Albert Kocourek, "Tabulae Minores Jurisprudentiae," *Yale Law Journal*, XXX (1920–21), 222–25.
156. Kocourek, "Plurality of Advantage and Disadvantages," 56.

In this table *contrary* means the opposite direction of the relations; powers run from dominus to servus, while claims go from servus to dominus. Privileges and immunities are the so-called subcontraries, as can be seen by the directions of the arrows in the table of correlatives. *Reciprocals* means that privilege is a variation of power, while immunity is a negative form of claim. *Negatives* refers to the substance of the actions: in the case of "power," dominus can take action against servus; in case of "immunity," servus cannot take action against dominus. In the case of "claim," servus may be coerced to engage in a particular behavior; in the case of "privilege," dominus cannot be coerced to behave in a particular way. These relations are merely of a verbal nature; they are meaningful only when the complex terms of relation are accepted as reality.[157]

The most detailed tables are extensions of the development of the general and specific correlative negatives of the nexal relation. The negative of power, for example, is no-power and can signify any one of the seven concepts that constitute no-power. The specific negative is disability, because in its specific meaning no-power belongs (1) to the passive group and must (2) designate an inability, clearly determining its place. The table reads:[158]

157. To show the diversity of concrete jural situations, Kocourek developed a table of permutations given the conditions: (a) that only two persons participate in the relation; (b) that no more than two jural or quasi-jural relations be involved; and (c) that the temporal priority be ignored. The result is the following table ("Purality of Advantage and Disadvantage," 58):

A	D
a	d
AA	DD
Aa	Dd
aa	dd
AD	DA
Ad	Da
aD	dA
ad	da

A and D stand for advantage and disadvantage in the nexal relation; a and d signify advantage and disadvantage in the quasi-jural relation. To designate specific relations, indices can be introduced—A1 for power, A2 for privilege, and so on. This table of permutations also depends for its meaning on the utility of the terms.

Negative Correlatives

3	2	1	1	3	2
Negatives		Dominant	Servant	Negatives	
Specific	General	Correlatives		General	Specific
Inability	No-claim	Claim	Duty	No-privilege	Privilege
Liability	No-immunity	Immunity	Disability	No-disability	Power
Duty	No-privilege	Privilege	Inability	No-inability	Claim
Disability	No-power	Power	Liability	No-liability	Immunity

A second table indicates the technical points from which the negatives are derived:

Forms of Jural Negation

Negatives		Correlatives		Negatives	
Serv. pass.	Dom. pass.	Claim	Duty	Serv. act.	Dom. act.
Serv. pass.	Dom. pass.	Immunity	Disability	Serv. act.	Dom. act.
Serv. act.	Dom. act.	Privilege	Inability	Serv. pass.	Dom. pass.
Serv. act.	Dom. act.	Power	Liability	Serv. pass.	Dom. pass.

When, for example, the specific negation of duty is to be determined, we will first find that duty is a "servient-active concept"; in that case the negation must be "dominant-active" —that is, privilege or power. Since duty includes legal coercion of behavior toward another person, the specific negative must lack the legal coercion, so that the decision points to privilege.

This example clearly illustrates the lack of content in the diagram, since Kocourek decides in favor of privilege as the specific negative of duty by claiming that it contains "no legal compulsion to act towards another." But this phrase applies just as much to power, since power, too, is legally uncoerced behavior. The formula that leads to "privilege" should read: the relation to be sought must testify to the *refusal* of a coercion to act. To act the negation of the

---

158. Kocourek, "Tabulae Minores," 219.

coercion contained in "duty," however, we can no longer find the *absence* of coercion cited by Kocourek; the idea of refusal is a random addition arising from the conceptual construction. The decision is therefore reached without sufficient reason merely in order to preserve the geometric form of the schema originally constructed by Hohfeld. The fact that the connection between the formal construction and the meaning of the concepts has been destroyed becomes obvious through the circumstance that Kocourek, using different concepts and the same formal reflections, aims at the same result Hohfeld proclaimed. The intellectual operation has become detached from concretion and becomes a game with its own value, pursued for its own sake.

5

On John R. Commons

I

John R. Commons was born in Hollandsburg, Ohio, in 1862, during the Civil War. His father's family, who were Quakers, had left their home in Virginia because of slavery and had settled in Richmond, Indiana, the western center of Quaker settlements. Commons' father was born in the North, outside the sphere of influence of the slave economy. His mother, whose family came from Vermont and had settled in northern Ohio (roughly the area that is now Cleveland), was a schoolteacher in Richmond, where she married Commons' father. The families of both Commons' parents were farmers. In addition, his father practiced the trade of harness maker and owned a share in the local newspaper.

Commons' youth, until his twentieth year—when he left Winchester, Indiana, where his parents now lived, to attend Oberlin College—was marked by this environment. The Quaker religious aristocracy, personal dignity, and the idea of a brotherly community coincide with the sense of independence of the pioneer farmer and the conscious struggle for freedom from slavery. His mother, and later Commons himself, was educated at Oberlin, the Congregationalist college that was the first, beginning in 1833, to admit blacks and women. Commons' father's independent personality developed to the point where he abandoned any determinate form of religion and turned to positivist philosophy. Discussions about Spencer, the philosophy of individualism, and its relation to the problem of slavery are among Commons' earliest memories. He became a printer, a trade he practiced starting at fourteen and continued even during his college years—during vacations as a typesetter in various print shops and during the school year as printer of the college newspaper. In 1883 he joined Local 53 of the Typographical Union, and to this day he is an honorary member.

When he first arrived at Oberlin, he spent a year in the college's preparatory school, since the local school in Winchester did not adequately prepare its students for admission to college. In 1885 he enrolled in the college. That same year, between his studies and his work as a printer, he was so overworked that he suffered a nervous breakdown and had to take a year's leave of absence. He spent the summer of 1885 as a typesetter in various localities in Michigan, Ohio, and Indiana. In October he accompanied his brother to Florida. They took the train when they could afford it or could manage to hoodwink a conductor; the rest of the time they walked, and eventually they arrived in Tampa. In payment for a job, their father had been given a piece of property in Florida, and to the best of their ability the brothers cultivated part of the land, living on the proceeds of the harvest and on the money they had earned through occasional printing jobs picked up in the course of their travels. In 1886 they sold a ten-acre orange grove very profitably.

Their improved financial situation and his newfound health allowed John to continue his studies in the fall of 1886, and two years later he graduated. During his time at Oberlin he was particularly influenced and helped by James Monroe, professor of economics, who lectured on Henry George's economic theory and was a supporter of the abolition movement. After Commons' graduation Monroe persuaded a wealthy acquaintance to make a loan to Commons that allowed him to study at Johns Hopkins University for an additional two years. It was there that Commons became familiar with the German school of history through Richard T. Ely (who had studied with [Karl Gustav Adolf] Knies) and Herbert B. Adams, who was the first in the United States to apply the methodical approaches he had acquired in Germany to the study of state and local government. Fellow students at Johns Hopkins, influenced by the same teachers, were the historian [Frederick Jackson] Turner, the sociologist A. W. Small, and the editor of the New York *Times*, John Finley. Commons ended his student days when Oberlin conferred the M. A. degree on him in 1890.

The years that followed, which involved teaching, theoretical writings, and practical research in economics, but most important the first works on distribution of wealth and proportional representation, cannot be understood without considering the problematic situation into which Commons was born. His life overlaps the shaping of the American nation, and his work is woven into this process; but its beginnings hark back to a period before his birth, the decades in the first half of the nineteenth century. The Civil War put an end to the period of limitless expansion, and with the completion of the transcontinental Union Pacific railroad in 1869, the frontiers in their relation to the population became increasingly noticeable, until in the decade 1890–1900 the population of the American middle states was decreasing rather than growing.[1] With the progressive transition to an industrial system, the farmer-pioneer population began to flow back to the urban centers of the Pacific and Atlantic coasts and the Middle West. Long before these overt symptoms indicating that the American space was beginning to be exhausted, the industrial revolution and the emergence of a class of wage labor had led to cooperative and communistic experiments in an attempt to do away with the unpleasant phenomena of capitalism by introducing a completely different economic system. With the exceptions of a few communities built on religious foundations, these experiments failed, though in the United States they lasted longer and were more numerous than in any other area within the capitalist economic system because of the extent, the affordability, and the outstanding quality of the land along with freedom from government interference. Between these attempts at the utopian negation of capitalism and Commons' philosophy of economics and government stands the person of Josiah Warren.

Warren (1798–1874) came from a Puritan New England family. At the age of twenty he married, moved west, and settled on the frontier in Cincinnati. He made a living as a music teacher and orchestra conductor, invented a lamp that burned cheap fat instead of tallow, and in 1823 founded what became a highly successful lamp factory. Around this time Robert Dale Owen came to Cincinnati on a lecture tour, and Warren became such an enthusiastic promoter of Owen's social program that in 1825 he sold the factory and joined the New Harmony community. The two years that

1. Frederick L. Paxson, *History of the American Frontier, 1763–1893* (Boston, 1924). Two maps on p. 550 chart the population distribution in 1890 and 1900 respectively. The frontier is defined as the outer limits of an area where the population is less than six per square mile.

followed converted him from the idea of cooperation to an individualistic economic philosophy. Looking back, he wrote of his experiences:

Many a time while I dwelled in the midst of them did I say to myself, Oh! if the world could only assemble on these hills around and look down upon us through all these experiences, what lessons they would learn! There would be no more French Revolutions, no more patent political governments, no more organizations, no more constitution-making, no more law-making, no more human contrivances for the foundation of society. And what a world of disappointment and suffering this experience might save them! But they could not get our experience, and so they kept on organizing communities, phalansteries, political parties, and national revolutions, only to fail, of course, as we did, and to destroy by degrees the little hope that existed of making the world more fit to live in.[2]

This lament shows that Warren was fully persuaded of the hopelessness of the cooperative experiment, but it also reveals an excessive faith in the perfectibility of man and in the half-sentimental, half-pathetic rhetoric of a state of mind that does not require mastery of complex economic and political situations. In the end, the substance of his litany indicates his anarchist doctrine.

Warren's doctrine may be called anarchist, and in traditional intellectual history he himself is given the title of "first American anarchist." The label is based on his theory of the sovereignty of the individual and the incompatibility of government use of force with the right to a maximum of individual liberty. He gives the most precise version of this thesis in the chapter "Liberty" in his *Equitable Commerce*, where he attempts to define the conditions of self-sovereignty: If an individual person, his work, his responsibilities, the ground on which he dwells, his property, and all his interests are so completely disconnected, disunited from those of all others that he can always control them or rid himself of them without in the process controlling or disturbing those of others; and if he is the only one to set foot on his land, if his person is not touched, if others do not make demands on his time and attention against his will; then that individual can for all practical purposes

2. Quoted in William Bailie, *Josiah Warren, the First American Anarchist: A Sociological Study* (Boston, 1906), 5. Details of Warren's life and career have been taken from this work.

be called the sovereign of himself and of all that belongs to him.[3]

His experiences at New Harmony gave rise to these uncompromising claims and definitions of the individual's sphere of liberty and property, unattached to any social relations; and practical arguments, rather than theoretical speculations, justify the radical rejection of government. The "experience of the whole world" has demonstrated that the business of an organization is carried out, not by all its members, but by a select group; this group must be granted powers commensurate with the matters it is authorized to deal with, and this authority and these powers accordingly diminish individual sovereignty. If the leadership group represents all the individual's interests, his sovereignty is totally destroyed; if it represents only half, the individual retains the other half. But since these quantities cannot be measured precisely, giving up even the smallest part of self-sovereignty will in practice tend to lead to its complete abnegation, so that the individual is not secure under any form of government.[4] Sovereignty is not an abstract principle; it is the concrete sphere of action of the individual or of the leadership group. Warren advocates the individual's concrete freedom from control, and from this point of view he criticizes the inadequacy of democratic institutions. He considers those who hold to the theory of the "general will," the result of individual votes, "fatally mistaken." Only a small fraction of the voters understand the measures submitted for a vote, and very few are able to foresee all practical consequences. The majority will be disappointed because in practice a law does not have the effect they expected. Furthermore, some will change their minds after casting their ballots. A single individual can cast the deciding vote and thus establish a law that is against the wishes of half of all members of the community. Accordingly, in general a situation exists that threatens the individual's liberty and sovereignty to the utmost degree. The only redress is the complete separation of all individual interests and the strictest observance of self-sovereignty.[5] Warren's practical view leads him to realistic sociological observations about Lamartine's

3. [Paraphrasing] Josiah Warren, *Equitable Commerce: A New Development of Principles as Substitutes for Laws and Governments, for the Harmonious Adjustment and Regulation of the Pecuniary, Intellectual, and Moral Intercourse of Mankind, Proposed as Elements of New Society* (1846; rev. ed. New York, 1852), 61.

4. *Ibid.*, 60.

5. *Ibid.*, 24, 25.

history of the French Revolution. For example, he quotes Couthon's address: "Citizens, Capet is accused of great crimes, and in my opinion he is guilty. Accused, he must be judged, for eternal justice demands that every guilty man shall be condemned. By whom shall he be condemned? By you, whom the nation has constituted the great tribunal of the state." Warren's comment on the passage reads:

> Here, by a jumble of sounding words, "great crimes," "eternal justice," "great tribunal of the state," all of which mean nothing whatever but the barbarian imagination of the speaker, a phantom is got up called *the state*, which is made to absolve the murderers from the responsibility of the murder. If this responsibility had rested individually upon Couthon, where, in truth, the whole of all that he was talking about existed, he would have shrunk back from taking the first step. But throwing all the responsibility upon the soulless phantom called *the state*, there was no longer any check to crime! This is raising institutions of the state *above* the Individual![6]

The myth of the nation and the state is exposed, the democratic ideology is shown to be foreign to reality, and its place is taken by an interpretation of history achieved by determining individual responsibility and conduct.

The doctrine of individual sovereignty is supplemented by an economic policy intended to make possible a life in which the individual sphere is entirely separate. Warren's guiding principle is that prices should be established according to the cost of labor, not subjective value. Supposing person A urgently requires a loan, and person B is in a position to offer it—then the amount of interest should be determined not with a view to A's need but only by B's labor time to satisfy the technical delivery of granting the loan. The occasion for promoting the cost principle is the shrinking of the American space for expansion. The machine, Warren notes, has deprived the laborer of his work, and the machine belongs to those who did not make it and gave no equivalent of their own labor for it. The hungry laborer must flee to the countryside. But here, too, he finds the land controlled by those who did not work it and paid no equivalent for it. "At this point of starvation, we *must* have remedy, or confusion."[7] The way out is the calculation of labor

6. *Ibid*, 27.
7. *Ibid.*, 41.

costs according to the time, difficulty, and "repugnancy" of the labor and the risk of loss involved. What must not be counted in calculating a price is subjective value (for example, high rents in the workers' quarters of a city) and the various forms of monopoly control—land, natural skills (the better doctor preferred to the worse one), patents, and other artificial monopolies. The adoption of Warren's system would not abolish private property but would essentially reduce it to a single object—labor time—and this democratic reduction makes the individual the manager of the naturally provided means of satisfying needs without creating monopolies that make it possible to extort from the consumer a maximum of profit and bring about the conditions of dependency. Warren believed that his system would retain all the advantages of the capitalist system—foremost among them the division of labor.[8]

Warren advocated his views not with the intention of overturning the social order but to show how concrete cases provide the opportunity to begin on a more satisfactory solution to social problems. He himself turned his idea into practice in 1827 by opening the first "Time-Store" in Cincinnati. His principle was that each item was clearly marked with its sale price; for the time spent in making a purchase the buyer would give the seller a "work note" that might, for example, read: Miss XY owes JW ten minutes of needlework. The store was a success—so much so that a competitor at a nearby corner lost his customers and was forced to rebuild his business on the same basis in order to win them back. After two years Warren gave up the store in order to test in production the principle that had been so successful on the distribution level. First he tried it on a small scale with four acquaintances and was encouraged to found a small community with a half dozen families in Tuscarawas County, Ohio. This enterprise failed because the area turned out to be infested with malaria. His next attempt was to reorganize the unsuccessful Claremont Phalanx, a Fourierist cooperative in Cincinnati, in 1847. With this group he founded the village of Utopia along the Ohio River, and here he was once again successful. In a short time the families, who at the beginning of the experiment had $10 among them, owned houses and thriving farms of their own. The community disbanded when still better oppor-

8. *Ibid.*, 43ff.

tunities beckoned farther west, in Minnesota. His last and greatest success was the 1851 founding of Modern Times, a village of about a hundred houses on Long Island. The community exists to this day, but Warren's principles in their strictest form have been abandoned. The reason is similar to the cause of the dissolution of Utopia: the group had no capacity to expand. In Utopia the far West offered new possibilities to the settlers; in Modern Times the opportunities lay in industry (the village is sixty kilometers from New York). Besides differences in theory, Warren's settlements differed from all Fourier's and Owen's communist or socialist enterprises in the actual problems they tried to solve. In a short time the poor, who had nothing except their labor power, became owners of modest landholdings and homes and were full participants in a pleasant communal life. Warren knew that nearly insurmountable difficulties stood in the way of expanding his program to larger economic units; but compared with the collapsed experiments of the New Harmony type, he was successful, since he demonstrated for at least a limited area the solution of a particular group problem—to establish a community without formal organization, whether autocratic or majority-democratic.[9]

The new doctrine of self-sovereignty—as distinct from earlier sovereignty in the hands of princes, parliaments, or the people—contains elements that have special significance for the United States and others that continue to have an effect on European-American history. What is particular to developments in the United States are the cost principle, the fight against monopolies, and the idea of the independent individual who, in a free community, accepts the service of others and himself serves their needs. The critique of democracy and the majority system belongs to Western history in general. In his 1859 essay *On Liberty*, for example, John Stuart Mill advocates the principle of self-sovereignty. As the most important precursor of the idea he names only Wilhelm von Humboldt; but in the *Autobiography* he refers to the

9. See the circular of the Modern Times population reprinted in Josiah Warren, *Practical Details in Equitable Commerce*, with a Preface by Stephen Pearl Andrews (New York, 1852), I, vii: "There is no society formed by us. We are as distinctly Individuals in property relations, in business, in responsibilities, in modes of thought, opinion, and action, as the citizens of New York or any other city . . . we have no corporation of any description, nor any organised or connected responsibilities whatsoever."

general European trend to individualism as decisive for the essay, naming Goethe as its outstanding representative and William Maccall's *Elements of Individualism* as a work that deals with principles similar to his own. Finally he writes about Warren:

> A remarkable American, Mr. Warren, had framed a System of Society, on the foundation of "the Sovereignty of the Individual," had obtained a number of followers, and had actually commenced the formation of a Village Community (whether it now exists I know not), which, though bearing a superficial resemblance to some of the projects of Socialists, is diametrically opposed to them in principle, since it recognizes no authority whatever in society over the individual, except to enforce equal freedom of development for all individuals . . . in one passage I have borrowed from the Warrenites' their phrase, the sovereignty of the individual.[10]

Mill's statements are not entirely correct. His own essay had as its subject matter the principle that state power may interfere in the individual sphere of liberty only to protect other persons.[11] Warren rejects any organized government power without exception, and he could take this stand in practice because his communities were so small that presumably his personal authority, public opinion, and most of all the character of the selected community members were sufficient guarantees of undisturbed development. Nevertheless, the contrast between Warren's anarchist rejection of any sort of organization and its recognition in utilitarian liberalism is less than it would appear to be in theoretical terms. Both men fought against the democracy of their day, and what is important is this shared practical situation, not pedantic categorization of theories of the state. Mill, too, delivers himself of observations on the French Revolution, finding that a people that exercises power differs markedly from a people that is ruled, and that self-restraint is less the rule of the individual over himself than of others over him.[12] Because Warren's experiences, on which he based his theory, were derived from smaller communities of farmers and artisans, without specific clashes of interests—that is, from communities in which each individual represented himself and could be sovereign

---

10. John Stuart Mill, *Autobiography*, "published for the first time without alterations or omissions from the original manuscript in the possession of Columbia University" (New York, 1924), 179.
11. John Stuart Mill, *On Liberty* (London, 1859), 21.
12. *Ibid.*, 12.

because in fact no one pursued objectives that differed from those of the other members—he could replace the political theory of representational democracy with his apparently anarchist philosophy. His doctrine is not completely understood if its theoretical content is the only object of study. The strong, unreflective collective life of primitive communities must be seen as the basis on which a sphere of "freedom from the state" could be promoted, because the group is held together more tightly by the power of shared history, origin, and economic hardships than could be attained by any governmental power apparatus. Warren's critical position does not differ from Mill's, but under the influence of a specific set of experiences, it leads to a theory with a particular content that in its most extreme form has hardly anything in common with Mill's political science, which—taking into account further communal problems—results in the theory of proportional representation.

If we do not consider a theory according to its ultimate formulation but interpret it in terms of its development and its critical function, we can understand Warren's anarchism as a proposal for proportional representation in which the represented unit is the individual. Understood in this way, Warren is one of the first to elaborate those principles of a social system that, by way of the political theory of proportional representation, leads to Commons' doctrine of the "reasonableness" of administrative commissions and the representation of other interests besides political ones.

The first solution of the proportional system that was technically successful originated with Thomas Hare. His concrete problem was the change in the English political situation after 1832; that year's parliamentary reform broadened popular representation but retained an evil that Hare formulated as the attempt to combine representation of interests and of persons. The old idea of a constituency as a unit of interests made impossible the representation of individual persons with divergent opinions within this constituency. Hare constructed his system to solve this problem.[13] In establishing an authority, he refers particularly to the political writings of [John C.] Calhoun, who suggested that the majority problem in the United States could be solved by forming representation of separate interests in the form of separate chambers; legislation

13. Thomas Hare, *A Treatise on the Election of Representatives, Parliamentary and Municipal* (Rev. ed.; London, 1861), v, vi.

could not be enacted without the agreement of all representatives.[14] Calhoun considered this constitutional form the only way to prevent the abuse of minorities. In the English constitution Calhoun's idea was realized in the upper and lower houses of Parliament, but the problem nevertheless persisted in the House of Commons. The special value of his system, Hare said, is that it solved the problem of proportional representation *within* a representative assembly.[15] Hare was followed by an extensive literature on the technical questions of the system, but the formulation of the problem itself was hardly affected. Fawcett's 1860 essay, "Mr. Hare's Reform Bill Simplified and Explained," indicates its subject right in the title.[16] The 1871 work by Simon Sterne, *On Representative Government*, is a discussion of Hare's system as it has significance for American conditions. John Stuart Mill's "Considerations on Representative Government" adopts Hare's system as well. Since Warren, nothing new has been added to the critical position.

Warren's political science can be functionally combined with other suggestions for complete representation and be interpreted as a borderline case of proportional representation. But the special social experiences it grew out of give it a feature that was not found or considered significant outside the United States. Mill's advocacy of liberty harks back to the natural-right tradition of liberty, and his idea of the individual is purely and simply one of men born equal, of human beings as members of an abstract humanity, of human beings endowed with a right to the development of all their faculties and protected from encroachment by the state (the organized form of society, as opposed to the community). His and Hare's doctrine of proportional representation looks for an ideal machinery to safeguard the differences and the interests of the individual, who is imagined as an isolated being, and to ensure they have their fair share of influence on government actions.

Warren's idea of the individual is completely different. He does not see him as an exemplar of humanity, whose individual specialness must be supported in opposition to the collective. He iden-

14. John Caldwell Calhoun, *A Disquisition on Government and a Discourse on the Constitution of the United States* (Charleston, 1851), 24.

15. Hare, *Treatise*, 7.

16. See also Henry Fawcett and Millicent G. Fawcett, "Proportional Representation and Hare's Scheme Explained," in *Essays and Lectures on Social and Political Subjects* (London, 1872).

tifies the individual as a member of a concrete community, related to all others in spite of personal differences by the idea of service and labor, and thus completely one with them and so undifferentiated in all social actions that control of the collective becomes unnecessary. This idea of the individual is derived from the model of the American pioneer. Warren himself was a pioneer, living on the frontier, and his social system was derived from the primitive laboring and living communities of farmers and artisans. The fundamental experience of his anarchism is not the abstract individual of the human-rights period but the coherence of the social group— living on newly settled land and still exposed to the original inhabitants—that faced the task of economic survival and conquest. Such a group has no need of formal organization because the hardships of their situation form the interests of everyone so equally that any differences become inconsequential. Warren can point to the sovereignty of the individual because the sphere of liberty on which the individual has set his sights is so small and the sphere of lack of liberty is so large—though accepted as a matter of course and not really felt as lack of freedom—that no system of force could carry out the protection of reciprocal interests as effectively as the unconscious homogeneity of his group.

Commons' origins lie in the same social surroundings as Warren's. At the time of his birth the settlement of the West was more advanced, but the pioneering spirit was still in full bloom and is so effective to this day that the Middle West is considered an independent cultural zone within American society, on a par with the cultures of New England and the South. Just as it is for Warren, therefore, the experience of the pioneer community is fundamental to all Commons' works, and it is on this basis that he constructs his practical and theoretical work. However, because it is so all-pervasive, it is accepted so much as a matter of course that no conscious reflections of its significance surface, and distinguishing this element from others is made very much more difficult. Its particularity and significance for American thought can be more clearly shown in cases in which it was made the subject matter of separate observation in the sociological literature and the principle of American sociology.

The first of these significant cases is found in Henry Franklin Giddings' *Principles of Sociology*. Giddings takes the "original and elementary subjective fact" of society to be "the consciousness of kind."[17] The definition of this subjective relation uses the terminology of states of consciousness and insists that this condition lies in the recognition of another conscious being as of the same species. The broadness of its meaning becomes clear by contrasting it with the state of consciousness of kind understood as a purely social behavior and with specific economic, political, and religious conduct, as well as with the supporting examples. If, Giddings writes, the worker followed his economic interests, he would accept the highest wages he is offered; but in fact he prefers taking part in a strike that he does not understand to exiling himself from the society of his fellows as a strikebreaker. The example makes no sense in economic terms, but it demonstrates that "consciousness of kind" is intended to designate the experience of pure group membership, without reflection on the rational sense of the action. This "consciousness of kind" is merely the "primary factor" of human nature; not self-interest but man's social nature is the principle on which society is built and the origin of progress.[18] Viewed objectively, progress means an increase in commerce among people, a multiplication of relations, an improvement in the standard of living, population growth, and development toward rational conduct. Subjectively it is the "expansion of the consciousness of kind." Growth in empathy and the development of reason are merely secondary phenomena. The important and causative sequence lies in the development of consciousness of kind. At first this awareness was limited to family and tribe, expanding in levels to clan, race, and nation, and opened the view to a new phase of development encompassing all mankind. The Persian, Macedonian, and Roman empires paved the way for universal brotherhood, and when Saint Paul had transformed the Christian teaching derived from the esoteric certainty that all men are brothers and the children of one father into the dynamic doctrine that all men can become brothers through being born again—then Christianity became the integrating historical force. It began to realize its mission, and today Christian philanthropies and missionary activity are dedicated to the spread of knowledge, the improvement of material conditions, character building, and uniting human classes and races into one

17. Henry Franklin Giddings, *The Principles of Sociology* (New York, 1896), 17.
18. *Ibid.*, 225.

spiritual humanity.[19] The ideal human condition is presented as a maximum of social relations and the experience of social solidarity, with an adequate standard of living and the dominance of reason. Leaving aside the dominance of reason—a later and more incidental desire, fueled by an exaggerated belief in the importance of science—this ideal adds nothing to what could be found in Warren's anarchist pioneer communities. Giddings identified this peculiarly American social system as the ideal objective of a human society.

Santayana takes a more skeptical view of the matter. He distinguishes between democracy as a constitutional system and as a condition of social equality—social democracy. Genetically, social democracy is primitive and unintentional, peculiar to communities in which everyone takes an active part in all tasks and no one stands out. "It is the democracy of Arcadia, Switzerland, and the American pioneers."[20] This form has no room either for an aristocracy or for prestige; instead there is universal readiness to put one's shoulder to the wheel and share in executing the work at hand, not under anyone's leadership but "by a kind of conspiring instinct and contagious sympathy." But Santayana realizes that this social system is by nature the form of a primitive culture, that extending it to larger groups makes for extraordinary difficulties, that a strong power organization is necessary to suppress tendencies to aristocracy as the consequence of natural talents, and that it would be a very questionable achievement if all humankind were reduced to the standing of the contemporary working class. "To abolish aristocracy, in the sense of social privilege and sanctified authority, would be to cut off the source from which all culture has hitherto flowed."[21] Such a community would have to be made up of members who are "plebeian in position, patrician in spirit."[22] Such a society must be inspired by fanatical patriotism and a shared faith and would have to bear the consequences of this state of mind, as was observed in the Spartan polity. Collective virtue turns only too easily to fanaticism, becomes superstition and convention, and ceases to be an advantage.

Dewey shared Giddings' optimistic view and advocated the same

19. *Ibid.*, 359–60.
20. George Santayana, *Reason in Society* (New York, 1905), 114, Vol. II of Santayana,*The Life of Reason; or, The Phases of Human Progress*, 5 vols.
21. *Ibid.*, 125.
22. *Ibid.*, 132.

theory in every essential point. He replaced "consciousness of kind" with "likemindedness"[23] and ascribes to it the obligating power behind all specifics of social action. Like Giddings, he uses awkward psychological terminology for his description. He states that in order to live communally, people should have common goals, beliefs, knowledge, and finally—summarily—mutual "understanding."[24] For "understanding" Dewey has no other concept ready than the rationalistic one of consciousness of community. He cites an example: A person automatically catches a thrown ball, automatically throws it again so that another person receives it and automatically throws it back—these people do not form a community. But if both knew where the ball was coming from and that another person would catch it—that is, if their actions were purposeful—they would be in a relation of "likemindedness."

He, too, espoused the concept of expansion and progress to higher levels of communalization, and his criterion for the goodness of a society is the variety and number of different associations among individuals.[25] And again these quantitative determinants are the sufficient definition of a democratic community, since the content of the aims is such a matter of course for Dewey that any discussion aiming to lay doubts to rest is superfluous: the content is the labor and service of all members of the community. In the democratic communities currently in existence, Dewey notes, appreciation of manual labor, of commercial enterprises, and of tangible efforts in the service of the whole group is growing. In theory we nowadays expect from men and women something in return for the intellectual and economic support they get from the community. It is true that some still admire a life lived in luxury and idleness, but "a better moral sentiment" rules against such a way of life.[26] The community of labor, in the sense of material well-being, with the most numerous and most varied association of the members, is the ideal.

In Commons' concrete investigations and philosophical formulations, the pioneer society is always the first premise, and it is only on this basis that the special problems he addresses have meaning. In his first book, *The Distribution of Wealth*, the con-

23. For the presumable religious root of this theory, see Rom. 12:16 and 15:5–7.
24. John Dewey, *Democracy and Education: An Introduction to the Philosophy of Education* (New York, 1916), 5.
25. *Ibid.*, 96.
26. *Ibid.*, 366.

nection is not yet as fully elaborated as in his later work. The economic theory of the Austrian school, especially Böhm-Bawerk's *Rechte und Verhältnisse* (Rights and Conditions) and *Positive Theorie des Kapitales* (Positive Theory of Capital), predominates in his thinking, though the adaptation to the specific American situation is very clear. Commons' early work deals with the questions of wage distribution in the given historical economic system and reduces the problems of subjective value theory to a minimum by a thorough analysis. The point of departure is not subjective value but the objective price and the location of financial expenditures by the economic subject that corresponds to his wealth and his savings in terms of objective prices. This point of departure allows him to conclude that the economic problem is historically conditioned, which is the reason why the price of a particular commodity is set by the customary supply and the customary demand of this commodity in relation to the customary supply and demand of all other commodities in the same economic category. In this way the crucial question about the reasons for scarcity of supply in relation to demand is raised: it is the scarcity of natural resources and the intervention by the state in creating private property, monopolies, patents, taxes, and tariffs. The institution of private property especially allows the owners to establish arbitrary levels of supply, in order to exploit demand by aiming at higher profits exceeding their costs. As in Warren's analysis, Commons contrasts a cost principle and a value principle, the difference being, however, that Commons does not consider the cost principle the better choice in establishing an economy in every case.

The total economic system is permeated by temporary and permanent monopoly gains, and their creation by the legal order separates the economic problems of production from those of distribution. To arrive at a clear distinction, Commons criticized Böhm-Bawerk's theory of private and social capital, maintaining instead that all goods are capital—that is, instruments of production—until the moment of their actual consumption. The piece of meat in the kitchen, for example, is capital and is subject to additional amounts of labor up until it is brought to the table to be consumed. Precisely speaking, therefore, there is no such thing as consumer goods; rather, consumption is the boundary that separates the homogeneous mass of (capital) goods from their disappearance from economic life. It is not possible to separate social and private capital, as Böhm-Bawerk does, treating them as partially different masses of goods. Commons argues that there is only one mass of economic goods; seen from the point of view of production and consumption, this mass is social capital, whereas from the view of the legal system, it is private capital.

The doctrine of production factors of land, capital, and labor becomes simplified into the antithesis of man/nature. In his detailed analysis of the land problem Commons finds that the natural resources commonly thought of as scarce (wood, iron, fertility of the soil) under present conditions are free goods just as air and sunshine, and that the sought-for conditioning factor is the *situational* quality of the land in proportion to human settlements. Thus, to give one example, there is no shortage of wood, but there is a scarcity of wood on favorably situated soil. Land must not be considered a special production factor, since it is a stable integrating element for laborers in the form of the soil on which they act, just as the machine constitutes the factor that constrains spatial expansion. "Land merely furnished room for nature to work upon the surface of the earth, just as it furnishes room for man to work. And when the forces, energies, and material of nature are combined with the labor of man, land furnishes room for the two to work together in the production of utilities."[27] The special trait of the "situation" is the fact that it is irreplaceable, in contrast to all other elements involved in production, and that is why surpluses after replacement of costs will be channeled to this element. It is not because the materials as such are scarce, but because they are scarce in this special situation that the surplus is channeled to the owner of the situational monopoly.

The significance of this form of the theory in the American tradition is evident in practical application. In 1921 the Wisconsin legislature was considering the Grimstad Bill, which, along with other measures, advocated a tax on the worth of "bare" land. The "bare" value for an urban parcel of land is the value of the property when the cost of buildings on it has been deducted. It was suggested that farmland be subject to a special assessment, which would deduct not only the costs of buildings, livestock, and the like, but also

27. John R. Commons, *The Distribution of Wealth* (New York, 1893), 29.

50 percent of the net worth of the land for productivity, taxing only the remainder of the bare land. The motivation behind the bill is the same as Warren's determination of prices according to the cost principle: the labor expended is the permitted factor in determining price or, in this case, the value of land, whereas the increase in value through a situational monopoly is subject to a levy for the benefit of the entire community that works it. As a scientific adviser to the budget committee of the Wisconsin legislature, Commons supported the measure, and in a treatise he specifically pointed out its connection with Henry George's single-tax doctrine.

George's proposal was based on the ethical doctrine that land is nature's gift to *all* people and on the economic theory that land consists of natural forces that produce a value surplus beyond the product of labor. The Grimstad Bill improved on the economic theory and eliminated from the land that amount of productivity that must be worked for and renewed by the expenditure of labor and capital in order to keep the property productive within the particular economic system; these efforts were considered the product of labor. The ethical doctrine of remuneration for labor is retained. The consequence of this calculation of value is the equal taxing of rural and urban properties. In 1919 the following land and building values were registered for Wisconsin:[28]

Rural Property

Without improvements	$1,289,332,819	79.08%
Improvements	$ 340,771,127	20.92%
	$1,630,103,946	100.00%

Urban Property

Without improvements	$ 460,256,606	40.13%
Improvements	$ 686,795,320	59.87%
	$1,147,051,926	100.00%

The calculation of value in the Grimstad Bill would deduct from the 79.08 percent of rural property another 50 percent—roughly 40 percent of the taxes was productivity value—so that only about 40

28. John R. Commons, "A Progressive Tax on Bare Land Values," *Political Science Quarterly*, XXXVII (March, 1922), 56. See also Commons, "A Comparison of the Nolan, Grimstad, and Keller Bills" (Typescript, November, 1923).

percent remained taxable, just as was true for urban properties. The state of Wisconsin considered 40 percent of the land value as situation monopoly—a source of income that originates not in the owners' labor but in the shared efforts of the commonwealth and therefore also obligated to pay tribute to the commonwealth.

One temporary monopoly is distinguished from "unearned" gains, and Commons wants to see its privileged standing protected: the position of the entrepreneur. On this point he deviates from Warren's economic idea of the pioneer community and his strict cost principle, accepting instead the capitalist system with its captains of industry and, more recently, its venture capitalists. The politics of the commonwealth require that preference be given to any sign of progress in the economic order; since the elements within the system are interdependent, economic improvements in one place are effective in every place. Higher profits resulting from reorganization of the means of production are to flow entirely to the creative mind, in order to spur it on to still greater achievements. These monopoly gains are not dangerous, because the new enterprises benefit the economy directly and the gains are merely temporary: as soon as the enterprise is sold or the preferred status is capitalized, compensation for the monopoly status falls on the debit side of the concern and fills the pockets of the permanent monopoly owner, becoming "unearned" income, which will be subject to special taxes. In the construction of Commons' economic theory, such practical considerations arise through the grouping of all forms of income around the center represented by the entrepreneur. He formulates the concept of private capital as the legal monopoly aspect of the means of production, and he treats the forms of monopolies to which the income is distributed as an item of expenditure for the entrepreneur who sets the economic process in motion. The entrepreneur distributes income to the owners of monopolies. In only two instances is the system of distribution based on the cost principle: in wages for the lowest class of laborers and in capital taxes, the amount of which is determined by the margin where the current satisfaction of need seems more valuable than withholding gains for future use.

One can see a linear increase in a sense of reality from the unsuccessful social experiments of the first half of the nineteenth century through Warren's communities to Commons' economic theory. A vague intellectual dissatisfaction and an excessive faith in utopian solutions of social problems grew into an individualistic pioneer psychology and a system of promissory labor notes and costs, useful in a limited situation. In Commons' formulation this situation was so well adapted to the tasks of a mixed agricultural and industrial commonwealth that a practicable system of taxes could indicate the precise percentage the system of individual enterprise owed to the community. Radical, dogmatic individualism is reduced, and the person of the entrepreneur is assigned the position due him.

A similar increase of reality is shown in Commons' work on proportional representation.[29] The political inadequacies he mentions are the same ones Warren, Hare, Calhoun, and Mill complained of, but the critical argument is not focused on the theory of democracy and the principle of majority rule; instead, Commons explains the historical function of representative assemblies in shaping a unified nation out of comparatively independent local associations separated by vast territories. Nation building is now complete in England, and almost complete in America, so that the territorial structure has taken on secondary importance and the function of representation by territories has come to an end. The new economic and political situation requires new forms of organization, especially the proportional representation of interests.

The new forms are necessary to break up the American system of conventions and "bossism" and the ensuing political corruption. Since not only representatives to state assemblies and the federal Congress but also governors, judges, and the president must be nominated and elected, a hierarchy of nominating conventions has arisen on the foundation of local political clubs, which vote for delegates who nominate representatives; these delegations elect their representatives to the state conventions, and the state conventions elect delegates to the national conventions. Parallel with the system of conventions, which occur occasionally, there is a hierarchy of standing committees that keep the party machinery going; this is the party organization in the narrower sense: the boss, elected by the local political club, as a rule presides over the stand-

29. John R. Commons, *Proportional Representation* (1896; 2d ed. New York, 1907). Quotations are from the second edition. See also Commons, *Representative Democracy* (New York, 1900), 29.

ing committees. These lowest of bosses elect the city boss, and party leaders at this level vote for the county boss, and so on through the state boss to the national party chairman. The power of the party is strengthened by patronage and by control of public utilities, which are private corporations whose fiscal policy and price determination are under government supervision. Since the territorially based two-party system prevents the representation of divergent interests, it is necessary to nominate candidates who are untouched by any particular color and who can therefore unite a majority for themselves because they are colorless. For all practical purposes the political machine is thus powerless, being merely a business arrangement behind which a third organization arises that injects an agenda into the activities of the politicians. This is the lobby—a loose representation of interests, not regulated by law; because it has no legal organization and no public control, it is an inexhaustible source of corruption. The mission of proportional representation is to break the organization of the bosses and the lobbies, with their systematic corruptions, and to create a legitimate representation of all interests of the commonwealth.

The same superior insight into reality marks Commons' understanding of the commonwealth's position in the society of nations. Such sociologists and educators as Giddings and Dewey adopt the concept of the pioneer association and expand it without qualification until it becomes the ideal objective for the development of an undifferentiated humanity. Commons, however, reflecting on Jefferson's "All men are created equal," explains that the essence of American democracy is the fact that every citizen is offered equal opportunity; but he adds to the principle the demand that all must be in an equal position to make use of the opportunities. "Two things, therefore, are necessary, for a democratic government such as that which the American people have set before themselves: equal opportunities before the law, and equal ability of classes and races to use those opportunities."[30] The added demand is directed to the colored races in the American polity and to the immigrant laborers who, because of their insufficient mastery of the language and their lack of education, are not able to live as equal members

30. John R. Commons, *Races and Immigrants in America* (1907; 2d ed. with a new introduction, New York, 1920), 3.

of the American system. Seen from this perspective, the "greatest injury" that was inflicted on the United States was

the stimulation given to that spirit of suppression which, in the end, brought anarchy to Europe. For we are by history a nation of frontiersmen and rough riders. We make concessions only to our equals. If to our population is added negroes, we do not fraternize as do the French, but we keep them in the place which we think fit for them, and lynch law repeals the Fourteenth Amendment. If we add successively Irish, Chinese, Slavs, Italians, we use the later races as "hunkies" to displace the children of the earlier races who have begun to aspire, and, if they too demand an equal voice in their treatment, then, forgetting how we used them, we denounce them as foreigners, aliens, un-American, led on by anarchists and revolutionists, and reach for our guns.[31]

These words describe a historical situation as inevitable, and they do so without sentimentality. They merely report the facts and do not try to introduce some metaphysical doctrine of superiority to justify past events. They resonate with a consciousness of responsibility. The spirit of aristocratic rule over lesser peoples and Commons' frank, skeptical acknowledgment of the situation, contemptuous of any criticism, can be seen most clearly in the short section describing the annexation of Hawaii:

It is not enough that we have opened our gates to the millions of divergent races in Europe, Asia, and Africa; we have in these latter days admitted to our fold new types by another process—annexation.

The Hawaiians are the latest of these oversea races to be brought under our flag, although in the course of eighty years they have been brought under our people. Nowhere else in the world has been seen such finished effect on an aboriginal race of the paradoxes of Western civilization—Christianity, private property, and sexual disease. With a population of some 300,000 at the time of discovery they had dwindled by domestic wars and imported disease to 140,000 when the missionaries came in 1820, then to 70,000 in 1850 when private property began its hunt for cheap labor, and now they number but 30,000. A disease eliminating the unfit of a race protected by monogamy decimates this primitive people on a lower stage of morals. Missionaries from the most intellectual type of American Protestantism converted the diminishing nation to Christianity in fifty years. A soil and climate the most favorable in the world for sugar-cane inspired American planters and sons of missionaries to displace the unsteady Hawaiians with industrious coolies, and finally to overthrow the government they had undermined and then annex it to America.[32]

31. *Ibid.*, xviii.
32. *Ibid.*, 104–105.

If the imperialist community of equals wants to maintain its sovereignty abroad, it cannot tolerate domestic social discontent. The treaty of 1868 still guarantees reciprocal favored-nation status for immigration between China and the United States. Since then the labor movement has become strong enough to pass legislation preventing the importation of cheap labor and after the war to reduce immigration from Europe to a fraction of what it had been. The political influence of labor grew alongside the expansion of the industrial system, since "Democracy, like commodities, responds to the law of supply and demand. If there are thousands and millions whom we can use as we please we place but little human value on them. If they are scarce we begin to consult their wishes and to treat them as beings like ourselves."[33] Reactionary entrepreneurs were in favor of immigration because it supplied cheap labor, and they supported their position with the argument that cheap foreign labor is necessary to national growth; that American natural resources are infinite, but that not enough American laborers can be found to utilize them; that in the future, as in the past, America was to be the haven for all the oppressed of other nations; and that the principles of American democracy could not be communicated better to all the peoples of the earth than through the absorption of all immigrants into the commonwealth. The laborers, on the other hand, themselves immigrants or the children of immigrants, are determined to keep others from having whatever has been given to them, and they can justify their attitude by the reminder that the future of American democracy is the future of the American wage earner. In order to have an intelligent and patriotic citizenry, wages and the standard of living for the bulk of citizens must be protected. The rising economic group of wage earners must have equal rights with the descendants of the older economic strata when it comes to a way of life and political influence in order to secure the unity and domestic peace of the commonwealth of equals. How much the internal structure of this society is different from the European ones is shown by some remarks Commons made in 1920: America, he noted, was facing the decision about which type of labor union was to predominate, the revolutionary kind or the negotiating sort. If we open our gates again and if the aroused proletariat of Europe

33. *Ibid.*, xviii–xix.

once more rushes into the American factories, we nourish our industry with revolution, and the nation will be forced to support the dictatorship of the capitalists. If immigration is limited enough and the new arrivals are given enough time to acquire experience and enjoy education in self-government, a middle way, by recognizing collective bargaining, will become possible. The unions ask for limitation, the capitalists call for immigration. But the nation, which pays the bill, which cannot tolerate revolutions even if the alternative is despotism, which must suppress or deport any revolutionaries the entrepreneurs bring in, cannot assume the burden.[34]

We have said that Commons' life coincided with the period when the American nation took shape. The most important event in this process is the workers' struggle for equality in the community, with its disappointments caused by the waves of immigration that flooded everything, and the final closing of immigration after the World War. Participation in this process of rebuilding a community of equals, encompassing the entire nation, after the earlier pioneer communities were destroyed by the exhaustion of space and by industrialization, is the subject of Commons' further research and theory.

II

The full complexity of Warren's theory and experiments had its roots in settlements of farmers and artisans. Only their barest outlines—the closeness of the pioneer community and the cost principle—remain as an objective in American society and as theory in Commons' work. The details inherent in the task of creating a democratic community change completely. A symbolic representative may be found in the man who from the beginning of the labor movement led American labor to a level of organization where its future position of power as an equal member in the industrial system was no longer in question. This man is Samuel Gompers. After his death Commons wrote of him: "Twenty-seven years have passed since I met Gompers in person, and from that time on I counted myself among his followers."[35] Like Commons, he lived

34. *Ibid.*, xxii.
35. John R. Commons, "The Passing of Samuel Gompers," *Current History*, XXI (1925), 670.

during the period of national rebuilding, but his effectiveness is closely entwined in the economic and political struggle, whereas Commons' work, to the extent that it has practical ramifications, is performed in the areas of research, consultancy, government, investigating committees, and legislation and in participation in welfare organizations outside the union struggle itself. Commons' origins in the world of farmers and artisans link him with the goals of labor and enable him to understand them on the basis of a similar background. But the difference between the economic sectors in which they were active—that of the scholar versus that of the worker—gives Gompers the immediate symbolic force in an area of American life that is merely one of many sources of and materials for Commons' thinking.

We have called Gompers' person symbolic because today he seems to Commons the symbol of the workers' struggle for participation in democracy: "One of the ten or twelve greatest Americans" was born in England in 1850, the son of Dutch Jewish parents. He came to the United States as one of the millions of immigrant industrial workers—strangers in an American society made up of farmers, a prospering middle class, and intellectuals. A labor movement within the chaos of immigrants of different languages, religions, races, and political convictions could find only *one* common basis: the struggle for higher wages, shorter hours, more liberty. Theories and intellectuals were extraneous and dangerous to such a program, "industrially impossible." More radical and more class-conscious than Marx, Gompers eliminated from the movement all social reformers who came from a different social stratum. By this move he preserved the American unions from the collapse that befell the international labor movement as the result of the socialism and anarchism of its intellectual members.

This antitheoretical policy drew the attention of the movement to the rules and regulations within industries that control the workers' daily lives. The worker is seen as a concrete person, required every day to protect himself from the entrepreneur in all the minutiae of the workplace. He must struggle to keep his wages from eroding and to maintain his job security, and he must do so as an individual, not as a member of the "class" whose "solidarity" is demanded in the abstract. Gompers and his teacher [Karl] Laurrell were thoroughly familiar with Marx's writings, but they viewed workers' problems not as the struggle between labor and capital, not as a noisy demand for improvements in the situation of the working classes, but as the fight for more favorable regulation of particulars in industry: recognition of the union, grievance committees, business agents, union cards, arbitration, hiring and firing, imposed work speeds, promotions and transfers, priority in the quality of the workplace. For it was on the regulation of these details that the concrete liberty of the industrial worker rested, and Gompers was one of them. From the very beginning, every connection with European socialist and revolutionary theories, which were rooted in a class society and had no meaning for the American idea of society, was severed. It was not a stigmatized group that confronted the rest of society; rather, the individual worker struggled for recognition as an economic equal. What drives the movement is not "class consciousness" but "wage consciousness."

From the first, Gompers also took his place in the American political system. He did not seek political representation for workers in Congress; he understood that the American parties are large cooperative institutions of professional politicians and bosses, who compete for control of the administration and for political position; they are not representatives of the citizens to advocate the public weal. The unions cannot assert themselves against these organizations of political specialists. A labor party would be just as impossible in politics as a socialist movement is impossible in industry. The relationship to the political party must be the same as that of all other interests: not participation but negotiation for protection against government interference, so that negotiations with the employers can proceed under the unhampered pressure of economic power. The organization of unions in the American Federation of Labor is completely nonpolitical. Every affiliated international union is completely independent in regulating its internal affairs and sends a delegate to the conventions with a number of votes determined by the particular union's membership. Local unions too small to become allied with international trade unions have only *one* vote at the convention. This structure allows the weight of decisions to lie with the responsible, conservative, experienced leaders of the large unions, and the representatives of small local groups with radical tendencies can speak about them but cannot implement them. Commons reports: "At these conventions I have heard the most radical and most eloquent outbursts from delegates of local associations; then a brief answer by Gompers or another member of the executive board; then a vote of 99 to 1 against the irresponsible local. . . . It is a council of responsible leaders, not a house of popular representatives."[36] Gompers created a "machine" of the greatest internal unanimity and solidarity and the utmost external effectiveness. It is an organization brought into being by the needs of modern America and is more representative of American national life than the Constitution, which is based on the eighteenth-century European natural-right doctrine. The A. F. of L. combines a maximum of self-administration by its members and a central organ formed by the leaders, the responsible parties themselves, and not by intellectual representatives who speak not for themselves but for others and whose decisions therefore lack moral weight.

An immigrant Jewish worker born in England; the rejection of European socialist doctrine; the fostering of wage consciousness instead of class consciousness; the acceptance of the American system of negotiating with the political parties instead of politicizing the labor movement; the creation of an organization based in the needs of the current situation of American democracy; the national attitude during the World War: in every stage of his life and work, Gompers became for Commons the symbolic leader on the road to rebuilding the nation—symbolic still in his last words, "God bless our American institutions. May they grow better and better," and in the national recognition he was given in death by a military escort at his funeral.

In his autobiography Gompers himself left behind a detailed report on the stages of his growth from immigrant to labor leader. But the work is merely a source of information about his person. It is not "source material," because the events of his life he recounts are consciously selected and arranged in such a way that they depict Gompers in the way he wants to be seen. Though the book therefore loses its value as a collection of historical facts, it gains as the description of the typical transformation of the European worker into an American. Gompers has a clear view of the situation and arranges matters accordingly, and he makes precise distinctions among the levels of experience that shaped his life.

36. *Ibid.*

His earliest childhood belonged to Europe; it was composed of impressions from workers' lives that apply universally to a capitalist economy, but for Gompers they became the beginnings of practical-political principles in the United States. The earliest of these impressions was unemployment among the silk weavers of Spitalfields. Gompers relates:

> Many of our neighbors were descendants of French Huguenots who fled from France after the revocation of the Edict of Nantes and built their characteristic houses with little leaded window-panes and in that new home plied their wonderful skill in silk weaving that brought fame and wealth to Spitalfields. But the passing of time had brought shadows to the buildings and changes to the industry. One of my most vivid early recollections is the great trouble that came to the silk weavers when machinery was invented to replace their skill and take their jobs. No thought was given those men whose trade was gone. Misery and suspense filled the neighborhood with a depression air of dread. The narrow street echoed with the tramp of men walking the street in groups with no work to do. Burned into my mind, was the indescribable effect of the cry of these men, "God, I've no work to do. Lord strike me dead—my wife, my kids want bread and I've no work to do." Child that I was, that cry taught me the worldwide feeling that has ever bound the oppressed together in a struggle against those who hold control over the lives and opportunities of those who work for wages. That feeling became a subconscious guiding impulse that in later years developed into the dominating influence in shaping my life. . . . They were our neighbors, whose daily lives we shared. We could not but share their suffering and their feeling of injustice.[37]

The neighborly closeness, the empathy with the suffering of others, the feeling of belonging among people of similar fates, and the lack of stability in the lives of workers—all these Gompers stresses as decisive impressions. Both the recognition of the social position of a worker and the defenses against uncertainty assume a form in America that differs sharply from the European model. His first few weeks in America did not change him; his work—cigar making—was the same as in London. But gradually experience and new acquaintances "made me feel the freedom of opportunity and the bigness of the ideal on which American conditions and institutions were founded."[38] His feelings were fed by the cosmopolitan nature

37. Samuel Gompers, *Seventy Years of Life and Labor: An Autobiography* (2 vols.; New York, 1925), I, 4–5.
38. *Ibid.*, 25.

of New York in the 1860s and 1870s: revolutionaries and the economically dissatisfied from all the world gathered on the East Side. "We were daily accustomed to hear foreign tongues, to learn through personal contact the distinguishing demarcations of races and national cultures—not that we understood these things but rather sensed them. Such a background is in itself of educational value to those who would understand and direct masses of men. . . . In the early 1870s New York looked like Paris during the Commune."[39] Every period of reaction in the chain of European revolutions had brought a wave of revolutionaries to New York: followers of Garibaldi, Forty-Eighters, Chartists, Carbonari, Home Rulers, Danes, Austrians, Russians gathered together and spread their revolutionary gospel. Men of this type were not inclined to adopt the customs of a new country. Instead, they put their singular stamp on their surroundings. "The spirit of adventure and the sincerity to risk much for an ideal had left their mark even upon the second generation which I met among my boy friends as well as upon those I later met in the shop."[40] Here foreigners penetrated American life, and the process of Americanization was just as much a shaping of America by immigrants as it was the foreigners' adaptation to the new land; they brought with them an enterprising spirit, and what they found was a wealth of possibilities.

The adaptation took place in the formation of communities. Gompers mentions the fellow feeling with the neighbors' children; the shared Fourth of July celebrations; the formation of a "judge and jury club"; education through lectures and reading circles at Cooper Union; joining in the Odd Fellows; the shared mourning at the death of Lincoln.[41]

Closer ties came from the factory community. The skilled practice of a manual trade left the mind free for conversation: the workers chose a good reader from their midst and compensated him for the loss in work; the reading was followed by discussions, and the workers came to know one another better and became friends. A cigarmaking shop "was a world in itself—a cosmopolitan world.

39. *Ibid.*, 26.
40. *Ibid.*
41. "Like some cataclysm came the report that an assassin had struck down the great Emancipator. It seemed to me that some great power for good had gone out of the world. . . . I cried and cried all that day and for days I was so depressed that I could scarcely force myself to work." *Ibid.*, 27.

Shopmates came from everywhere—some had been nearly everywhere. When they told us of strange lands and peoples, we listened eagerly. No one ever questioned another as to his past life, for many were revolutionists who sought new opportunity and safety by leaving the past a blank."[42]

When he was seventeen, Gompers married, and at this early age the responsibility of a family and children lent maturity and gravity to his thoughts and actions. "I could not understand irresponsibility of word or act," he wrote in discussing the radicalism of the No. 12 International [Local 12 of the Cigarmakers' International Union of America], which was made up of intellectuals and which advocated anarchy, free love, and the like. This position did serious damage to the upwardly striving trade union movement.

The insecurity in workers' economic situation, the willingness, influenced by the New York revolutionaries, to fight; acclimatization to American society, with its greater chances for promotion; the love of work;[43] the rejection of radical measures and of intellectuals, who "do not understand that experiments with the labor movement are experiments with people's lives"—all these were the beginnings of Gompers' personality and continue to be decisive elements in the life of all American workers.

During the period 1920–1922, Whiting Williams, at that time personnel director of the Hydraulic Pressed Steel Company, tried to familiarize himself with the situation of workers in the United States, Great Britain, and France by taking part in their lives. He planned to use the knowledge thus gained in his job. The three volumes—partly in diary form, partly summarizing reflection—provide the latest material on the situation of industrial workers in the United States and set out comparisons with European workers.[44] His findings are in total agreement with the picture Gompers

42. Ibid., 79.
43. Ibid., 45: "The craftsmanship of the cigarmaker was shown in his ability to utilize wrappers to the best advantage, to shave off the unusable to a hairbreadth, to roll so as to cover holes in the leaf and to use both hands so as to make a perfectly shaped and rolled product. . . . I had earned the mind-freedom that accompanied skill as a craftsman." Ibid., 56–57: "I loved the touch of soft velvety tobacco and gloried in the deft sureness with which I could make cigars grow in my fingers, never wasting a scrap of material. . . . I gave all that was in me to that which was at hand, task or pleasure."
44. Whiting Williams, What's on the Worker's Mind: By One Who Put on Overalls to Find Out (New York, 1920); Williams, Full Up and Fed Up: The Worker's Mind in Crowded Britain (New York, 1921); Williams, Horny Hands and Hampered Elbows: The Worker's Mind in Western Europe (New York, 1922).

paints of his life. What most affects it is the fear of unemployment—of job loss. The situation of the American worker in general is unprotected, and he can be dismissed from one day to the next. Williams describes his experiences when he went to look for work in several steel mills: waiting for hours in long lines of the unemployed outside the factory gates in winter; the despair when, after days of looking, no work is found, the money is gone, and there seems no way out; the demoralization and the loss of self-respect. These periods of unemployment severely damage a man's ability to work well, and especially his morale in the workplace. The fear of a few such weeks rouses in the worker grave doubts about any technical innovation that temporarily puts a man out of work and makes him "very hesitant to accept the calm assurance of the economists that he need have no fear because the whole thing is bound to work out in the long run through increased production and the resultant cheapening of goods. Naturally enough, with his family on his mind, he fears this 'long run' may be so long that his self-respect may be destroyed, even though starvation be avoided, before the slack is taken up."[45] Like Gompers, Williams expresses mistrust of the "intellectual," who sees the economic process only as a production mechanism and forgets that it affects real human beings with daily needs, who are the ones most affected and suffer the greatest damage, especially to their "self-respect."

Williams stresses this particular circumstance over and over because given American conditions, which are not organized to practice class-based solidarity or class mutual aid, it seems the worst thing that can happen to a worker: that he gives up on himself and accepts work on any conditions, that he turns to drink and loses the feeling of independence and of equality with all other people. He shows that the importance of "the job," the fear of losing one's job and consequently being left at a great disadvantage in the social and economic machinery, is not restricted to manual labor but is equally valid for the higher grades of workers. Even the captain of industry takes the view that he is amassing his fortune primarily to protect himself and his family against times of illness or when age puts an end to his yearly income as the director of a business. The main difference between his "job" and that of the laborer is

45. [Williams, *What's on the Worker's Mind*, 284.]

that he is hired and paid by the month or the year instead of the hour or week and that he has some guarantees against dismissal without cause. But he as well as the worker is always under the cloud of fear of a reduction in his income or of unemployment. Opportunities and savings lessen the fear but do not eliminate it. The difference is not grounded in membership in a class of workers or entrepreneurs but in the margin of security.

In America labor and management do not confront each other as classes and there is no revolutionary proletariat. To characterize this situation Williams refers to the theory of relative success: Any normal human being is spurred on in his work by the desire to surpass his fellows by a small amount, to gain the feeling of getting ahead, to do more than merely stay in place. The main thing is the feeling of movement and advancement. The "high spots" in the life of a sheet-metal worker and a banker proceed by the same formula—they are high spots because they measure progress from the starting point. "It is this satisfaction in the distance travelled, rather than in the point arrived at, that permits millions of us to have our separate, individual satisfactions without wanting to crowd each other out of the pleasure of the same, or competing, ultimate destination."[46] These "high spots" are of special significance to the wage laborer, more than to the man who holds a job on a higher level. Heavy labor and especially the long twelve-hour shifts do not allow the manual worker the possibility of leading a private life like that of the higher employees. The worker leads his life mainly at his job, and more than the members of other occupations, he must find his satisfaction in work precisely because the work makes it impossible for him to look for amusement and distraction outside the workplace. The respectful treatment of the worker on the job and the prospects of promotion are therefore the most important aspects of a good personnel director's job, in order to prevent bad feelings and maintain the workers' "self-respect."

When Williams wrote his book on the American worker, his experiences had left him with the impression that the worker is not given enough hope for improvement in his situation in American concerns. The misfortune is that the workers feel "a conviction that for them there is no chance to break through" and rise to the

46. [Ibid., 297–98.]

higher levels of skilled workers and foremen. After he had familiarized himself with conditions in England and France, he found
that the crucial difference between the American and European industrial systems was the wealth of possibilities and hopes of the
American worker:

> Without any doubt the status enjoyed and the figure cut by the
> American worker as an integral part of the community is higher and
> greater than in Europe. Also, because of the absence of anything like
> Europe's lines of class, immensely more hopeful. One sign of all this
> is the surprisingly slight difference in the wage of the skilled laborers
> of Europe as compared with semiskilled and unskilled workers. With
> us these differences are so great, not only in wages but in dignity and
> responsibility, that there is undoubtedly a greater distance between
> our skilled workers and our unskilled, foreign-born laborers than be
> tween thoses same skilled workers and the superintendents and other
> representatives of capital. This simply means that the whole body of
> hand workers abroad is restricted in a more nearly uniform and cer
> tainly more definitely characterized group than here, where at the top
> our worker group shades off almost imperceptibly into the administra
> tive body. The restricted compactness of the workers tends in turn to
> persuade the rest of the citizenry in Europe to the comfortable assump
> tion that, in the nature of the case, the life of the "working classes"
> cannot be expected to give any real satisfaction.[47]

The hierarchy of the labor force, with its maximum of division
of labor and mobility of laborers to higher positions, is in fact
worked out in such a way that it serves as a superb instrument to
fight the labor movement. According to the principle of relative
success, promotions within the hierarchy allow restless elements
to rise, and stifle the beginning of class hatred. "I have often come
upon fiery socialists and ardent trade unionists thus transformed
and vaporized by this elevating process," Commons wrote.[48]

Williams found, conversely, that it was characteristic for European workers, especially those in England, to have a stifling class
consciousness. For a long time England has been a country with a
narrow margin between the number of jobs and the number of
workers applying for them. English political and social life is crucially determined by the narrowness of this ratio, by the expectation of keeping a job for life once it has been obtained and never

47. Williams, *Horny Hands and Hampered Elbows*, 250–51.
48. John R. Commons, *Labor and Administration* (New York, 1913) 77.

again having to risk the horror of unemployment, and by the obligation of the ruling class to stay away from business activity so as not to deprive someone else of work and risk one's wealth. The worker who leaves his job to his son is the extreme consequence of this situation. Holding on to a job has an incomparably higher significance than its creation and development—the typical trait of the American economy. Earning a living has been stripped of any excitement because the job is too important to be dealt with lightly, as the American worker does. The satisfaction of a primitive need to expand, the feeling of freedom of movement and individual activity must be sought outside the workplace. Williams sees this necessity as the cause of the extraordinary interest in horse racing and the high rate of alcoholism among the British working class, especially in the Glasgow area. Holding on to the job is the determining factor for the formation of the "class." "When you can get, at the age of fourteen or at twenty-one, the job which you can pretty confidently expect—with good luck—to hold on to until you're old and pensioned, then you have the making of class lines. . . . Nothing is more important to understand and at all times remember than this: that among an industrial people social levels . . . tend to follow job levels."[49] Where skills bring recognition and the expectation of a better job, the worker at any level will make every effort to end his life on a level higher than the one where he began. Those who succeed at this game know nothing of "classes," since the growth of skills and the broadening of responsibilities change these workers' "class" every time they rise another rung in the industrial hierarchy.

The abundance of natural resources and their extensive cultivation, the extent of the domestic market, and mass production and division of labor make possible an industrial system with such a high level of mobility and such abundance of relative opportunities to rise higher that the contrast of capital and labor hardly furnishes a reason for solidarity within the labor movement. A worker who has a comfortable income, owns a four-room house and a Ford cannot be persuaded that he is exploited and must unite with workers in other countries to bring about the fall of capitalism. Williams explained the contradiction that many American entrepreneurs saw Gompers, with his cautious policies of collective bargaining, as an

49. [Williams, *Full Up and Fed Up*, 290.]

238

archradical, while European labor leaders considered him hopelessly conservative, by pointing out that Gompers and his followers, even before they begin the bargaining process, feel themselves so much closer to the employer than ever happens in Europe; by their acceptance of the capitalist system they are so at one with it that actual negotiations deal only with technical details, and agreement on these is arrived at relatively easily.

The labor movement cannot become aggressive so long as it is not the expression of a class. Solidarity and discipline are impossible when the individual can expect to advance more successfully when he is not lumped in with a movement. The fact that Gompers and the A. F. of L. firmly reject socialist and communist theories and the politicization of the labor movement is only a negative indication of the existence of a social philosophy that cannot be reconciled with theories of class struggle. Since this positive theory of class struggle was not formulated systematically from the ranks of labor, its existence is frequently ignored, and the politics of the A. F. of L., as compared with European labor organizations, are described as being thirty or more years "behind the times." The philosophy of the American trade union lives in the tradition of the pioneer community; its theoretical principle, as noted above, is treated in the sociological literature, but even here it is considered such a matter of fact that the historically conditioned idea of "likemindedness" or "consciousness of kind" appears as an a priori principle in forming an association. A very realistic interpretation is found in Commons' addition to the democratic idea of equality of the condition of equal qualifications and imperialist propaganda. Because the labor movement itself is so entangled in daily skirmishes, the obvious foundations of the community of equals, the acceptance of the capitalist system as an excellent production machine in its service, and the narrowing of the struggle's objective to a fair participation in the imperialistic community so equipped are not brought to consciousness.

The pragmatic policy and the rejection of socialist ideas is not a symptom of a lack of theory; rather, it indicates that the fundamental demands of social philosophy have been realized to such an extent and are so unquestioned that union activities need only deal with details within the social order, and basically employers and employees are agreed on basic arrangements. The relation between the overt

239

policy and the unspoken underlying philosophy of society is similar
to that between Warren's anarchist dogmatism and the concrete situation above which it rises. Warren's anarchism is not the result of
profound philosophical considerations, he does not reach back to the
origins of metaphysical speculations, as, for example, Fichte's socialism does. It is a doctrine that forms a comparatively irrelevant
conclusion to a life situation; Warren does not at all see and understand its extent and its overall significance. The premises are unconscious and the thinking is restricted to the level of superficial phenomena. A. F. of L. politics did not develop a theory akin to Warren's.
But compared with an empirical labor movement infused with philosophy, its antitheoretical tactic of bargaining over concrete problems of the worker's situation has a similar relation to its unconscious
premises as Warren's doctrine does to its own presuppositions. The
unique trait of this relationship may be formulated as follows: that
the rational-active sphere of thought encompasses merely a small and
superficial sector of the total life, that it is merely an intellectual
annex to life, not a world with its own origins.

❧

Commons' thinking takes a related form. His analytic skills and
the breadth of his personality extend the intellectual universe to
such an extent that it encompasses the metaphysical problems of
time and finitude, duration and *élan vital*. Its origin, however, does
not lie in an immediate metaphysical experience; the formulations
are the result of decades of accumulated research into the concrete
facts of the American economy. Commons is very serious when he
notes that he finds it incredible that thinkers develop certain views
on metaphysical problems or arrive at conclusions in the theory of
law without studying the development of common law and American labor law. Between his first work in economic theory, published in 1893, and *The Legal Foundations of Capitalism*, published
in 1924, lie thirty years of studies on American legal and economic
history and on the current situation of the American economic system. His philosophy is grounded in this material, and it is these
facts that determine the problems he addresses. The world of metaphysics is touched only by the inevitable speculative form, not by
speculative will.

The beginning and the end of research into the facts are represented by works that encompass American economic life in its totality: the creation of index numbers and the dissertation on the function of the Federal Reserve Board. During the period 1890–1899 Commons was granted professorships at various universities. In 1890–1891 he taught economics at Wesleyan University, succeeding Woodrow Wilson, but his contract was not renewed because he could not adapt himself to teaching according to the syllabus. The following year, at Oberlin, he was free to conduct his classes in the form of discussions of concrete cases in economics, and he was successful. In the period 1892–1895 he taught sociology and political science at the University of Indiana and from 1895 to 1899 he was professor of sociology at Syracuse University. Because of his "radicalism," Syracuse fired him; he had participated in a Sunday discussion group of men who debated anarchist, communist, socialist, and single-tax doctrines; he himself was a supporter of William Jennings Bryan and had advocated free silver, municipal control of public utilities, and labor unions. The president of the university informed him that though he was free to express his opinion in his lectures within the department, such expressions in public threatened the university's financial stability.

Abandoning teaching altogether, he became the head of the Bureau of Economic Research, an organization financed by George H. Shibley to promote Bryan's 1900 campaign. The bureau lasted only a short time, and Commons issued only two bulletins, in July and October, 1900. But these were the first publications to contain American index numbers that can bear comparison with those worked out by Sauerbeck in England and Conrad in Germany.[50] Until the publication of Commons' index figures, the indices in the Aldrich Reports were the only ones offering useful points of departure over a period of time, but these only went through 1891, and the supplementary figures issued by the Department of Labor were incompatible with the preceding ones. Furthermore, the numbers were based on a single quotation for January 1 of each year, and since factory owners' ledger entries were used, the basis changed from year to year. In addition, comparison with the British and

50. John R. Commons, "Index Numbers of Prices, Freight Rates, Stock Quotations for the years 1878 to 1900, Shown by Percentages of Index Numbers," *Quarterly Bulletin of the Bureau of Economic Research*, I (July, 1900), 1–34; Commons, "Wholesale Prices by Monthly and Quarterly Averages, 1896 to 1900 and 1878 to 1882, Shown by Index Numbers and Diagrams," *ibid.*, II (October, 1900), 35–54.

German figures was impossible because the figures of the Aldrich Reports were made up primarily of goods at a higher level of production. Commons' figures were based on the price quotations of the standard professional journals and limited to staples that were of uniform commercial quality and were sold on the open market. The unit chosen was the harvest year, beginning on July 1, and certain rules were established for the quotations: weekly averages for strongly fluctuating items, monthly averages for more stable goods, such as chemicals and building materials; top prices were quoted for items with wide deviations (especially cattle), while a mean between top and bottom quotations was given for others. The items included were classified according to their responsiveness to changing demands and according to their distance from the raw material. The first class consisted of cattle, which adapted very slowly to demand and whose prices therefore rose sharply during periods of prosperity. The other classes are animal products; agricultural products; metals, minerals, and wood; and industrial products. The compilation of this index, which included practically all significant products of American commerce, gave Commons the first overall view of the system and insights into the relations among his various levels. Commons' statistical curves show the interrelationship between prices of stocks and bonds, wholesale prices, and retail prices on the one hand and wages and salaries on the other, and they demonstrate that for specific intervals the movement of one can be derived from the others, with railroad-stock fluctuations having special significance in predicting future economic conditions.

The establishment of the Federal Reserve System resulted in an organization capable of regulating American price levels and interest rates. The 1913 bill listed among the purposes of the Federal Reserve Board's discount policy the establishment of price stability, but the House committee eliminated this provision. In April, 1923, the FRB passed a resolution: "That the time, manner, character, and volume of open-market investments purchased by federal reserve banks be governed with primary regard to the accommodation of commerce and business and to the effect of such purchases or sales on the general credit situation." The phrase "the general credit situation" expresses a price-stabilization policy that the FRB had implemented several months before issuing the resolution, in order to prevent convulsions in the regular economic process that result from credit inflations and recessions. The policy was carried out with a fair amount of consistency. In practice, in February, 1923, slight increases (0.5 percent) in the rediscount rates of three reserve banks and insignificant sales on the open market were sufficient to direct the credit policies of the member banks in the desired direction.

Commons agreed fully with a policy of price stabilization, but we can only speculate on his reasons. His actual motivation is unclear and can hardly be elicited from documents, since he himself did not write on the subject but treated the demand for stabilization as a matter of course. In terms of dogma, the demand for a stable price level is understandable as a safety measure to prevent "unearned" losses and gains through changes in monetary value, and the factual situation alone furnishes ample grounds for raising the demand, since in the long run the FRB was not able or willing to carry out its policy of stabilization. The successful prevention of credit inflation was therefore followed by a period of price deflation that—increasingly after 1924—led to the farm crisis. During the period of postwar prosperity mortgages, which had reached a high point of inflation, could not be paid off in an economy of lowered prices for farm products and higher monetary value; the incongruity caused by appreciation went so far that in cases of loans on cattle, the sale price of the cattle would not have covered the loan. The crisis spread to the local banks that had granted such loans and mortgages and led to numerous cases of bankruptcy. The philosophy of a community of equals and of price setting according to the cost principle must consistently strive for a stable price level in order to prevent the unjust plundering of debtors by the holders of the loans. In view of the dynamic character of the American economy, the demand is less easy to explain. A price level—that is, an index figure—does not exist per se; it is compiled from the actual prices of particular goods, as Commons was the first to do on a large scale in the United States. In every nonstationary economy, but especially in one with such a high rate of expansion as the American economy, prices change continually. Technical improvements in production, sales, and financing; the introduction of new products; the elimination of older products through standardization; the shift in the relation between agricultural and factory workers—all these affect prices. On the whole, it does not matter whether the price level rises or falls; in either case, an increase in the supply of real goods, which destroys the value of a comparison of price levels, must be anticipated. Even if it were possible to keep the index figures constant, it would be impossible to draw from them conclusions concerning the real supply and the constancy of the real wealth relationship between various population groups—especially farmers and industrial workers.

The farm crisis is an excellent example of the complicated situation: The American farmer is not merely a producer of agricultural goods, he is also traditionally a speculator in land. He is used to seeing a considerable part of his income and increments in his assets result from the increased value of his farm as a consequence of overall American expansion. And the criticism has been leveled at farmers that their current crisis is first of all the result of unsuccessful speculation. In the case of farmers, such an element of speculation has been a well-known factor in American economic history since colonial times, and occasionally it leads to crises because the market is unorganized and unpredictable. But essentially this element is no different from the overcapitalization of industrial projects, which require twenty years (for something like the U.S. Steel Corporation) or ten years (in the bread business) before expansion can absorb the costs, or from overvaluation of land in the innumerable country towns, each of which strives to grow into a metropolis.

Price setting within the total American economy in big business, trade, and agricultural production is threatened with the discontinuation of expected expansion—that is, periodic growth in value, which if it is based not merely on inflation, necessitates expansion of the real supply. Given such expansion, however, the index would have to be adjusted to the current situation by, for example, giving less weight to foodstuffs while increasing the value assigned to automobiles and building materials. Such a change would rob the index of a basis for comparison. The constancy of the index in a strongly expansive economy indicates nothing unless it is assumed that the growth in wealth runs parallel to population growth, so that the individual's quota of wealth remains unchanged, as does the relationship between the two classes of goods; it would be the situation of an economy that grows proportionally in every sector, so that a later stage will show the same profile except that it is enlarged. Although now the complications of the dynamic make it harder or even impossible to construct a constant price level, Commons clings to his dogma, going so far as to declare that the trend of the abstract price level, regulated by the FRB, is not directly connected with the trends followed by concrete prices and that an influence on the price level in the abstract through the manipulation of interest rates does not influence the concrete price of goods—that therefore the stabilization of the index achieves its purpose of stabilizing monetary value without depriving the private sector of the control of actual prices.

Rationally, this view is contradictory, and the insistence on the dogma of stability must be interpreted from the perspective of typical American irrationalities. It is possible that the idea of an abstract price level without connection with concrete prices, on the assumption that this price level has some sort of significance and can be manipulated, presents a case of intellectualism similar to that contained in Kocourek's theory of law. Here too the concept of the index is developed from the concrete situation, turning it into the subject matter of a theory that no longer bears any relation to the reality it is meant to explain. The motivation of the theory lies in the desirability of maintaining the society of equals, but the concepts are not firmly rooted in reality, working instead through an emotional intention (as distinct from a logical intention) to refer to reality. If "reality" is defined by certain premises, the claim can in fact be made that a stable index is necessary to prevent undeserved losses and gains; but when "reality" so construed is identified with complete reality, and when the construed dogma is referred to the concrete historical situation—a reference not of rational analysis but a requirement of will—it can be designated as emotional intention. The same form of relation characterizes Warren's anarchic dogmatism and the reality of the pioneer community. Intellectually only a part of the theory is absorbed into the reality, but emotionally the fragment is made to refer to the total reality.[51]

51. Professor Commons disagrees with this analysis. He summarized his criticism in a letter: "I do not have a merely intellectual idea of stabilization, but I have a definite purpose, namely, the regularization of employment, the regular functioning of industry, and justice as between creditors and debtors." In spite of this opposite opinion, my analysis stands, since I see no contradiction between it and Professor Commons'. I do not dispute Professor Commons' claim that his stabilization theory serves to pursue a practical purpose; my analysis refers merely to the internal structure of the theory, regardless of its purpose. It was precisely the inadequacy of the practical purpose and the theory that was the striking phenomenon.

The first attempts at constructing the index and the comments on the policy of the FRB frame the study of separate sectors of the American economy. Commons uses the index figures of the Aldrich Reports and his own in connection with his work for the Industrial Commission; the index curve is combined with immigration figures to demonstrate the connection between periods of rising prices and favorable market conditions on the one hand and immigration curves on the other. The reports of the Industrial Commission occupy eighteen volumes of evidence and one of summation. In compliance with a law of June 18, 1896, the commission was empowered "to investigate questions pertaining to immigration, to labor, to agriculture, to manufacturing, and to business, and to report to Congress and to suggest such legislation as it may deem best upon these subjects." It was further to collect data and make suggestions for legislation that could serve as support for uniform legislation in the various states of the Union "in order to harmonize conflicting interests and to be equitable to the laborer, the employer, the producer, and the consumer."

The formulation of this law is of particular significance in connection with Commons' philosophy, since the idea of harmonizing all interests in an economic conflict is his central concept; a solution that is "reasonable" can be found only by consulting all interested parties and by an "equitable" compromise, just as was called for by the Industrial Commission law.

The substance of Commons' systematic argument, far from being new, developed out of the American tradition. What is new is the organization of separate principles in a rational context and the development of a specifically American system of economics, the first and so far the only major one in America. From the beginning of his practical economic research Commons has focused on the objectives that were subsequently to become the structure of his theory.

The Industrial Commission reports contain material on trusts and industrial combines, on convict labor, and transportation; on labor legislation; on the situation of workers in industry, trade, and agriculture; on the distribution of farm products, taxation, mining, immigration, education, labor organizations, and industrial combinations in Europe. The eighteen volumes provide a thorough picture of the American economy around 1900 (Thorsten Veblen's *Business Enterprise* is based on these data). In gathering this material, Commons became familiar with the details of the production and distribution machinery that he had earlier come to know as a phenomenon of prices.

The commission assigned to Commons himself the volume on immigration. This work, more than any other, introduces the American social problem at the same time that it communicates the most accurate knowledge of almost all branches of industry, because the immigration problem affects every aspect of the economy equally. The introductory chapters of the report therefore present a general overview of the occupations in which immigrants engage and very detailed studies of the influence of immigration on wages and unemployment compared with such other causes as cyclical depressions, living standards, unequal distribution of immigrants, labor organization, machines and division of labor, and competition from work performed by women and children. The most thorough investigation, detailed in subsequent chapters, was devoted to the garment industry, since it is exclusively in the hands of immigrants and therefore provides the best picture of problems connected with immigration to the United States.

At the time the reports were compiled, the garment industry was given its definitive form by the Jewish immigrants who had emigrated to the United States in massive number after the Russian pogrom of 1881. Practically all attempts at establishing Jewish agricultural communities failed, and the garment industry became the principal area of occupation for this group of workers. Until the Jewish tailors took over, production in the garment field was organized in such a way that employers passed on the material to a "middleman." These middlemen lived in the same parts of town as the immigrants. They might run a saloon or some other business, they knew the language of the immigrants around them, and they were able to pass the work on to individual tailors. The Jewish tailors displaced the middlemen because their knowledge of the trade gave them a superior position in dealing with the workers. Under their influence a carefully structured system of division of labor came into being that brought an abrupt end to the type of tailor who understands all the facets of his trade, replacing him with small coordinated groups, each assigned a different part of the job. Each of these groups, led by a "contractor," had to compete with all the others to be assigned work by the employer, and this more difficult situation drove up the speed of production and the number of working hours, while piecework prices dropped. The pace increased to such an extent that women were driven out of the industry because they were not physically able to keep up.

When the trade union movement tried to take over this industry, it encountered great difficulties. Besides the Jews, who primarily spoke Yiddish, the work force consisted of Swedes, Czechs, Poles, Germans, and Italians, none of whom knew English. Organizing a particular workers' district usually took about three years, just long enough for the immigrants to become sufficiently familiar with the institutions of the country and its language to enable them to turn to more promising work. At the end of a three-year period, generally speaking, the original immigrants were replaced by more recent ones, so that the work of organizing had to begin all over again. It was not until after the strike of 1910–1911 that the union made enough headway for at least some districts, especially in Chicago, to achieve tolerable working conditions. Another large impediment to organizing was opposition by the more skilled workers to the union policy of lowering the work rate; those who were able to work more quickly could, if they made use of their full capabilities, earn comparatively high wages, which soon provided them with independence and transition to the small-entrepreneurial class. This expectation was made possible by the technical peculiarities of the garment trade, which required no investment capital or over-head besides rent for the workplace and the price of sewing mach-ines, since the material was provided without a security deposit by the employers. The lack of solidarity among the more highly skilled workers tended to raise the standard of work rates and therefore depressed the pay for piecework.

The most important aspects of the problem of incorporating im-migrant workers into the society of equals are all contained here: the multiplicity of languages, making organization more difficult (the organ of the Amalgamated Clothing Workers is published in seven languages); the waves of immigration, bringing new unorga-nized masses to replace earlier cohorts; the wide range of possibil-ities, placing the interests of the more skilled workers in conflict with union policies and attracting the best workers into the ranks of employers; occasionally it even happens that there is a transition from labor leader to highly paid director in the industrial group that had previously been the enemy.

The garment industry was dominated by the immigrants, and its internal organizational problems can demonstrate in almost total purity the process by which newly arrived workers adapt to the older community and win a tolerable place within it. An entire branch of industry is "foreign"—so foreign that the ACW is not a member of the A. F. of L. because of its radical position—and is secure in its position. Another type of problem is shown in cases of mixed work forces. In the garment industry the problems of the industrial worker and the immigrant overlap; they are separate in more diffused industries, so that the influence of the immigrant situation can be more clearly distinguished from the social contradictions of the labor-capital relationship. The expansion of the pioneer community is not a simple increase in the number of members; it is also a shift in the economic system from the prevalence of agriculture and manual labor to industry. The native-born Americans who had entered the economic group of industrial workers were forced, like the immigrants, to fight for social equality in the economically reorganized community. And it was precisely this group of indigenous Americans who were resistant to situations where the work force was mixed; this resistance was eventually overcome by the immigrants' union policies. Here the foreigners did not look for a position of equality with the earlier settlers; the foreign-born group of workers forced the natives to raise their own position so that the newcomers would not find their efforts thwarted. In specific cases in mixed industries the coincidence of the conditions of immigrants and workers turns immigrants into the aggressive group, which forces onto native-born Americans an equality that had almost been lost and in this way, in response to their own needs, begins the reorganization of the American community on a new economic foundation.

An example of this type is the income policy of the miners' union in Illinois. The workers were distributed among the seven district divisions in such a way that in the two northern divisions (1 and 2) the immigrants were predominant, while in the southern districts (6 and 7) American-born workers made up the great majority. The contrast in distribution was paralleled by a difference in coal deposits: the northern ones had poor seams, the southern ones were richer. The production costs in the north were considerably higher, so that in order to compete with the south, wages had to be lowered. The following tables give an overview of the position:[52]

(1) Comparison of Foreign and Native Miners in Illinois, 1899

Division	Total Number	% Americans	% Foreigners
1	7,498	11	89
2	6,631	28	72
3	1,799	69	31
4	4,655	38	62
5	6,401	52	48
6	5,008	49	51
7	4,999	80	20

(2) Income Before and After Organization

Division	Average Tonnage per Man per Day, 1896	Average Daily Income ($) 1896	1899	Increase	Average Yearly Income ($) 1896	1899
1	2.70	1.90	2.01	5.8	299.39	378.00
2	2.69	1.68	1.96	16.6	232.38	415.31
3	3.04	1.78	1.80	6.8	280.34	288.96
4	4.22	1.53	2.31	37.8	324.22	465.06
5	5.69	1.97	2.15	9.2	383.91	416.49
6	4.44	1.72	2.30	33.7	329.65	436.37
7	5.53	1.58	2.40	51.3	235.01	388.89

52. [Some of the figures in the second table are obviously wrong. For example, the reported increase in Division 3 daily income, from $1.78 to $1.80, does not represent 6.8 percent, as stated, but slightly more than 1 percent; the increase from $1.53 to $2.31 in Division 4 does not work out to 37.8 percent but to roughly 50 percent; nor is it apparent how the Division 2 miners' yearly income could rise by 75 percent while their daily income went up by only 16.6 percent. Voegelin cites no source for the material—presumably it came from Commons—and it is not clear how these discrepancies arose. In any case, they have little effect on the discussion that follows.]

What separates the years 1896 and 1899 is a strike. Besides achieving an overall increase in wages, it also succeeded in establishing a wage scale that enabled the northern coal mines to compete with those to the south. Wages in the southern mines were adjusted in such a way that they evened out the advantages of better coal seams, thus putting competition among all the mines on an even footing. The union, which was brought in and dominated by the immigrants, forced the Americans to accept such high wages that the indigenous workers in the southern mines earned higher incomes than the immigrants in the northern pits. The principle of this wage policy, which goes beyond merely securing decent wages, attempts to bring about uniform production conditions in order to preserve the jobs in the less favorable pits. In this way it helps not only the workers but also the owners of the less productive mines. This case as well as the foregoing are good examples of the type of problems encountered and solved by the union movement, and for the subject matter of Commons' studies. A philosophy of class conflict is entirely absent, and the "labor question" consists almost entirely of a continuing chain of solutions to situations of the sort described here.

The next large-scale research project in which Commons participated was carried out by the National Civic Federation for the United States Bureau of Labor. It focused on limitations and regulation of production in America and England.[53] In the "Letter of Transmittal" Commons' participation is described: "The materials for this report were collected and prepared in the main by Prof. John R. Commons, assisted by John H. Gray, Ph.D.; Walter E. Weyl, Ph.D., and several of the special agents of this Bureau. . . . The work has been edited by Professor Commons."[54] The work is in two parts, one dealing with America, the other with England. The second section is edited by Gray, whereas Commons had primary responsibility for the sections dealing with American conditions. The material covered printing, the machine and iron industries, the steel industry, construction, cigarmaking, the manufacture of shoes, glass, and pottery, slaughterhouses, and the preserved-meat

53. John R. Commons *et al.*, "Report on Regulation and Restriction of Output," *Eleventh Special Report of the Commissioner of Labor*, H.R. Doc. No. 734, 58th Cong., 2d. Sess. (Washington, D.C., 1904), rpr. as "Restrictions by Trade Unions" in Commons, *Labor and Administration*, chap. 9.
54. *Ibid.*

industry. Only some of the English data can be compared with the American—printing, shoes, construction, coal mining. The others—shipbuilding, furniture making, street paving, textiles—have no parallel in the American data. The reason why the studied fields are so disparate lies in the fact that only those industries were investigated in which regulation and restriction of production had actually taken place or were suspected of having taken place, and these industries do not entirely overlap in the two countries.

When it comes to particulars, parallels can be drawn for only part of the fields, but Gray analyzes in detail his overall impressions of the English workers' situation and arrives at the same results as Whiting Williams was to do almost twenty years later. He, too, sees the crucial difference to lie in England's class conflict and the absence of class in America. He draws something like the following picture: The average Englishman believes that the entire social, political, and industrial order would collapse if the worker or his children had any expectation of rising above their class and that sudden or substantial wage raises would destroy the worker's "status." It is assumed that a worker should not require or receive more than a specific income, and the employers are not inclined to reward great skill and outstanding achievement, no matter how remarkable, beyond a certain amount. Since the worker also accepts this theory as unalterable, he directs all his efforts, not to special achievements in order to win a higher social standing, but more to assuring that his place within the working class is secure and comfortable.

The result of the mutual recognition of status is a particular trait in the policy of restricting output—a trait that is typically absent in America. What the two nations have in common is the tendency to regulate performance and maintain some sort of average in order not to put a fellow worker out of work. But the acceptance of the idea of status also generates an atmosphere of indifference to good performance and a tendency to do as little as possible, since doing more does not pay. Given this attitude, when technical improvements are introduced in America the result is greater productivity, but they lead to a decline in worker productivity and therefore no increase in output in Great Britain. Gray cites an example from the shipbuilding industry, where production did not rise at all (there were, however, universal complaints about inadequate utilization of technical equipment). When the pressure of wages and despair drive the workers to go on the offensive, they lead to the uniquely British phenomenon of the ca' canny. The theory behind ca' canny is a value theory of labor; the circular of October 2, 1896, states, "Pay workmen the good wages and they will give you their best labor and their best skill."[55] Unfair wages can expect to be repaid only with shoddy work. Behind this original ca' canny and subsequent attempts at restricting output lies the idea of status, with its principle of the minimum in performance in exchange for the wages the employer is prepared to pay. The difference between American and English work performance can best be seen in the case of typesetters because the kind of composing machine used and the method by which output is calculated are the same. The best performance by an individual single worker in London was 4,500 ems per hour; the American best performance was 10,000 ems. The practical minimum required of an English worker is 3,000 ems per hour, whereas 4,000 ems is expected in America.

The comparison discloses the principal characteristics of the American economy better than research on it alone could do and shows that even where the common theme of work restrictions and distribution applies to a larger number of workers, this effect takes on very different forms when under the influence of class pressure on the one society, rather than an abundance of opportunities for upward mobility on the other. Unlike the case of the English shipbuilding industry, in which a technical innovation resulted merely in a decrease in individual performance, the other extreme is represented by the case of the introduction of the linotype machine, cited over and over by Commons as an example of a brilliant stroke of union policy. Until 1891 not more than a half dozen Mergenthaler linotype machines were in use in the United States. That year the Mergenthaler Company began to make greater efforts at introducing the machines and informed the union that it would insist on getting the machines accepted and would not shrink from any battle. Experience had already shown that strikes against machines are hopeless, and the union officers arrived at a verbal agreement with the Mergenthaler Company according to which the union persuaded its members to learn to work the machine and not

55. *Ibid.,* "Letter of Transmittal," p. 9.

to oppose its introduction. In return, the manufacturing company would refuse to support employers' efforts to exploit the installation of the machines in order to break the union; likewise, work using the linotype machine would not be used to unfairly lower wages. The agreement was observed by both sides; only one strike was started—in Zanesville, Ohio—and it collapsed at once when the union sent workers to the town to replace the strikers. The introduction of the linotype machine ended with higher day wages and reduced hours, along with enormous profits for the company and the owners of printing shops.[56]

The third major research project Commons undertook at the request of the National Civic Federation dealt with the business structure of public utilities in England and America.[57] It was a matter of establishing the advantages and disadvantages of municipal and of private operation of gasworks, electricity works, waterworks, and streetcars. This project was chiefly responsible for a broadening of the material foundations of Commons' thinking. For the first time he had to deal directly with the entire complex of problems faced by public utilities—with commissions that determine their value, with price setting under state or municipal control, and with political control of an industrial enterprise. The difference between British and American municipal administrations, the integrity of one against the corruption of the other, conditioned by the tradition of the governing class in England and the lack of such a tradition in a nation of immigrants, became clear to him through what he saw and

56. This case illustrates what a union can do in an industry that, because of its nature, requires workers who are of above-average intelligence and education. The printers' union is one of the oldest and most respected in the United States and for all practical purposes free from immigrants who speak other languages. Thus the case, as a type of "native-born" industry, can be joined to the other types of immigrant-dominated and mixed industries.

57. *Municipal and Private Operation of Public Utilities: Report to the National Civic Federation Commission on Public Ownership and Operation* (New York, 1907). The most important summary articles in this volume are: Walter L. Fisher, "The American Municipality"; Frank J. Goodnow, "The British Municipality"; J. W. Sullivan, "The Labor Report"; and John R. Commons, "Labor and Politics." This last essay is subdivided into the following sections: (1) "Political Employees"; (2) "Efficiency of Municipal Operation"; (3) "Organisation of Municipal Employees"; (4) "Private Companies and Municipal Councils"; (5) "Trade Unions and Wages"; and (6) "Minimum Wages." [Commons' essay is reprinted as "Labor and Municipal Politics" in *Labor and Administration*, chap. 12.]

The purpose of the study is given in the introduction by Edward A. Moffett as research into the gasworks, electric light and power plants, waterworks, and streetcars "in its relation to the municipality, the consumer, and the citizen generally."

learned during an extended trip to England. The comparison he carried out in person lends sharpness and detail to his knowledge of the contrasts between the American and the English social order and political systems.[58]

III

In this third essay Commons himself wrote the report on labor and politics. Among other questions he addressed the organization of municipal employees, the influence of the union on wages, and the problem of minimum hourly rates. He combined this material with the report on immigration and the study of restrictions on output to analyze the condition of workers in a changing and reorganizing society. These analyses were not limited to relating the facts Commons found, leaving interpretation to the reader—if for no other reason than that facts are always an interpretative selection. Instead, sometimes the work grew immediately out of a legislative purpose; at other times he was moved by the hope of contributing to the improvement of unsatisfactory conditions by informing public opinion. In each case the purpose was to find a solution to a socioeconomic problem; the material was arranged and the analysis carried in such a way that the problems of the situation and the direction of a possible solution were clear to the reader. The basis for the solution at which Commons' interpretive analysis aimed is structured by his own specific view of the development of the capitalist system in the past and its probable further development in the near future, based on precise knowledge of American economic history.

58. The foregoing citations do not exhaust Commons' practical writings. In his complete works his method is experimental and focused on the immediate study of collective bargaining, and not only by external observation, but also in active participation. As economic adviser to committees of the Wisconsin legislature he worked on the following legislation: civil service law, public utility law, industrial commission and accident-insurance laws, and the minimum wage law. He was further involved with the bills for unemployment compensation and a bill for application of an unearned increment tax for land values and privileges. Other significant functions were his activity in organization unemployment insurance in Chicago's garment industry, work with La Follette on the Federal Trade Commission Bill, representing the western states (along with Fetter and Ripley) in the Pittsburgh Plus Case brought against the U.S. Steel Corporation to the Federal Trade Commission, participation in organizing the National Bureau of Economic Research, which Commons heads intermittently. Finally, Commons has for the last three years been president of the National Consumer League. [A complete bibliography of Commons' writings, prepared by Robert G. Spitze, appears in Commons, *The Economics of Collective Action* (New York, 1950), 377–407.]

Systematically—though not chronologically—these great research projects represent the conclusion of another series of Commons' studies of the history of American labor up to the point at
which contemporary history and documentation begin. This research was carried out not by Commons alone but by Commons
working with a staff of students and collaborators. The most significant result of this cooperation is the ten-volume *Documentary
History of American Industrial Society* (1910–1911), edited by
Commons, Phillips, Gilmore, Sumner, and Andrews. Eight years
later *History of Labor in the United States* was published, compiled
by Commons and another generation of scholars—Saposs, Sumner,
Mittelman, Hoagland, Andrews, and Perlman. Both the documentary and the narrative histories laid the groundwork for scholarly
research in labor history in the United States. They inspired and
formed the basis of more recent publications. Subsequent scholarly
generations continue the history of labor into the immediate present; the third generation collected the materials combined in the
volume *Industrial Government,* and a fourth is currently at work
on monographs giving the history of individual unions.[59]

Any discussion of Commons' work must take his students' contributions into account. It is an essential aspect of his overall personality that he extended his efforts to form teams that continued
his work in his spirit and adopted his ideas and his personality,
allowing them to live on all over America. The phenomenon of

59. John R. Commons *et al.,* eds., *Documentary History of American Industrial
Society* (10 vols.; Cleveland, 1910–11), prepared under the auspices of the American
Bureau of Industrial Research with the cooperation of the Carnegie Institution of
Washington, D.C., with Preface by Richard T. Ely and Introduction by John B. Clark.
The collection is arranged as follows:

Volumes 1, 2: *Plantation and Frontier,* by U. B. Phillips.
Volumes 3, 4: *Labor Conspiracy Cases, 1806–1842,* by Commons, E. A.
    Gilmore.
Volumes 5, 6: *Labor Movement, 1820–1840,* by Commons, H. L. Sumner.
Volumes 7, 8: *Labor Movement, 1840–1860,* by Commons.
Volumes 9, 10: *Labor Movement, 1860–1880,* by Commons, J. B. Andrews.

See also Commons *et al.,* eds., *History of Labor in the United States* (2 vols.; New
York, 1918), and Commons, *Industrial Government* (New York, 1921). For the latter, from July to September, 1919, a group of students collected data on "industrial
government" in thirty concerns (among them Ford, Dennison, and Hart Schaffner
& Marcks [sic]). The results are arranged in such a way that the report on each
concern forms a separate chapter in the book. Commons himself wrote the Introduction as well as the chapter titled "The Opportunity of Management" in the section called "Inferences."

cooperation in the form of a "school" and "contribution" to a particular project was examined earlier, in the discussion of legal logic, and in that section it was shown that the ethical-religious undertone of work on the problem is itself by no means advantageous; it leads to a situation where the autonomy of the subject matter is forgotten because of problems that are not essentially related to it. The problems that were intended to be solved cooperatively—insufficient organization of legal norms, the clumsiness of the system of precedents, the inadequate training of lawyers—had no immediate bearing on the questions of legal analysis in general and the structure of a law in particular. Practical-political intentions were mingled with unrelated purposes of rational analysis. But in the work of Commons and his students the collaboration was successful because their kind of ethical research stands in a particularly advantageous relationship to their scholarly tasks.

The political purpose was earlier characterized in detail as the integration of a group of people—industrial workers—in the commonwealth. Developments in industry had destroyed the early pioneer community. These developments gave rise to a new practical-political objective by creating people with economic interests outside the traditional order, a new democratic community that included the new people as equals. The practical realization of the ideal of the community of equals was threatened by the emergence of an industrial proletariat that was looked down upon; the struggle for the workers is thus the struggle for internal reformation and stabilization of American society. The fact that in jurisprudence the combination of scholarly and legal-political tasks failed is not because the two are methodologically incompatible but because in actual cases the two barely touch on each other. But the examination of the contemporary situation of workers in America and research into its history directly serve American political ideals. To turn these ideals into reality requires detailed knowledge of the current crisis in American democracy and its causes. The spread of Commons' work to his school may therefore have a more important effect on policies and the shaping of the community than does its success as scholarly investigation.

Commons gave a precise description of the political goal of the internal reorganization of the American community in its historical position and present-day objectives in an essay on Karl Marx and capitalist and socialist trends in the modern economy.[60] The *Communist Manifesto* was written at a time when the European proletariat had suffered great miseries following the ten-year depression beginning in 1837, and it was Commons' belief that the theories Marx elaborated in the next twenty years were fundamentally grounded in the conditions of this period. Had that world remained unchanged, Commons believed, Marx's predicted evolution to communism would have set in quite soon. But 1850 saw the beginning of an internal reorganization of the capitalistic system, especially allowing corporations to grow freely. A corporation could now be founded without a charter, and though this release from licensing did not prevent the concentration of capital, it allowed the decentralization of ownership rights—first through the great increase in the number of corporations everywhere, and today in America through the deliberate spread of small stock ownerships, which directly involve the interest of thousands of people in maintaining the capitalist system, to the great sorrow of anticapitalist labor leaders. The second essential element in the reorganization of capitalism is social legislation. Besides these measures of state intervention, which Marx could not have foreseen, there is the special evolution undergone by today's labor movement in the United States. Commons points out that "in every case that I know of, and in every country, where workingmen have formed the so-called producers' cooperatives, in order to become, as they say, their own employers, and have thus elected their own foremen, superintendents, and directors, they have failed. Laborers, as a class, are incompetent to elect the boss."[61] Today the labor movement recognizes that workers as a class cannot manage a capitalist economy, that capturing the capitalist system would end in total collapse, and that the expectation of personal material success is necessary for successful business management; that the role of labor is different, though just as important to society—through bargaining and the pressure of its economic power to restrict and limit control of personal interest in such a way that workers as a class do not suffer from it but can participate in the system's successes through reduced working hours, higher living standards, and

60. John R. Commons, "Marx Today: Capitalism and Socialism," *Atlantic Monthly*, CXXXVI (November, 1925), 682–93.
61. *Ibid.*, 685.

greater security. Today the capitalist system has grown out of the period of cutthroat competition and class conflict between capital and labor into a period of stabilization, marked in America by the conservative policies of the unions, the rejection of the suit brought against the U.S. Steel Corporation in 1919,[62] and the stabilization policies of the FRB discussed above.[63]

The predictions contained in Marxist philosophy of history were revealed to be false because Marx did not and could not foresee the internal reorganization of the capitalist system. Aside from this error of historical prophecy, Commons finds in Marx's metaphysics basic flaws that render an understanding of the social problems impossible and make the Marxist view of history unsuitable as the basis for practical politics. Marx and Hegel share the view of a process of history that, either as the unfolding of the idea or as necessary development of the economic form, takes place by way of individuals but according to a law that transcends their will. "Consequently," writes Commons, "in both cases the actual historical evolution of collective wills was overlooked."[64]

The words *historical* and *collective will* are used here with a particular meaning. Marx and Hegel also speak about historical development and attempt to describe its laws, but the metaphysical status of a law beyond actual individual actions causes Commons to contrast the concrete sphere of action, as the "actual" historical one, with all action-transcending law. The "collective will" is not a mystical person, but "custom." "In Anglo-American history we find this collective will moving forward as the common law, including under this designation the law-merchant, or the custom of capitalists, as well as the law-agriculture, or the custom of feudal

62. *Ibid.*, 689. "The court declared that the Steel Corporation had not reduced wages, had not lowered the quality of its product, had not created artificial scarcity, had not coerced or oppressed competitors, had not undersold competitors in one locality and maintained prices in other localities, had not obtained customers by secret rebates or departures from published prices. Neither competitors nor customers, said the court, testified to any oppression or coercion on the part of the company, and they testified to a general satisfaction with the well known and published policy of stabilization of prices and deliveries pursued by the Corporation."

63. *Ibid.*, 690. "For the past two years this stabilization has been surprisingly effective, preventing general inflation in spite of the surplus of gold, and, while there may be need of improvements in procedure or in representation of interests other than those of the bankers, which experience will reveal, yet no greater service toward the self-recovery of capitalism can be suggested than this stabilization of credit, business, and prices for America and the world."

64. *Ibid.*

landlords and farmers, and the law-labor, or the custom of labor and trade-unions."[65] The totality of historical development lies in the chain of concrete action, whose continuity is safeguarded by custom, and this supervision and gradual change through a hierarchy of conciliatory authorities culminates in America in the Supreme Court. "Custom" and the process of change are therefore the core problem of all sociological research.[66]

The process does not, as Marx believed, spend itself in conflicts of interest and struggles between two economic groups, ending in a communist situation of harmonized interests. Nor is it possible to bring reality to Adam Smith's idea of harmony brought about by the famous free play of economic forces. The idealism of a capitalist or communist harmony of interests collapses in the face of the fact that social conflict is the basic form of historical evolution, conditioned by the tension between the scarcity of goods and land and the pressure of population. But the social conflict is not, as Marx predicted, a two-sided class struggle; it is individual conflict multiplied into the thousands, and it arises wherever the scarcity of goods puts impediments in an individual's—or a group's or nation's—efforts to expand. It is the conflicts between buyer and seller, employer and employee, landlord and tenant, between groups of taxpayers about the distribution of burdens, between railroads and their riders, between the widely divergent interests of the lobbies in their efforts to enlist professional politicians. It is not a struggle between "classes" but between "classifications"—"for no individual is tied up to a single class, as Marx contended, and as might be true in Europe, but every individual belongs to as many classifications as he may have conflicting economic interests."[67]

The rigid identification of a person with a more or less accidental economic interest—the essence of a class society—is abolished; the individual is returned to his full personality and is placed at the center of multiple conflicts of interest; but there is no intention of finding a strictly utopian harmonic solution corresponding to an ideal. On the contrary: the significance of these conflicts is precisely that they must be settled daily without historical pathos and

65. *Ibid.*, 691.
66. This statement may be taken as formulating the underlying motivation for the achievements of the entire school of institutional economics.
67. Commons, "Marx Today," 693.

"without waiting for ultimate ideals."[68] Every concrete conflict must be treated as an everyday matter at the moment it arises, and it must be resolved "day by day."[69] The historical process is robbed of the pathos that idealistic interpretations, influenced by the wish for a particular ending, confer on it so generously. It loses the quality of romantic opiate that makes it possible to forget oneself in identification with it and its objective in an intoxication of greatness without responsibility. Every day it becomes, simply and very humanly, the change of daily custom in which all participate by their ordinary actions. It is a democratic historical process. It has no heroes burning with high ideals—the day-to-day objectives are not extravagant, brilliant, or heroic. It is not an exciting drama in which masses wrestle each other. It has no utopian goal of ultimately reconciling all contradictions. Murkily it rolls along, without an end in sight. Millions of people participate in it—all of them individuals who will never become a mass (because no single other confronts them); they merely cancel each other out by their incalculable number. They desire nothing great, merely to get along "as well as they can." The aimless unpretentiousness of this phrase shows the special form of solemnity that supports it. Without making any definitive classification, a distinction must be made between the self-conscious pathos, which loses the person in the process of history, and the strict damming up of its sources into concrete actions initiated by the individual, and only by him.

The rejection of ultimate goals and ideal laws does not abolish the values by which actions are judged; it is merely that these values are so near, so nearly accomplished and real, that the distance induced by pathos, which always has about it something sentimental, in the pejorative sense of the word, has disappeared. The goals are not so distant that they have to be inscribed on tablets to be kept in mind. They are so implicit in every action, and every action is so imbued with them, that there is no need to mention them. Warren's anarchic doctrine of society shows that the entire form of life is presupposed, so that practical demands deal merely with superficial details. A similar theoretical structure is evident in Giddings' and Dewey's sociology and in the apparently anti-theoretical stance of the union movement. Commons' interpreta-

68. *Ibid.*
69. *Ibid.*

tion of the historical process is a variation of the same structure, presented in a somewhat different manner.

The anarchic theory came about through ignoring and forgetting its nonanarchic basis. After the closing of the frontier as a historical environment that also incorporates the workers into the commonwealth, Dewey and Giddings, though they have not the least doubt about the absoluteness of the democratic ideal—a maximum of both numbers and options for association—nevertheless see this ideal as still in the distance, as an end toward which development is moving. Commons views it from its inception. Between Warren on the one side and Dewey and Giddings on the other are several decades of historical development that gave to the problem of American democracy a new aspect and new possibilities of expression. Between Giddings and Dewey and Commons there is an essential difference in the metaphysical stance: For the first two, a historical difference exists between current concrete individual actions and the ideal goal; for Commons, there exists a metaphysical tension, which cannot be resolved by any historical objective in concrete actions at any time. Commons' historical research and his philosophical analyses have their origin in the awareness of this tension, in enduring it, and in the desire to help those who, through a historical accident, are externally handicapped in the unending chain of overcoming it.

⟡

It is not possible to discuss in detail Commons' vast system of philosophy of law and economics, developed in *The Legal Foundations of Capitalism* (1924). Here only one basic thought can be explained and its historical basis discussed: the transformation of the concepts of liberty and property for the purpose of protecting the workers. A series of decisions of the highest state courts and the Supreme Court extends into the present. These, taking their point of departure from the eighteenth-century rationalist concept of liberty, rendered null and void legislatures' measures to protect workers. The history of these decisions was presented in detail by Roscoe Pound in his essay "Liberty of Contract."[70] A few examples will suffice. An 1884 decision overturned an ordinance that miners'

---

70. Roscoe Pound, "Liberty of Contract," *Yale Law Journal*, XVIII (1908–1909), 454–87.

wages must conform to the weight of the coal they supplied, because the law could not be reconciled with the right of entering freely into contracts. In 1895 a law limiting hours of work for women in the garment industry was overturned with the reasoning: "The legislature has no right to deprive one class of persons of privilege allowed to other persons under like conditions." A law stating that workers must be given their wages in cash was struck down in Kansas in 1899 with the argument that "while it might be desirable and profitable to the employee of such corporation to receive a horse a cow or a house and lot in payment for his wages, yet the legislature prohibits payment in that way and places the laborer under guardianship, classifying him in respect of freedom of contract with the idiot, the lunatic, or the felon in the penitentiary."[71] Currently, the most important measure that is the object of the fight between state legislatures and the Supreme Court is the attempt at setting minimum wages.

All these judgments are based on a concept of volition that Commons refers to as a will *in vacuo*, as distinguished from will *in concreto*. It is the concept of volition as a capacity underlying concrete behavior, a substance or thing in itself, separate from its expression in individual actions. It permits distinguishing between an action and its neglect as a nonaction; it permits the idea of free will and the claims based on it, according to which a worker is free to enter on a work contract if he so wishes and the legislature is in error if it rules that his working day may not exceed a maximum of ten hours.

Will *in concreto* is not a power in itself, opposed to the stream of concrete actions; it is real only as it is expressed in the choice of actions. It cannot choose between an action and its neglect; it can select only between two actions—not between a positive and a negative one, but only between two positive alternatives. The concept of neglect of action becomes possible and meaningful only when a single action, picked out of the stream of life, is observed without connecting it with the stream, as is typified by criminal-court proceedings. In this connection itself, the omission of one action always means establishing another. The stream of life in all its parts simply is; the contrast of positive and negative is imposed on it

71. *Jones* v. *People*, 110 Ill. 590, *Ritchie* v. *People*, 155 Ill. 99, *State* v. *Haun*, 61 Kan. 146, all quoted *ibid.*

from outside through selected orders of value. The action that stands in opposition to a neglect of action is not a simple behavioral element; it is complicated by being assigned a meaning. Will *in concreto* is always real action—neglect of action is real only to the extent that establishing it of necessity eliminates the possibility of all other actions—and yet it is not simple and determined as the plain word might imply; it is dimensionalized through forbearance: "The will is the only force that can place a limit on its own performance. Other forces always go to the limit of their power in overcoming resistance. What gravitation does, what electricity does, is all that it possibly can do in that direction under the circumstances. This might be found true also of the will if we knew all about its physiological and unconscious sub-structure. But consciously, as we know it in our persuading, coercing and commanding one another, the will alone forbears to go to the limit of its possible power of performance." [72]

Physical laws are equations with interchangeable sides; that a physical force goes to the limits of its ability indicates that an event fills the equation. The "consciousness" of the will, which is limited, is a meaningful order of life without an equation. In the physiological substructure—that is, in the world of natural law—actions may appear as indifferent fulfillments of a law, whereas in the order of meaning they also have the opportunity to be different. Commons' formulation that physical force reaches the limits of its ability does not quite adequately characterize the contrast with will. Its limit of capacity is not only the maximum it can reach but also a minimum below which it cannot fall—the action is indifferent.

Forbearance on the concrete will is carried out in another medium of vital power, which can be economized according to an order of value in the multiplicity of its expressions. Forbearance in one direction opens the possibility of new behavior in another. The will draws energy from a limited supply, the individual's life, and the limitation of life gives its meaning to the limitation as a dimension of behavior. In any case, physical energy, finite or infinite, is not aware of the problem of the visible limit and of conscious economy, and it is the indifference of energy, as it is expressed in legalistic terms, of which Commons speaks as a going to the limits.

72. John R. Commons, *The Legal Foundations of Capitalism* (New York, 1924), 77.

Campbell's example of the gradual construction of a clock by one's own labor as the derivation of the right to property traced property back to the assignation of personal labor and its incorporation in economic goods. The product, which has absorbed a part of the limited vital energy, became a part of life itself and was "naturally" the property of the source of power to which it owed its existence. In this reasoning man and nature stand in opposition. The economization of life in its relation to the nature that serves to preserve it is the root of the phenomena of the economy and the law. Commons starts with the same idea, but he refines the analysis of the problem of scarcity and provides a metaphysical background for the theory as a whole. For him there are not scarce goods but a scarcity caused by the "situation" of necessary things. But in the last analysis a situational scarcity is nothing more than the amount of work required for any effort, so that it cannot be traced back to scarcity of life and the biological and mental organization of people associated with it. Quite often an object is turned into the occasion of economic evaluation and legal protection by its relation to a creative individual stream of life. "Property is not a physical object but is the relationship which a person necessarily sets up between his personal abilities and the world about."[73] To the extent that the concept of abstract will has changed to belief in concrete will, rational freedom supporting action to a concrete act of choice in action, the concept of property changes from a firm, clear, tangible object to the concrete multiplicity of relations between person and world. Property has stopped being a mere piece of land or cattle, with immediate economic value; it has become anything that is possessed of exchange value in the individual's social life: a good reputation, ability to work, business goodwill, patents, access to a market, protection from unfair competition, stocks, bonds, bank accounts, credit. Property has become an "intangible," encompassing everything "that enables one to obtain from others an income in the process of buying and selling, borrowing and lending, hiring and hiring out, renting and leasing, in any of the transactions of modern business."[74] Property is not a thing in the material world, but the expectation of my freedom of action in relation to the world outside; it is congruent with the prospects

73. *Ibid.,* 156.
74. *Ibid.,* 19.

of chosen acts—that is, with the expressions of will *in concreto*.

Even tangible objects are not property; what matters is the use to which they are put within the framework of the legal order and the customs of a society. Tangible property is itself an expression of intangible freedom. The congruence of the two is shown even more clearly by such examples as the right of workers to join a union or to go on strike or to validate their economic power through their union's confronting their employer. All these workers' "freedoms" are their property and valuable economic goods. For value has also been withdrawn from substantive property and assigned to the function of expected action—just as freedom of the substantial will has shifted to the chances of the chosen act. Thus the specific object is no longer valuable, that value residing in "expected desirable behavior regarding it"; value resides in the "expected will in action."[75] Freedom, property, and value are joined in the expected behavior of a person, in the significance of this behavior in the entire vital organization of the person.[76]

The separate problems of legal and economic theory were grasped at the point that allows their essential connections in the structure of the personality to be understood. Coming from the concrete person, the meaning of its sphere of behavior—represented as freedom, property, and value—is perceived in its given social context. These dimensions of individual action stand outside what is traditionally thought of as legal and economic theory, at a center that, to give it a name, may be called a metaphysics of law and economics. And only at a second stage is there discussion of a cluster of concepts that gives richness to the concretization of action and whose overall structure was described as being derived from the forbearance of life. These are the concepts of efficiency, custom, and sovereignty. The first refers to the constraint of behavior to the laws of nature; the second refers to the social customs that restrict a person's actions; the third is the constitutional regulation of behavior.

These concepts raise analysis above the narrow boundary of the person to include nature and society. Commons dealt most thoroughly with the third, the problem of law, and his work reshaped the results of American analytic jurisprudence and incorporated it into the system. First, in *Legal Foundations of Capitalism*, he ac-

75. *Ibid.*, 20.
76. *Ibid.*, 156.

cepted the general scheme of basic legal concepts elaborated by Hohfeld and his school. But later, to be consistent with his own theories, he found himself compelled to change the meaningful content of the schema and the problem as a whole.[77] In any concrete social situation the individual is not dealing with an imaginary opponent; an economic action does not take the form of an exchange between A and B; rather, the element of social behavior is a "transaction" among three or five persons. When buying is concerned, the transaction is conducted between A and B, guaranteed by a constitutional order with sanction opportunities S (Commons inserts a judge as the third person), and is more narrowly defined by the competing buyer C and seller D.

Thus a transaction involves three typically different relations: the principal relation between A and B, the collateral relations of A to C and B to D, and the "sovereignty" relation to court officials. The latent or open social conflict, with the threatened or openly intervening physical power of the state, is the unit of social relations. It is a unit of a very complex nature, since the transaction was given this neutral name because it was not intended to convey either a legal or an economic concept; both forms of relation, traditionally separated by the fact that they are studied by scholars in different departments, are aspects of the same transaction, and without claiming definitiveness for his analysis, Commons attempted to dissect the complex of relational processes into conceptual chains. The concrete transaction is held together by the dual expectation of economic gain and legal sanction. It is occasioned by the expectation of the economic advantage arising from it, and the legal order's threat of sanctions guarantees execution. If the expectation of sanctions is considered primary, then the area of possible transactions breaks into two fields of relations between people—one guaranteed by an expectation of sanction, the other field containing nonguaranteed relations. If the purpose of economic gain is postulated as primary, then the situation of a person

77. John R. Commons, "The Problems of Correlating Law, Economics, and Psychology" (Manuscript dated September, 1926, bearing the notation "To be revised"). [This manuscript was never published. It is available in Commons Scrapbook, USS Mss 21A/7, pp. 225–71, Commons Papers, Wisconsin Historical Society, Madison.] See also K. M. Llewellyn, "The Effect of Legal Institutions upon Economics," *American Economic Review*, XV (1925), 664–83, and Commons, "Law and Economics," *Yale Law Journal*, XXXIV (1924–25), 371–82.

is either advantageous or in jeopardy. If the two divisions are connected, the person who participates in a transaction is faced with four possible situations: (1) economic advantage combined with expectation of sanctions (case of an outstanding debt); (2) economic disadvantage with absence of the expectation of sanctions (jeopardizing the business through legally sanctioned competition); (3) economic advantage with the absence of the expectation of sanctions (when the person damages another in the competitive struggle); (4) economic disadvantage with the expectation of sanctions (compulsion to pay a debt).

To cover the four situations, Commons introduces the names *security, exposure, privilege,* and *conformity;* he sums them up as the "economic consequences" of the legal expectation of sanctions and seems to place greater weight on the economic nature of the situation than on its legal aspect. This tendency is shown clearly in the structure of a second chain of concepts alongside the situational possibilities. This chain, named "legal relations," contains the concepts of right, no-right, no-duty, and duty; these are meant to describe the special legal aspect of the basic social relation created by the expectation of sanctions. The legal concept of right corresponds to the situation of security, exposure to no-right, privilege to no-duty, and conformity to duty. If the series of legal concepts were to stand alone, it would as such be an advance on Hohfeld's schema, since Commons recognizes as jural relations only the correlatives right-duty, while he expressly calls the relation no-right–no-duty "nonjural," though he does recognize it as a relation. By "nonjural" is meant the situation in which, because the threat of sanctions is absent, there is no relation to a legal process, and it is therefore impossible to speak of a legal relation and legal concepts. But the tradition of Hohfeld's school is so overwhelming that the two terms intended to indicate an absence of legal relation, a nonexistence, are nevertheless incorporated in the series of "legal relations" and given the name of nonlegal relations—a name that is in itself contradictory. The dissection of Hohfeld's schema has thus gone so far that jural concepts are reduced to those closest to process and sanction. That even these are not tenable was shown in the chapter on analytic jurisprudence.

The total of the four concepts—including the negative ones—made their way into Commons' analysis because the chain from security to conformity as a specific economic situation was mis-understood, so that in order to give a full description of social re-lations, it seemed necessary to add a parallel series of concepts of jural relations. In order to complete the parallelism, four concepts had to be found, and this exigency caused the formation of the ques-tionable nonjural legal relation. In fact the four concepts designated as "economic consequences" contain all the material that went into structuring the transaction concept, as can be seen in the way they develop, since they come into being through crossing the pos-itive and negative possibilities of the profit and sanction expecta-tions. We are not dealing with four economic consequences, each independent of the others, standing side by side; rather, there are only two that are multiplied into four by being doubled with the expectation of sanction. This situation is evident in some remarks Commons made on the problem of concrete freedom: security and privilege are the two favorable situations, and they are combined into the field of concrete freedom—the field where no external pres-sure affects behavior. It was therefore possible successfully to shape concepts of a social reality in such a way that they can summarize both the legal and the economic problem. The parallelism of the jural relations is a remnant of the Hohfeld tradition, and though no good case can be made for it, it changes nothing in the value of the primary concepts. Commons gives an overview of his analysis in the following table:

Opposite Persons

Legal Relations	Economic Consequences	Legal Expectations	Economic Consequences	Legal Relations
Right	Security	Sanction	Conformity	Duty
No-right	Exposure	No-sanction	Privilege	No-duty
No-duty	Privilege	No-sanction	Exposure	No-right
Duty	Conformity	Sanction	Security	Right

This scheme does not solve all the problems of Commons' anal-ysis. Following the tradition of legal theory, he also constructed a diagram of auxiliary verbs parallel with the other chains of concepts. The significance of such a table is that it describes not situations or relations but concrete individual behavior separated according to action or neglect of action on a value scale. A simple diagram of this sort was earlier (in theory of law) given in the words *must, may, must not, may not,* indicating the dimensions of possible behavior by person A, broken by the idea of desired or undesirable outcome of this behavior for A. Instead Commons constructs the following table, parallel with the basic concepts:

A		B
Security . . . Can		Must, must not . . Conformity
Exposure . . . Cannot		May, need not . . Privilege
Privilege . . . May, need not		Cannot . . . . . Exposure
Conformity . . Must, must not		Can . . . . Security

To understand the significance of this conceptual order, the first row must be dissected into its elements so as to determine its content as precisely as possible. The situation of security comes about by combining a threat of sanction against B with an economic advantage for A. This interpretation of the concept can be presented in the formula $A^{p\leftarrow}B^{s\leftarrow}$, with S and P indicating respectively the sanction and the profit; the arrows indicate the relation to person A and person B. Exposure is brought about by a lack of the threat of sanctions against B in relation to jeopardizing profits for A: $A^{\rightarrow p}$ $B^{\rightarrow s}$. Privilege is the lack of a threat of sanctions along with profit for A: $^{s\leftarrow}A^{p\leftarrow}B$. Conformity combines a sanction against A with an advantage for B: $^{\rightarrow s}A$ $^{\rightarrow p}B$.

$$A^{p\leftarrow} \quad B^{s\leftarrow}$$
$$A^{\rightarrow p} \quad B^{\rightarrow s}$$
$$^{s\leftarrow}A \quad ^{p\leftarrow}B$$
$$^{\rightarrow s}A \quad ^{\rightarrow p}B$$

Along with the concept of person A, the essential element of a person B is also contained in the situational concepts. They cannot therefore be arranged simply in a schema of behavioral concepts for one or the other of these persons. If for the moment we leave Commons' attribution out of account and add the corresponding auxiliary verbs to the analytic formula, the following picture emerges:

A —	B must
A —	B may
A may	B —
A must	B —

It follows that, though all the situational concepts can be established for A, only two of them (privilege and conformity) encompass A's behavior, whereas the two others (security and exposure) deal with B's behavior. The words *need not, may not* and *can, cannot*, which Commons incorporated, are lacking here. The negations of *must* and *may* can be added easily without changing anything in the schema. If *may* alone is added to A, it neutrally stands for a behavior; if *need not* is added, the behavior is dissected into action and neglect of action. But the words *can* and *cannot* lead to an entirely different chain of concepts: they do not designate the behavior of A when faced with a *must* or a *may* by B within a given situation; rather, they refer to a behavior that causes the sanction— for example, a lawsuit in case B does not behave in the expected manner. If in these cases we wanted to introduce words for A's behavior that confront and supplement *may* and *must*, they must be something like "may receive" and "must tolerate." Thus a detailed schema has the following form:

A may receive	B must
A must tolerate	B may
A may	B must tolerate
A must	B may receive

The concepts "can" and "cannot," indicating the area of the right to sue, have been taken from the behavioral problems of jurisprudence, and as correlatives of the behaviors "must" and "may" they have no meaning.

Every detail of Commons' conceptual apparatus points to its origins. The series of jural relations was left in position next to the series of situational concepts because even though the new problem of the social situation was seen as the concrete unit of jural and economic reality, it could not be entirely detached from the images and tables of American analysis. The schema of auxiliary words was adopted, but its function of naming behavior in situations was not so clearly grasped as to leave the behavioral concepts standing. The situational concepts contain the natural-law idea of the right-duty correlation between two persons. But the defects of an insufficient effort to overcome the tradition are nowhere more deeply embedded than in the structure of the concepts. The remnants of earlier theoretical forms stand as external reminders next to Commons' new concepts. The error of placing the jural concepts separately alongside the others that contain both sanction and profit can be remedied by omitting them and not wasting another word on them; they have no function in the overall structure of Commons' theory. The behavioral analysis through auxiliary words is incomplete in a complicated way, but it too has no further effect upon the system. The full significance is concentrated in the situational concepts. They too contain traditional material, but its systematic value has changed completely. The pattern of the natural-right relation was the right-duty correlation between two persons, so that the right of one equaled the duty of the other. The significance cannot always be clearly grasped, but where understanding comes close to being possible, as in Supreme Court decisions, it has the significance of an abstract relation, in the appropriate style connected with the concept of abstract will. Commons' concretization of the relation leads to a new interpretation of the relations of people with each other. They no longer confront each other as equal abstract individuals, no longer having any rights—such as the right to enter into contracts—*in abstracto;* now their concrete situations are weighed against each other to determine the concrete "reciprocity" of the spheres of freedom. When, for example, an employer with a thousand employees discharges one of them, the work force is diminished by .1 percent, but the worker in question loses 100 percent of his livelihood; thus it makes no sense to speak of the equal right of employer and employee to terminate employment, for the only thing that is important is the relation of "reciprocity."

Just as equality, abstract freedom, the abstract individual, and the will behind actions belong to a particular world of thought, so are the structure and significance of reciprocity linked with the concrete concepts of freedom, property, limitation, and will. The abstract equality of people and will views individuals as identical copies of the model of man, paying no attention to the concrete differences of the behavioral spheres. The correlation of right and duty in the jural relation determines, for example, that the sum A is entitled to demand equals the sum B must pay, or that my right to entice customers away from another by lowering my prices equals the duty of the other to tolerate this behavior. Reciprocity does not take the object brought about by the relation (debt or capturing customers) as a thing in itself; it considers the effect on the overall life of the persons involved in the situation; more precisely, it does not focus on the object at all, concentrating instead on the changes in the various lives and contrasting certain behaviors (which are related by virtue of having a shared object). The connecting links of a life, with its forbearance, that differs from all physical occurrences determine the meaning of the concrete changes and their reciprocity.

The contrast with the abstract correlation of right and duty can be most clearly understood in the new temporal element that enters the concept of reciprocity. The abstract nature of the jural relation is based on the fact that a momentary picture is taken at the instant the two lives touch, so that in this moment, without regard to before and after, the solid shared point stands alone, away from the reasons for its creation and its consequences. Reciprocity also highlights one point, but reciprocity keeps separate the corresponding moments of the two lives in their fullness. It allows them to be raised out of their diversity by turning attention to them, but it does not denature them; instead, more carefully than the concept of correlation, it leaves their total reality in flux. And complete reality happens to contain the quality of flow. The momentarily elevated point is only one, raised above a meaningfully organized life; the present given behavior encapsulates not only the past it has accumulated so far but also the expectation of future consequences of present behavior. The futurity of time is discounted in the present behavior; all interpretations of the present moment, and all the value assigned it, flow from the expectation of future events.

Commons sees here a displacement of the concept of time, whose continuity can be proved in the history of the national economy. In the first period the value of a good is sought in accumulated power from the past; Quesnay sees it in the accumulation of natural powers; Ricardo and Marx, in labor power stored in the product. The doctrine of marginal utility shifts the source of value into the feelings of pleasure and pain in the present. Böhm-Bawerk's theory of interest begins the latest form that derives economic value from expectations. It is the transition from a theory of past quantity to a theory of future expectation. Only in a system of expectations do present behavior and the present situation have specific meaning, and it is with regard to this origin of meaning that the concepts of social behavior must be constructed.

Commons fulfilled the demands of this method of construction in every single concept. His thorough knowledge of labor history and the emergence of fundamental principles in Supreme Court decisions were the occasion for his concretizing equality into reciprocity, the object into expectation, abstract freedom into the opportunity to choose. Finally, the process also includes the concept of the center of meaning. The dissection of the concepts of the individual and of substantial will, begun in the eighteenth century, came to completion in Commons, and his formulation is sufficient for all current systematic requirements. The individual is dissolved in a chain of behavior, linked with the presumption of future events in the point of the present. The connection is not produced by an entity behind the event but resides in the meaning and purpose that make the event understandable, so that Commons establishes the equation of substance and purpose; he allows no metaphysical substance behind the appearance but only its understandable meaning. The equation eliminates all methodological problems arising from contrasting the individual and society, for if the individual is no more than a pattern of meaningfully connected behavior, it is not—at least in this instance—different from any other understandable pattern of actions, whether these be stock corporations, family, state, or a religious community. Commons includes all behavior patterns composed of a majority of people under the rubric of "going concerns," expressed in the simple formula: "The going concern may be looked upon as a person with a composite will, but this so-called 'will' is none other than the working rules of the concern operating through the actions and transactions of those who observe the rules."[78]

For an economic institution, for example, the "will" of the going concern lies in the discretionary acts of selection of everyone in-

78. Commons, *Legal Foundations of Capitalism,* 147.

volved with it, from the company president down to the lowliest worker who has his sphere of freedom in managing his tools. "The collective will is the organized symposium of all the discretionary acts of all participants as they go along from day to day, according to the rules of the organization. It is an organized mass movement."[79] The collective will also reaches back to the participation of former members of the going concern. Current discretionary actors behave within a historical medium of customs, habits, precedents, and work methods that has accumulated during a longer or shorter timespan and sets concrete limits on today's freedom of choice. Past contracts, agreements, stockholders' resolutions, and the like are binding in the present; the social contract, legal agreements with shareholders, and the like are binding far into the future. The strongest obligation, finally, is the legal system, which confers on the undertaking its legal standing and regulates each individual transaction, such as buying and selling, hiring, granting agencies, and the like.

The state itself is merely one going concern among others. "The state is not 'the people,' nor 'the public,' it is the working rules of the discretionary officials of the past and present who have had and now have the legal power to put their will into effect within the limits set by other officials, past and present, and through the instrumentality of other officials or employees, present and future."[80] Government is the series of transactions that occur between officials and citizens or between officials of the same state or of different states. The state is the meaningful process of continuous discretionary changes in legal rules; its coherence does not come from the constitution; it is "held together by thinking alike."[81] The fundamental social fact on which Commons—as Giddings, Santayana, and Dewey did before him—bases the functioning of the democratic state is the concrete agreement of the will.

෴

The dissolution and concretion of abstract entities into meaningful series of actions has brought people and institutions to a new methodological plane. Further, it has destroyed gradations in value

79. *Ibid.*, 146–47.
80. *Ibid.*, 149.
81. *Ibid.*, 363.

and reduced the traditional snobbery prevalent in social life. Though the state was still called sovereign, this designation was adapted to a customary title and is not intended to contrast the superior powers of the person of the state with the lesser will of the individual. Even the state was dissolved into a series of actions within individual spheres of discretion, and Commons considered it an expression of assimilation that the civil servant can be called to account by the same court of law that settles private quarrels. This process of assimilation leaves nothing standing except equal members of the commonwealth. He goes even further, demanding a form of organization for large areas of social existence that deviates substantially from the traditional forms. His study of union constitutions revealed a principle that developed out of American social problems and was therefore more significant than the constitutional principles of the eighteenth century. It was the principle of responsible business leadership through leaders, as opposed to representation by intellectuals—that is, people who do not in their own right belong to the pattern of meaningful behaviors in whose name they act but acquire legitimation merely through a more or less deep understanding from the outside. The quality of the responsible leaders is derived from the philosophy of the stream of life and from the accumulation of past experience. Only someone whose own life is rooted in a concrete meaningful connection, only someone who by his personal history has stored within himself life in this sense, only someone who is not separated from life in this sense by the chasm of secondary understanding may speak for this life—that is, for himself. Life does not need an advocate, it can represent itself. Representation as a political idea as such is irreconcilable with this philosophy of life, but under the special forms of the American Constitution and politics, the contradiction stands out more clearly and has led to a system of institutions based on the new principle. The break between the mass of the people and their congressional representatives is sharpened by the principle of ministerial lack of responsibility to the parliament—that is, to Congress—and Congress is independent of the party machine, which does not represent any population group in particular, so that representation of various interests in fact proceeds through the instrument of the lobby.

Given these circumstances, it seemed appropriate to withdraw a number of administrative departments from the normal system of political corruption, structuring them as fairly independent offices. What resulted were the Interstate Commerce Commission, the Federal Trade Commission, the Federal Reserve Board, the Tax Commission, the Tariff Commission, and innumerable state commissions. The purpose of nonpartisan administration was achieved in some cases, while in others the system failed completely. The beginnings of the system go back to the end of the nineteenth century, but its principles were not clearly formulated until Commons did so in 1913. In that year industrial disturbances and strikes took on such dimensions that President Woodrow Wilson saw himself compelled to entrust a commission "on Industrial Relations" with investigating the incidents and their grounds and to recommend possible remedies. Through Robert La Follette's good offices he offered the chairmanship to Commons. For financial reasons Commons could not accept and became an ordinary member of the commission, while Frank P. Walsh headed it.

The final report of the commission consisted of two documents, one of which was signed by Commons and Florence J. Harriman.[82] It proposed the establishment of a federal industrial commission, and an outline was given for its organization. The paper stated as the rationale for its recommendation that state and federal governments alone cannot be expected to remedy all grievances. "As soon as people come to look upon the coercive power of government as the only means of remedying abuses, then the struggle for control of government is substituted for the private initiative through private associations, from which the real substantial improvements must come."[83] The state as "going concern"—that is, in practice, the administration and the Congress—is to have the least possible effect on the critical situation, and its function should be limited

82. John R. Commons and Florence J. Harriman, "Report of Commissioners," in *Industrial Relations: Final Report and Testimony Submitted to Congress by the Commission on Industrial Relations*, Senate Doc. No. 615, 64th Cong., 1st Sess. (2 vols.; Washington, D.C., 1916), I, 171–230.

83. *Ibid.*, 172. Page 173 refers to Commons' experiences in his position as a member of the Industrial Commission of Wisconsin (1911–13). The commission is structured according to principles similar to those developed in the text. See John R. Commons, *The Industrial Commission of Wisconsin: Its Organization and Methods* (Madison, 1913) [rpr. as "Constructive Investigation and the Industrial Commission of Wisconsin," *Survey*, XXIX (1913), 440–48, and in *Labor and Administration*, chap. 22].

to rendering the necessary administrative-technical aid to organizing private initiative. The proposed structure of the new organization provided for the employers' organization (such as the Association of Coal Operators, National Metal Trades Association,
Association of Railroad Presidents, and the brewers) and workers'
groups (including the A. F. of L., the Railroad Brotherhoods, and the
Women's Trade Union League) to submit lists from which the president (for a federal commission) or the governor (for a state commission) would name ten members to an advisory representative
council. The secretary of labor and the secretary of commerce
would be additional members of the council. The council recom-
mended that the president (or governor) name three commissioners
with the Senate's advice and consent. This nominating procedure
would bring together on the council the leaders of the parties immediately involved in the conflict; further, they must agree to the
proposals of persons trusted by both sides. The three commissioners (serving a six-year term) therefore would not owe their position
to climbing the ladder of the bureaucratic system but would be
elected by the parties themselves for the purpose of self-administration of their affairs. The commission's function would be to apply the laws governing working conditions, safety measures, health
provisions, workers' compensation for accidents, employment
agencies, child labor, industrial training, statistics, immigration,
and the like. It would have the right to issue decrees and regulations
implementing the laws, as it would the right to initiate and publish
studies concerning all problems under its jurisdiction.

The quality that was to be assured for administration and decisions by this form of self-administration Commons called "reasonableness," following the terminology of common law and the Supreme Court. The resolution of a conflict is to be reasonable.
Commons sees the significance of this concept also in the fact that
it can be derived from the philosophy of concrete life. A reasonable
solution or decision, the determination of reasonable value or price,
can be achieved not by subsuming a case under a legal regulation
but by the form of the procedure. It is found by the judgment of
"reasonable men"—men with common sense. And the man and
his judgment can be reasonable only when he weighs all the relevant facts and allows them to enter into the decision—"giving due
weight to all of the facts" is the formula for reasonable procedure.

"It is not a 'program' or a 'platform' or a schedule of 'inalienable rights' that bridges over the periods of hardship and depression, but it is the spirit of true democracy, which investigates, takes into account all of the facts, gives due weight to each, and works out, not an ideal, but a reasonable solution day by day."[84] The reasonable solution is a "question of personality, and that final test of personality, reasonableness."[85] It can be acquired only through participation in the life process that has led to the conflict, so that the reasonable solution acquires the form of a compromise between the two antagonistic parties themselves. The ideal case would see the elimination of all persons not personally involved in the conflict. In Commons' view, interference by outsiders is valid only when the disputing parties cannot envisage a solution other than force. And even then the greatest service the outsider can offer the parties is "the elimination of himself as soon as possible."[86]

Animosity toward the intellectual—already evident in Gompers—is not based on his lack of knowledge or on any absence of understanding, which could be alleviated by industrious study, but has its metaphysical roots in the belief that the process of social life must not be borne by an organization alien to it but that the healing of the consequences of the conflicts in whose form it takes its course must emerge from social life itself. The "genuine democratic spirit," to which Commons refers occasionally, knows only one class of equals, who must get along with each other. Intervention by the states or supervision and arbitration by specialists would destroy the unity of the commonwealth and establish authorities in a community whose guiding principle is the equality of all its members, without any authority. Life's limitations have given rise to social conflict; because the cost to life energy of overcoming natural impediments must be economized, conflicts of interest arise whenever an individual finds himself in a situation that stands in the way of another's advantage. The same life, however, that by its basic traits of limitation and foresight brings about conflicts and makes them tangible also allows individuals to accumulate experience leading to reasonableness, compromise, and day-to-day compatibility.

84. John R. Commons, *Industrial Goodwill* (New York, 1919), 185.
85. *Ibid.*, 176.
86. *Ibid.*, 177.

Expressed in this way, the solution cannot be taken for granted. Whenever a conflict arises, it might appear simpler to remove the opponent and to appropriate the desired advantage by force. It is not clear why the accumulation of experience must lead to common sense and reasonable compromise. Commons' thinking, with its dialectic of life's self-healing, can only be understood by constantly remembering its tacit premise in the conditions of American life. Warren's political program made a neat separation between the anarchic theory and its tacit assumptions. The aversion to theory evident in Gompers' actions and in union policies was based on unquestioning acceptance of the social ideal, so that only the resolution of concrete conflicts became a problem within the accepted order. Giddings and Dewey went so far as to turn the actual all-pervasiveness of the American ideal into an a priori of sociology. Commons' philosophy raised the problem to a higher level; in his system all concepts are understood from the vantage point of the center of the outlook on life, and his concepts of reasonable behavior and reasonable decisions attain the level of sophistication where the form and content of life, its conflicts and resolutions, fuse into one, simply stated into the meaning: the necessity of getting along as well as one can.

The anarchic necessity and lack of specific purpose in quarreling and making up have practical and historical meaning in present-day America because they form the basis for the idea of equality, of "thinking alike": an actual reduction of individual intellectual differences to such a degree that the historical-accidental high standard of living is reinterpreted on the intellectual level in the modest ideal of getting along with one's fellow man, who is one's intellectual equal. The equality of the pioneer community was materially conditioned by a shared predicament; such a community represented a fighting unit in hostile territory. Today these necessities no longer exist, and equality has remained as an intellectual value and a requisite for its own sake. Equality was so much taken for granted by Warren and Gompers that they saw no need to mention it; though Giddings and Dewey saw it as a problem, they crudely changed it from historical fact into a priori necessity; in Commons' writings equality has turned into a philosophy of life, thus obtaining its metaphysical significance.

It differs from all European attempts, especially those of Bergson and Simmel, primarily by one trait that on first glance looks like dilettantism. The thoughts are developed without any significant prior philosophical education. The technique of treating the concepts is highly inadequate, and the intention of putting down in writing a philosophical system is missing completely. It almost looks as though this theory of law and economics had accidentally grown into a major philosophy. But it is precisely the apparent dilettantism and the inadvertent element in forming the system that have their origins in the typically American approach to problems; that is, they originate not in the structure of the system, as is true in the writings of Bergson and Simmel, but in its tangibly experienced everyday events. The researches of American scholars into the country's history and current situation, the formation of legal history, and the analysis of Supreme Court decisions furnish Americans with an approach to the problems of life, and there, where it was grasped most deeply, its metaphysical content could become most brilliantly visible. The same philosophy of life that presents itself in Europe as the final product of individual philosophical culture, seen by selected people and aimed at an intellectual elite, is discovered in America by an exceedingly modest and amiable man who, coming from a farmers' and workers' environment, spent decades working through his historical and political experiences. His perspective was so astute that, almost without being aware of what he was doing, he needed only to say what he saw in order to give the highest philosophical expression to the significance of the society in which and for which he lived. His technical flaws are part of his being: in a society of equals, the perfection of the apparatus— to which every European philosopher worthy of the name aspires— is considered improper and merely an attempt to be better than one's neighbor. The construction of a structure of thought from the love of intellectual perfection, from a passion for objectivity, and for the system itself isolates its builder, draws him away from the human community, from the values of living together, toward others whose enjoyment is of necessity solitary. Santayana is unpopular in America and is considered un-American because he was too good a philosopher. Dewey owes his reputation more to his questionable books on education than to his sound work in metaphysics. The deficiencies of the system follow of necessity from underestimating the solitary value of intellectual maturity and perfection against the social values of helping and getting along. The extent to which the value systems have been humanized—that is, robbed of their objectivity—is demonstrated by a single passage from Commons' essay "Utilitarian Idealism":

> I do not see why there is not as much idealism of its kind in breeding a perfect animal or a Wisconsin No. 7 ear of corn, or in devising an absolutely exact instrument for measuring a thousand cubic feet of gas, or for measuring exactly the amount of butter or casein in milk, as there is in chipping out a Venus de Milo or erecting a Parthenon. . . . Of course a cow is just a cow, and can never become a Winged Victory. But within her field of human endeavour she is capable of approaching an ideal. And, more than that, she is an ideal that every farmer and farmer's boy—the despised slaves and helots of Greece—can aspire to.[87]

87. John R. Commons, "Utilitarian Idealism," *Western Intercollegiate Magazine*, December, 1909, pp. 267–69 [rpr. in *Labor and Administration*, chap. 1].

Index

A priori principles, 4–5, 6
Adams, Herbert B., 206
Adventure [in *Life of Reason*], 107–108
Agapism, 39
Age, 110–13
Aldrich Reports, 241–42
Allen, Alexander G. V., 141
Altamira, Rafael, 178
Alvarez, A., 179
Amalgamated Clothing Workers, 248
American Federation of Labor, 230–31, 238–40, 249
American character [and generalism], 181
American Law Institute, 177–78n114
Amos, Sheldon, 155, 177
Anarchism [Warren's], 13, 208, 213–14, 216–17, 280
Andrews, J. B., 256
Andrews, James de Witt, 174
Andrews, Stephen Pearl, 212
Animality, 26, 27–28, 101–102, 107
Anxiety, 11
Appropriation, 171–72
Aristocracy, 218
Aristotle, 73, 108
Art, 112
Atomic theory, 108
Austin, John, 144–59

Bailie, William, 208
Bar, Carl Ludwig von, 179
Baudelaire, Charles, 14
Bayle, Pierre, 141
Bentham, Jeremy, 144, 166
Bergeson, Henri, 50, 114, 115, 281
Berkeley, George, 27–29, 50, 54, 115, 127, 140, 141
Berolzheimer, Fritz, 180
Bismarck, Otto von, 115
Boethius, Hector, 86
Böhm-Bawerk, Eugen, 188, 221, 274

Borchard, Edwin M., 174, 175, 193
Bossism, 224–25
Boston Platform, 129ff.
Boundary concept, essence as, 81
Bradley, Francis H., 37, 57
Brentano, Franz, 3, 8, 19, 66–83, 98, 127
Brissaud, Jean, 178, 179
Broom, Herbert, 151–52
Brown, Thomas, 31, 44
Brunner, Heinrich, 178
Bryan, William Jennings, 241
Burke, Edmund, 179
Butler, Nicholas M., 192

Ca' canny, 253
Calhoun, John C., 215, 224
Calisse, Carlo, 178
Calling [religious], 128ff.
Calvin, John, 127, 129
Calvinist dogma, 127ff.; mentioned, 3, 11
Campbell, Edward L., 169, 171, 265
Capital, capitalism, 207, 219ff., 258ff.
Captains of industry, 223–24, 235–36
Cardozo, Benjamin N., 178
Carlyle, Thomas, 37
Carter, James C., 169
Case method [in law], 176–77
Casebooks, 150–51
Categories: personal, 7ff.; peripheral, 7–8, 10ff.; empirical, 9; standardization of, 11. *See also* Stylistic categories
Chaos, 40–41, 46, 99–100, 121, 141, 143
Choice, 263–64, 274
Christianity, 217–18
Civil War, U.S., 205, 207
Claremont Phalanx, 211
Clark, John B., 256
Class, class consciousness, 231, 236, 237ff., 263

283

Classification, 260
Codification, 158, 174, 177ff.
Coercion, 160–61, 196–97
Coexistence, 31, 34, 44–45
Cohen, Morris R., 39, 179
College presidents, 192–93
Collier, Arthur, 140
Commands. *See* Orders
Commission on Industrial Relations,
    277–78
Common sense philosophy, 29ff.
Common law, 144, 169, 240
Commons, John R., 3, 11, 12, 15–17,
    21, 36, 47, 62, 63, 131, 170, 189,
    205–82 *passim*
Commonwealth, 223, 225
Communist Manifesto, 258
Communitas spirituum, 105–107
Concepts of perception, 3, 8, 66ff.
Concretion in discourse, 13–14, 83,
    101, 119–20, 183–84, 195, 198ff.
Conduct: order of, 152–54
Conrad, Johannes, 241
Conrad, Joseph, 84
Consciousness of kind, 217 ff. *See also*
    Likemindedness
Consumer goods, 220–21
Continental Legal History Series, 178,
    178n115
Contingency, 220–21
Continuity, 40ff.
Contribution [as term], 194
Conversation, 95, 97
Conviction, natural, 25–26
Cook, Walter W., 182, 190–95, 196,
    199
Corbin, Arthur L., 183–90, 194, 196,
    199
Cost principle, 210–11, 212, 220ff.,
    227. *See also* Labor, cost principle of
Culture [in Santayana's thought],
    107ff.

Dewey, John, 4, 38, 218–19, 225,
    261–62, 275, 280
Dante, 94, 112
Darwin, Charles, 115
Death, 40–41, 46, 61–62, 101ff., 106,
    111
Del Vecchio, Giorgio, 180
Democratic community [U.S.], 218ff.,
    228, 231, 257, 262
Democritus, 108, 121
Detective stories, as art form, 13–14
Dialectic of consciousness, 49–50
Dialectical functions, 81

Dialectics: and open/closed self, 9ff.,
    141; of skepticism, 9, 28–29; of
    identity, 13; absence of (in Peirce),
    48ff., (in James) 50–51, 127; of
    present moment (Hodgson), 51–52;
    and act-object relation, 68ff.;
    "synthetically a priori," 93;
    avoidance of (Peirce, James,
    Santayana), 127
Dilettantism, 12, 281
Disillusionment, 109ff., 122
Distribution of wealth, 219ff.
Divination, 48
Doubt, 24–25
Drake, Joseph H., 179
Dualism, 51
Duguit, Léon, 177
Duration: Hume on, 26–27, 30–31; and
    memory, 29–30; dialectical
    treatment of, 31ff., 70–71
Duty: 145, 148ff., 157; relative and
    absolute, 148–49; primary and
    secondary, 149–50
Dwight, Sereno E., 135, 137

Edwards, Jonathan, 4, 11, 127, 131–43
Effort, 33–34
Elan vital, 240
Ely, Richard T., 206, 256
Emanation of good, 141–42
Emerson, Ralph Waldo, 96
Engelmann, Arthur, 179
Entrepreneurs, 224
Environment, 60
Equivalence [of style], 21
Eros, 47, 85ff., 93–94, 106
Esmain, Adhemar, 178
Essence, 66–67, 72ff., 97ff., 104ff., 116,
    127. *See also* Residue
Eternity, 103ff.
Evil, 61, 143
Evolution [of the mind], 105–106
Existence: 23–63 *passim*; as function,
    23, 26ff.; Hume on, 26–27; Berkeley
    on, 27; Locke on, 27; Reid on,
    29–30; and essence, 98–99;
    biological, over generations,
    102–103
Experience, 97ff., 101, 109
External documentation [novels as],
    10–11

Familiarity [closeness], 10–11, 239
Farm crisis, 243
Farming, 243–44
Fawcett, Henry, 215

Fawcett, Millicent G., 215
Fechner, Gustav T., 50
Federal organization [of U.S.], 176
Federal Reserve Board, 3, 8, 13, 242ff.
Fichte, Johann G., 240
Finiteness, 46, 60, 170ff.
Finley, John, 206
Fisher, Walter L., 254
Football coach, 192–93
Forbearance, 264
Foreignness, 84, 96, 117, 121ff., 126
Form(s): criteria for study of herein,
    4ff.; and intellectual formations, 5ff.,
    20; and self-expressive phenomena,
    7–8; categories of, as discussed
    herein, 8ff.; as shaped historically;
    14ff.; describing, 19–20; provisional
    nature of, 20; and truth, 20; and
    structure(s), 22; speculative, 99–100;
    literary, 120–21
Fouille, Alfred J. E., 180
Fourier, François, 212
Freedom, 102, 162ff., 170ff., 262ff., 272
Freud, Sigmund, 94
Friendship, 94–95
Frontier, 207ff.

Gardiner, H. Norman, 137, 140
Gareis, Karl von, 180
Garment industry, 249
General will, 209
Generalization, 45
Genteel tradition, 96
Gentleman [as term], 85
George, Henry, 206, 222
German school of history, 206
Giddings, Henry F., 217–18, 225,
    261–62, 275, 280
Gierke, Otto von, 177
Gilmore, E. A., 256
God: as personal, 47–48, 62; Puritan
    concept of, 127ff.; Edwards on,
    128–43 passim; as space, 138; and
    philosophical idealism, 139ff.
Goethe, Johann, 1, 112, 213
"Going concern" [as used by
    Commons], 274–75, 277
Gompers, Samuel, 15, 228–35, 238–39,
    279
Goodnow, Frank J., 254
Gray, John C., 147, 172, 173, 177, 187
Gray, John H., 251–53
Greatness, Santayana on, 116–17
Green, Thomas H., 37
Grimstad Bill, 221ff.

Grossart, Alexander B., 138
Gurney, Edmund, 130

Habit, 40, 41
Hamel, Joust A. van, 178
Hamilton, Sir William, 31
Hare, Thomas, 214
Harriman, Florence J., 277
Hearn, William E., 154–55, 156, 164
Hegel, Georg, 9, 33, 35, 57, 106, 259
Heraclitus, 108
Hertzberg, Ebbe, 178
Historical method, 14–15
History: forms of, 14ff.; continuum of,
    17–18; Commons on Marxist view
    of, 259ff.
Hoagland, H. E., 256
Hobbes, Thomas, 32, 144
Hodgson, Shadworth H., 3, 8, 19,
    32–34, 43–44, 51, 66, 69–73, 82, 127
Hohfeld, Wesley N., 165, 177, 181–85,
    189–91, 198–200, 267
Holland, Thomas E., 150, 155–59, 164
Holmes, Oliver Wendell, 179, 186
Huber, Eugen, 178
Hübner, Rudolf, 178
Hugo, Gustave, 145
Humboldt, Wilhelm von, 212
Hume, David, 9, 16, 20, 25–31, 50–51,
    53–54, 56, 116, 126–27, 132, 141,
    168
Husserl, Edmund, 3, 77–78, 81–82, 98
Huvelin, Paul, 179
Hyle, 77, 78, 81–82, 98–99

Idea(s): general, 45ff.; person as, 46; as
    thought and object, 54; Platonic,
    79–80, 108; in Santayana's poetry,
    89, 91, 93
Ideal passion, 116
Ideal types, 17–18
Idealism: of Edwards, 139ff.;
    utilitarian, 281–82
Identity, 26, 76–77
Identity philosophy, 57–58, 72
Illumination, 129, 130ff.
Immanent object, 8, 75ff.
Immigration, 126, 228, 247ff.
Immortality, 101ff., 105–106; ideal of,
    104, 105
Imperialism, 11, 206–207
Indermaur, John, 150
Index numbers, 240ff.
Industrial Commission, 246–47
Infinity, 60
Injustice, 148, 153, 165

Institutionalism, 188
Intellectuals, intellectualism, 12ff., 195ff., 231, 280–81
Intent, 83
Interest [monetary], 210
Intuition, 74–75, 115–16, 169–70, 174
Irony, 109–10

James, William, 3, 4, 8–12, 16, 19, 21, 25, 36–39, 49–63, 116, 126, 127, 130–31, 141, 143
Jefferson, Thomas, 225
Jhering, Rudolf von, 177, 180
Job security, 237–38
Job levels, 238
Jural relations. *See* Legal relations
Jurisprudence, 144–204 *passim*
Justice: Broom on, 152; Salmond on administration of, 160ff., 167; and natural-rights doctrine, 168–69

Kallen, Horace M., 95, 126
Kant, Immanuel, 101, 115
Karl Knies, 206
Knower and known, 51–52
Knowledge, problem of, 52–53
Kocourek, Albert, 179, 184, 195–204, 245
Kohler, Josef, 180
Korkunov, Nikolai M., 180

Labor, cost principle of, 210–11, 212, 220ff., 227
Labor movement, U.S., 228ff.
La Follette, Robert, 255, 277
Lamartine, Alphonse, 209
Language, 4, 19
Laurrell, Karl, 229
Law, 144–204 *passim*; written and unwritten, 145, 169; primary and secondary, 150, 157; rights of "at rest and in motion," 157, 195; divine, 170; lowest common denominators of, 183; multitales, unitales, and paucitales, 188
Legal facts, 159
Legal materials, standardization and codification of, 174ff.
Legal maxims, 151–52
Legal relations, 153–54, 182, 185ff., 195ff.; nexal and quasi-, 200
Leopardi, Giacomo, 86
Lewis, Sinclair, 11
Life, 101ff.
Life of Reason [Santayana], 101–104, 107–10

Likemindedness, 219, 275, 280. *See also* Consciousness of kind
Limitations, 264–65, 275
Lincoln, Abraham, 233
Linguistic expression, 4, 7
Linotype machine, 254
Literary psychology, 119ff.
Llewellyn, K. M., 267
Lobbying, 225, 260
Locke, John, 27–29, 54, 137, 141
Logicalization, 147
Loneliness, 10, 11, 28, 85, 90, 121–22, 126
Lorenzen, Ernest G., 179
Lotze, Rudolf, 57
Love, 46–47, 91ff.
Lucretius, 65, 112

Maccall, William, 213
MacCracken, John H., 132
Magic, 54
Maitland, Frederic W., 177, 178
Malebranche, Nicolas de, 141
Man of letters [as term], 85–86
Mankind, 217–18, 225
Mansfield, Lord, 152
Marx, Karl, 229, 257–61, 273
Mass production, 2
Material of the universe, 40, 51, 127
Material, 99–100
Mather, Cotton, 128
Matter, 140. *See also* Material of the universe
Meaning [and death], 46
Mechem, Floyd R., 179
Meiklejohn, Alexander, 193
Memory, 99, 103
Message [as term], 191ff.
Methodology, 4–5
Middle Ages, 2
Millikan, Robert, 193
Mills, John Stuart, 212–13, 215, 224
Mind: movement of, 17, 120; approach to problem of, 19–20; exhausted, as matter, 40; "law of," 41; and love, 47–48; continuity of, 48; nature and, 109–10; age and, 110
Miraglia, Luigi, 180
Mittelman, Edward B., 256
Modern Times, New York, 212
Modern Legal Philosophy Series, 179ff.
Modernism, 114–15
Monahan, James H., 152, 155, 159
Monism, 50–51, 57, 59–60
Monopolies, 211, 221, 222–23
Monroe, James, 206

Moore, John B.,175
Morgan, Thomas H., 193
Multiverse, 51
Musset, Alfred de, 86

Natural law, 152, 161–62, 168–69,
    172–73
Natural laws, 39, 186
Nature, 101ff., 109, 111
Negation of life, 26
New Harmony, Indiana, 207ff.
Newton, Isaac, 141
Next step, 62
Nietzsche, Friedrich, 115
Noema, 77ff., 98
Nonrational junctures, 100, 110
Norris, John, 140
"Noted educator," 192–93
Nothingness, 122–23

Objectivity, 11–12, 281
Obscenity, 10
Orders [legal], 146, 152, 156–57, 159,
    182–83
Originality, 11–12, 189–95 passim
Owen, Robert Dale, 207, 212

Page, W., 193
Pantheism, 59, 133, 142–43
Pathos, 260–61
Paul, Saint, 217
Paxson, Frederick L., 207
Peirce, Charles S., 3, 4, 8, 9, 16, 20, 21,
    36, 38, 39–50, 62, 126, 139–41, 143
Perlman, Selig, 256
Petrarch, 91
Phillips, U. B., 256
Philosophical system, 82–83, 118
Philosophy, scientific nature of,
    64–65, 116
Pioneer community, 216, 218, 219–20,
    223, 228, 280
Plagiarism, 12, 189ff.
Plato, 35, 79, 94, 106, 108, 127, 141
Platt, Charles M., 157
Plebeianism, 218
Pluralism, 50, 56, 57–58, 62–63, 130
Poe, Edgar A., 13–14
Political organizations, 145ff.
Positive law, 144–45, 155, 156,
    159–60, 172–73
Pound, Roscoe, 177, 179, 195, 262
Pragmatism, 12–13, 115, 183ff.
Precedents [legal], 176
Predestination, 128ff.

Predicates: negative, 80; positive, 104
Prediction, 186
Price stabilization, 5, 8, 242
Prices, 210–11, 220–21
Probability, 130ff.
Production: factors in, 220–21;
    restrictions on, 252–53
Promiscuity, 10
Property, 170ff., 211, 220, 222–23,
    262ff.
Proportional representation, 214–15,
    224ff.
Public utilities, 254–55
Pure experience, 25, 50ff., 56, 127
Puritan mysticism, 3, 11, 127–43
    passim

Quakers, 205
Quesnay, François, 273

Radical Empiricism, 25, 51, 56–57, 139
Rattigan, W. H., 155
Ratzel, Friederich, 2
Raumvolk, 2
Reason, 86ff., 107ff., 116–17
Reasonableness, 214, 246, 279
Reciprocity, 272–73
Reconsideration, 83
Redemption, 90, 100
Reduction: phenomenological, 79;
    skeptical, 79ff., 98
Reflection, 92, 103
Reid, Thomas, 29–31, 141
Relations: experiential, 57
Religious affection [Edwards on],
    133–34
Residue: and essence, 66, 104; of
    skepticism, 80
Responsibility, 10
Ricardo, David, 273
Right: as concept in legal system, 145;
    relation of rights, 154
Riley, I. Woodbrige, 138
Root, Elihu, 178
Rousseau, Jean, 115, 174
Royce, Josiah, 4, 127
Rule of law, 185
Russell, Bertrand, 114, 116

Salmond, John W., 155, 160–66, 167,
    182, 189, 190
Sanborn, Frank B., 132
Sanctions, 146–47, 153, 165
Santayana, George, 3–4, 6–7, 14, 16,
    19, 21, 34–36, 64–125 passim, 127,
    141, 143, 183, 218, 275

Saposs, D. J., 256
Sauerbeck, Augustus, 241
Schema of auxiliary words, 187, 196–97, 271ff.
Schopenhauer, Arthur, 37, 108
Schröder, R., 178
Seigel, H., 178
Self: open, 9, 10, 11, 12, 62–63; closed, 9, 63; flight from, 53; dimensionless, 53ff.; suffering, 85, 87ff., 98; solitary, 88ff.; and love of God, 88–89
Self-sovereignty. See Sovereignty
Shelley, Percy, 114, 116
Shibley, George H., 241
Shock, 34
Shortages, 170ff.
Simmel, Georg, 64, 281
Single tax, 222
Singularity-in-duality, 24
Situational concepts, 271
Situational quality of land, 221–22
Skepticism: Hume's, 9, 25ff., 50, 126; dialectic of, 28–29; transformation of, 29–31
Slavery: freedom from, 205
Small, A. W., 206
Smith, Adam, 260
Smith, George H., 166–67, 171, 174
Smith, J. W., 250
Smyth, Egbert C., 140–41
Sociability, 10
Social body, 5
Social conflict: and Marx, 260–61; as transaction, 267ff.; and "reasonableness," 278ff.
Social reality, 147, 154, 162, 164, 271
Socrates, 80, 108, 127
Solipsism, 25, 85, 98, 110, 124
Sonnets [Santayana's], 14, 86ff., 98, 112–13
Sovereignty: 145ff., 173, 267; of the individual, 208ff., 212
Space, 2, 138; exhaustion of, 207, 228
Spatial people. See Raumvolk
Special interests, 187–88
Speculation: and prespeculative material, 82–83; and speculative reason, 98ff.
Spence, Thomas, 179
Spencer, Herbert, 37, 205
Spenser, Arthur W., 179
Spinoza, Benedict, 108, 141
Spiritual differences between sexes [in Santayana], 94–95
Splitting of law, 174
Spreading of feelings, 43–44

Stammler, Rudolf, 180
State, the, 158, 160, 170, 187, 213, 276
Stewart, Dugald, 31
Stintzing, von Roderich, 178
Stobbe, Otto, 178
Stream of consciousness. See Stream of things
Stream of things, 65, 70–71, 82, 108
Strindberg, August, 94
Structural thematics, 19, 21–22
Structure of the universe, 57–59
Stylistic categories, 21
Substance and purpose: Commons' equation of, 274
Sullivan, J. W., 254
Sumner, Helen L., 256
Supreme Court, 174, 259, 274
Symbolic being, 23–24
Symbols, 82, 153
Synechism, 39

Taking twice over, 58
Terry, Herbert T., 147, 155, 158, 159, 166, 190
Thatness, 32, 51, 69, 98
Theism, 59, 174
Theory: definition of, 4; practical functions of, 12
Thought, idea as, 54
Time, 2, 3, 21, 23–63 passim, 99, 103, 171–72, 240, 273; intervals of, 26; and timelessness, 60; as illusion, 63; reason and, 103; futurity and, 273–74
Time-Store, 211
Tocqueville, Alexis de, 181
Tourtoulon, Pierre de, 180
Transaction, 267ff.
Trust, 10, 25
Truths, 8, 20
Tuscarawas County, Ohio, 211
Tychism, 39

Unified procedure, 173
Union Pacific, 207
Unions, 227–40 passim; 248ff.; 258–59
Utopia, Ohio, 211

Value: personal, 102; monetary, 211; systematic, 264, 272–73
Vanni, Cavaliere, 180
Vision, 38ff.

Wage consciousness, 230
Wages, 223, 229, 249ff.

Walker, Timothy, 179
Walsh, Frank P., 277
Warren, Josiah, 13, 208–12, 214,
   215–16, 224, 261, 280
Weber, Max, 17, 147
Wedekind, Frank, 94
Weininger, Otto, 94
Weyl, Walter E., 251
Whatness, 32, 51, 69, 98
Wickersham, George, 178
Wigmore, John H., 177, 179
Wilde, Oscar, 94
Will, 263ff., 272

Willard, Samuel, 130
Williams, Whiting, 234–39
Wilson, Woodrow, 241, 277
Woman, 94–95
Woodbridge, F. J. E., 132
Working class [American versus
   European], 234ff.
World of self, 88–89

Youth, 107–108, 110

Zola, Emile, 94
Zöpfel, H., 178